The World of the Victorians

THE WORLD OF THE VICTORIANS

An Anthology of Poetry and Prose

Selected and Edited
with Critical Commentary by

E. D. H. Johnson

PROFESSOR OF ENGLISH
PRINCETON UNIVERSITY

CHARLES SCRIBNER'S SONS
New York

ACKNOWLEDGMENTS

Grateful acknowledgment is due to the following:

For "Nature's Questioning" and "In Tenebris II" by Thomas Hardy. From *Collected Poems* by Thomas Hardy. Copyright 1925 by The Macmillan Company. Reprinted with permission of The Macmillan Company, the Trustees of the Hardy Estate, and Macmillan & Co., Ltd.

For "Terence, this is stupid stuff . . ." by A. E. Housman. From "A Shropshire Lad"—Authorized Edition—from *The Collected Poems of A. E. Housman.* Copyright 1939, 1940, © 1967, 1968 by Robert E. Symons. Reprinted by permission of Holt, Rinehart and Winston, Inc., by permission of the Society of Authors as the literary representative of the Estate of the late A. Housman, and by permission of Messrs. Jonathan Cape, Ltd., publishers of A. E. Housman's *Collected Poems.*

For "God's Grandeur" and "That Nature is a Heraclitean Fire . . ." by Gerard Manley Hopkins. From *Poems of Gerard Manley Hopkins,* Third Edition, edited by W. H. Gardner. Copyright 1948 by Oxford University Press, Inc. Reprinted by permission.

For "The Latest Decalogue" by Arthur Hugh Clough. From *The Poems of Arthur Hugh Clough,* edited by H. F. Lowry, A. C. P. Norrington, and F. L. Mulhauser, copyright 1951. Reprinted by permission of The Clarendon Press, Oxford.

For an extract from *The New Republic; or Culture, Faith and Philosophy in an English Country House* by W. H. Mallock. Reprinted by permission of Chatto & Windus, Ltd.

The ornamental design reproduced on the cover of this book was originally executed by William Morris for the Kelmscott Press. From Aymer Vallance, *The Art of William Morris* (London: George Bell, 1897). Courtesy, Art Division, New York Public Library.

Contents

Note to the Reader *ix*
General Introduction *xi*

PART ONE. SIGNS OF THE TIMES

Introduction *3*

THOMAS BABINGTON MACAULAY (1800-1859)
Southey's *Colloquies* *11*

THOMAS CARLYLE (1795-1881)
Signs of the Times *37*

ALFRED TENNYSON (1809-1892)
Ulysses *62*
Locksley Hall *64*

MATTHEW ARNOLD (1822-1888)
Stanzas from the Grande Chartreuse *72*
Dover Beach *79*

Suggestions for Additional Reading *80*

PART TWO. THE INDIVIDUAL AND SOCIETY

Introduction *85*

JOHN STUART MILL (1806-1873)
Of Individuality, as One of the Elements of Well-Being *93*

THOMAS CARLYLE (1795-1881)
Democracy *113*

JOHN RUSKIN (1819-1900)
The Nature of Gothic *127*

WILLIAM MORRIS (1834-1896)
Useful Work versus Useless Toil: The Socialist Platform *143*

Suggestions for Additional Reading *163*

CONTENTS

PART THREE. THE SEARCH FOR FAITH

Introduction *167*

JOHN HENRY NEWMAN (1801-1890)
History of My Religious Opinions to the Year 1833 *176*

THOMAS CARLYLE (1795-1881)
Natural Supernaturalism *203*

ALFRED TENNYSON (1809-1892)
In Memoriam *214*

JAMES THOMSON (1834-1882)
The City of Dreadful Night *222*

THOMAS HARDY (1840-1928)
Nature's Questioning *230*
In Tenebris II *231*

ALFRED EDWARD HOUSMAN (1859-1936)
"Terence, this is stupid stuff . . ." *233*

ALGERNON CHARLES SWINBURNE (1837-1909)
Prelude to *Songs before Sunrise* *236*

GEORGE MEREDITH (1828-1909)
Hard Weather *243*

GERARD MANLEY HOPKINS (1844-1889)
God's Grandeur *247*
That Nature is a Heraclitean Fire . . . *248*

Suggestions for Additional Reading *249*

PART FOUR. THE ROLE OF THE ARTIST

Introduction *253*

JOHN RUSKIN (1819-1900)
Of the Real Nature of Greatness of Style *263*

ROBERT BROWNING (1812-1889)
Fra Lippo Lippi *284*
Andrea del Sarto *296*

vi

CONTENTS

MATTHEW ARNOLD (1822-1888)
The Study of Poetry *305*

WALTER HORATIO PATER (1839-1894)
Preface *318*
La Gioconda *323*
Conclusion *325*

DANTE GABRIEL ROSSETTI (1828-1882)
The Portrait *329*

Suggestions for Additional Reading *333*

PART FIVE. THE ENDS OF EDUCATION

Introduction *337*

THOMAS HENRY HUXLEY (1825-1895)
Science and Culture *345*

MATTHEW ARNOLD (1822-1888)
Literature and Science *360*

CHARLES ROBERT DARWIN (1809-1882)
Autobiography *380*

WALTER HORATIO PATER (1839-1894)
The Child in the House *404*

Suggestions for Additional Reading *419*

PART SIX. THE MASK OF COMEDY

Introduction *423*

ARTHUR HUGH CLOUGH (1819-1861)
The Latest Decalogue *425*

WILLIAM MAKEPEACE THACKERAY (1811-1863)
How to Live Well on Nothing a Year *427*

CHARLES DICKENS (1812-1870)
Podsnappery *437*

vii

CONTENTS

ALGERNON CHARLES SWINBURNE (1837-1909)
The Higher Pantheism in a Nutshell *444*

SAMUEL BUTLER (1835-1902)
The Musical Banks *447*

GEORGE MEREDITH (1828-1909)
Prelude to *The Egoist* *455*

CHARLES LUTWIDGE DODGSON—"Lewis Carroll" (1832-1898)
A Mad Tea-Party *461*

EDWARD LEAR (1812-1888)
Limericks *470*

WILLIAM HURRELL MALLOCK (1849-1923)
The New Republic *476*

WILLIAM SCHWENK GILBERT (1836-1911)
Etiquette *484*
Patience; or Bunthorne's Bride *489*

OSCAR WILDE (1854-1900)
Epigrams *494*

Suggestions for Additional Reading *498*

Selective Bibliography *499*
I. General Works on the Victorian Age *499*
The Historical Setting *499*
The Intellectual Climate *499*
The Literary Background *501*
II. Individual Authors *504*

Notes for Illustrations *513*

Index of Authors *517*

Note to the Reader

The following selections preserve the form in which they appear in editions of their respective authors' works accepted as standard. Biblical and classical quotations and allusions are sufficiently identified by references and explanatory notes; and translations have been supplied for phrases in foreign languages. Otherwise, footnotes are for the most part confined to terms, proper names, and geographical locations not readily traceable in *Webster's New Collegiate Dictionary.*

General Introduction

Again and again I have insisted how those are the happy moments of humanity, how those are the marking epochs of a people's life, how those are the flowering times for literature and art and all the creative power of genius, when there is a *national* glow of life and thought, when the whole of society is in the fullest measure permeated by thought, sensible to beauty, intelligent and alive.

In these words from *Culture and Anarchy* Matthew Arnold provided a touchstone for assessing the greatness of historical eras. The Greece of Aeschylus, the England of Shakespeare, as he goes on to say, had exhibited the hallmarks of true cultural distinction; not so the England of Tennyson and Dickens. Indeed, the purpose underlying all of Arnold's prose writings, literary, social, or religious, was to show how disastrously Victorian England was betraying the noblest traditions of its own past and of other civilizations. Yet, to the thousands who daily thronged the Crystal Palace which housed the Great Exhibition of 1851, or who a generation later in 1887 took part in Queen Victoria's Golden Jubilee, it may well have seemed that they had been fortunate enough to live through England's finest time. Of what, they might have asked, were these great celebrations expressive, if not of "a national glow of life," proudly manifesting Britain's destiny in shaping the modern world?

The full name of the Exhibition of 1851, predecessor of today's World Fairs, was the Great Exhibition of the Works of Industry of All Nations. In his opening address on May 1 Prince Albert stated that the planning of the whole affair was an example of what could be accomplished by "goodwill and cordial co-operation among nations, aided by the means that modern science had placed at our command." Implicit in everything that he and the other speakers had to say was the twofold faith in material and moral progress that characterized the age. If the displays that the 13,000 contributors sent to the Exhibition proclaimed the gospel of work, they no less fervently testified to the belief that man's growing mastery over natural forces was ushering in an era of universal peace. Indeed, England's dream of peace was to survive unbroken for a full century from Waterloo in 1815 to the outbreak of the First World War in 1914, disturbed only by the relatively minor interruptions of the Crimean War (1854-1856) and the Boer War (1899-1902).

Yet, paradoxically, Victoria's long rule (1837-1901) saw more revolutionary changes in the habits of mind and ways of life of her people than any comparable period in the history of nations. In this connection one thinks primarily, perhaps, of the Industrial Revolution, which originated in Great Britain thanks to the speculative daring and mechanical ingenuity of her inventors and was then taken in hand by the emergent middle class, which maintained England's economic ascendancy as the "workshop of the world" throughout most of the century. But it must also be remembered that in a century when the birthpangs of modern states on the Continent and in the Americas were attended by civil discord and wars of aggression, England was peacefully democratizing its inherited system of parliamentary government through the successive Reform Bills of 1832, 1867, and 1884. Meanwhile, the Pax Britannica, substituting law and administrative efficiency for fire and sword, reached out across the globe to open up new markets, until by 1900 the British sovereign presided over an empire thirteen million square miles in extent and numbering 320 million subjects. One historian has aptly described Victoria's reign as "a great revolutionary age—an age in which Britain did more to change the world than she has ever done before or since." [1]

Among the wares which crowded the eighteen acres of exhibition space within the towering palace of glass and cast iron which Joseph Paxton designed for the Great Exhibition, mechanical marvels preponderated. It was as though a vast horn of plenty had been turned upside down, spilling out the machinery from which the wealth of nations would henceforth be derived. The story of the Industrial Revolution has often been told. The principal scientific developments occurred

---

[1] Christopher Dawson, in *Ideas and Beliefs of the Victorians* (London, 1949), p. 27. This volume, a collection of radio talks prepared by a large number of scholars for presentation on the Third Programme of the British Broadcasting Corporation, passes in lively review virtually every aspect of Victorian life and letters.

in the seventy-five years preceding the period covered by this volume. It was left, however, for Victorian businessmen to capitalize on the inventions of such engineers as Watt, Hargreaves, Arkwright, Crompton, and Stephenson. England's industrial supremacy in the nineteenth century was thus the result of a happy wedding of technological skill to commercial enterprise. The fact that in 1835 England was manufacturing sixty-seven per cent of the cotton used in the world is jointly attributable to improvements in methods of spinning and weaving and to the establishment of the factory system. The Manchester and Liverpool Railway began to run in 1830; by the year of the Exhibition Great Britain was covered by a network of railway lines totalling nearly 7,000 miles, entirely built by private capital.

Wherever they looked Victorian optimists could find statistical support for their faith in material progress. There was, however, another and darker side to the picture disclosed to all responsible thinkers. The changing face of England was symbolic of deeper changes which radically affected the lives of the entire people. Between 1800 and 1900 the population nearly quadrupled from ten and one-half to thirty-seven millions. This expansion was accompanied by a no less portentous shift from the age-old agricultural economy which still prevailed at the beginning of the century to an industrial economy which by the 1880's had converted two-thirds of the populace into town dwellers. So rapid and fundamental were the alterations in the patterns of social life that there was no time to make ready for them, even had there been any agency experienced enough to do so. As early as 1844 a thoughtful observer remarked: "The Factory system is a modern creation. History throws no light on its nature. . . . The steam engine had no precedent, the mule and the power-loom entered on no prepared heritage; they sprang into sudden existence . . . passing so rapidly through their stage of infancy that they had taken their position in the world and firmly established themselves before there was time to prepare a place for their reception."

What the Industrial Revolution did was to create a wholly new environment to which human beings had then to seek to accommodate themselves. One of the most influential books of the age was Charles Lyell's *Principles of Geology* (1830-33), in which the author demonstrated that the history of the earth was inscribed on its surface and that the evidences of its antiquity included fossils of many extinct species. It remained for Charles Darwin to suggest a generation later in his great *The Origin of Species* (1859) that myriad earlier forms of life had lost out in their struggle for survival through inability to adapt to environmental change. The dilemma which confronted Victorian society under the Industrial Revolution was similar, with this exception: that whereas in biological evolution the organism is called on to meet new conditions imposed from outside in accordance with natural laws, social evolution is an artificial process through which man creates his own opportunities and accepts responsibility for whether they affect his lot for better or worse.

There is no need to rehearse the horrors which the industrialization of Victorian England inflicted on the working classes which made up the majority of the population. The literature of the period is filled with appalling accounts of the conditions under which men, women, and children labored in mines, factories, and sweatshops, and of the overcrowded and fetid slum-tenements which were their homes. What is less often taken into account is that under steady pressure from reformers the worst evils were alleviated in the course of the period. Among the measures enacted by the first reformed parliaments in a continuing effort to improve living conditions were the New Poor Law of 1834, which was aimed at abolishing outdoor relief; the Municipal Corporations Act of 1835, which laid the groundwork for efficient town administration; the repeal of the Corn Laws (1846), by which the principle of free trade was established; Fielden's Factory Act of 1847, known as the "Ten Hours Bill," which effectively limited and regularized working hours for women and children; and the Public Health Act of 1848, which under the shadow of a cholera epidemic enforced sanitary measures on urban centers of population. Admittedly, these laws arrived somewhat tardily and were more often than not inadequate in scope and administration. But this is the less surprising in view of the unprecedented measures that were called for; nor does it seriously reflect on the intellectual honesty and moral courage with which the authorities confronted and sought to remedy abuses which were, according to the teaching of the orthodox economists of the day, unavoidable in an industrialized social order whose continuing prosperity depended on conformity to the theories of *laissez-faire* or free competition. As one commentator has remarked: "The people of this age were unwilling to accept anomalies and sufferings as necessary or beyond remedy and they were profoundly convinced that of all the evils which beset mankind and all the dangers which threatened it, none was beyond the reach of human intelligence to analyse or of human resolve to cure." [2]

The great achievements of the Victorians nearly all relate to a single mastering impulse: their sense of public morality. Because Peel put the welfare of his country above political affiliation, he broke the Conservative party over the issue of repealing the Corn Laws of 1846, just as Gladstone's advocacy of Home Rule for Ireland split the Liberals in 1886. This same quality of selfless devotion to large social goals imparts a family likeness to the characters held up for our admiration in the pages of Victorian literature: whether it be Millbank, the philanthropic millowner of Disraeli's *Coningsby* or the mythic King Arthur of Tennyson's *Idylls of the King*; Dorothea Brooke, the saintly heroine of George Eliot's *Middlemarch* or Strickland, Kipling's model police officer in *Plain Tales from the Hills*.

When private clashed with public interest, there was no doubt in the mind of the true Victorian as to which should be given precedence; but it was the part of wisdom and virtue so to live that the two should go hand in hand. No book in the period enjoyed wider popularity than Samuel Smiles' *Self-Help* (1859), which with its insistence on the sturdy virtues of prudence, frugality, self-reliance, and hard work became the standard manual for worldly success. Yet the author's message was in no sense limited to arousing the acquisitive instincts of his readers. "Money is power after its sort, it is true," he wrote; "but intelligence, public spirit and moral virtue are powers too, and far nobler ones." The same note sounds in the testimonial which a number of distinguished figures from public life presented in 1885 to the aging John Ruskin in gratitude for his lifelong advocacy of the doctrines:

That Political Economy can furnish sound laws of national life and work only when it respects the dignity and moral destiny of man.

[2] Viola Klein, in *Ideas and Beliefs of the Victorians*, p. 261.

That the wise use of wealth, in developing a complete human life, is of incomparably greater moment both to men and nations than its production or accumulation, and can alone give these any vital significance.

That honourable performance of duty is more truly just than rigid enforcement of right; and that not in competition but in helpfulness, not in self-assertion but in reverence, is to be found the power of life.

Where public morality prevails there will also be present a regard for traditions as the safeguard and sanction of the institutions on which any stable social order is founded. Ever since G. K. Chesterton wrote his brilliant but erratic little book on *The Victorian Age in Literature* (1913), it has been customary to speak in a pejorative sense of Victorian England as pre-eminently the Age of Compromise. The implication is that the Victorians existed in a perpetual state of hovering between alternatives, never able to commit themselves to clear-cut programs of action, at best "muddlin' through." But this is to take a greatly oversimplified view of an ingrained conservatism that led English thinkers of the school of Burke and Coleridge to interpret the present in the light of everything that could be learned from the past. "The Victorian compromise was the work of idealists," one historian remarks, "and the more intense and sincere was their idealism, the stronger was their devotion to compromise." [3] A well-known stanza from Tennyson crystallizes the Victorian ideal of progress, not as innovation but as organic process; England is apostrophized as

A land of settled government,
A land of just and old renown,
Where Freedom slowly broadens down
From precedent to precedent . . . .

The revolutionary systems of such continental thinkers as Auguste Comte and Karl Marx made little headway in England, where doctrinaire blueprints for social betterment had always been regarded with distrust. Benthamism began as a moderate program of legal reform; and the Fabian Socialists with their motto of the "inevitability of gradualness" were committed to the policy of re-educating existing political parties.

[3] Christopher Dawson, in *Ideas and Beliefs of the Victorians*, p. 28.

Yet, implicit in the very meaning of compromise as a means of harmonizing the best features of opposing values is an element of tension. And it is this unwearied straining after the ideal within the actual rather than any tame begging of issues that imparts so invigorating a tone to Victorian social life. John Stuart Mill's eloquent plea for freedom of discussion sets his age's attitude towards compromise in its proper light. In *On Liberty* he writes: "Truth, in the great practical concerns of life, is so much a question of the reconciling and combining of opposites, that very few have minds sufficiently capacious and impartial to make the adjustment with an approach to correctness, and it has to be made by the rough process of a struggle between combatants fighting under hostile banners."

There was at least one issue on which complete unanimity prevailed among the Victorians. This was the desirability of providing education for the growing populace. Government officials, industrialists, religious leaders were at one in promoting the spread of literacy as a panacea for the troubles of the day. Taught to read and write, men would become more law-abiding citizens, more skilled and reliable workers, more God-fearing homemakers. The impetus towards primary education, initially provided by two religious organizations, the Church of England's National Society for Promoting the Education of the Poor and the non-sectarian British and Foreign School Society, culminated with the passage in 1870 of an act which made elementary education available on a nation-wide basis. The father of adult education was Henry Brougham, whose Society for the Diffusion of Useful Knowledge, founded in 1827, led to the Mechanics' Institutes and Workingmen's Colleges of the mid-century.

The immediate result of the movement for mass education was to bring into existence an entirely new reading public among the middle and lower classes, to whom the rapid developments in the art of printing, which was one of the important products of the Industrial Revolution, made available not only newspapers and magazines, but a flood of popular literature. The rise of the novel, as a medium for entertainment comparable to the theater in Elizabethan times, is perhaps the most important literary phenomenon of the age. Of the audience to which the Victorian novelist addressed himself, Wilkie Collins, author of the first true detective story, *The Moonstone,* had this to say in an article written in 1858:

> The Unknown Public is, in a literary sense, hardly beginning, as yet, to learn to read. . . . The future of English fiction may rest with this Unknown Public, which is now waiting to be taught the difference between a good book and a bad. It is probably a question of time only. The largest audience for periodical literature, in this age of periodicals, must obey the universal law of progress, and must, sooner or later, learn to discriminate. When that period comes, the readers who rank by millions, will be the readers who give the widest reputations, who return the richest rewards, and who will, therefore, command the service of the best writers of their time. A great, an unparalleled prospect awaits, perhaps, the coming generation of English novelists. To the penny journals of the present time belongs the credit of having discovered a new public. When that public shall discover its need of a great writer, the great writer will have such an audience as has never yet been known.

The first serious writer to reach this Unknown Public was Charles Dickens. How eagerly it was awaiting discovery is illustrated by the history of the publication of *Pickwick Papers,* which began to appear in 1836 when the author was twenty-four. Dickens' customary method was to bring out his novels serially in monthly parts of three or four chapters, priced at a shilling. His publishers cautiously limited the edition of the first part of Pickwick to 400 copies, but so spectacular was the increase in demand that by the fifteenth number the printing figures had risen to 40,000. In none of Dickens' subsequent fiction did the parts publication ever fall much below 25,000. When the Victorian habit of reading aloud within the family circle is taken into account, it may be reliably estimated that on the average one out of ten readers in England kept up with the monthly installments. The more usual practice was to publish stories in three volumes, the so-called three-decker; but although much more expensive, these novels enjoyed hardly less vogue thanks to the appearance on the literary scene of lending libraries, the first and most successful of which, Mudie's, began accepting subscriptions in 1842. Six years later the powerful publishing house of W. H. Smith and Son leased stalls in the new railway stations through which to circulate best sellers by the thousands in cheap reprints.

It must not be inferred, however, that the reading tastes of the Victorian public were formed exclusively on prose fiction. With their religious background of Puritan dissent, the middle and lower classes tended to look with disfavor on novel-reading as a distraction from the serious concerns of life; and many publishers were reluctant to accept novels, as being harmfully frivolous in tendency. Indeed, there are grounds for arguing that until well along in the age the influential literary forms were the sermon, the tract, and the periodical essay. Of the 45,000 titles published in England between 1816 and 1851, more than ten thousand were works of divinity; and as late as 1880 listings in this category still outnumbered novels two to one. So earnest was the Victorian thirst for knowledge that the weightiness of its contents constituted no bar to a volume's appeal. Within a year of its publication in 1850, sixty thousand copies had been printed of *In Memoriam,* Tennyson's long and often abstruse elegiac poem which became a kind of Bible to his age; and the twelve hundred and fifty copies of the initial printing of Darwin's *The Origin of Species* were bought up on the first day. The nineteenth century was, furthermore, the golden age of the serious quarterlies and monthlies, to which most of the writers included in this anthology made major contributions.

There is, however, another and more significant way in which Victorian England may be said to have produced a great popular literature. The leading writers shared a sense of mission, born of wholehearted commitment to the problems of the age; and this led them to speak to their audience with a peculiar directness and urgency. Dickens' willing acceptance of the demanding conditions of serial publication is an example in point. Of this mode of writing, Thackeray, another of its practitioners, said that it promoted a "communion between the writer and the public . . . something continual, confidential, something like personal affection." Fluctuating sales of the monthly parts served as a kind of barometer in terms of which Dickens could assess the response to his novels. Thus, when the demand for instalments of *Martin Chuzzlewit* began to drop off, he despatched his protagonist to the United States as a means of recapturing attention. The hundreds of despondent letters which he received from his readers bore testimony to their sorrow over the pathetic deaths of Paul Dombey in *Dombey and Son* and of Little Nell in *The Old Curiosity Shop.* The intimate relationship of Dickens with his public has been compared to that between the ancient bardic poets and their auditors; like a great actor, he needed to feel the presence of a live audience to do his best work. It was, indeed, this need that led him late in life to undertake the exhausting series of public readings from his novels which precipitated his death.

The Victorian man of letters regarded himself as a kind of lay preacher, with the periodicals of the day for his pulpit. Here is the reason that much of that writing sounds to modern ears didactic and hortatory in tone, expressive of the arts of the preacher, the debater, and the lecturer. It is in De Quincey's phrase a "literature of power," originating in "divine discontent" with the *status quo,* passionately informed by a striving "to set the crooked straight." In his fine essay "The Function of Criticism at the Present Time" Matthew Arnold defines the role of the critic as that of cultural mediator within his society. The business of criticism, says Arnold, is "simply to know the best that is known and thought in the world, and by in its turn making this known, to create a current of true and fresh ideas." To this view of their literary function all representative men of letters in nineteenth-century England would have unhesitatingly subscribed.

A recent historian of Victorian ideas has stated: "The intimate connection between literature and life is a significant feature of the Victorian age and one of its chief glories." [4] As the following selections will demonstrate, the writers of the time were no specialists; they took all knowledge for their province. Their writings, ranging through historical, political, economic, religious, and educational, as well as literary and artistic fields of inquiry, illuminate in a remarkably vivid way the complex interrelationships of Victorian life. At the same time they are an index to those qualities of inexhaustible vitality, moral idealism, and faith in human resources which underlie the other crowning achievements of the period. To read this literature is to enter and be at home in the world of the Victorians.

[4] Walter E. Houghton, *The Victorian Frame of Mind, 1830-1870* (New Haven, 1957), p. xvii.

The World of the Victorians

PART ONE

Signs of the Times

Introduction

It is always instructive for the student of past times to start by trying to determine what an age thought about itself. Such an investigation is rendered the easier in the case of the Victorians because they thought about themselves constantly, out of an intensity of self-consciousness which has no analogue in earlier periods. Many associated factors help to explain the introspective bias of the Victorian mind: the persistence among the middle classes of the nonconformist conscience with its emphasis on personal conduct; the legacy of Romantic subjectivism, as illustrated by the strongly autobiographical complexion of so much Victorian writing; the isolation of individuals, ensuant on the dissolution of societal ties (to which Friedrich Engels called attention in *The Condition of the Working-Class in England in 1844*). Out of a need to objectify and gain perspective on its predicament, the age turned increasingly to consult history.

The great eighteenth-century historians, Gibbon, Hume, Voltaire, had tended to view preceding epochs as disjunctive or self-contained, relevant to the present only to the extent that they provided theoretical grounds for illustrating the virtues and vices of men. The modern science of history is an outgrowth of German idealistic philosophy in the late eighteenth and nineteenth centuries, as embodied in the teachings, among others, of Herder, Kant, and Hegel. The historical writing which resulted, of which Carlyle is the principal exemplar in England, regarded history as a ceaselessly unfolding continuum, with the past existing in organic relation to the present. The study of origins thus acquired a greatly enhanced importance; for it was now perceived that existing institutions are the product of an agelong process of evolutionary development. Carlyle represented this process by a poetic metaphor derived from the Norse legend of the Tree of Life:

I like, too, that representation they have of the Tree Igdrasil. All Life is figured by them as a Tree. . . . At the foot of it, in the Death-kingdom, sit three *Nornas,* Fates,—the Past, Present, Future; watering its roots from the Sacred Well. Its 'boughs,' with their buddings and disleafings,—events, things suffered, things done, catastrophes,—stretch through all lands and times. Is not every leaf of it a biography, every fibre there an act or word? Its boughs are Histories of Nations. The rustle of it is the noise of Human Existence, onwards from of old. . . . It is Igdrasil, the Tree of Existence. It is the past, the present, and the future; what was done, what is doing, what will be done; 'the infinite conjugation of the verb *To do*.'

Among the diverse phenomena to be associated with nineteenth-century historiography are the study of myth and the growth of nationalism, not to speak of such fateful aberrations as racism and other doctrines derived from the Historic Right school.

The new historical sense accompanied and was at least in part connected with the great shift in emphasis from the physical to the biological sciences, from the spatially conditioned mind of an eighteenth century dominated by the towering figure of Newton to the time-haunted consciousness of the age of Darwin. Man's faith in absolutes based on *a priori* reasoning gave way to a relativistic habit of mind which profoundly influenced the nature of historical judgments. Thus, John Stuart Mill would argue

That the human mind has a certain order of possible progress, in which some things must precede others, an order which governments and public instructors can modify to some, but not to an unlimited extent: that all questions of political institutions are relative, not absolute, and that different stages of human progress not only *will* have, but *ought* to have, different institutions: that government is always either in the hands, or passing into the hands, of whatever is the strongest power in society, and that what this power is, does not depend on institutions, but institutions on it. . . .

No concept held more imaginative appeal for the Victorians than that of a *Zeitgeist* or Time Spirit as the agent of historical change. To its operation they attributed their successes or failures in measuring up to the ideals which they had set for themselves.

In his essay on "The Function of Criticism at the Present Time" Matthew Arnold discriminates between what he calls "epochs of expansion" and "epochs of concentration." The former are the supreme periods of imaginative endeavor, such as the Renaissance; the latter, transitional in character, encourage critical, rather than creative activity (and here, of course, Arnold has his own era in mind). A similar distinction is developed by John Stuart Mill in his remarkable *Autobiography*. Recording his debt to the St. Simonians, an early French group of Socialist thinkers, he says how greatly he was "struck with the connected view which they for the first time presented to me, of the natural order of human progress; and especially with their division of all history into organic and critical periods." He goes on:

During the organic periods . . . mankind accept with firm conviction some positive creed, claiming jurisdiction over all their actions, and containing more or less of truth and adaptation to the needs of humanity. Under its influence they make all the progress compatible with the creed, and finally outgrow it; when a period follows of criticism and negation, in which mankind lose their old convictions without acquiring any new ones, of a general or authoritative character, except the conviction that the old are false.

So widespread was the notion of periodicity that there is hardly a Victorian writer who does not adopt some version of it in seeking to analyze the temper of the age, or who is not disposed to agree with Arnold and Mill that the signs of the times all pointed to the fact that England was passing through a transitional phase. Typical of the half-rueful, half-hopeful perplexity with which the Victorians gazed out on the world about them is Tennyson's statement about the theme of his Arthurian epic, *Idylls of the King:*

All ages are ages of transition, but this is an awful moment of transition. It seems to me as if there were much less of the old reverence and chivalrous feeling in the world than there used to be. I am old and I may be wrong, for this generation has assuredly some spirit of chivalry. We see it in acts of heroism by land and sea, in fights against the slave trade, in our Arctic voyages, in philanthropy, etc. The truth is that the wave advances and recedes. I tried in my "Idylls" to teach men these things, and the need of the Ideal.

In this connection we recall the King's dying words in the "Morte d'Arthur" after the symbolic relinquishing of his sword:

The old order changeth, yielding place to new,
And God fulfils Himself in many ways,
Lest one good custom should corrupt the world.

Victorian society was the creation of its middle classes, Arnold's
Philistines; this much was clear to every social critic who addressed
himself to what became known as "the condition-of-England question."
As early as 1820 James Mill, the political philosopher and father of
John Stuart Mill, had forecast their role in the new age and on this
prophecy had based his argument for their right to the franchise, to be
granted by the Reform Bill of 1832:

There can be no doubt that the middle rank, which gives to science, to
art, and to legislation itself, their most distinguished ornaments, the
chief source of all that has exalted and refined human nature, is that
portion of the community of which, if the basis of representation were
ever so far extended, the opinion would ultimately decide. Of the people
beneath them, a vast majority would be sure to be guided by their advice
and example.

According to John Stuart Mill, Victorian middle-class culture had
resulted from the fusion "of the two influences which have chiefly
shaped the British character since the days of the Stuarts: commercial
money-getting business and religious Puritanism." With this opinion
all historians of the period are in virtual agreement. Utilitarianism and
Evangelical Christianity, subscribed to not as rigid bodies of doctrine,
but rather as sanctioning pre-existent beliefs and practices, constitute
the two great ground swells which, beneath all surface ripples, sway
the currents of ideas in nineteenth-century England.

For all their apparent incongruity, there are points of identity between the ruthlessly competitive spirit which guided the business
methods of Victorian capitalists and their humanitarian zeal for social
betterment. R. H. Tawney's *Religion and the Rise of Capitalism*
(1926) is, as its title suggests, the classic exemplification of the inter-
dependence of the two. As A. V. Dicey, another authority, has noted:
"Benthamism and Evangelicalism represented the development in widely
different spheres of the same fundamental principle, the principle of

individualism." [1] In the final analysis, the sole authority to whom the Protestant holds himself accountable is his Creator, under a system of rewards which places a premium on those prudential qualities of industry, continence, and thrift, which spell worldly prosperity. Traceable to this pragmatic morality are such proverbial expressions as "God helps those who help themselves" or "honesty is the best policy." The pervasive influence of Calvinist doctrine on English dissent produced an additional incentive to amassing the world's goods, since material success could so readily be construed as a token that one had a place among the elect predestined to salvation. Contemporary critics were not slow to draw attention to the resulting paradox. Thus, Charles Kingsley, whose social novels present a burning indictment of the age, declared in one of his sermons: "It is most sad, but most certain, that we are like those Pharisees of old in this . . . that we too have made up our mind that we can serve God and Mammon at once; that the very classes among us who are most utterly given up to money-making, are the very classes which, in all denominations, make the loudest religious profession; that our churches and chapels are crowded on Sundays by people whose souls are set, the whole week through, upon gain and nothing but gain." Bulstrode, the hypocritical banker of George Eliot's *Middlemarch*, may stand for the type that Kingsley had in mind. The author describes her character's self-deluding motives as follows:

It was a principle with Mr. Bulstrode to gain as much power as possible, that he might use it for the glory of God. He went through a great deal of spiritual conflict and inward argument in order to adjust his motives, and make clear to himself what God's glory required. . . . Profitable investments in trades where the power of the prince of this world showed its most active devices, became sanctified by a right application of the profits in the hands of God's servant.

Yet, despite their uneasy alliance in much of the reform agitation of the period, Utilitarianism and Evangelicalism rested on diametrically opposed ontological assumptions. The Utilitarians, also known as the

---

[1] A. V. Dicey, *Lectures on the Relation between Law and Public Opinion in England during the Nineteenth Century* (London, 1930), p. 401.

Philosophic Radicals or Benthamites (after the name of their leading thinker, Jeremy Bentham), were rationalists in the empirical tradition of English philosophy. They accepted the sensationalist psychology of John Locke, who had maintained that there can be no such things as innate ideas and that all knowledge is derived from experience, the mind being regarded as a kind of recording mechanism for sensory stimuli. Bentham, who sought to construct a system for quantitatively codifying these stimuli (his "felicific calculus"), argued that all men are selfishly impelled to seek pleasure and avoid pain, although with proper education they can be brought to see that the happiness of each is contingent on the good of the whole. It then becomes the business of government to guarantee, in Bentham's favorite phrase, "the greatest happiness of the greatest number" through emancipating the citizen from all restraints which might inhibit the free development of his individuality. Translated into economic terms by Adam Smith, author of *Wealth of Nations,* and his disciples, this teaching yields the doctrine of *laissez-faire;* in a freely competitive society each trader will be the best judge of his own profit. Thoroughgoing materialists, the Utilitarians distrusted religion along with literature and the arts as emotional distortions of the hard realities of existence. On the other hand, with their democratic faith in the perfectibility of human institutions, provided a suitable environment, they were enthusiastically optimistic advocates of progress.

Very different was the Evangelical cast of mind, whether its possessor was affiliated with the Established Church of England or with one of the many nonconforming sects of the period. To the Christian, physical welfare is of relatively little moment as compared with the state of his everlasting soul. The highest truths are spiritual, transmitted through the Bible by divine revelation and substantiated by intuition. Human nature is flawed by the ineradicable taint of Original Sin; and this world is properly to be regarded as a vale of sorrowful struggling towards possible felicity in the afterlife. Innate propensities towards good or evil sufficiently testify that men are neither free nor equal. It is the Christian's bounden duty to relieve suffering wherever he encounters it; but progress is not measurable in economic terms, nor will legislative or governmental machinery avail to alter the ordained class structure of society, as exemplified in the words of a popular jingle of the day:

> The rich man in his castle,
> The poor man at his gate,
> God made them, high or lowly,
> And order'd their estate.

In broad distinction, it may be asserted that Victorians read the signs of the times in an essentially pessimistic way if they had been brought up in an Evangelical atmosphere, and in an essentially optimistic way if they had been educated according to the tenets of Utilitarianism. The revolutionary aspects of an age in which every access of new knowledge called in question traditional values could not appear in the same light to individuals whose minds and hearts were filled with a vision of the City of God as to their fellows who were content with building the earthly paradise. Yet, as Christopher Dawson has pointed out, the antagonism between these points of view nourished the best elements in the life of Victorian England:

The beliefs of early Victorian England may seem to us a strange compound of mutually inconsistent orthodoxies—the bleak rationalism of the Utilitarians and the narrow pietism of the Evangelicals, but they were like flint and steel to one another, and from their contact there sprang the spirit of moral idealism and the passion for reform which burn like fire beneath the hard surface of the age of iron and steam.[2]

No one of the authors of the following selections, chosen to illustrate the differing ways that the Victorians assessed the cultural temper of the age, can be strictly aligned with the tenets of either Utilitarianism or Evangelical Christianity. Their writings, however, range between the extremes of optimism and pessimism associated with those groups, and are representative of prevailing attitudes. Thomas Babington Macaulay and Thomas Carlyle, both historians, stand at the farthest remove from each other in their reading of the signs of the times. Macaulay, as spokesman of the Whigs or Liberals who carried the First Reform Bill, shared to the full his party's ebullient faith in progress, whereas Carlyle, who never shed his gloomy Calvinist origins, waged unremitting

---

[2] Christopher Dawson, in *Ideas and Beliefs of the Victorians*, p. 30.

warfare on every manifestation of Victorian liberalism. Through their poetry, Alfred Tennyson, the Poet Laureate, and Matthew Arnold, the apostle of Culture, responded more imaginatively, but not less incisively to the *Zeitgeist*. The former appealed to the vitalistic spirit which accepted the *Zeitgeist* as a challenge to heroic action, while the latter espoused withdrawal from active engagement to the end of preserving individual integrity.

Thomas Babington Macaulay

1800-1859

Southey's *Colloquies*

Macaulay's review of Southey's *Sir Thomas More: or,
Colloquies on the Progress and Prospects of Society*
(1829), portions of which are here omitted, appeared
in the *Edinburgh Review,* January 1830. Robert
Southey (1774-1843) became Poet Laureate in 1813,
by which time the revolutionary ardors of his youth
had cooled down into uniform conservatism. His
Colloquies supplied a platform to "Young England,"
a political movement of the 1840's which, under the
leadership of Disraeli, opposed the prevailing
philosophy of *laissez-faire.*

. . . We now come to the conversations which pass between Mr. Southey and Sir Thomas More,[1] or rather between two
Southeys, equally eloquent, equally angry, equally unreasonable, and
equally given to talking about what they do not understand. Perhaps we
could not select a better instance of the spirit which pervades the whole
book than the passages in which Mr. Southey gives his opinion of the
manufacturing system. There is nothing which he hates so bitterly. It
is, according to him, a system more tyrannical than that of the feudal
ages, a system of actual servitude, a system which destroys the bodies
and degrades the minds of those who are engaged in it. He expresses

---

[1] Sir Thomas More (1478-1535), the great sixteenth-century humanist, author of
Utopia (1516), and Lord Chancellor and Privy Counsellor to Henry VIII, who had
him indicted for high treason and beheaded. More was canonized in 1935. He is
one of the speakers in Southey's *Colloquies.*

a hope that the competition of other nations may drive us out of the field; that our foreign trade may decline; and that we may thus enjoy a restoration of national sanity and strength. But he seems to think that the extermination of the whole manufacturing population would be a blessing, if the evil could be removed in no other way.

Mr. Southey does not bring forward a single fact in support of these views; and, as it seems to us, there are facts which lead to a very different conclusion. In the first place, the poor-rate is very decidedly lower in the manufacturing than in the agricultural districts. If Mr. Southey will look over the Parliamentary returns on this subject, he will find that the amount of parochial relief required by the labourers in the different counties of England is almost exactly in inverse proportion to the degree in which the manufacturing system has been introduced into those counties. The returns for the years ending in March 1825, and in March 1828, are now before us. In the former year we find the poor-rate highest in Sussex, about twenty shillings to every inhabitant. Then come Buckinghamshire, Essex, Suffolk, Bedfordshire, Huntingdonshire, Kent, and Norfolk. In all these the rate is above fifteen shillings a head. We will not go through the whole. Even in Westmoreland and the North Riding of Yorkshire, the rate is at more than eight shillings. In Cumberland and Monmouthshire, the most fortunate of all the agricultural districts, it is at six shillings. But in the West Riding of Yorkshire, it is as low as five shillings: and when we come to Lancashire, we find it at four shillings, one-fifth of what it is in Sussex. The returns of the year ending in March 1828 are a little, and but a little, more unfavourable to the manufacturing districts. Lancashire, even in that season of distress, required a smaller poor-rate than any other district, and little more than one-fourth of the poor-rate raised in Sussex. Cumberland alone, of the agricultural districts, was as well off as the West Riding of Yorkshire. These facts seem to indicate that the manufacturer is both in a more comfortable and in a less dependent situation than the agricultural labourer.

As to the effect of the manufacturing system on the bodily health, we must beg leave to estimate it by a standard far too low and vulgar for a mind so imaginative as that of Mr. Southey—the proportion of births and deaths. We know that, during the growth of this atrocious system, this new misery, to use the phrases of Mr. Southey, this new enormity, this birth of a portentous age, this pest which no man can approve whose heart is not seared or whose understanding has not been darkened, there has been a great diminution of mortality, and that this diminution has been greater in the manufacturing towns than anywhere else. The mortality still is, as it always was, greater in towns than in the country. But the difference has diminished in an extraordinary degree. There is the best reason to believe that the annual mortality of Manchester, about the middle of the last century, was one in twenty-eight. It is now reckoned at one in forty-five. In Glasgow and Leeds a similar improvement has taken place. Nay, the rate of mortality in those three great capitals of the manufacturing districts is now considerably less than it was, fifty years ago, over England and Wales, taken together, open country and all. We might with some plausibility maintain that the people live longer because they are better fed, better lodged, better clothed, and better attended in sickness, and that these improvements are owing to that increase of national wealth which the manufacturing system has produced.

Much more might be said on this subject. But to what end? It is not from bills of mortality and statistical tables that Mr. Southey has learned his political creed. He cannot stoop to study the history of the system which he abuses, to strike the balance between the good and evil which it has produced, to compare district with district, or generation with generation. We will give his own reason for his opinion, the only reason which he gives for it, in his own words:—

We remained a while in silence looking upon the assemblage of dwellings below. Here, and in the adjoining hamlet of Millbeck, the effects of manufactures and of agriculture may be seen and compared. The old cottages are such as the poet and the painter equally delight in beholding. Substantially built of the native stone without mortar, dirtied with no white lime, and their long low roofs covered with slate, if they had been raised by the magic of some indigenous Amphion's[2] music, the materials could not have adjusted themselves more beautifully in accord with the surrounding scene; and time has still further harmonized them with weather stains, lichens, and moss, short grasses, and short

[2] Son of Zeus and Antiope. The walls of Thebes built themselves in response to the magic of his music on the lyre.

fern, and stone-plants of various kinds. The ornamented chimneys, round or square, less adorned than those which, like little turrets, crest the houses of the Portuguese peasantry; and yet not less happily suited to their place, the hedge of clipt box beneath the windows, the rose-bushes beside the door, the little patch of flower-ground, with its tall hollyhocks in front; the garden beside, the bee-hives, and the orchard with its bank of daffodils and snowdrops, the earliest and the profusest in these parts, indicate in the owners some portion of ease and leisure, some regard to neatness and comfort, some sense of natural, and innocent, and healthful enjoyment. The new cottages of the manufacturers are upon the manufacturing pattern—naked, and in a row.

"How is it," said I, "that everything which is connected with manufactures presents such features of unqualified deformity? From the largest of Mammon's temples down to the poorest hovel in which his helotry are stalled, these edifices have all one character. Time will not mellow them; nature will neither clothe nor conceal them; and they will remain always as offensive to the eye as to the mind."

Here is wisdom. Here are the principles on which nations are to be governed. Rose-bushes and poor-rates, rather than steam-engines and independence. Mortality and cottages with weather-stains, rather than health and long life with edifices which time cannot mellow. We are told, that our age has invented atrocities beyond the imagination of our fathers; that society has been brought into a state compared with which extermination would be a blessing; and all because the dwellings of cotton-spinners are naked and rectangular. Mr. Southey has found out a way, he tells us, in which the effects of manufactures and agriculture may be compared. And what is this way? To stand on a hill, to look at a cottage and a factory, and to see which is the prettier. Does Mr. Southey think that the body of the English peasantry live, or ever lived, in substantial or ornamented cottages, with box-hedges, flower-gardens, bee-hives, and orchards? If not, what is his parallel worth? We despise those mock philosophers, who think that they serve the cause of science by depreciating literature and the fine arts. But if anything could excuse their narrowness of mind, it would be such a book as this. It is not strange that, when one enthusiast makes the picturesque the test of political good, another should feel inclined to proscribe altogether the pleasures of taste and imagination.

Thus it is that Mr. Southey reasons about matters with which he thinks himself perfectly conversant. We cannot, therefore, be surprised to find that he commits extraordinary blunders when he writes on points of which he acknowledges himself to be ignorant. He confesses that he is not versed in political economy, and that he has neither liking nor aptitude for it; and he then proceeds to read the public a lecture concerning it which fully bears out his confession.

· · · · ·

"A people," he tells us, "may be too rich, but a government cannot be so."

"A state," says he, "cannot have more wealth at its command than may be employed for the general good, a liberal expenditure in national works being one of the surest means of promoting national prosperity; and the benefit being still more obvious, of an expenditure directed to the purposes of national improvement. But a people may be too rich."

We fully admit that a state cannot have at its command more wealth than may be employed for the general good. But neither can individuals, or bodies of individuals, have at their command more wealth than may be employed for the general good. If there be no limit to the sum which may be usefully laid out in public works and national improvement, then wealth, whether in the hands of private men or of the Government, may always, if the possessors choose to spend it usefully, be usefully spent. The only ground, therefore, on which Mr. Southey can possibly maintain that a government cannot be too rich, but that a people may be too rich, must be this, that governments are more likely to spend their money on good objects than private individuals. But what is useful expenditure? "A liberal expenditure in national works," says Mr. Southey, "is one of the surest means for promoting national prosperity." What does he mean by national prosperity? Does he mean the wealth of the State? If so, his reasoning runs thus: The more wealth a state has the better; for the more wealth a state has the more wealth it will have. This is surely something like that fallacy, which is ungallantly termed a lady's reason. If by national prosperity he means the wealth of the people, of how gross a contradiction is Mr. Southey guilty. A people, he tells us, may be too rich: a government cannot: for a government can employ its riches in making the people richer. The wealth of the people is to be taken from them, because they have too much, and laid out in works, which will yield them more.

We are really at a loss to determine whether Mr. Southey's reason for recommending large taxation is that it will make the people rich, or that it will make them poor. But we are sure that, if his object is to make them rich, he takes the wrong course. There are two or three principles respecting public works, which, as an experience of vast extent proves, may be trusted in almost every case.

It scarcely ever happens that any private man or body of men will invest property in a canal, a tunnel, or a bridge, but from an expectation that the outlay will be profitable to them. No work of this sort can be profitable to private speculators, unless the public be willing to pay for the use of it. The public will not pay of their own accord for what yields no profit or convenience to them. There is thus a direct and obvious connection between the motive which induces individuals to undertake such a work, and the utility of the work.

Can we find any such connection in the case of a public work executed by a government? If it is useful, are the individuals who rule the country richer? If it is useless, are they poorer? A public man may be solicitous for his credit. But is not he likely to gain more credit by an useless display of ostentatious architecture in a great town than by the best road or the best canal in some remote province? The fame of public works is a much less certain test of their utility than the amount of toll collected at them. In a corrupt age, there will be direct embezzlement. In the purest age, there will be abundance of jobbing. Never were the statesmen of any country more sensitive to public opinion, and more spotless in pecuniary transactions, than those who have of late governed England. Yet we have only to look at the buildings recently erected in London for a proof of our rule. In a bad age, the fate of the public is to be robbed outright. In a good age, it is merely to have the dearest and the worst of everything.

Buildings for State purposes the State must erect. And here we think that, in general, the State ought to stop. We firmly believe that five hundred thousand pounds subscribed by individuals for railroads or canals would produce more advantage to the public than five millions voted by Parliament for the same purpose. There are certain old saws about the master's eye and about everybody's business, in which we place very great faith.

There is, we have said, no consistency in Mr. Southey's political system. But if there be in his political system any leading principle, any one error which diverges more widely and variously than any other, it is that of which his theory about national works is a ramification. He conceives that the business of the magistrate is, not merely to see that the persons and property of the people are secure from attack, but that he ought to be a jack-of-all-trades, architect, engineer, schoolmaster, merchant, theologian, a Lady Bountiful in every parish, a Paul Pry[3] in every house, spying, eavesdropping, relieving, admonishing, spending our money for us, and choosing our opinions for us. His principle is, if we understand it rightly, that no man can do anything so well for himself as his rulers, be they who they may, can do it for him, and that a government approaches nearer and nearer to perfection, in proportion as it interferes more and more with the habits and notions of individuals.

He seems to be fully convinced that it is in the power of government to relieve all the distresses under which the lower orders labour. Nay, he considers doubt on this subject as impious. We cannot refrain from quoting his argument on this subject. It is a perfect jewel of logic:—

"Many thousands in your metropolis," says Sir Thomas More, "rise every morning without knowing how they are to subsist during the day; as many of them, where they are to lay their heads at night. All men, even the vicious themselves, know that wickedness leads to misery: but many, even among the good and the wise, have yet to learn that misery is almost as often the cause of wickedness."

"There are many," says Montesinos,[4] "who know this, but believe that it is not in the power of human institutions to prevent this misery. They see the effect, but regard the causes as inseparable from the condition of human nature."

[3] Lady Bountiful, a benevolent country gentlewoman in George Farquhar's comedy *The Beaux' Stratagem* (1707); Paul Pry, the meddling hero of *Paul Pry* (1825), a farce by John Poole (1786?-1872).

[4] Legendary hero of Spanish romance, cited to voice Southey's Tory romanticism.

"As surely as God is good," replied Sir Thomas, "so surely there is no such thing as necessary evil. For, by the religious mind, sickness, and pain, and death, are not to be accounted evils."

Now if sickness, pain, and death, are not evils, we cannot understand why it should be an evil that thousands should rise without knowing how they are to subsist. The only evil of hunger is that it produces first pain, then sickness, and finally death. If it did not produce these, it would be no calamity. If these are not evils, it is no calamity. We will propose a very plain dilemma: either physical pain is an evil, or it is not an evil. If it is an evil, then there is necessary evil in the universe: if it is not, why should the poor be delivered from it?

Mr. Southey entertains as exaggerated a notion of the wisdom of governments as of their power. He speaks with the greatest disgust of the respect now paid to public opinion. That opinion is, according to him, to be distrusted and dreaded; its usurpation ought to be vigorously resisted; and the practice of yielding to it is likely to ruin the country. To maintain police is, according to him, only one of the ends of government. The duties of a ruler are patriarchal and paternal. He ought to consider the moral discipline of the people as his first object, to establish a religion, to train the whole community in that religion, and to consider all dissenters as his own enemies.

"Nothing," says Sir Thomas, "is more certain, than that religion is the basis upon which civil government rests; that from religion power derives its authority, laws their efficacy, and both their zeal and sanction; and it is necessary that this religion be established as for the security of the state, and for the welfare of the people, who would otherwise be moved to and fro with every wind of doctrine. A state is secure in proportion as the people are attached to its institutions; it is, therefore, the first and plainest rule of sound policy, that the people be trained up in the way they should go. The state that neglects this prepares its own destruction; and they who train them in any other way are undermining it. Nothing in abstract science can be more certain than these positions are."

"All of which," answers Montesinos, "are nevertheless denied by our professors of the arts Babblative and Scribblative: some in the audacity of evil designs, and others in the glorious assurance of impenetrable ignorance."

The greater part of the two volumes before us is merely an amplification of these paragraphs. What does Mr. Southey mean by saying that religion is demonstrably the basis of civil government? He cannot surely mean that men have no motives except those derived from religion for establishing and supporting civil government, that no temporal advantage is derived from civil government, that men would experience no temporal inconvenience from living in a state of anarchy? If he allows, as we think he must allow, that it is for the good of mankind in this world to have civil government, and that the great majority of mankind have always thought it for their good in this world to have civil government, we then have a basis for government quite distinct from religion. It is true that the Christian religion sanctions government, as it sanctions everything which promotes the happiness and virtue of our species. But we are at a loss to conceive in what sense religion can be said to be the basis of government, in which religion is not also the basis of the practices of eating, drinking, and lighting fires in cold weather. Nothing in history is more certain than that government has existed, has received some obedience, and has given some protection, in times in which it derived no support from religion, in times in which there was no religion that influenced the hearts and lives of men. It was not from dread of Tartarus, or from belief in the Elysian fields,[5] that an Athenian wished to have some institutions which might keep Orestes from filching his cloak, or Midias from breaking his head.[6] "It is from religion," says Mr. Southey, "that power derives its authority, and laws their efficacy." From what religion does our power over the Hindoos derive its authority, or the law in virtue of which we hang Brahmins its efficacy? For thousands of years civil government has existed in almost every corner of the world, in ages of priestcraft, in ages of fanaticism, in ages of Epicurean indifference, in ages of enlightened piety. However pure or impure the faith of the people might be, whether they adored a beneficent or a malignant power, whether they thought the soul mortal or immortal, they have, as soon as they ceased to be absolute savages, found out their need of civil government, and instituted it accordingly. It is as universal as the practice of cook-

---

[5] Hell and Heaven in Greek mythology.
[6] Characters in Aristophanes' satiric comedy *The Birds*.

ery. Yet, it is as certain, says Mr. Southey, as anything in abstract science, that government is founded on religion. We should like to know what notion Mr. Southey has of the demonstrations of abstract science. A very vague one, we suspect.

The proof proceeds. As religion is the basis of government, and as the State is secure in proportion as the people are attached to public institutions, it is therefore, says Mr. Southey, the first rule of policy that the government should train the people in the way in which they should go; and it is plain that those who train them in any other way are undermining the State.

Now it does not appear to us to be the first object that people should always believe in the established religion and be attached to the established government. A religion may be false. A government may be oppressive. And whatever support government gives to false religions, or religion to oppressive governments, we consider as a clear evil.

The maxim, that governments ought to train the people in the way in which they should go, sounds well. But is there any reason for believing that a government is more likely to lead the people in the right way than the people to fall into the right way of themselves? Have there not been governments which were blind leaders of the blind? Are there not still such governments? Can it be laid down as a general rule that the movement of political and religious truth is rather downwards from the government to the people than upwards from the people to the government? These are questions which it is of importance to have clearly resolved. Mr. Southey declaims against public opinion, which is now, he tells us, usurping supreme power. Formerly, according to him, the laws governed; now public opinion governs. What are laws but expression of the opinion of some class which has power over the rest of the community? By what was the world ever governed but by the opinion of some person or persons? By what else can it ever be governed? What are all systems, religious, political, or scientific, but opinions resting on evidence more or less satisfactory? The question is not between human opinion and some higher and more certain mode of arriving at truth, but between opinion and opinion, between the opinions of one man and another, or of one class and another, or of one generation and another. Public opinion is not infallible; but can Mr.

Southey construct any institutions which shall secure to us the guidance of an infallible opinion? Can Mr. Southey select any family, any profession, any class, in short, distinguished by any plain badge from the rest of the community, whose opinion is more likely to be just than this much abused public opinion? Would he choose the peers, for example? Or the two hundred tallest men in the country? Or the poor Knights of Windsor? [7] Or children who are born with cauls? Or the seventh sons of seventh sons? We cannot suppose that he would recommend popular election; for that is merely an appeal to public opinion. And to say that society ought to be governed by the opinion of the wisest and best, though true, is useless. Whose opinion is to decide who are the wisest and best?

Mr. Southey and many other respectable people seem to think that, when they have once proved the moral and religious training of the people to be a most important object, it follows, of course, that it is an object which the government ought to pursue. They forget that we have to consider, not merely the goodness of the end, but also the fitness of the means. Neither in the natural nor in the political body have all members the same office. There is surely no contradiction in saying that a certain section of the community may be quite competent to protect the persons and property of the rest, yet quite unfit to direct our opinions, or to superintend our private habits.

So strong is the interest of a ruler to protect his subjects against all depredations and outrages except his own, so clear and simple are the means by which this end is to be effected, that men are probably better off under the worst governments in the world than they would be in a state of anarchy. Even when the appointment of magistrates has been left to chance, as in the Italian Republics, things have gone on far better than if there had been no magistrates at all, and if every man had done what seemed right in his own eyes. But we see no reason for thinking that the opinions of the magistrate on speculative questions are more likely to be right than those of any other man. None of the modes by which a magistrate is appointed, popular election, the accident of the lot, or the accident of birth, affords, as far as we can perceive, much security for his being wiser than any of his neighbours. The chance of his being

[7] Military pensioners, lodged in the precincts of Windsor Castle.

wiser than all his neighbours together is still smaller. Now we cannot understand how it can be laid down that it is the duty and the right of one class to direct the opinions of another, unless it can be proved that the former class is more likely to form just opinions than the latter.

The duties of government would be, as Mr. Southey says that they are, paternal, if a government were necessarily as much superior in wisdom to a people as the most foolish father, for a time, is to the most intelligent child, and if a government loved a people as fathers generally love their children. But there is no reason to believe that a government will have either the paternal warmth of affection or the paternal superiority of intellect. Mr. Southey might as well say that the duties of the shoemaker are paternal, and that it is an usurpation in any man not of the craft to say that his shoes are bad and to insist on having better. The division of labour would be no blessing, if those by whom a thing is done were to pay no attention to the opinion of those for whom it is done. The shoemaker, in the *Relapse*,[8] tells Lord Foppington that his Lordship is mistaken in supposing that his shoe pinches. "It does not pinch; it cannot pinch; I know my business; and I never made a better shoe." This is the way in which Mr. Southey would have a government treat a people who usurp the privilege of thinking. Nay, the shoemaker of Vanbrugh has the advantage in the comparison. He contented himself with regulating his customer's shoes, about which he had peculiar means of information, and did not presume to dictate about the coat and hat. But Mr. Southey would have the rulers of a country prescribe opinions to the people, not only about politics, but about matters concerning which a government has no peculiar sources of information, and concerning which any man in the streets may know as much and think as justly as the King, namely religion and morals.

Men are never so likely to settle a question rightly as when they discuss it freely. A government can interfere in discussion only by making it less free than it would otherwise be. Men are most likely to form just opinions when they have no other wish than to know the truth, and are exempt from all influence, either of hope or fear. Government, as government, can bring nothing but the influence of hopes and

---

[8] *The Relapse, or Virtue in Danger* (1696), an immensely successful comedy by Sir John Vanbrugh (1664-1726).

fears to support its doctrines. It carries on controversy, not with reasons, but with threats and bribes. If it employs reasons, it does so, not in virtue of any powers which belong to it as a government. Thus, instead of a contest between argument and argument, we have a contest between argument and force. Instead of a contest in which truth, from the natural constitution of the human mind, has a decided advantage over falsehood, we have a contest in which truth can be victorious only by accident.

And what, after all, is the security which this training gives to governments? Mr. Southey would scarcely propose that discussion should be more effectually shackled, that public opinion should be more strictly disciplined into conformity with established institutions, than in Spain and Italy. Yet we know that the restraints which exist in Spain and Italy have not prevented atheism from spreading among the educated classes, and especially among those whose office it is to minister at the altars of God. All our readers know how, at the time of the French Revolution, priest after priest came forward to declare that his doctrine, his ministry, his whole life, had been a lie, a mummery during which he could scarcely compose his countenance sufficiently to carry on the imposture. This was the case of a false, or at least of a grossly corrupted religion. Let us take then the case of all others most favourable to Mr. Southey's argument. Let us take that form of religion which he holds to be the purest, the system of the Arminian part of the Church of England. Let us take the form of government which he most admires and regrets, the government of England in the time of Charles the First. Would he wish to see a closer connection between Church and State than then existed? Would he wish for more powerful ecclesiastical tribunals? for a more zealous King? for a more active primate? Would he wish to see a more complete monopoly of public instruction given to the Established Church? Could any government do more to train the people in the way in which he would have them go? And in what did all this training end? The Report of the state of the Province of Canterbury, delivered by Laud [9] to his master at the close of 1639, represents the Church of England as in the highest and most palmy state. So effectually

---

[9] William Laud (1573-1645), Archbishop of Canterbury and a vigorous opponent of nonconformity.

had the Government pursued that policy which Mr. Southey wishes to see revived that there was scarcely the least appearance of dissent. Most of the bishops stated that all was well among their flocks. Seven or eight persons in the diocese of Peterborough had seemed refractory to the Church, but had made ample submission. In Norfolk and Suffolk all whom there had been reason to suspect had made profession of conformity, and appeared to observe it strictly. It is confessed that there was a little difficulty in bringing some of the vulgar in Suffolk to take the sacrament at the rails in the chancel. This was the only open instance of nonconformity which the vigilant eye of Laud could detect in all the dioceses of his twenty-one suffragans, on the very eve of a revolution in which primate, and Church, and monarch, and monarchy were to perish together.

At which time would Mr. Southey pronounce the Constitution more secure: in 1639, when Laud presented this report to Charles; or now, when thousands of meetings openly collect millions of dissenters, when designs against the tithes are openly avowed, when books attacking not only the Establishment, but the first principles of Christianity, are openly sold in the streets? The signs of discontent, he tells us, are stronger in England now than in France when the States-General met: and hence he would have us infer that a revolution like that of France may be at hand. Does he not know that the danger of states is to be estimated, not by what breaks out of the public mind, but by what stays in it? Can he conceive anything more terrible than the situation of a government which rules without apprehension over a people of hypocrites, which is flattered by the press and cursed in the inner chambers, which exults in the attachment and obedience of its subjects, and knows not that those subjects are leagued against it in a free-masonry of hatred, the sign of which is every day conveyed in the glance of ten thousand eyes, the pressure of ten thousand hands, and the tone of ten thousand voices? Profound and ingenious policy! Instead of curing the disease, to remove those symptoms by which alone its nature can be known! To leave the serpent his deadly sting, and deprive him only of his warning rattle!

When the people whom Charles had so assiduously trained in the good way had rewarded his paternal care by cutting off his head, a new kind of training came into fashion. Another government arose which, like the former, considered religion as its surest basis, and the religious discipline of the people as its first duty. Sanguinary laws were enacted against libertinism; profane pictures were burned; drapery was put on indecorous statues; the theatres were shut up; fast-days were numerous; and the Parliament resolved that no person should be admitted into any public employment, unless the House should be first satisfied of his vital godliness. We know what was the end of this training. We know that it ended in impiety, in filthy and heartless sensuality, in the dissolution of all ties of honour and morality. We know that at this very day scriptural phrases, scriptural names, perhaps some scriptural doctrines excite disgust and ridicule, solely because they are associated with the austerity of that period.

Thus has the experiment of training the people in established forms of religion been twice tried in England on a large scale, once by Charles and Laud, and once by the Puritans. The High Tories of our time still entertain many of the feelings and opinions of Charles and Laud, though in a mitigated form; nor is it difficult to see that the heirs of the Puritans are still amongst us. It would be desirable that each of these parties should remember how little advantage of honour it formerly derived from the closest alliance with power, that it fell by the support of rulers and rose by their opposition, that of the two systems that in which the people were at any time drilled was always at that time the unpopular system, that the training of the High Church ended in the reign of the Puritans, and that the training of the Puritans ended in the reign of the harlots.

This was quite natural. Nothing is so galling to a people not broken in from the birth as a paternal, or, in other words, a meddling government, a government which tells them what to read, and say, and eat, and drink, and wear. Our fathers could not bear it two hundred years ago; and we are not more patient than they. Mr. Southey thinks that the yoke of the Church is dropping off because it is loose. We feel convinced that it is borne only because it is easy, and that, in the instant in which an attempt is made to tighten it, it will be flung away. It will be neither the first nor the strongest yoke that has been broken asunder and trampled under foot in the day of the vengeance of England.

SIGNS OF THE TIMES

. . . . .

The signs of the times, Mr. Southey tells us, are very threatening. His fears for the country would decidedly preponderate over his hopes, but for a firm reliance on the mercy of God. Now, as we know that God has once suffered the civilised world to be overrun by savages, and the Christian religion to be corrupted by doctrines which made it, for some ages, almost as bad as Paganism, we cannot think it inconsistent with his attributes that similar calamities should again befall mankind.

We look, however, on the state of the world, and of this kingdom in particular, with much greater satisfaction and with better hopes. Mr. Southey speaks with contempt of those who think the savage state happier than the social. On this subject, he says, Rousseau never imposed on him even in his youth. But he conceives that a community which has advanced a little way in civilisation is happier than one which has made greater progress. The Britons in the time of Cæsar were happier, he suspects, than the English of the nineteenth century. On the whole, he selects the generation which preceded the Reformation as that in which the people of this country were better off than at any time before or since.

This opinion rests on nothing, as far as we can see, except his own individual associations. He is a man of letters; and a life destitute of literary pleasures seems insipid to him. He abhors the spirit of the present generation, the severity of its studies, the boldness of its inquiries, and the disdain with which it regards some old prejudices by which his own mind is held in bondage. He dislikes an utterly unenlightened age; he dislikes an investigating and reforming age. The first twenty years of the sixteenth century would have exactly suited him. They furnished just the quantity of intellectual excitement which he requires. The learned few read and wrote largely. A scholar was held in high estimation. But the rabble did not presume to think; and even the most inquiring and independent of the educated classes paid more reverence to authority, and less to reason, than is usual in our time. This is a state of things in which Mr. Southey would have found himself quite comfortable; and, accordingly, he pronounces it the happiest state of things ever known in the world.

26

The savages were wretched, says Mr. Southey; but the people in the time of Sir Thomas More were happier than either they or we. Now we think it quite certain that we have the advantage over the contemporaries of Sir Thomas More, in every point in which they had any advantage over savages.

Mr. Southey does not even pretend to maintain that the people in the sixteenth century were better lodged or clothed than at present. He seems to admit that in these respects there has been some little improvement. It is indeed a matter about which scarcely any doubt can exist in the most perverse mind that the improvements of machinery have lowered the price of manufactured articles, and have brought within the reach of the poorest some conveniences which Sir Thomas More or his master could not have obtained at any price.

The labouring classes, however, were, according to Mr. Southey, better fed three hundred years ago than at present. We believe that he is completely in error on this point. The condition of servants in noble and wealthy families, and of scholars at the Universities, must surely have been better in those times than that of day-labourers; and we are sure that it was not better than that of our workhouse paupers. From the household book of the Northumberland family, we find that in one of the greatest establishments of the kingdom the servants lived very much as common sailors live now. In the reign of Edward the Sixth the state of the students at Cambridge is described to us, on the very best authority, as most wretched. Many of them dined on pottage made of a farthing's worth of beef with a little salt and oatmeal, and literally nothing else. This account we have from a contemporary master of St. John's. Our parish poor now eat wheaten bread. In the sixteenth century the labourer was glad to get barley, and was often forced to content himself with poorer fare. In Harrison's introduction to Holinshed [10] we have an account of the state of our working population in the "golden days," as Mr. Southey calls them, "of good Queen Bess." "The gentilitie," says he, "commonly provide themselves sufficiently of wheat for their own tables, whylest their household and poore neigh-

[10] William Harrison (1534-1593), author of "Description of England," included in Holinshed's *Chronicles* (1577), which was an important source book of British history for Shakespeare and other Elizabethan dramatists.

bours in some shires are inforced to content themselves with rye or barleie; yea, and in time of dearth, many with bread made eyther of beanes, peason, or otes, or of altogether, and some acornes among. I will not say that this extremity is oft so well to be seen in time of plentie as of dearth; but if I should I could easily bring my trial: for albeit there be much more grounde eared nowe almost in everye place than hathe beene of late yeares, yet such a price of corne continueth in eache towne and markete, without any just cause, that the artificer and poore labouring man is not able to reach unto it, but is driven to content himself with horse-corne." We should like to see what the effect would be of putting any parish in England now on allowance of "horse-corne." The helotry of Mammon are not, in our day, so easily enforced to content themselves as the peasantry of that happy period, as Mr. Southey considers it, which elapsed between the fall of the feudal and the rise of the commercial tyranny.

"The people," says Mr. Southey, "are worse fed than when they were fishers." And yet in another place he complains that they will not eat fish. "They have contracted," says he, "I know not how, some obstinate prejudice against a kind of food at once wholesome and delicate, and everywhere to be obtained cheaply and in abundance, were the demand for it as general as it ought to be." It is true that the lower orders have an obstinate prejudice against fish. But hunger has no such obstinate prejudices. If what was formerly a common diet is now eaten only in times of severe pressure, the inference is plain. The people must be fed with what they at least think better food than that of their ancestors.

The advice and medicine which the poorest labourer can now obtain, in disease, or after an accident, is far superior to what Henry the Eighth could have commanded. Scarcely any part of the country is out of the reach of practitioners, who are probably not so far inferior to Sir Henry Halford as they are superior to Dr. Butts.[11] That there has been a great improvement in this respect, Mr. Southey allows. Indeed he could not well have denied it. "But," says he, "the evils for which these sciences

---

[11] Sir Henry Halford (1766-1844), royal physician successively to George III, George IV, William IV, and Queen Victoria; Sir William Butts (d. 1545), physician to Henry VIII.

are the palliative, have increased since the time of the Druids, in a proportion that heavily overweighs the benefit of improved therapeutics." We know nothing either of the diseases or the remedies of the Druids. But we are quite sure that the improvement of medicine has far more than kept pace with the increase of disease during the last three centuries. This is proved by the best possible evidence. The term of human life is decidedly longer in England than in any former age, respecting which we possess any information on which we can rely. All the rants in the world about picturesque cottages and temples of Mammon will not shake this argument. No test of the physical well-being of society can be named so decisive as that which is furnished by bills of mortality. That the lives of the people of this country have been gradually lengthening during the course of several generations, is as certain as any fact in statistics; and that the lives of men should become longer and longer, while their bodily condition during life is becoming worse and worse, is utterly incredible.

Let our readers think over these circumstances. Let them take into the account the sweating sickness and the plague. Let them take into the account that fearful disease which first made its appearance in the generation to which Mr. Southey assigns the palm of felicity, and raged through Europe with a fury at which the physician stood aghast, and before which the people were swept away by myriads. Let them consider the state of the northern counties, constantly the scene of robberies, rapes, massacres, and conflagrations. Let them add to all this the fact that seventy-two thousand persons suffered death by the hands of the executioner during the reign of Henry the Eighth, and judge between the nineteenth and the sixteenth century.

We do not say that the lower orders in England do not suffer severe hardships. But, in spite of Mr. Southey's assertions, and in spite of the assertions of a class of politicians, who, differing from Mr. Southey in every other point, agree with him in this, we are inclined to doubt whether the labouring classes here really suffer greater physical distress than the labouring classes of the most flourishing countries of the Continent.

It will scarcely be maintained that the lazzaroni who sleep under the porticoes of Naples, or the beggars who besiege the convents of Spain, are in a happier situation than the English commonalty. The distress which has lately been experienced in the northern part of Germany, one of the best governed and most prosperous regions of Europe, surpasses, if we have been correctly informed, anything which has of late years been known among us. In Norway and Sweden the peasantry are constantly compelled to mix bark with their bread; and even this expedient has not always preserved whole families and neighbourhoods from perishing together of famine. An experiment has lately been tried in the kingdom of the Netherlands, which has been cited to prove the possibility of establishing agricultural colonies on the waste lands of England, but which proves to our minds nothing so clearly as this, that the rate of subsistence to which the labouring classes are reduced in the Netherlands is miserably low, and very far inferior to that of the English paupers. No distress which the people here have endured for centuries approaches to that which has been felt by the French in our own time. The beginning of the year 1817 was a time of great distress in this island. But the state of the lowest classes here was luxury compared with that of the people of France. We find in Magendie's *Journal de Physiologie Expérimentale*[12] a paper on a point of physiology connected with the distress of that season. It appears that the inhabitants of six departments, Aix, Jura, Doubs, Haute Saone, Vosges, and Saone-et-Loire, were reduced first to oatmeal and potatoes, and at last to nettles, beanstalks, and other kinds of herbage fit only for cattle; that when the next harvest enabled them to eat barley-bread, many of them died from intemperate indulgence in what they thought an exquisite repast; and that a dropsy of a peculiar description was produced by the hard fare of the year. Dead bodies were found on the roads and in the fields. A single surgeon dissected six of these, and found the stomach shrunk, and filled with the unwholesome aliments which hunger had driven men to share with beasts. Such extremity of distress as this is never heard of in England, or even in Ireland. We are, on the whole, inclined to think, though we would speak with diffidence on a point on which it would be rash to pronounce a positive judgment without a much longer and closer investigation than we have bestowed upon it, that the labouring classes of this island, though they have their grievances and distresses, some

[12] François Magendie (1783-1855), noted French physiologist.

produced by their own improvidence, some by the errors of their rulers, are on the whole better off as to physical comforts than the inhabitants of an equally extensive district of the old world. For this very reason, suffering is more acutely felt and more loudly bewailed here than elsewhere. We must take into the account the liberty of discussion, and the strong interest which the opponents of a ministry always have to exaggerate the extent of the public disasters. There are countries in which the people quietly endure distress that here would shake the foundations of the State, countries in which the inhabitants of a whole province turn out to eat grass with less clamour than one Spitalfields weaver would make here, if the overseers were to put him on barley-bread. In those new commonwealths in which a civilised population has at its command a boundless extent of the richest soil, the condition of the labourer is probably happier than in any society which has lasted for many centuries. But in the old world we must confess ourselves unable to find any satisfactory record of any great nation, past or present, in which the working classes have been in a more comfortable situation than in England during the last thirty years. When this island was thinly peopled, it was barbarous: there was little capital; and that little was insecure. It is now the richest and most highly civilised spot in the world; but the population is dense. Thus we have never known that golden age which the lower orders in the United States are now enjoying. We have never known an age of liberty, of order, and of education, an age in which the mechanical sciences were carried to a great height, yet in which the people were not sufficiently numerous to cultivate even the most fertile valleys. But, when we compare our own condition with that of our ancestors, we think it clear that the advantages arising from the progress of civilisation have far more than counterbalanced the disadvantages arising from the progress of population. While our numbers have increased tenfold, our wealth has increased a hundredfold. Though there are so many more people to share the wealth now existing in the country than there were in the sixteenth century, it seems certain that a greater share falls to almost every individual than fell to the share of any of the corresponding class in the sixteenth century. The King keeps a more splendid court. The establishments of the nobles are more magnificent. The esquires are richer; the merchants are richer; the shopkeepers are richer. The serving-man, the artisan, and the husbandman, have a more copious and palatable supply of food, better clothing, and better furniture. This is no reason for tolerating abuses, or for neglecting any means of ameliorating the condition of our poorer countrymen. But it is a reason against telling them, as some of our philosophers are constantly telling them, that they are the most wretched people who ever existed on the face of the earth.

We have already adverted to Mr. Southey's amusing doctrine about national wealth. A state, says he, cannot be too rich; but a people may be too rich. His reason for thinking this is extremely curious.

A people may be too rich, because it is the tendency of the commercial, and more especially of the manufacturing system, to collect wealth rather than to diffuse it. Where wealth is necessarily employed in any of the speculations of trade, its increase is in proportion to its amount. Great capitalists become like pikes in a fish-pond who devour the weaker fish; and it is but too certain, that the poverty of one part of the people seems to increase in the same ratio as the riches of another. There are examples of this in history. In Portugal, when the high tide of wealth flowed in from the conquests in Africa and the East, the effect of that great influx was not more visible in the augmented splendour of the court, and the luxury of the higher ranks, than in the distress of the people.

Mr. Southey's instance is not a very fortunate one. The wealth which did so little for the Portuguese was not the fruit either of manufacturers or of commerce carried on by private individuals. It was the wealth, not of the people, but of the Government and its creatures, of those who, as Mr. Southey thinks, can never be too rich. The fact is, that Mr. Southey's proposition is opposed to all history, and to the phenomena which surround us on every side. England is the richest country in Europe, the most commercial country, and the country in which manufactures flourish most. Russia and Poland are the poorest countries in Europe. They have scarcely any trade, and none but the rudest manufactures. Is wealth more diffused in Russia and Poland than in England? There are individuals in Russia and Poland whose incomes are probably equal to those of our richest countrymen. It may be doubted whether there are not, in those countries, as many fortunes of eighty thousand a year as here. But are there as many fortunes of two thousand a year, or of one thousand a year? There are parishes in England which contain more people of between three hundred and three thousand pounds a year than could be found in all the dominions of the Emperor Nicholas. The neat and commodious houses which have been built in London and its vicinity, for people of this class, within the last thirty years, would of themselves form a city larger than the capitals of some European kingdoms. And this is the state of society in which the great proprietors have devoured a smaller!

The cure which Mr. Southey thinks that he has discovered is worthy of the sagacity which he has shown in detecting the evil. The calamities arising from the collection of wealth in the hands of a few capitalists are to be remedied by collecting it in the hands of one great capitalist, who has no conceivable motive to use it better than other capitalists, the all-devouring State.

It is not strange that, differing so widely from Mr. Southey as to the past progress of society, we should differ from him also as to its probable destiny. He thinks, that to all outward appearance, the country is hastening to destruction; but he relies firmly on the goodness of God. We do not see either the piety or the rationality of thus confidently expecting that the Supreme Being will interfere to disturb the common succession of causes and effects. We, too, rely on his goodness, on his goodness as manifested, not in extraordinary interpositions, but in those general laws which it has pleased him to establish in the physical and in the moral world. We rely on the natural tendency of the human intellect to truth, and on the natural tendency of society to improvement. We know no well-authenticated instance of a people which has decidedly retrograded in civilisation and prosperity, except from the influence of violent and terrible calamities, such as those which laid the Roman Empire in ruins, or those which, about the beginning of the sixteenth century, desolated Italy. We know of no country which, at the end of fifty years of peace and tolerably good government, has been less prosperous than at the beginning of that period. The political importance of a state may decline, as the balance of power is disturbed by the introduction of new forces. Thus the influence of Holland and of Spain is much diminished. But are Holland and Spain poorer than formerly? We doubt it. Other countries have outrun them. But we suspect that they have been positively, though not relatively, advancing. We suspect that Holland is richer than when she sent her navies up the Thames, that Spain is richer than when a French king was brought captive to the footstool of Charles the Fifth.

History is full of the signs of this natural progress of society. We see in almost every part of the annals of mankind how the industry of individuals, struggling up against wars, taxes, famines, conflagrations, mischievous prohibitions, and more mischievous protections, creates faster than governments can squander, and repairs whatever invaders can destroy. We see the wealth of nations increasing, and all the arts of life approaching nearer and nearer to perfection, in spite of the grossest corruption and the wildest profusion on the part of rulers.

The present moment is one of great distress. But how small will that distress appear when we think over the history of the last forty years; a war, compared with which all other wars sink into insignificance; taxation such as the most heavily taxed people of former times could not have conceived; a debt larger than all the public debts that ever existed in the world added together; the food of the people studiously rendered dear; the currency imprudently debased, and imprudently restored. Yet is the country poorer than in 1790? We firmly believe that, in spite of all the misgovernment of her rulers, she has been almost constantly becoming richer and richer. Now and then there has been a stoppage, now and then a short retrogression; but as to the general tendency there can be no doubt. A single breaker may recede; but the tide is evidently coming in.

If we were to prophesy that in the year 1930 a population of fifty millions, better fed, clad, and lodged than the English of our time, will cover these islands; that Sussex and Huntingdonshire will be wealthier than the wealthiest parts of the West Riding of Yorkshire now are; that cultivation, rich as that of a flower-garden, will be carried up to the very tops of Ben Nevis and Helvellyn; that machines constructed on principles yet undiscovered will be in every house; that there will be no highways but railroads, no travelling but by steam; that our debt, vast as it seems to us, will appear to our great-grandchildren a trifling encumbrance which might easily be paid off in a year or two—many people would think us insane. We prophesy nothing; but this we say: If any person

34

had told the Parliament which met in perplexity and terror after the crash in 1720 [13] that in 1830 the wealth of England would surpass all their wildest dreams, that the annual revenue would equal the principal of that debt which they considered as an intolerable burden, that for one man of ten thousand pounds then living there would be five men of fifty thousand pounds, that London would be twice as large and twice as populous, and that nevertheless the rate of mortality would have diminished to one-half of what it then was, that the post-office would bring more into the exchequer than the excise and customs had brought in together under Charles the Second, that stage coaches would run from London to York in twenty-four hours, that men would be in the habit of sailing without wind, and would be beginning to ride without horses, our ancestors would have given as much credit to the prediction as they gave to *Gulliver's Travels.* Yet the prediction would have been true; and they would have perceived that it was not altogether absurd, if they had considered that the country was then raising every year a sum which would have purchased the fee-simple of the revenue of the Plantagenets, ten times what supported the Government of Elizabeth, three times what, in the time of Cromwell, had been thought intolerably oppressive. To almost all men the state of things under which they have been used to live seems to be the necessary state of things. We have heard it said that five per cent. is the natural interest of money, that twelve is the natural number of a jury, that forty shillings is the natural qualification of a county voter. Hence it is that, though in every age everybody knows that up to his own time progressive improvement has been taking place, nobody seems to reckon on any improvement during the next generation. We cannot absolutely prove that those are in error who tell us that society has reached a turning point, that we have seen our best days. But so said all who came before us, and with just as much apparent reason. "A million a year will beggar us," said the patriots of 1640. "Two millions a year will grind the country to powder," was the cry in 1660. "Six millions a year, and a debt of fifty millions!" exclaimed Swift; "the high allies have been the ruin of us." "A hundred and forty millions of debt!"

[13] Year of acute financial depression, ensuant on the bursting of the fraudulent scheme known as the South Sea Bubble.

said Junius;[14] "well may we say that we owe Lord Chatham more than we shall ever pay, if we owe him such a load as this." "Two hundred and forty millions of debt!" cried all the statesmen of 1783 in chorus; "what abilities, or what economy on the part of a minister, can save a country so burdened?" We know that if, since 1783, no fresh debt had been incurred, the increased resources of the country would have enabled us to defray that debt at which Pitt, Fox, and Burke stood aghast, nay, to defray it over and over again, and that with much lighter taxation than what we have actually borne. On what principle is it that, when we see nothing but improvement behind us, we are to expect nothing but deterioration before us?

It is not by the intermeddling of Mr. Southey's idol, the omniscient and omnipotent State, but by the prudence and energy of the people, that England has hitherto been carried forward in civilisation; and it is to the same prudence and the same energy that we now look with comfort and good hope. Our rulers will best promote the improvement of the nation by strictly confining themselves to their own legitimate duties, by leaving capital to find its most lucrative course, commodities their fair price, industry and intelligence their natural reward, idleness and folly their natural punishment, by maintaining peace, by defending property, by diminishing the price of law, and by observing strict economy in every department of the State. Let the Government do this: the People will assuredly do the rest.

[14] Pseudonym of the unidentified author of *Letters of Junius* (1772), attacking George III and his Tory ministers.

Thomas Carlyle

1795-1881

Signs of the Times

This essay was published anonymously in the *Edinburgh Review,* June 1829. According to James Anthony Froude, Carlyle's biographer, it was "the first of the essays in which he brought out his views on the condition of modern English society." As the official organ of the progressive Whigs, the *Edinburgh Review* would not, it may be assumed, have endorsed most of the "views" here presented.

It is no very good symptom either of nations or individuals, that they deal much in vaticination. Happy men are full of the present, for its bounty suffices them; and wise men also, for its duties engage them. Our grand business undoubtedly is, not to *see* what lies dimly at a distance, but to *do* what lies clearly at hand.

> Know'st thou *Yesterday,* its aim and reason;
> Work'st thou well *Today,* for worthy things?
> Calmly wait the *Morrow's* hidden season,
> Need'st not fear what hap soe'er it brings.

But man's "large discourse of reason" *will* look "before and after";[1] and, impatient of the "ignorant present time," will indulge in anticipation far more than profits him. Seldom can the unhappy be persuaded that the evil of the day is sufficient for it; and the ambitious will not be content with present splendour, but paints yet more glorious triumphs, on the cloud-curtain of the future.

[1] See *Hamlet* iv.iv.36-37.

The case, however, is still worse with nations. For here the prophets are not one, but many; and each incites and confirms the other; so that the fatidical fury spreads wider and wider, till at last even Saul must join in it. For there is still a real magic in the action and reaction of minds on one another. The casual deliration of a few becomes, by this mysterious reverberation, the frenzy of many; men lose the use, not only of their understandings, but of their bodily senses; while the most obdurate unbelieving hearts melt, like the rest, in the furnace where all are cast as victims and as fuel. It is grievous to think, that this noble omnipotence of Sympathy has been so rarely the Aaron's-rod of Truth and Virtue,[2] and so often the Enchanter's-rod of Wickedness and Folly! No solitary miscreant, scarcely any solitary maniac, would venture on such actions and imaginations, as large communities of sane men have, in such circumstances, entertained as sound wisdom. Witness long scenes of the French Revolution, in these late times! Levity is no protection against such visitations, nor the utmost earnestness of character. The New-England Puritan burns witches, wrestles for months with the horrors of Satan's invisible world, and all ghastly phantasms, the daily and hourly precursors of the Last Day; then suddenly bethinks him that he is frantic, weeps bitterly, prays contritely, and the history of that gloomy season lies behind him like a frightful dream.

Old England too has had her share of such frenzies and panics; though happily, like other old maladies, they have grown milder of late: and since the days of Titus Oates have mostly passed without loss of men's lives; or indeed without much other loss than that of reason, for the time, in the sufferers. In this mitigated form, however, the distemper is of pretty regular recurrence; and may be reckoned on at intervals, like other natural visitations; so that reasonable men deal with it, as the Londoners do with their fogs,—go cautiously out into the groping crowd, and patiently carry lanterns at noon; knowing, by a well-grounded faith, that the sun is still in existence, and will one day reappear. How often have we heard, for the last fifty years, that the country was wrecked, and fast sinking; whereas, up to this date, the country is entire and afloat! The "State in Danger" is a condition of things, which we have

[2] Cf. Numbers xvii.

witnessed a hundred times; and as for the Church, it has seldom been out of "danger" since we can remember it.

All men are aware that the present is a crisis of this sort; and why it has become so. The repeal of the Test Acts, and then of the Catholic disabilities,[3] has struck many of their admirers with an indescribable astonishment. Those things seemed fixed and immovable; deep as the foundations of the world; and lo, in a moment they have vanished, and their place knows them no more! Our worthy friends mistook the slumbering Leviathan for an island; often as they had been assured, that Intolerance was, and could be nothing but a Monster; and so, mooring under the lee, they had anchored comfortably in his scaly rind, thinking to take good cheer;[4] as for some space they did. But now their Leviathan has suddenly dived under; and they can no longer be fastened in the stream of time; but must drift forward on it, even like the rest of the world: no very appalling fate, we think, could they but understand it; which, however, they will not yet, for a season. Their little island is gone; sunk deep amid confused eddies; and what is left worth caring for in the universe? What is it to them that the great continents of the earth are still standing; and the polestar and all our loadstars, in the heavens, still shining and eternal? Their cherished little haven is gone, and they will not be comforted! And therefore, day after day, in all manner of periodical or perennial publications, the most lugubrious predictions are sent forth. The King has virtually abdicated; the Church is a widow, without jointure; public principle is gone; private honesty is going; society, in short, is fast falling in pieces; and a time of unmixed evil is come on us.

At such a period, it was to be expected that the rage of prophecy should be more than usually excited. Accordingly, the Millennarians have come forth on the right hand, and the Millites on the left. The Fifth-monarchy men prophesy from the Bible, and the Utilitarians from Bentham. The one announces that the last of the seals is to be opened, positively, in the year 1860; and the other assures us that "the greatest-

---

[3] The Test Acts, which had imposed civil restrictions on Catholics and Dissenters, were repealed in 1828; Catholic emancipation, as a result of which Catholics could be elected to Parliament, followed in 1829.

[4] Cf. *Paradise Lost* 1.200-208.

happiness principle" is to make a heaven of earth, in a still shorter time. We know these symptoms too well, to think it necessary or safe to interfere with them. Time and the hours will bring relief to all parties. The grand encourager of Delphic or other noises is—the Echo. Left to themselves, they will the sooner dissipate, and die away in space.

Meanwhile, we too admit that the present is an important time; as all present time necessarily is. The poorest Day that passes over us is the conflux of two Eternities; it is made up of currents that issue from the remotest Past, and flow onwards into the remotest Future. We were wise indeed, could we discern truly the signs of our own time; and by knowledge of its wants and advantages, wisely adjust our own position in it. Let us, instead of gazing idly into the obscure distance, look calmly around us, for a little, on the perplexed scene where we stand. Perhaps, on a more serious inspection, something of its perplexity will disappear, some of its distinctive characters and deeper tendencies more clearly reveal themselves; whereby our own relations to it, our own true aims and endeavours in it, may also become clearer.

Were we required to characterise this age of ours by any single epithet, we should be tempted to call it, not an Heroical, Devotional, Philosophical, or Moral Age, but, above all others, the Mechanical Age. It is the Age of Machinery, in every outward and inward sense of that word; the age which, with its whole undivided might, forwards, teaches and practises the great art of adapting means to ends. Nothing is now done directly, or by hand; all is by rule and calculated contrivance. For the simplest operation, some helps and accompaniments, some cunning abbreviating process is in readiness. Our old modes of exertion are all discredited, and thrown aside. On every hand, the living artisan is driven from his workshop, to make room for a speedier, inanimate one. The shuttle drops from the fingers of the weaver, and falls into iron fingers that ply it faster. The sailor furls his sail, and lays down his oar; and bids a strong, unwearied servant, on vaporous wings, bear him through the waters. Men have crossed oceans by steam; the Birmingham Fire-king has visited the fabulous East; and the genius of the Cape, were there any Camoens now to sing it, has again been alarmed, and with far stranger thunders than Gamas. There is no end to machinery. Even the horse is stripped of his harness, and finds a fleet fire-horse yoked in his stead. Nay, we have an artist that hatches chickens by steam; the very brood-hen is to be superseded! For all earthly, and for some unearthly purposes, we have machines and mechanic furtherances; for mincing our cabbages; for casting us into magnetic sleep. We remove mountains, and make seas our smooth highways; nothing can resist us. We war with rude Nature; and, by our resistless engines, come off always victorious, and loaded with spoils.

What wonderful accessions have thus been made, and are still making, to the physical power of mankind; how much better fed, clothed, lodged and, in all outward respects, accommodated men now are, or might be, by a given quantity of labour, is a grateful reflection which forces itself on every one. What changes, too, this addition of power is introducing into the Social System; how wealth has more and more increased, and at the same time gathered itself more and more into masses, strangely altering the old relations, and increasing the distance between the rich and the poor, will be a question for Political Economists, and a much more complex and important one than any they have yet engaged with.

But leaving these matters for the present, let us observe how the mechanical genius of our time has diffused itself into quite other provinces. Not the external and physical alone is now managed by machinery, but the internal and spiritual also. Here too nothing follows its spontaneous course, nothing is left to be accomplished by old natural methods. Everything has its cunningly devised implements, its pre-established apparatus; it is not done by hand, but by machinery. Thus we have machines for Education: Lancastrian machines; Hamiltonian machines;[5] monitors, maps and emblems. Instruction, that mysterious communing of Wisdom with Ignorance, is no longer an indefinable tentative process, requiring a study of individual aptitudes, and a perpetual variation of means and methods, to attain the same end; but a secure, universal, straightforward business, to be conducted in the gross, by proper mechanism, with such intellect as comes to hand. Then, we have Religious

---

[5] Lancastrian machines, a reference to the monitorial method of teaching introduced by Joseph Lancaster (1778-1838); Hamiltonian machines, a reference to the system of foreign language instruction promoted by James Hamilton (1769-1829).

machines, of all imaginable varieties; the Bible-Society, professing a far higher and heavenly structure, is found, on inquiry, to be altogether an earthly contrivance: supported by collection of moneys, by fomenting of vanities, by puffing, intrigue and chicane; a machine for converting the Heathen. It is the same in all other departments. Has any man, or any society of men, a truth to speak, a piece of spiritual work to do; they can nowise proceed at once and with the mere natural organs, but must first call a public meeting, appoint committees, issue prospectuses, eat a public dinner; in a word, construct or borrow machinery, wherewith to speak it and do it. Without machinery they were hopeless, helpless; a colony of Hindoo weavers squatting in the heart of Lancashire. Mark, too, how every machine must have its moving power, in some of the great currents of society; every little sect among us, Unitarians, Utilitarians, Anabaptists, Phrenologists, must have its Periodical, its monthly or quarterly Magazine;—hanging out, like its windmill, into the *popularis aura*,[6] to grind meal for the society.

With individuals, in like manner, natural strength avails little. No individual now hopes to accomplish the poorest enterprise single-handed and without mechanical aids; he must make interest with some existing corporation, and till his field with their oxen. In these days, more emphatically than ever, "to live, signifies to unite with a party, or to make one." Philosophy, Science, Art, Literature, all depend on machinery. No Newton, by silent meditation, now discovers the system of the world from the falling of an apple; but some quite other than Newton stands in his Museum, his Scientific Institution, and behind whole batteries of retorts, digesters, and galvanic piles imperatively "interrogates Nature," —who, however, shows no haste to answer. In defect of Raphaels, and Angelos, and Mozarts, we have Royal Academies of Painting, Sculpture, Music; whereby the languishing spirits of Art may be strengthened, as by the more generous diet of a Public Kitchen. Literature, too, has its Paternoster-row[7] mechanism, its Trade-dinners, its Editorial conclaves, and huge subterranean, puffing bellows; so that books are not only printed, but, in a great measure, written and sold, by machinery.

National culture, spiritual benefit of all sorts, is under the same

[6] Popular breeze.
[7] Paternoster Row, a street in London where the publishing trade was centered.

management. No Queen Christina, in these times, needs to send for her Descartes; no King Frederick for his Voltaire, and painfully nourish him with pensions and flattery: any sovereign of taste, who wishes to enlighten his people, has only to impose a new tax, and with the proceeds establish Philosophic Institutes. Hence the Royal and Imperial Societies, the Bibliothèques, Glyptothèques, Technothèques,[8] which front us in all capital cities; like so many well-finished hives, to which it is expected the stray agencies of Wisdom will swarm of their own accord, and hive and make honey. In like manner, among ourselves, when it is thought that religion is declining, we have only to vote half-a-million's worth of bricks and mortar, and build new churches. In Ireland it seems they have gone still farther, having actually established a "Penny-a-week Purgatory-Society"! Thus does the Genius of Mechanism stand by to help us in all difficulties and emergencies, and with his iron back bears all our burdens.

These things, which we state lightly enough here, are yet of deep import, and indicate a mighty change in our whole manner of existence. For the same habit regulates not our modes of action alone, but our modes of thought and feeling. Men are grown mechanical in head and in heart, as well as in hand. They have lost faith in individual endeavour, and in natural force, of any kind. Not for internal perfection, but for external combinations and arrangements, for institutions, constitutions,— for Mechanism of one sort or other, do they hope and struggle. Their whole efforts, attachments, opinions, turn on mechanism, and are of a mechanical character.

We may trace this tendency in all the great manifestations of our time; in its intellectual aspect, the studies it most favours and its manner of conducting them; in its practical aspects, its politics, arts, religion, morals; in the whole sources, and throughout the whole currents, of its spiritual, no less than its material activity.

Consider, for example, the state of Science generally, in Europe, at this period. It is admitted, on all sides, that the Metaphysical and Moral Sciences are falling into decay, while the Physical are engrossing, every day, more respect and attention. In most of the European nations there is now no such thing as a Science of Mind; only more or less advance-

[8] Libraries, museums of sculpture, and museums of arts and crafts.

ment in the general science, or the special sciences, of matter. The French were the first to desert Metaphysics; and though they have lately affected to revive their school, it has yet no signs of vitality. The land of Malebranche, Pascal, Descartes and Fénelon, has now only its Cousins and Villemains;[9] while, in the department of Physics, it reckons far other names. Among ourselves, the Philosophy of Mind, after a rickety infancy, which never reached the vigour of manhood, fell suddenly into decay, languished and finally died out, with its last amiable cultivator, Professor Stewart.[10] In no nation but Germany has any decisive effort been made in psychological science; not to speak of any decisive result. The science of the age, in short, is physical, chemical, physiological; in all shapes mechanical. Our favourite Mathematics, the highly prized exponent of all these other sciences, has also become more and more mechanical. Excellence in what is called its higher departments depends less on natural genius than on acquired expertness in wielding its machinery. Without under-valuing the wonderful results which a Lagrange or Laplace[11] educes by means of it, we may remark, that their calculus, differential and integral, is little else than a more cunningly-constructed arithmetical mill; where the factors, being put in, are, as it were, ground into the true product, under cover, and without other effort on our part than steady turning of the handle. We have more Mathematics than ever; but less Mathesis.[12] Archimedes and Plato could not have read the *Mécanique Céleste;* but neither would the whole French Institute see aught in that saying, "God geometrises!" but a sentimental rodomontade.

Nay, our whole Metaphysics itself, from Locke's time downward, has been physical; not a spiritual philosophy, but a material one. The singular estimation in which his Essay[13] was so long held as a scientific work

[9] Victor Cousin (1792-1867), historian of philosophy, and Abel-François Villemain (1790-1870), literary critic, were minor figures compared with the four great French thinkers whose names precede theirs.

[10] Dugald Stewart (1753-1828), professor of moral philosophy at the University of Edinburgh, whose empiricism was antipathetic to Carlyle.

[11] Joseph Louis Lagrange (1736-1813) and Pierre Simon, Marquis de Laplace (1749-1827), were eminent French mathematicians and astronomers. The latter was author of *Traité de Mécanique Céleste,* 5 vols. (1799-1825).

[12] Mathematics considered as a pure rather than an applied science.

[13] John Locke's *An Essay Concerning Human Understanding* (1690).

(an estimation grounded, indeed, on the estimable character of the man) will one day be thought a curious indication of the spirit of these times. His whole doctrine is mechanical, in its aim and origin, in its method and its results. It is not a philosophy of the mind: it is a mere discussion concerning the origin of our consciousness, or ideas, or whatever else they are called; a genetic history of what we see *in* the mind. The grand secrets of Necessity and Freewill, of the Mind's vital or non-vital dependence on Matter, of our mysterious relations to Time and Space, to God, to the Universe, are not, in the faintest degree touched on in these inquiries; and seem not to have the smallest connexion with them.

The last class of our Scotch Metaphysicians had a dim notion that much of this was wrong; but they knew not how to right it. The school of Reid[14] had also from the first taken a mechanical course, not seeing any other. The singular conclusions at which Hume,[15] setting out from their admitted premises, was arriving, brought this school into being; they let loose Instinct, as an undiscriminating ban-dog, to guard them against these conclusions;—they tugged lustily at the logical chain by which Hume was so coldly towing them and the world into bottomless abysses of Atheism and Fatalism. But the chain somehow snapped between them; and the issue has been that nobody now cares about either, —any more than about Hartley's, Darwin's, or Priestley's contemporaneous doings in England.[16] Hartley's vibrations and vibratiuncles, one would think, were material and mechanical enough; but our Continental neighbours have gone still farther. One of their philosophers has lately discovered, that "as the liver secretes bile, so does the brain secrete thought"; which astonishing discovery Dr. Cabanis,[17] more lately still, in his *Rapports du Physique et du Morale de l'Homme,* has pushed into its minutest developments.

The metaphysical philosophy of this last inquirer is certainly no

[14] Thomas Reid (1710-1796), professor of moral philosophy at the University of Glasgow, a leading figure in the "common sense" school of Scottish philosophy.

[15] David Hume (1711-1776), the great Scottish historian and sceptical thinker.

[16] David Hartley (1705-1757), psychologist who developed the doctrine of the association of ideas; Erasmus Darwin (1731-1802), physician and poet, who anticipated his grandson's evolutionary hypothesis; Joseph Priestley (1733-1804), scientist and freethinker.

[17] Pierre Cabanis (1757-1808), French physiologist and materialist.

shadowy or unsubstantial one. He fairly lays open our moral structure with his dissecting-knives and real metal probes; and exhibits it to the inspection of mankind, by Leuwenhoek[18] microscopes, and inflation with the anatomical blowpipe. Thought, he is inclined to hold, is still secreted by the brain; but then Poetry and Religion (and it is really worth knowing) are "a product of the smaller intestines"! We have the greatest admiration for this learned doctor: with what scientific stoicism he walks through the land of wonders, unwondering; like a wise man through some huge, gaudy, imposing Vauxhall,[19] whose fireworks, cascades and symphonies, the vulgar may enjoy and believe in, —but where he finds nothing real but the saltpetre, pasteboard and catgut. His book may be regarded as the ultimatum of mechanical metaphysics in our time; a remarkable realisation of what in Martinus Scriblerus[20] was still only an idea, that "as the jack had a meat-roasting quality, so had the body a thinking quality,"—upon the strength of which the Nurembergers were to build a wood-and-leather man, "who should reason as well as most country parsons." Vaucanson[21] did indeed make a wooden duck, that seemed to eat and digest; but that bold scheme of the Nurembergers remained for a more modern virtuoso.

This condition of the two great departments of knowledge,—the outward, cultivated exclusively on mechanical principles; the inward, finally abandoned, because, cultivated on such principles, it is found to yield no result,—sufficiently indicates the intellectual bias of our time, its all-pervading disposition towards that line of inquiry. In fact, an inward persuasion has long been diffusing itself, and now and then even comes to utterance. That, except the external, there are no true sciences; that to the inward world (if there be any) our only conceivable road is through the outward; that, in short, what cannot be investigated and understood mechanically, cannot be investigated and understood at all. We advert the more particularly to these intellectual propensities, as to prominent symptoms of our age, because Opinion is

[18] Anton van Leuwenhoek (1632-1723), Dutch naturalist who invented a simplified microscope.

[19] Pleasure resort in London on the south side of the Thames.

[20] *Memoirs of Martinus Scriblerus* (1741), an anonymous satire on "false tastes in learning."

[21] Jacques de Vaucanson (1709-1782), French inventor.

at all times doubly related to Action, first as cause, then as effect; and the speculative tendency of any age will therefore give us, on the whole, the best indications of its practical tendency.

Nowhere, for example, is the deep, almost exclusive faith we have in Mechanism more visible than in the Politics of this time. Civil government does by its nature include much that is mechanical, and must be treated accordingly. We term it indeed, in ordinary language, the Machine of Society, and talk of it as the grand working wheel from which all private machines must derive, or to which they must adapt, their movements. Considered merely as a metaphor, all this is well enough; but here, as in so many other cases, the "foam hardens itself into a shell," and the shadow we have wantonly evoked stands terrible before us and will not depart at our bidding. Government includes much also that is not mechanical, and cannot be treated mechanically; of which latter truth, as appears to us, the political speculations and exertions of our time are taking less and less cognisance.

Nay, in the very outset, we might note the mighty interest taken in *mere political arrangements,* as itself the sign of a mechanical age. The whole discontent of Europe takes this direction. The deep, strong cry of all civilised nations,—a cry which, every one now sees, must and will be answered, is: Give us a reform of Government! A good structure of legislation, a proper check upon the executive, a wise arrangement of the judiciary, is *all* that is wanting for human happiness. The Philosopher of this age is not a Socrates, a Plato, a Hooker, or Taylor,[22] who inculcates on men the necessity and infinite worth of moral goodness, the great truth that our happiness depends on the mind which is within us, and not on the circumstances which are without us; but a Smith, a DeLolme, a Bentham,[23] who chiefly inculcates the reverse of this,—that our happiness depends entirely on external circumstances; nay, that the strength and dignity of the mind within us is itself the creature and consequence of these. Were the laws, the

[22] Richard Hooker (1554?-1600) and Jeremy Taylor (1613-1667), English divines and the authors of important theological works.

[23] Adam Smith (1723-1790), political economist who wrote *An Enquiry into the Nature and Causes of the Wealth of Nations* (1776); Jean Louis DeLolme (1740-1806), Swiss jurist and author of a work on the English Constitution; Jeremy Bentham (1748-1832), legal reformer and originator of Utilitarianism.

government, in good order, all were well with us; the rest would care for itself! Dissentients from this opinion, expressed or implied, are now rarely to be met with; widely and angrily as men differ in its application, the principle is admitted by all.

Equally mechanical, and of equal simplicity, are the methods proposed by both parties for completing or securing this all-sufficient perfection of arrangement. It is no longer the moral, religious, spiritual condition of the people that is our concern, but their physical, practical, economical condition, as regulated by public laws. Thus is the Body-politic more than ever worshipped and tendered; but the Soul-politic less than ever. Love of country, in any high or generous sense, in any other than an almost animal sense, or mere habit, has little importance attached to it in such reforms, or in the opposition shown them. Men are to be guided only by their self-interests. Good government is a good balancing of these; and, except a keen eye and appetite for self-interest, requires no virtue in any quarter. To both parties it is emphatically a machine: to the discontented, a "taxing-machine"; to the contented, a "machine for securing property." Its duties and its faults are not those of a father, but of an active parish-constable.

Thus it is by the mere condition of the machine, by preserving it untouched, or else by reconstructing it, and oiling it anew, that man's salvation as a social being is to be ensured and indefinitely promoted. Contrive the fabric of law aright, and without farther effort on your part, that divine spirit of Freedom, which all hearts venerate and long for, will of herself come to inhabit it; and under her healing wings every noxious influence will wither, every good and salutary one more and more expand. Nay, so devoted are we to this principle, and at the same time so curiously mechanical, that a new trade, specially grounded on it, has arisen among us, under the name of "Codification," or code-making in the abstract; whereby any people, for a reasonable consideration, may be accommodated with a patent code;—more easily than curious individuals with patent breeches, for the people does *not* need to be measured first.

To us who live in the midst of all this, and see continually the faith, hope and practice of every one founded on Mechanism of one kind or other, it is apt to seem quite natural, and as if it could never have been otherwise. Nevertheless, if we recollect or reflect a little, we shall find both that it has been, and might again be otherwise. The domain of Mechanism,—meaning thereby political, ecclesiastical or other outward establishments,—was once considered as embracing, and we are persuaded can at any time embrace, but a limited portion of man's interests, and by no means the highest portion.

To speak a little pedantically, there is a science of *Dynamics* in man's fortunes and nature, as well as of *Mechanics*. There is a science which treats of, and practically addresses, the primary, unmodified forces and energies of man, the mysterious springs of Love, and Fear, and Wonder, of Enthusiasm, Poetry, Religion, all which have a truly vital and *infinite* character; as well as a science which practically addresses the finite, modified developments of these, when they take the shape of immediate "motives," as hope of reward, or as fear of punishment.

Now it is certain, that in former times the wise men, the enlightened lovers of their kind, who appeared generally as Moralists, Poets or Priests, did, without neglecting the Mechanical province, deal chiefly with the Dynamical; applying themselves chiefly to regulate, increase and purify the inward primary powers of man; and fancying that herein lay the main difficulty, and the best service they could undertake. But a wide difference is manifest in our age. For the wise men, who now appear as Political Philosophers, deal exclusively with the Mechanical province; and occupying themselves in counting-up and estimating men's motives, strive by curious checking and balancing, and other adjustments of Profit and Loss, to guide them to their true advantage: while, unfortunately, those same "motives" are so innumerable, and so variable in every individual, that no really useful conclusion can ever be drawn from their enumeration. But though Mechanism, wisely contrived, has done much for man in a social and moral point of view, we cannot be persuaded that it has ever been the chief source of his worth or happiness. Consider the great elements of human enjoyment, the attainments and possessions that exalt man's life to its present height, and see what part of these he owes to institutions, to Mechanism of any kind; and what to the instinctive, unbounded force, which Nature herself lent him, and still continues to him. Shall we say, for example, that Science and Art are indebted principally to the founders of Schools and Universities? Did not Science originate rather, and gain advancement, in the obscure closets of the Roger Bacons, Keplers, Newtons; in the workshops of the Fausts and the Watts; wherever, and in what guise soever Nature, from the first times downwards, had sent a gifted spirit upon the earth? Again, were Homer and Shakespeare members of any beneficed guild, or made Poets by means of it? Were Painting and Sculpture created by forethought, brought into the world by institutions for that end? No; Science and Art have, from first to last, been the free gift of Nature; an unsolicited, unexpected gift; often even a fatal one. These things rose up, as it were, by spontaneous growth, in the free soil and sunshine of Nature. They were not planted or grafted, nor even greatly multiplied or improved by the culture or manuring of institutions. Generally speaking, they have derived only partial help from these; often enough have suffered damage. They made constitutions for themselves. They originated in the Dynamical nature of man, not in his Mechanical nature.

Or, to take an infinitely higher instance, that of the Christian Religion, which, under every theory of it, in the believing or unbelieving mind, must ever be regarded as the crowning glory, or rather the life and soul, of our whole modern culture: How did Christianity arise and spread abroad among men? Was it by institutions, and establishments and well-arranged systems of mechanism? Not so; on the contrary, in all past and existing institutions for those ends, its divine spirit has invariably been found to languish and decay. It arose in the mystic deeps of man's soul; and was spread abroad by the "preaching of the word," by simple, altogether natural and individual efforts; and flew, like hallowed fire, from heart to heart, till all were purified and illuminated by it; and its heavenly light shone, as it still shines, and (as sun or star) will ever shine, through the whole dark destinies of man. Here again was no Mechanism; man's highest attainment was accomplished Dynamically, not Mechanically.

Nay, we will venture to say, that no high attainment, not even any far-extending movement among men, was ever accomplished otherwise. Strange as it may seem, if we read History with any degree of thoughtfulness, we shall find that the checks and balances of Profit and Loss have never been the grand agents with men; that they have never been roused into deep, thorough, all-pervading efforts by any computable prospect of Profit and Loss, for any visible, finite object; but always for some invisible and infinite one. The Crusades took their rise in Religion; their visible object was, commercially speaking, worth nothing. It was the boundless Invisible world that was laid bare in the imaginations of those men; and in its burning light, the visible shrunk as a scroll. Not mechanical, nor produced by mechanical means, was this vast movement. No dining at Freemasons' Tavern, with the other long train of modern machinery; no cunning reconciliation of "vested interests," was required here: only the passionate voice of one man,[24] the rapt soul looking through the eyes of one man; and rugged, steel-clad Europe trembled beneath his words, and followed him whither he listed. In later ages it was still the same. The Reformation had an invisible, mystic and ideal aim; the result was indeed to be embodied in external things; but its spirit, its worth, was internal, invisible, infinite. Our English Revolution[25] too originated in Religion. Men did battle, in those old days, not for Purse-sake, but for Conscience-sake. Nay, in our own days, it is no way different. The French Revolution itself had something higher in it than cheap bread and a Habeas-corpus act. Here too was an Idea; a Dynamic, not a Mechanic force. It was a struggle, though a blind and at last an insane one, for the infinite, divine nature of Right, of Freedom, of Country.

Thus does man, in every age, vindicate, consciously or unconsciously, his celestial birthright. Thus does Nature hold on her wondrous, unquestionable course; and all our systems and theories are but so many froth-eddies or sandbanks, which from time to time she casts up, and washes away. When we can drain the Ocean into mill-ponds, and bottle-up the Force of Gravity, to be sold by retail, in gas jars; then may we hope to comprehend the infinitudes of man's soul under formulas of Profit and Loss; and rule over this too, as over a patent engine, by checks, and valves, and balances.

[24] Peter the Hermit (1050?-1115), French monk who sounded the call to the First Crusade.
[25] The Cromwellian Revolution of 1642-60.

Nay, even with regard to Government itself, can it be necessary to remind any one that Freedom, without which indeed all spiritual life is impossible, depends on infinitely more complex influences than either the extension or the curtailment of the "democratic interest"? Who is there that, "taking the high *priori* road," shall point out what these influences are; what deep, subtle, inextricably entangled influences they have been and may be? For man is not the creature and product of Mechanism; but, in a far truer sense, its creator and producer: it is the noble People that makes the noble Government; rather than conversely. On the whole, Institutions are much; but they are not all. The freest and highest spirits of the world have often been found under strange outward circumstances: Saint Paul and his brother Apostles were politically slaves; Epictetus was personally one. Again, forget the influences of Chivalry and Religion, and ask: What countries produced Columbus and Las Casas? Or, descending from virtue and heroism to mere energy and spiritual talent: Cortes, Pizarro, Alba, Ximenes? The Spaniards of the sixteenth century were indisputably the noblest nation of Europe: yet they had the Inquisition and Philip II. They have the same government at this day; and are the lowest nation. The Dutch too have retained their old constitution; but no Siege of Leyden, no William the Silent, not even an Egmont or DeWitt any longer appears among them. With ourselves also, where much has changed, effect has nowise followed cause as it should have done: two centuries ago, the Commons Speaker addressed Queen Elizabeth on bended knees, happy that the virago's foot did not even smite him; yet the people were then governed, not by a Castlereagh, but by a Burghley;[26] they had their Shakspeare and Philip Sidney, where we have our Sheridan Knowles and Beau Brummel.[27]

These and the like facts are so familiar, the truths which they preach so obvious, and have in all past times been so universally believed and acted on, that we should almost feel ashamed for repeating

[26] Robert Stewart Viscount Castlereagh (1769-1822), ultraconservative Foreign Secretary during and immediately after the Napoleonic Wars; William Cecil, first Baron Burghley (1520-1598), Secretary of State and Lord High Treasurer under Queen Elizabeth.

[27] James Sheridan Knowles (1784-1862), minor English dramatist; George Bryan "Beau" Brummel (1778-1840), the famous dandy and friend of George IV.

them; were it not that, on every hand, the memory of them seems to have passed away, or at best died into a faint tradition, of no value as a practical principle. To judge by the loud clamour of our Constitution-builders, Statists, Economists, directors, creators, reformers of Public Societies; in a word, all manner of Mechanists, from the Cartwright up to the Code-maker; and by the nearly total silence of all Preachers and Teachers who should give a voice to Poetry, Religion and Morality, we might fancy either that man's Dynamical nature was, to all spiritual intents, extinct, or else so perfected that nothing more was to be made of it by the old means; and henceforth only in his Mechanical contrivances did any hope exist for him.

To define the limits of these two departments of man's activity, which work into one another, and by means of one another, so intricately and inseparably, were by its nature an impossible attempt. Their relative importance, even to the wisest mind, will vary in different times, according to the special wants and dispositions of those times. Meanwhile, it seems clear enough that only in the right coordination of the two, and the vigorous forwarding of *both*, does our true line of action lie. Undue cultivation of the inward or Dynamical province leads to idle, visionary, impracticable courses, and, especially in rude eras, to Superstition and Fanaticism, with their long train of baleful and well-known evils. Undue cultivation of the outward, again, though less immediately prejudicial, and even for the time productive of many palpable benefits, must, in the long-run, by destroying Moral Force, which is the parent of all other Force, prove not less certainly, and perhaps still more hopelessly, pernicious. This, we take it, is the grand characteristic of our age. By our skill in Mechanism, it has come to pass, that in the management of external things we excel all other ages; while in whatever respects the pure moral nature, in true dignity of soul and character, we are perhaps inferior to most civilised ages.

In fact, if we look deeper, we shall find that this faith in Mechanism has now struck its roots down into man's most intimate, primary sources of conviction; and is thence sending up, over his whole life and activity, innumerable stems,—fruit-bearing and poison-bearing. The truth is, men have lost their belief in the Invisible, and believe, and hope, and work only in the Visible; or, to speak it in other words: This is not a Religious age. Only the material, the immediately practical, not the divine and spiritual, is important to us. The infinite, absolute character of Virtue has passed into a finite, conditional one; it is no longer a worship of the Beautiful and Good; but a calculation of the Profitable. Worship, indeed, in any sense, is not recognised among us, or is mechanically explained into Fear of pain, or Hope of pleasure. Our true Deity is Mechanism. It has subdued external Nature for us, and we think it will do all other things. We are Giants in physical power: in a deeper than metaphorical sense, we are Titans, that strive, by heaping mountain on mountain, to conquer Heaven also.

The strong Mechanical character, so visible in the spiritual pursuits and methods of this age, may be traced much farther into the condition and prevailing disposition of our spiritual nature itself. Consider, for example, the general fashion of Intellect in this era. Intellect, the power man has of knowing and believing, is now nearly synonymous with Logic, or the mere power of arranging and communicating. Its implement is not Meditation, but Argument. "Cause and effect" is almost the only category under which we look at, and work with, all Nature. Our first question with regard to any object is not, What is it? but, How is it? We are no longer instinctively driven to apprehend, and lay to heart, what is Good and Lovely, but rather to inquire, as onlookers, how it is produced, whence it comes, whither it goes. Our favourite Philosophers have no love and no hatred; they stand among us not to do, nor to create anything, but as a sort of Logic-mills, to grind out the true causes and effects of all that is done and created. To the eye of a Smith, a Hume or a Constant,[28] all is well that works quietly. An Order of Ignatius Loyola, a Presbyterianism of John Knox, a Wickliffe or a Henry the Eighth, are simply so many mechanical phenomena, caused or causing.

The *Euphuist*[29] of our day differs much from his pleasant predecessors. An intellectual dapperling of these times boasts chiefly of his irresistible perspicacity, his "dwelling in the daylight of truth," and so

[28] Benjamin Constant de Rebecque (1767-1830), French writer and politician.

[29] One who uses highly artificial or affected language; the name is derived from *Euphues* (1579), a romance by John Lyly (1554?-1606).

forth; which, on examination, turns out to be a dwelling in the *rush-light* of "closet-logic," and a deep unconsciousness that there is any other light to dwell in or any other objects to survey with it. Wonder, indeed, is, on all hands, dying out: it is the sign of uncultivation to wonder. Speak to any small man of a high, majestic Reformation, of a high majestic Luther; and forthwith he sets about "accounting" for it; how the "circumstances of the time" called for such a character, and found him, we suppose, standing girt and road-ready, to do its errand; how the "circumstances of the time" created, fashioned, floated him quietly along into the result; how, in short, this small man, had he been there, could have performed the like himself! For it is the "force of circumstances" that does everything; the force of one man can do nothing. Now all this is grounded on little more than a metaphor. We figure Society as a "Machine," and that mind is opposed to mind, as body is to body; whereby two, or at most ten, little minds must be stronger than one great mind. Notable absurdity! For the plain truth, very plain, we think is, that minds are opposed to minds in quite a different way; and *one* man that has a higher Wisdom, a hitherto unknown spiritual Truth in him, is stronger, not than ten men that have it not, or than ten thousand, but than *all* men that have it not; and stands among them with a quite ethereal, angelic power, as with a sword out of Heaven's own armory, sky-tempered, which no buckler, and no tower of brass, will finally withstand.

But to us, in these times, such considerations rarely occur. We enjoy, we see nothing by direct vision; but only by reflection, and in anatomical dismemberment. Like Sir Hudibras,[30] for every Why we must have a Wherefore. We have our little *theory* on all human and divine things. Poetry, the workings of genius itself, which in all times, with one or another meaning, has been called Inspiration, and held to be mysterious and inscrutable, is no longer without its scientific exposition. The building of the lofty rhyme is like any other masonry or bricklaying: we have theories of its rise, height, decline and fall, —which latter, it would seem, is now near, among all people. Of our "Theories of Taste," as they are called, wherein the deep, infinite, un-

---

[30] The hero of a burlesque poem, *Hudibras* (1663-78), by Samuel Butler (1612-1680).

speakable Love of Wisdom and Beauty, which dwells in all men, is "explained," made mechanically visible, from "Association" and the like, why should we say anything? Hume has written us a "Natural History of Religion";[31] in which one Natural History all the rest are included. Strangely too does the general feeling coincide with Hume's in this wonderful problem; for whether his "Natural History" be the right one or not, that Religion must have a Natural History, all of us, cleric and laic, seem to be agreed. He indeed regards it as a Disease, we again as Health; so far there is a difference; but in our first principle we are at one.

To what extent theological Unbelief, we mean intellectual dissent from the Church, in its view of Holy Writ, prevails at this day, would be a highly important, were it not, under any circumstances, an almost impossible inquiry. But the Unbelief, which is of a still more fundamental character, every man may see prevailing, with scarcely any but the faintest contradiction, all around him; even in the Pulpit itself. Religion in most countries, more or less in every country, is no longer what it was, and should be,—a thousand-voiced psalm from the heart of Man to his invisible Father, the fountain of all Goodness, Beauty, Truth, and revealed in every revelation of these; but for the most part, a wise prudential feeling grounded on mere calculation; a matter, as all others now are, of Expediency and Utility; whereby some smaller quantum of earthly enjoyment may be exchanged for a far larger quantum of celestial enjoyment. Thus Religion too is Profit, a working for wages; not Reverence, but vulgar Hope or Fear. Many, we know, very many we hope, are still religious in a far different sense; were it not so, our case were too desperate: but to witness that such is the temper of the times, we take any calm observant man, who agrees or disagrees in our feeling on the matter, and ask him whether our *view* of it is not in general well-founded.

Literature too, if we consider it, gives similar testimony. At no former era has Literature, the printed communication of Thought, been of such importance as it is now. We often hear that the Church is in danger; and truly so it is,—in a danger it seems not to know of:

[31] The first of David Hume's *Four Dissertations* (1757) is entitled "The Natural History of Religion."

for, with its tithes in the most perfect safety, its functions are becoming more and more superseded. The true Church of England, at this moment, lies in the Editors of its Newspapers. These preach to the people daily, weekly; admonishing kings themselves; advising peace or war, with an authority which only the first Reformers, and a long-past class of Popes, were possessed of; inflicting moral censure; imparting moral encouragement, consolation, edification; in all ways diligently "administering the Discipline of the Church." It may be said too, that in private disposition the new Preachers somewhat resemble the Mendicant Friars of old times: outwardly full of holy zeal; inwardly not without stratagem, and hunger for terrestrial things. But omitting this class, and the boundless host of watery personages who pipe, as they are able, on so many scrannel straws,[32] let us look at the higher regions of Literature, where, if anywhere, the pure melodies of Poesy and Wisdom should be heard. Of natural talent there is no deficiency: one or two richly-endowed individuals even give us a superiority in this respect. But what is the song they sing? Is it a tone of the Memnon Statue,[33] breathing music as the *light* first touches it? A "liquid wisdom," disclosing to our sense the deep, infinite harmonies of Nature and man's soul? Alas, no! It is not a matin or vesper hymn to the Spirit of Beauty, but a fierce clashing of cymbals, and shouting of multitudes, as children pass through the fire to Moloch![34] Poetry itself has no eye for the Invisible. Beauty is no longer the god it worships, but some brute image of Strength; which we may call an idol, for true Strength is one and the same with Beauty, and its worship also is a hymn. The meek, silent Light can mould, create and purify all Nature; but the loud Whirlwind, the sign and product of Disunion, of Weakness, passes on, and is forgotten. How widely this veneration for the physically Strongest has spread itself through Literature, any one may judge who reads either criticism or poem. We praise a work, not as "true," but as "strong"; our highest praise is that it has "affected"

---

[32] Cf. *Lycidas,* 124.

[33] The Greek name for a statue of Amenhotep III which was said to emit sounds when struck by the sun at dawn.

[34] A Semitic deity to whom human sacrifices were offered; cf. *Paradise Lost* I.392-405.

us, has "terrified" us. All this, it has been well observed, is the "maximum of the Barbarous," the symptom, not of vigorous refinement, but of luxurious corruption. It speaks much, too, for men's indestructible love of truth, that nothing of this kind will abide with them; that even the talent of a Byron cannot permanently seduce us into idol-worship; that he too, with all his wild siren charming, already begins to be disregarded and forgotten.

Again, with respect to our Moral condition: here also he who runs may read that the same physical, mechanical influences are everywhere busy. For the "superior morality," of which we hear so much, we too would desire to be thankful: at the same time, it were but blindness to deny that this "superior morality" is properly rather an "inferior criminality," produced not by greater love of Virtue, but by greater perfection of Police; and of that far subtler and stronger Police, called Public Opinion. This last watches over us with its Argus[35] eyes more keenly than ever; but the "inward eye" seems heavy with sleep. Of any belief in invisible, divine things, we find as few traces in our Morality as elsewhere. It is by tangible, material considerations that we are guided, not by inward and spiritual. Self-denial, the parent of all virtue, in any true sense of that word, has perhaps seldom been rarer: so rare is it, that the most, even in their abstract speculations, regard its existence as a chimera. Virtue is Pleasure, is Profit; no celestial, but an earthly thing. Virtuous men, Philanthropists, Martyrs are happy accidents; their "taste" lies the right way! In all senses, we worship and follow after Power; which may be called a physical pursuit. No man now loves Truth, as Truth must be loved, with an infinite love; but only with a finite love, as it were *par amours*.[36] Nay, properly speaking, he does not *believe* and know it, but only *"thinks"* it, and that "there is every probability!" He preaches it aloud, and rushes courageously forth with it,—if there is a multitude huzzaing at his back; yet ever keeps looking over his shoulder, and the instant the huzzaing languishes, he too stops short.

In fact, what morality we have takes the shape of Ambition, of "Honour": beyond money and money's worth, our only rational blessed-

[35] In Greek myth, a monster with one hundred eyes.
[36] For the sake of love.

ness is Popularity. It were but a fool's trick to die for conscience. Only for "character," by duel, or in case of extremity, by suicide, is the wise man bound to die. By arguing on the "force of circumstances," we have argued away all force from ourselves; and stand leashed together, uniform in dress and movement, like the rowers of some boundless galley. This and that may be right and true; *but* we must not do it. Wonderful "Force of Public Opinion"! We must act and walk in all points as it prescribes; follow the traffic it bids us, realise the sum of money, the degree of "influence" it expects of us, *or* we shall be lightly esteemed; certain mouthfuls of articulate wind will be blown at us, and this what mortal courage can front? Thus, while civil liberty is more and more secured to us, our moral liberty is all but lost. Practically considered, our creed is Fatalism; and, free in hand and foot, we are shackled in heart and soul with far straiter than feudal chains. Truly may we say, with the Philosopher, "the deep meaning of the Laws of Mechanism lies heavy on us"; and in the closet, in the Marketplace, in the temple, by the social hearth, encumbers the whole movements of our mind, and over our noblest faculties is spreading a nightmare sleep.

These dark features, we are aware, belong more or less to other ages, as well as to ours. This faith in Mechanism, in the all-importance of physical things, is in every age the common refuge of Weakness and blind Discontent; of all who believe, as many will ever do, that man's true good lies without him, not within. We are aware also, that, as applied to ourselves in all their aggravation, they form but half a picture; that in the whole picture there are bright lights as well as gloomy shadows. If we here dwell chiefly on the latter, let us not be blamed: it is in general more profitable to reckon up our defects than to boast of our attainments.

Neither, with all these evils more or less clearly before us, have we at any time despaired of the fortunes of society. Despair, or even despondency, in that respect, appears to us, in all cases, a groundless feeling. We have a faith in the imperishable dignity of man; in the high vocation to which, throughout this his earthly history, he has been appointed. However it may be with individual nations, whatever melancholic speculators may assert, it seems a well-ascertained fact, that in all times, reckoning even from those of the Heraclides and Pelasgi,[37] the happiness and greatness of mankind at large have been continually progressive. Doubtless this age also is advancing. Its very unrest, its ceaseless activity, its discontent contains matter of promise. Knowledge, education are opening the eyes of the humblest; are increasing the number of thinking minds without limit. This is as it should be; for not in turning back, not in resisting, but only in resolutely struggling forward, does our life consist.

Nay, after all, our spiritual maladies are but of Opinion; we are but fettered by chains of our own forging, and which ourselves also can rend asunder. This deep, paralysed subjection to physical objects comes not from Nature, but from our own unwise mode of *viewing* Nature. Neither can we understand that man wants, at this hour, any faculty of heart, soul or body, that ever belonged to him. 'He, who has been born, has been a First Man'; has had lying before his young eyes, and as yet unhardened into scientific shapes, a world as plastic, infinite, divine, as lay before the eyes of Adam himself. If Mechanism, like some glass bell, encircles and imprisons us; if the soul looks forth on a fair heavenly country which it cannot reach, and pines, and in its scanty atmosphere is ready to perish,—yet the bell is but of glass; 'one bold stroke to break the bell in pieces, and thou art delivered!' Not the invisible world is wanting, for it dwells in man's soul, and this last is still here. Are the solemn temples, in which the Divinity was once visibly revealed among us, crumbling away? We can repair them, we can rebuild them. The wisdom, the heroic worth of our forefathers, which we have lost, we can recover. That admiration of old nobleness, which now so often shows itself as a faint *dilettantism,* will one day become a generous emulation, and man may again be all that he has been, and more than he has been. Nor are these the mere daydreams of fancy; they are clear possibilities; nay, in this time they are even assuming the character of hopes. Indications we do see in other countries and in our own, signs infinitely cheering to us, that Mechanism is not always to be our hard task-master, but one day to be our pliant, all-ministering servant; that a new and brighter spiritual era is slowly

[37] The Heraclides were descendants of Hercules who occupied the Peloponnesus; the Pelasgi were Hellenic dwellers in Greece and the Aegean islands.

evolving itself for all man. But on these things our present course forbids us to enter.

Meanwhile, that great outward changes are in progress can be doubtful to no one. The time is sick and out of joint.[38] Many things have reached their height; and it is a wise adage that tells us, "the darkest hour is nearest the dawn." Wherever we can gather indication of the public thought, whether from printed books, as in France or Germany, or from Carbonari rebellions[39] and other political tumults, as in Spain, Portugal, Italy, and Greece, the voice it utters is the same. The thinking minds of all nations call for change. There is a deep-lying struggle in the whole fabric of society; a boundless grinding collision of the New with the Old. The French Revolution, as is now visible enough, was not the parent of this mighty movement, but its offspring. Those two hostile influences, which always exist in human things, and on the constant inter-communion of which depends their health and safety, had lain in separate masses, accumulating through generations, and France was the scene of their fiercest explosion; but the final issue was not unfolded in that country: nay, it is not yet anywhere unfolded. Political freedom is hitherto the object of these efforts; but they will not and cannot stop there. It is towards a higher freedom than mere freedom from oppression by his fellow-mortal, that man dimly aims. Of this higher, heavenly freedom, which is "man's reasonable service," all his noble institutions, his faithful endeavours and loftiest attainments, are but the body, and more and more approximated emblem.

On the whole, as this wondrous planet, Earth, is journeying with its fellows through infinite Space, so are the wondrous destinies embarked on it journeying through infinite Time, under a higher guidance than ours. For the present, as our astronomy informs us, its path lies towards *Hercules,* the constellation of *Physical Powers*: but that is not our most pressing concern. Go where it will, the deep HEAVEN will be around it. Therein let us have hope and sure faith. To reform a world, to reform a nation, no wise man will undertake; and all but foolish men know, that the only solid, though a far slower reformation, is what each begins and perfects on *himself.*

[38] Cf. *Hamlet* I.v.189.
[39] A revolutionary political movement in early nineteenth-century Italy.

Alfred Tennyson
1809-1892

Ulysses
Locksley Hall

Both of the following poems were first published in
Tennyson's *Poems* of 1842. The poet derived his
conception of the aging Ulysses less from Homer than
from Dante's treatment of the Greek hero in the
twenty-sixth canto of the *Inferno*. Of "Locksley Hall,"
Tennyson stated that "the poem was a simple
invention as to place, incidents and people," designed
to represent "young life, its good side, its deficiencies,
and its yearnings."

ULYSSES

It little profits that an idle king,
By this still hearth, among these barren crags,
Match'd with an aged wife, I mete and dole
Unequal laws unto a savage race,
That hoard, and sleep, and feed, and know not me.
I cannot rest from travel; I will drink
Life to the lees. All times I have enjoy'd
Greatly, have suffer'd greatly, both with those
That loved me, and alone; on shore, and when
Thro' scudding drifts the rainy Hyades[1]   10
Vext the dim sea. I am become a name;

[1] A cluster of stars in the constellation of Taurus; literally, "rain bringers," from
the Greek.

For always roaming with a hungry heart
Much have I seen and known,—cities of men
And manners, climates, councils, governments,
Myself not least, but honour'd them all,—
And drunk delight of battle with my peers,
Far on the ringing plains of windy Troy.
I am a part of all that I have met;
Yet all experience is an arch wherethro'
Gleams that untravell'd world, whose margin fades   20
For ever and for ever when I move.
How dull it is to pause, to make an end,
To rust unburnish'd, not to shine in use!
As tho' to breathe were life! Life piled on life
Were all too little, and of one to me
Little remains; but every hour is saved
From that eternal silence, something more,
A bringer of new things; and vile it were
For some three suns to store and hoard myself,
And this gray spirit yearning in desire   30
To follow knowledge like a sinking star,
Beyond the utmost bound of human thought.
   This is my son, mine own Telemachus,
To whom I leave the sceptre and the isle,—[2]
Well-loved of me, discerning to fulfil
This labour, by slow prudence to make mild
A rugged people, and thro' soft degrees
Subdue them to the useful and the good.
Most blameless is he, centred in the sphere
Of common duties, decent not to fail   40
In offices of tenderness, and pay
Meet adoration to my household gods,
When I am gone. He works his work, I mine.
   There lies the port; the vessel puffs her sail;
There gloom the dark, broad seas. My mariners,

[2] The island of Ithaca, of which Ulysses was king; located off the west coast of Greece.

Souls that have toil'd, and wrought, and thought with me,—
That ever with a frolic welcome took
The thunder and the sunshine, and opposed
Free hearts, free foreheads,—you and I are old;
Old age hath yet his honour and his toil.   50
Death closes all; but something ere the end,
Some work of noble note, may yet be done,
Not unbecoming men that strove with Gods.
The lights begin to twinkle from the rocks;
The long day wanes; the slow moon climbs; the deep
Moans round with many voices. Come, my friends.
'Tis not too late to seek a newer world.
Push off, and sitting well in order smite
The sounding furrows; for my purpose holds
To sail beyond the sunset, and the baths   60
Of all the western stars, until I die.
It may be that the gulfs will wash us down;
It may be we shall touch the Happy Isles,[3]
And see the great Achilles, whom we knew.
Tho' much is taken, much abides; and tho'
We are not now that strength which in old days
Moved earth and heaven, that which we are, we are,—
One equal temper of heroic hearts,
Made weak by time and fate, but strong in will
To strive, to seek, to find, and not to yield.   70

LOCKSLEY HALL

Comrades, leave me here a little, while as yet 'tis early morn;
Leave me here, and when you want me, sound upon the bugle-horn.

'Tis the place, and all around it, as of old, the curlews call,
Dreary gleams about the moorland flying over Locksley Hall;

[3] Legendary abode of Greek heroes after their deaths; said to be located in the Atlantic Ocean beyond the Strait of Gibraltar.

Locksley Hall, that in the distance overlooks the sandy tracts,
And the hollow ocean-ridges roaring into cataracts.

Many a night from yonder ivied casement, ere I went to rest,
Did I look on great Orion[1] sloping slowly to the west.

Many a night I saw the Pleiads,[2] rising thro' the mellow shade,
Glitter like a swarm of fireflies tangled in a silver braid.   10

Here about the beach I wander'd, nourishing a youth sublime
With the fairy tales of science, and the long result of time;

When the centuries behind me like a fruitful land reposed;
When I clung to all the present for the promise that it closed;

When I dipt into the future far as human eye could see,
Saw the Vision of the world, and all the wonder that would be.—

In the spring a fuller crimson comes upon the robin's breast;
In the spring the wanton lapwing gets himself another crest;

In the spring a livelier iris changes on the burnish'd dove;
In the spring a young man's fancy lightly turns to thoughts of love.   20

Then her cheek was pale and thinner than should be for one so young,
And her eyes on all my motions with a mute observance hung.

And I said, 'My cousin Amy, speak, and speak the truth to me,
Trust me, cousin, all the current of my being sets to thee.'

On her pallid cheek and forehead came a colour and a light,
As I have seen the rosy red flushing in the northern night.

And she turn'd—her bosom shaken with a sudden storm of sighs—
All the spirit deeply dawning in the dark of hazel eyes—

Saying, 'I have hid my feelings, fearing they should do me wrong;'
Saying, 'Dost thou love me, cousin?' weeping, 'I have loved
      thee long.'   30

[1] A constellation of stars named after the mythical Greek hunter whom it was supposed to represent.

[2] A constellation named for the seven daughters of Atlas, and like Orion, traditionally associated with autumnal storms.

Love took up the glass of Time, and turn'd it in his glowing hands;
Every moment, lightly shaken, ran itself in golden sands.

Love took up the harp of Life, and smote on all the chords with might;
Smote the chord of Self, that, trembling, past in music out of sight.

Many a morning on the moorland did we hear the copses ring,
And her whisper throng'd my pulses with the fulness of the spring.

Many an evening by the waters did we watch the stately ships,
And our spirits rush'd together at the touching of the lips.

O my cousin, shallow-hearted! O my Amy, mine no more!
O the dreary, dreary moorland! O the barren, barren shore! 40

Falser than all fancy fathoms, falser than all songs have sung,
Puppet to a father's threat, and servile to a shrewish tongue!

Is it well to wish thee happy?—having known me—to decline
On a range of lower feelings and a narrower heart than mine!

Yet it shall be; thou shalt lower to his level day by day,
What is fine within thee growing coarse to sympathise with clay.

As the husband is, the wife is; thou art mated with a clown,
And the grossness of his nature will have weight to drag thee down.

He will hold thee, when his passion shall have spent its novel force,
Something better than his dog, a little dearer than his horse. 50

What is this? his eyes are heavy; think not they are glazed with wine.
Go to him, it is thy duty; kiss him, take his hand in thine.

It may be my lord is weary, that his brain is overwrought;
Soothe him with thy finer fancies, touch him with thy lighter thought.

He will answer to the purpose, easy things to understand—
Better thou wert dead before me, tho' I slew thee with my hand!

Better thou and I were lying, hidden from the heart's disgrace,
Roll'd in one another's arms, and silent in a last embrace.

Cursed be the social wants that sin against the strength of youth!
Cursed be the social lies that warp us from the living truth! 60

Cursed be the sickly forms that err from honest Nature's rule!
Cursed be the gold that gilds the straiten'd forehead of the fool!

Well—'tis well that I should bluster!—Hadst thou less unworthy proved—
Would to God—for I had loved thee more than ever wife was loved.

Am I mad, that I should cherish that which bears but bitter fruit?
I will pluck it from my bosom, tho' my heart be at the root.

Never, tho' my mortal summers to such length of years should come
As the many-winter'd crow that leads the clanging rookery home.

Where is comfort? in division of the records of the mind?
Can I part her from herself, and love her, as I knew her, kind?   70

I remember one that perish'd; sweetly did she speak and move;
Such a one do I remember, whom to look at was to love.

Can I think of her as dead, and love her for the love she bore?
No—she never loved me truly; love is love for evermore.

Comfort? comfort scorn'd of devils! this is truth the poet[3] sings,
That a sorrow's crown of sorrow is remembering happier things.

Drug thy memories, lest thou learn it, lest thy heart be put to proof,
In the dead unhappy night, and when the rain is on the roof.

Like a dog, he hunts in dreams, and thou art staring at the wall,
Where the dying night-lamp flickers, and the shadows rise and fall.   80

Then a hand shall pass before thee, pointing to his drunken sleep,
To thy widow'd marriage-pillows, to the tears that thou wilt weep.

Thou shalt hear the 'Never, never,' whisper'd by the phantom years,
And a song from out the distance in the ringing of thine ears;

And an eye shall vex thee, looking ancient kindness on thy pain.
Turn thee, turn thee on thy pillow; get thee to thy rest again.

Nay, but Nature brings thee solace; for a tender voice will cry.
'Tis a purer life than thine, a lip to drain thy trouble dry.

---

[3] Dante; cf. *Inferno* v.121-123.

Baby lips will laugh me down; my latest rival brings thee rest.
Baby fingers, waxen touches, press me from the mother's breast.   90

O, the child too clothes the father with a dearness not his due.
Half is thine and half is his: it will be worthy of the two.

O, I see thee old and formal, fitted to thy petty part,
With a little hoard of maxims preaching down a daughter's heart.

'They were dangerous guides the feelings—she herself was not exempt—
Truly, she herself had suffer'd'—Perish in thy self-contempt!

Overlive it—lower yet—be happy! wherefore should I care?
I myself must mix with action, lest I wither by despair.

What is that which I should turn to, lighting upon days like these?
Every door is barr'd with gold, and opens but to golden keys.   100

Every gate is throng'd with suitors, all the markets overflow.
I have but an angry fancy; what is that which I should do?

I had been content to perish, falling on the foeman's ground,
When the ranks are roll'd in vapour, and the winds are laid with sound.

But the jingling of the guinea helps the hurt that Honour feels,
And the nations do but murmur, snarling at each other's heels.

Can I but relive in sadness? I will turn that earlier page.
Hide me from my deep emotion, O thou wondrous Mother-Age!

Make me feel the wild pulsation that I felt before the strife,
When I heard my days before me, and the tumult of my life;   110

Yearning for the large excitement that the coming years would yield,
Eager-hearted as a boy when first he leaves his father's field,

And at night along the dusky highway near and nearer drawn,
Sees in heaven the light of London flaring like a dreary dawn;

And his spirit leaps within him to be gone before him then,
Underneath the light he looks at, in among the throngs of men;

Men, my brothers, men the workers, ever reaping something new;
That which they have done but earnest of the things that they shall do.

For I dipt into the future, far as human eye could see,
Saw the Vision of the world, and all the wonder that would be;   120

Saw the heavens fill with commerce, argosies of magic sails,
Pilots of the purple twilight, dropping down with costly bales;

Heard the heavens fill with shouting, and there rain'd a ghastly dew
From the nation's airy navies grappling in the central blue;

Far along the world-wide whisper of the south-wind rushing warm,
With the standards of the peoples plunging thro' the thunder-storm;

Till the war-drum throbb'd no longer, and the battle-flags were furl'd
In the Parliament of man, the Federation of the world.

There the common sense of most shall hold a fretful realm in awe,
And the kindly earth shall slumber, lapt in universal law.   130

So I triumph'd ere my passion sweeping thro' me left me dry,
Left me with the palsied heart, and left me with the jaundiced eye;

Eye, to which all order festers, all things here are out of joint.
Science moves, but slowly, slowly, creeping on from point to point;

Slowly comes a hungry people, as a lion, creeping nigher,
Glares at one that nods and winks behind a slowly-dying fire.

Yet I doubt not thro' the ages one increasing purpose runs,
And the thoughts of men are widen'd with the process of the suns.

What is that to him that reaps not harvest of his youthful joys,
Tho' the deep heart of existence beat for ever like a boy's?   140

Knowledge comes, but wisdom lingers, and I linger on the shore,
And the individual withers, and the world is more and more.

Knowledge comes, but wisdom lingers, and he bears a laden breast,
Full of sad experience, moving toward the stillness of his rest.

Hark, my merry comrades call me, sounding on the bugle-horn,
They to whom my foolish passion were a target for their scorn.

Shall it not be scorn to me to harp on such a moulder'd string?
I am shamed thro' all my nature to have loved so slight a thing.

Weakness to be wroth with weakness! woman's pleasure, woman's pain—
Nature made them blinder motions bounded in a shallower brain.   150

Woman is the lesser man, and all thy passions, match'd with mine,
Are as moonlight unto sunlight, and as water unto wine—

Here at least, where nature sickens, nothing. Ah, for some retreat
Deep in yonder shining Orient, where my life began to beat,

Where in wild Mahratta-battle[4] fell my father evil-starr'd;—
I was left a trampled orphan, and a selfish uncle's ward.

Or to burst all links of habit—there to wander far away,
On from island unto island at the gateways of the day.

Larger constellations burning, mellow moons and happy skies,
Breadths of tropic shade and palms in cluster, knots of Paradise.   160

Never comes the trader, never floats an European flag,
Slides the bird o'er lustrous woodland, swings the trailer from the crag;

Droops the heavy-blossom'd bower, hangs the heavy-fruited tree—
Summer isles of Eden lying in dark-purple spheres of sea.

There methinks would be enjoyment more than in this march of mind,[5]
In the steamship, in the railway, in the thoughts that shake mankind.

There the passions cramp'd no longer shall have scope and breathing
              space;
I will take some savage woman, she shall rear my dusky race.

Iron-jointed, supple-sinew'd, they shall dive, and they shall run,
Catch the wild goat by the hair, and hurl their lances in the sun;   170

Whistle back the parrot's call, and leap the rainbows of the brooks,
Not with blinded eyesight poring over miserable books—

[4] The Mahrattas were a fierce band of Hindus with whom the British in India
fought a number of local wars during the early nineteenth century.
[5] A current phrase signifying the faith in material progress shared by early Victorians. See the satiric chapter entitled "The March of Mind" in Thomas Love
Peacock's *Crotchet Castle* (1831).

Fool, again the dream, the fancy! but I *know* my words are wild,
But I count the gray barbarian lower than the Christian child.

I, to herd with narrow foreheads, vacant of our glorious gains,
Like a beast with lower pleasures, like a beast with lower pains!

Mated with a squalid savage—what to me were sun or clime?
I the heir of all the ages, in the foremost files of time—

I that rather held it better men should perish one by one,
Than the earth should stand at gaze like Joshua's moon in Ajalon! [6]   180

Not in vain the distance beacons. Forward, forward let us range,
Let the great world spin for ever down the ringing grooves of change. [7]

Thro' the shadow of the globe we sweep into the younger day;
Better fifty years of Europe than a cycle of Cathay.

Mother-Age,—for mine I knew not,—help me as when life begun;
Rift the hills, and roll the waters, flash the lightnings, weigh the sun.

O, I see the crescent promise of my spirit hath not set.
Ancient founts of inspiration well thro' all my fancy yet.

Howsoever these things be, a long farewell to Locksley Hall!
Now for me the woods may wither, now for me the roof-tree fall.   190

Comes a vapour from the margin, blackening over heath and holt,
Cramming all the blast before it, in its breast a thunderbolt.

Let it fall on Locksley Hall, with rain or hail, or fire or snow;
For the mighty wind arises, roaring seaward, and I go.

[6] Cf. Joshua x.12.

[7] This metaphor originated in an amusing misunderstanding on Tennyson's part, which he explained as follows: "When I went by the first train from Liverpool to Manchester (1830) I thought the wheels ran in a groove. It was a black night and there was such a vast crowd round the train at the station that we could not see the wheels. Then I made this line."

Matthew Arnold

1822-1888

Stanzas from the Grande Chartreuse
Dover Beach

Originally published in *Fraser's Magazine* in 1855, "Stanzas from the Grande Chartreuse" was reprinted in *New Poems*, 1867. The Grande Chartreuse of the title is the famous Carthusian monastery near Grenoble in the French Alps, which Arnold visited with his wife on their wedding trip in September 1851. Although composed much earlier, "Dover Beach" was first published in *New Poems*, 1867.

STANZAS FROM THE GRANDE CHARTREUSE

Through Alpine meadows soft-suffused
With rain, where thick the crocus blows,
Past the dark forges long disused,
The mule-track from Saint Laurent goes.
The bridge is cross'd, and slow we ride,
Through forest, up the mountain-side.

The autumnal evening darkens round,
The wind is up, and drives the rain;
While, hark! far down, with strangled sound
Doth the Dead Guier's stream complain,   10
Where that wet smoke, among the woods,
Over his boiling cauldron broods.

Swift rush the spectral vapours white
Past limestone scars with ragged pines,
Showing—then blotting from our sight!—
Halt—through the cloud-drift something shines!
High in the valley, wet and drear,
The huts of Courrerie appear.

Strike leftward! cries our guide; and higher
Mounts up the stony forest-way.   20
At last the encircling trees retire;
Look! through the showery twilight grey
What pointed roofs are these advance?—
A palace of the Kings of France?

Approach, for what we seek is here!
Alight, and sparely sup, and wait
For rest in this outbuilding near;
Then cross the sward and reach that gate.
Knock; pass the wicket! Thou art come
To the Carthusians' world-famed home.   30

The silent courts, where night and day
Into their stone-carved basins cold
The splashing icy fountains play—
The humid corridors behold!
Where, ghostlike in the deepening night,
Cowl'd forms brush by in gleaming white.

The chapel, where no organ's peal
Invests the stern and naked prayer—
With penitential cries they kneel
And wrestle; rising then, with bare   40
And white uplifted faces stand,
Passing the Host[1] from hand to hand;

---

[1] This is one of several misapprehensions in a poem which professedly gives an outsider's version of monastic life. It was not the Host (consecrated bread), but the Instrument of the Pax, a crucifix, that Arnold would have seen passed by the monks.

Each takes, and then his visage wan
Is buried in his cowl once more.
The cells!—the suffering Son of Man
Upon the wall—the knee-worn floor—
And where they sleep, that wooden bed,
Which shall their coffin be, when dead!

The library, where tract and tome
Not to feed priestly pride are there,   50
To hymn the conquering march of Rome,[2]
Nor yet to amuse, as ours are!
They paint of souls the inner strife,
Their drops of blood, their death in life.

The garden, overgrown—yet mild,
See, fragrant herbs are flowering there!
Strong children of the Alpine wild
Whose culture is the brethren's care;
Of human tasks their only one,
And cheerful works beneath the sun.   60

Those halls, too, destined to contain
Each its own pilgrim-host of old,
From England, Germany, or Spain—
All are before me! I behold
The House, the Brotherhood austere!
—And what am I, that I am here?

For rigorous teachers seized my youth,
And purged its faith, and trimm'd its fire,
Show'd me the high, white star of Truth,
There bade me gaze, and there aspire.   70
Even now their whispers pierce the gloom:
What dost thou in this living tomb?

Forgive me, masters of the mind!
At whose behest I long ago

[2] That is, the triumphal progress of Roman Catholicism.

So much unlearnt, so much resign'd—
I come not here to be your foe!
I seek these anchorites, not in ruth,
To curse and to deny your truth;

Not as their friend, or child, I speak!
But as, on some far northern strand,   **80**
Thinking of his own Gods, a Greek
In pity and mournful awe might stand
Before some fallen Runic stone—
For both were faiths, and both are gone.

Wandering between two worlds, one dead,
The other powerless to be born,
With nowhere yet to rest my head,
Like these, on earth I wait forlorn.
Their faith, my tears, the world deride—
I come to shed them at their side.   **90**

Oh, hide me in your gloom profound,
Ye solemn seats of holy pain!
Take me, cowl'd forms, and fence me round,
Till I possess my soul again;
Till free my thoughts before me roll,
Not chafed by hourly false control!

For the world cries your faith is now
But a dead time's exploded dream;
My melancholy, sciolists say,
Is a pass'd mode, an outworn theme—   **100**
As if the world had ever had
A faith, or sciolists been sad!

Ah, if it *be* pass'd, take away,
At least, the restlessness, the pain;
Be man henceforth no more a prey
To these out-dated stings again!
The nobleness of grief is gone—
Ah, leave us not the fret alone!

But—if you cannot give us ease—
Last of the race of them who grieve   110
Here leave us to die out with these
Last of the people who believe!
Silent, while years engrave the brow;
Silent—the best are silent now.

Achilles ponders in his tent,[3]
The kings of modern thought are dumb;
Silent they are, though not content,
And wait to see the future come.
They have the grief men had of yore,
But they contend and cry no more.   120

Our fathers[4] water'd with their tears
This sea of time whereon we sail,
Their voices were in all men's ears
Who pass'd within their puissant hail.
Still the same ocean round us raves,
But we stand mute, and watch the waves.

For what avail'd it, all the noise
And outcry of the former men?—
Say, have their sons achieved more joys,
Say, is life lighter now than then?   130
The sufferers died, they left their pain—
The pangs which tortured them remain.

What helps it now, that Byron bore,
With haughty scorn which mock'd the smart,
Through Europe to the Ætolian shore[5]
The pageant of his bleeding heart?

[3] Insulted by Agamemnon, the Greek leader, Achilles withdrew to his tent and refused to take part in the war against Troy. The suggestion is that the leading thinkers of modern times have withdrawn in bafflement before the problems confronting them.

[4] Arnold's precursors in the Romantic period, including the poets Byron and Shelley mentioned in succeeding stanzas.

[5] The original name of the part of Greece where Byron died in 1824, while fighting in the Greek War of Independence.

That thousands counted every groan,
And Europe made his woe her own?

What boots it, Shelley! that the breeze
Carried thy lovely wail away,   140
Musical through Italian trees
Which fringe thy soft blue Spezzian bay? [6]
Inheritors of thy distress
Have restless hearts one throb the less?

Or are we easier, to have read,
O Obermann! [7] the sad, stern page,
Which tells us how thou hidd'st thy head
From the fierce tempest of thine age
In the lone brakes of Fontainebleau,
Or chalets near the Alpine snow?   150

Ye slumber in your silent grave!—
The world, which for an idle day
Grace to your mood of sadness gave,
Long since hath flung her weeds away.
The eternal trifler breaks your spell;
But we—we learnt your lore too well!

Years hence, perhaps, may dawn an age,
More fortunate, alas! than we,
Which without hardness will be sage,
And gay without frivolity,   160
Sons of the world, oh, speed those years;
But, while we wait, allow our tears!

Allow them! We admire with awe
The exulting thunder of your race;
You give the universe your law,
You triumph over time and space!

[6] Shelley was drowned in the Bay of Spezzia on the Italian coast in 1822.
[7] Reference to Étienne Pivert de Senancour (1770-1846), the melancholy author of *Obermann* (1804), which Arnold much admired for its qualities of sensitivity to nature and subtle introspection. Senancour, who lived for a period of years in Switzerland, is buried at Fontainebleau near Paris.

Your pride of life, your tireless powers,
We laud them, but they are not ours.

We are like children rear'd in shade
Beneath some old-world abbey wall,   170
Forgotten in a forest-glade,
And secret from the eyes of all.
Deep, deep the greenwood round them waves,
Their abbey, and its close of graves!

But, where the road runs near the stream,
Oft through the trees they catch a glance
Of passing troops in the sun's beam—
Pennon, and plume, and flashing lance!
Forth to the world those soldiers fare,
To life, to cities, and to war!   180

And through the wood, another way,
Faint bugle-notes from far are borne,
Where hunters gather, staghounds bay,
Round some fair forest-lodge at morn.
Gay dames are there, in sylvan green;
Laughter and cries—those notes between!

The banners flashing through the trees
Make their blood dance and chain their eyes;
That bugle-music on the breeze
Arrests them with a charm'd surprise.   190
Banner by turns and bugle woo:
Ye shy recluses, follow too!

O children, what do ye reply?—
'Action and pleasure, will ye roam
Through these secluded dells to cry
And call us?—but too late ye come!
Too late for us your call ye blow,
Whose bent was taken long ago.

'Long since we pace this shadow'd nave;
We watch those yellow tapers shine,   200
Emblems of hope over the grave,
In the high altar's depth divine;
The organ carries to our ear
Its accents of another sphere.

'Fenced early in this cloistral round
Of reverie, of shade, of prayer,
How should we grow in other ground?
How can we flower in foreign air?
—Pass, banners, pass, and bugles, cease;
And leave our desert to its peace!'   210

DOVER BEACH

The sea is calm to-night.
The tide is full, the moon lies fair
Upon the straits;—on the French coast the light
Gleams and is gone; the cliffs of England stand,
Glimmering and vast, out in the tranquil bay.
Come to the window, sweet is the night air!
Only, from the long line of spray
Where the sea meets the moon-blanch'd land,
Listen! you hear the grating roar
Of pebbles which the waves draw back, and fling,   10
At their return, up the high strand,
Begin, and cease, and then again begin,
With tremulous cadence slow, and bring
The eternal note of sadness in.

Sophocles long ago
Heard it on the Ægæan, and it brought
Into his mind the turbid ebb and flow
Of human misery; we
Find also in the sound a thought,
Hearing it by this distant northern sea.   20

The Sea of Faith
Was once, too, at the full, and round earth's shore
Lay like the folds of a bright girdle furl'd.
But now I only hear
Its melancholy, long, withdrawing roar,
Retreating, to the breath
Of the night-wind, down the vast edges drear
And naked shingles of the world.

Ah, love, let us be true
To one another! for the world, which seems   30
To lie before us like a land of dreams,
So various, so beautiful, so new,
Hath really neither joy, nor love, nor light,
Nor certitude, nor peace, nor help for pain;
And we are here as on a darkling plain
Swept with confused alarms of struggle and flight,
Where ignorant armies clash by night.

SUGGESTIONS FOR ADDITIONAL READING

More extended acquaintance with the work of the authors of the foregoing selections will serve further to clarify and to give definition to their varying responses to the temper of the age. The following essays and poems are especially relevant in the context of the present section:

Thomas Babington Macaulay, "Francis Bacon" (1837); *History of England* (1849-61), the famous third chapter of the first volume

ADDITIONAL READING

Thomas Carlyle, "Characteristics" (1831); "Shooting Niagara: And After?" (1867)

Alfred Tennyson, *Maud: A Monodrama* (1855); "Locksley Hall Sixty Years After" (1886), a sequel to the poem printed above

Matthew Arnold, "Empedocles on Etna" (1852); "The Buried Life" (1852); any of Arnold's elegiac poems, including "Stanzas in Memory of the Author of 'Obermann,'" "The Scholar-Gipsy," "Thyrsis," "Obermann Once More," "Rugby Chapel"

John Stuart Mill's important essays on the two figures whom he regarded as the great seminal thinkers of the nineteenth century, "Bentham" (1838) and "Coleridge" (1840), have been published together under the title *Mill on Bentham and Coleridge* (London, 1950), with an illuminating introduction by F. R. Leavis.

The name of virtually every great social critic of the period is associated with a volume which yields profound theoretic insight into the habits of mind which shaped Victorian England. The student who aspires to understand the age in greater depth should pursue a course of reading in the following:

William Cobbett, *Rural Rides* (1830); see edition by G. D. H. Cole, 3 vols. (London, 1930)

Thomas Carlyle, *Past and Present* (1843)

John Stuart Mill, *On Liberty* (1859); see especially World's Classics edition (Oxford, 1924), with prefatory essay by Harold Laski

John Ruskin, *Unto This Last* (1862)

Matthew Arnold, *Culture and Anarchy* (1869); especially recommended in the edition by J. Dover Wilson (Cambridge, Eng., 1935)

John Morley, *On Compromise* (1874)

Walter Bagehot, *Physics and Politics* (1876); see recent edition with introduction by Jacques Barzun (New York, 1948)

Herbert Spencer, *The Man versus the State* (1884)

George Bernard Shaw and others, *Essays in Fabian Socialism* (1889); see the sixth edition (London, 1962), with an introduction by Asa Briggs

PART TWO

The Individual and Society

Introduction

Victorian social attitudes reflect the sharpened class consciousness which was a significant outgrowth of the Industrial Revolution. Nowhere are these attitudes more sensitively registered than in the Victorian novel, which during the 1840's and 1850's widened its focus to include all strata of English life. The earliest and one of the most perceptive of the so-called social novels was Disraeli's *Sybil, or The Two Nations* (1845). The meaning of the subtitle comes out in the following dialogue between the hero, an idealistic young aristocrat named Egremont, and two strangers of inferior station whom he encounters:

"This is a new reign," said Egremont, "perhaps it is a new era."
"I think so," said the younger stranger.
"I hope so," said the elder one.
"Well, society may be in its infancy," said Egremont, slightly smiling; "but, say what you like, our Queen reigns over the greatest nation that ever existed."
"Which nation?" asked the younger stranger, "for she reigns over two."
The stranger paused; Egremont was silent, but looked inquiringly.
"Yes," resumed the younger stranger after a moment's interval. "Two nations; between whom there is no intercourse and no sympathy; who are as ignorant of each other's habits, thoughts, and feelings, as if they were dwellers in different zones, or inhabitants of different planets; who are formed by a different breeding, are fed by a different food, are ordered by different manners, and are not governed by the same laws."
"You speak of—" said Egremont, hesitatingly.
"The Rich and the Poor."

The bleakness of this view of social relations was supported by a body of economic doctrine which Carlyle named the Dismal Science. According to its teaching, the dealings between men are prescribed by natural laws as inevitable and impersonal in their operation as those which govern the physical cosmos. A founding document in this school of thought was T. R. Malthus' *An Essay on the Principle of Population* (1798), in which the author undertook to prove that without such salutary checks as war, famine, and disease, overpopulation would soon threaten the extinction of the human race. Another leading economist of the day, David Ricardo, argued in his *Principles of Political Economy and Taxation* (1817) that trade cycles, fluctuating in accordance with the laws of supply and demand, will unavoidably subject the working classes to recurrent periods of unemployment and severe distress. In the opinion of the orthodox advocates of *laissez-faire*, furthermore, all governmental or legislative measures aimed at ameliorating hardship are ill-advised and ultimately harmful, since they upset the balance of the laws of political economy.

Pushed to its theoretical limit, *laissez-faire* countenances a kind of cutthroat competition wholly incompatible with the social ideal. That this extreme of individualism was unacceptable even to the most ruthless industrialists, the prevalence of private philanthropy in the age bears witness. More significant, however, was the accumulating evidence that corporate endeavor very generally produces better results than private enterprise. It was through banding together in the Anti-Corn Law League, under the leadership of Richard Cobden and John Bright, that commercial interests were able to force the repeal of tariffs on the importation of grain against the formidable opposition of the landowning classes. The railway boom of the 1840's, showing what could happen when large numbers of private investors acted in concord, led directly to the Limited Liability Act of 1855, which in turn began to transfer big business into the hands of joint stockholding companies.

The communal spirit, however, most clearly manifested itself among the working classes. Disappointed in their hopes that the First Reform Bill would give them a voice in government and not to be pacified by piecemeal legislative reforms or charitable benefactions, they undertook to act for themselves in a variety of ways. Popular agitation for a more democratic Parliament erupted in mass demonstrations in 1839, 1842, and 1848; but this movement, known as Chartism, was abortive because premature, serving only to emphasize the political disunion still existing among the lower orders. More productive was the socialist propaganda of Robert Owen, whose textile mills at New Lanark in Scotland provided an early model for employee participation in management. Owen's experiment lay behind the formation in 1844 of the Rochdale Pioneers, the first of the great English co-operative societies. The mid-century brought a wave of prosperity to Britain after the disorders of the "hungry '40's"; and this period of quietude favored the consolidation of trades unions, as labor, abandoning political maneuvers for the time, turned to organizing its growing industrial might. R. H. Hutton, an astute contemporary observer, commented in 1866 on the challenge which such working-class developments was offering to *laissez-faire* doctrine: "Only the working class have got a clear conception of how much individuals owe, by way of self-sacrifice to the larger social organization to which they belong. . . . What I think may fairly be hoped for, is the diversion of some of this high *esprit de corps* from the narrow organization of the Trade Society to the wider organization of the nation." The foregoing prophecy was to be amply confirmed by the passage of the Second and Third Reform Bills, brought about through the mobilization of this new force of public opinion. With each passing decade of the nineteenth century the tide of social thinking in England set more strongly away from individualism and towards collectivism. In the words of A. V. Dicey, a distinguished authority on the period:

The great Reform Act was carried by and for the benefit of the middle classes. It was the work of men who desired to change the constitution of Parliament because they wished for legislation in conformity with the principles of individualism. The Reform Acts, 1867-1884, were carried in deference to the wishes and by the support of the working classes, who desired, though in a vague and indefinite manner, laws which might promote the attainment of the ideals of socialism or collectivism.[1]

At the outset of the Victorian period political power in England was still shared between the Whigs and Tories (or Liberals and Conservatives). These two great parties perpetuated radically different traditions with regard to the individual's status in society. The Liberals derived their political philosophy from John Locke's *Two Treatises of Government* (1690). In terms of Lockean philosophy government comes into being as the result of a contractual pact among its members. Through the social contract men agree to delegate to the state sufficient powers to ensure the preservation of their private property, while still retaining certain inalienable rights, chief among which are life, liberty, and the pursuit of happiness. The basis of government is thus the consent of the

[1] A. V. Dicey, *Lectures on the Relation between Law and Public Opinion in England during the Nineteenth Century* (London, 1930), p. 254.

governed, the state being regarded in the guise of a necessary evil, as a kind of policing agency whose *raison d'être* is to restrain the strong from victimizing the defenseless. In essence Locke's theory of government is atomistic; that is to say, each citizen within the state is treated as a separate unit entitled to perfect freedom in determining his course of action, so long as his conduct does not interfere with a like freedom on the part of all the other units. It is hardly necessary to point out how congenial this way of thinking was to the *laissez-faire* economics of Adam Smith and his followers.

While accepting the individualistic assumptions of Locke's system, the Benthamites or Utilitarians significantly revised his negative attitude towards the duties of government. To Bentham's pragmatic bent of mind, the premises on which Whig statesmen rested their case for restricting governmental authority, the social contract, natural rights, a natural identity of interests, were nothing but meaningless abstractions. The question to be asked of any law or institution or mode of belief was "What useful purpose does it serve?" According to the principle of "utility," the best form of social organization is that which promotes the greatest happiness of the greatest number of its members. And while all Benthamites agreed that representative government offered the surest theoretical guarantee of universal happiness, they were unwilling to grant that this democratic goal could ever be achieved so long as the state confined its activities to safeguarding the privileges of the property-holding classes. Clearly then, and this was the great revolution in political thinking wrought by the Utilitarians, the powers vested in government must be converted to a more positive program, that of actually fostering the public welfare of the entire community. To Bentham and his disciples goes the credit for educating Victorian England to the need for centralized administration as the most efficient and humane method of dealing with the social problems of the age.

The classic apology for Victorian liberalism is John Stuart Mill's *On Liberty* (1859). In at least two important respects Mill, who possessed extraordinary insight into the dominant tendencies of his age, as well as the capacity to move with it, expanded the vision of his predecessors among the Utilitarians. He records in his *Autobiography* how, rebelling against the rigidly mechanistic view of human nature which his father had sought to instill in him, he developed an altogether more humanistic faith in man's inherent potentialities. As he put it: "Those only are happy . . . who have their minds fixed on some object other than their own happiness; on the happiness of others, on the improvement of mankind, even on some art or pursuit, followed not as a means, but as itself an ideal end." Thus, in Mill's definition true liberty is to be measured not by the amount of physical well-being that prevails within society, but rather by the opportunities open to each individual to achieve full self-realization. Secondly, Mill's study of the French sociologist Auguste Comte led him to the relativistic conclusion that forms of government are historically circumstanced by the differing social conditions which give rise to them. In opposition to the *a priori* Benthamite position that democratic freedom is absolutely and under all conditions to be desired, he maintained: "Liberty, as a principle, has no application to any state of things anterior to the time when mankind have become capable of being improved by free and equal discussion." Furthermore, although Mill was convinced that England's existing form of parliamentary government was most suitable to his countrymen in their present state of civilization, his faith in progress, based on the perfectibility of human beings and their institutions, was such that in his later years he could confidently look forward to the day when individual needs would be better served by some form of socialism: "The social problem of the future we considered to be, how to unite the greatest individual liberty of action, with a common ownership in the raw material of the globe, and an equal participation of all in the benefits of combined labour."

The real impetus towards socialism, however, was generated by long-established political traditions contrary in tendency to the doctrines associated with Locke and Bentham. As Mill represented Victorian liberalism at its best, so Carlyle was the leading spokesman for the authoritarian tendency. Here is what Carlyle has to say in *Past and Present* about the kind of society promoted by *laissez-faire* individualism:

True, it must be owned, we for the present, with our Mammon-Gospel, have come to strange conclusions. We call it a Society; and go about professing openly the totalest separation, isolation. Our life is not a mutual helpfulness; but rather, cloaked under due laws-of-war, named 'fair competition' and so forth, it is a mutual hostility. We have profoundly forgotten everywhere that *Cash-payment* is not the sole relation of human beings; we think, nothing doubting, that *it* absolves and liquidates all engagements of man. "My starving workers?" answers the rich mill-owner: "Did I not pay them, to the last sixpence, the sum covenanted for? What have I to do with them more?"—Verily Mammon-worship is a melancholy creed.

The shift in perspective between the individualist and the collectivist points of view can be illustrated by juxtaposing two forms of the same word, thus: state—State. When capitalized the term at once calls up the concept of nations existing as unique entities, each imbued with some kind of mysterious reality apart from and beyond, though still including the lives of its citizens. In this connection it is again relevant to remember how profoundly nineteenth-century habits of mind were influenced by the rise of the biological sciences. Locke's theory of government, as has been seen, is atomistic in a Newtonian sense; within the social framework individuals function as autonomous or self-directing particles. During the Victorian age this mechanistic outlook gave way increasingly to the notion that society exhibits the characteristics of a living organism and that its members are vitally interrelated in the same way as molecules within the human body.

The collectivist attitude is thus profoundly at odds with the liberal's insistence on individual freedom. If the state is endowed with powers beyond purely protective ones, if it is granted the authority to legislate over its citizens for the good of the whole, then it must follow that men can lay claim to no rights which are not conferred upon them by society at large. Implied here is a reversal of the Lockean formula for good government which regards the state as the servant of private interests. Now, on the contrary, individual welfare is conceived as being subordinate to and contingent on the continuing health of the larger organism in which each is intrinsically involved.

Authoritarian theories of political philosophy are, of course, very ancient; they are advanced in Plato's *Republic* and inhere in all societies organized on hierarchic principles. Their appeal was especially strong to nineteenth-century revolutionary thinkers on the Continent, where they signaled the emergence of statism. Power politics on the European model were, however, alien to the cautious British mentality; and the collectivist impulse in England has its origins in traditional Toryism, as reinterpreted for the new age by Burke and Coleridge. Transplanted into an industrial environment, collectivism took root in the Victorian labor movement, where it contributed to the growing solidarity of the working classes in their efforts to gain political power. Channeled through the co-operative and trades union activities of the mid-century, it shaped the influential socialist organizations that grew up in the 1880's and led ultimately to the formation in 1892 of the Independent Labour Party.

The great mass of Victorian social criticism reflects a parallel effort to reconstitute the social sense in opposition to the rampant individualism of the times. Carlyle's writings attest to his passionate conviction that all men are brothers, united to each other by "organic filaments." The same view of society as a homogeneous fabric of interwoven relationships is shared by most Victorian novelists, and, indeed, supplies the unifying principle for the panoramic settings and labyrinthine plots of so many of their stories. In Dickens' *Bleak House,* for example, the movement of events is so conducted as to show how the fate of the haughty Lady Dedlock at one end of the social scale is inextricably involved with that of Jo, the illiterate crossing-sweeper, at the other extreme. In their constant evocations of the past, furthermore, Victorian writers were motivated not so much by romantic nostalgia for the picturesque aspects of bygone times, as by the desire to revivify that communal devotion to transcendent ideals which had irradiated foregoing periods of high civilization. What Carlyle and Ruskin and Morris looked for and found in the hierarchic structure of mediæval society, and Arnold in the harmonious expansion of classical Greek culture, were sanctions for social cohesion of a kind so conspicuously lacking in their own fragmented world.

The implications for the Victorian public of the swing from individualism to collectivism are admirably summarized by A. V. Dicey in the following passage:

Benthamite Liberals have looked upon men mainly, and too exclusively, as separate persons, each of whom must by his own efforts work out his own happiness and well-being; and have held that the prosperity of the community—as, for example, of the English nation—means nothing more than the prosperity or welfare of the whole, or of the majority of its members. They have also assumed, and surely not without reason, that if a man's real interest be well understood, the true welfare of each citizen means the true welfare of the State. . . . Collectivists, on the other hand, have looked upon men mainly, and too exclusively, not so much as isolated individuals, but as beings who by their very nature are citizens and parts of the great organism—the State—whereof they are members. Reformers, whose attention has thus been engrossed by the social side of human nature, have believed, or rather felt, that the happiness of each citizen depends upon the welfare of the nation, and have held that to ensure the welfare of the nation is the only way of promoting the happiness of each individual citizen.[2]

Underlying the great debate over men's self-regarding instincts as opposed to their social responsibilities are different assumptions about the needs of human nature. The liberal like Mill would say that the best form of social organization is that which allows each individual the fullest possible liberty to pursue his own ends. To this the collectivist would reply that society exists primarily to provide security for its members. The distinction can be made in terms of two ways of defining freedom: the freedom *to* and the freedom *from*—the freedom to choose between differing courses of action, or the freedom from having to choose. By the first definition authority is lodged in the individual, by the second it is transferred to society.

Each of the four prose selections which follows offers typical speculations about the relationship of the individual to society in Victorian England. John Stuart Mill is the champion of individualism, although he searchingly scrutinizes the antagonistic forces which were mining the liberal ideal from within. Like E. M. Forster, in whom his spirit lives on, Mill is disposed to give only two cheers for democracy! At the farthest remove, the authoritarian Carlyle decries the leveling tendencies in modern society which militate against the appearance of strong leaders of the caliber of those heroic figures who in past times have provided patterns for lesser men. John Ruskin, while he shares Carlyle's predilection for hierarchic societies and for paternalistic governments, shows deeper and more sympathetic insight into the plight of the workingman under the dehumanizing forces of the Industrial Revolution. The socialism of William Morris is of a peculiarly indigenous variety, harking back to the mediæval guild system; and alert readers will not fail to note that he stands in the direct line of descent from Carlyle and Ruskin. Indeed, when Morris established his famous Kelmscott Press in 1891, Carlyle's *Past and Present* and Ruskin's "The Nature of Gothic" were among the first works to bear its imprint.

[2] Dicey, pp. 300-301.

John Stuart Mill

1806-1873

Of Individuality, as One of the Elements of Well-Being

The selection here printed is Chapter Three of *On Liberty* (1859). Mill was a close student of Alexis de Tocqueville (1805-1859), the French political philosopher, whose *Democracy in America* (1835-40) helped formulate his belief that the great threat to democratic freedom is "collective mediocrity," resulting from social pressures on individuals to conform to mass opinion.

Such being the reasons which make it imperative that human beings should be free to form opinions, and to express their opinions without reserve; and such the baneful consequences to the intellectual, and through that to the moral nature of man, unless this liberty is either conceded, or asserted in spite of prohibition; let us next examine whether the same reasons do not require that men should be free to act upon their opinions—to carry these out in their lives, without hindrance, either physical or moral, from their fellow men, so long as it is at their own risk and peril. This last proviso is of course indispensable. No one pretends that actions should be as free as opinions. On the contrary, even opinions lose their immunity, when the circumstances in which they are expressed are such as to constitute their expression a positive instigation to some mischievous act. An opinion that corn-dealers are starvers of the poor, or that private property is robbery, ought to be unmolested when simply circulated through the press, but may justly incur punishment when delivered orally to an excited mob assembled before the house of a corn-dealer, or when handed about among the same mob in the form of a placard. Acts, of whatever kind, which, without justifiable cause, do harm to others, may be, and in the more important cases absolutely require to be, controlled by the unfavourable sentiments, and, when needful, by the active interference of mankind. The liberty of the individual must be thus far limited; he must not make himself a nuisance to other people. But if he refrains from molesting others in what concerns them, and merely acts according to his own inclination and judgement in things which concern himself, the same reasons which show that opinion should be free, prove also that he should be allowed, without molestation, to carry his opinions into practice at his own cost. That mankind are not infallible; that their truths, for the most part, are only half-truths; that unity of opinion, unless resulting from the fullest and freest comparison of opposite opinions, is not desirable, and diversity not an evil, but a good, until mankind are much more capable than at present of recognizing all sides of the truth, are principles applicable to men's modes of action, not less than to their opinions. As it is useful that while mankind are imperfect there should be different opinions, so is it that there should be different experiments of living; that free scope should be given to varieties of character, short of injury to others; and that the worth of different modes of life should be proved practically, when any one thinks fit to try them. It is desirable, in short, that in things which do not primarily concern others, individuality should assert itself. Where, not the person's own character, but the traditions or customs of other people are the rule of conduct, there is wanting one of the principal ingredients of human happiness, and quite the chief ingredient of individual and social progress.

In maintaining this principle, the greatest difficulty to be encountered does not lie in the appreciation of means towards an acknowledged end, but in the indifference of persons in general to the end itself. If it were felt that the free development of individuality is one of the leading essentials of well-being; that it is not only a co-ordinate element with all that is designated by the terms civilization, instruction, education, culture, but is itself a necessary part and condition of all those things; there would be no danger that liberty should be undervalued, and the adjustment of the boundaries between it and social control would present no extraordinary difficulty. But the evil is, that individual spontaneity is hardly recognized by the common modes of thinking, as having any intrinsic worth, or deserving any regard on its own account. The majority, being satisfied with the ways of mankind as they now are (for it is they who make them what they are), cannot comprehend why those ways should not be good enough for everybody; and what is more, spontaneity forms no part of the ideal of the majority of moral and social reformers, but is rather looked on with jealousy, as a troublesome and perhaps rebellious obstruction to the general acceptance of what these reformers, in their own judgement, think would be best for mankind. Few persons, out of Germany, even comprehend the meaning of the doctrine which Wilhelm von Humboldt, so eminent both as a savant and as a politician, made the text of a treatise—that "the end of man, or that which is prescribed by the eternal or immutable dictates of reason, and not suggested by vague and transient desires, is the highest and most harmonious development of his powers to a complete and consistent whole;" that, therefore, the object "towards which every human being must ceaselessly direct his efforts, and on which especially those who design to influence their fellow men must ever keep their eyes, is the individuality of power and development;" that for this there are two requisites, "freedom, and variety of situations;" and that from the union of these arise "individual vigour and manifold diversity," which combine themselves in "originality." [1]

Little, however, as people are accustomed to a doctrine like that of Von Humboldt, and surprising as it may be to them to find so high a value attached to individuality, the question, one must nevertheless think, can only be one of degree. No one's idea of excellence in conduct is that people should do absolutely nothing but copy one another. No one would assert that people ought not to put into their mode of life, and into the conduct of their concerns, any impress whatever of their own judgement, or of their own individual character. On the other hand, it would be absurd to pretend that people ought to live as if nothing whatever had been

---

[1] *The Sphere and Duties of Government,* from the German of Baron Wilhelm von Humboldt, pp. 11-13. [Mill's note.] Karl Wilhelm von Humboldt (1767-1835) was a distinguished German statesman, philologist, and man of letters.

known in the world before they came into it; as if experience had as yet done nothing towards showing that one mode of existence, or of conduct, is preferable to another. Nobody denies that people should be so taught and trained in youth, as to know and benefit by the ascertained results of human experience. But it is the privilege and proper condition of a human being, arrived at the maturity of his faculties, to use and interpret experience in his own way. It is for him to find out what part of recorded experience is properly applicable to his own circumstances and character. The traditions and customs of other people are, to a certain extent, evidence of what their experience has taught *them;* presumptive evidence, and as such, have a claim to his deference: but, in the first place, their experience may be too narrow; or they may not have interpreted it rightly. Secondly, their interpretation of experience may be correct, but unsuitable to him. Customs are made for customary circumstances, and customary characters; and his circumstances or his character may be uncustomary. Thirdly, though the customs be both good as customs, and suitable to him, yet to conform to custom, merely *as* custom, does not educate or develop in him any of the qualities which are the distinctive endowment of a human being. The human faculties of perception, judgement, discriminative feeling, mental activity, and even moral preference, are exercised only in making a choice. He who does anything because it is the custom makes no choice. He gains no practice either in discerning or in desiring what is best. The mental and moral, like the muscular powers, are improved only by being used. The faculties are called into no exercise by doing a thing merely because others do it, no more than by believing a thing only because others believe it. If the grounds of an opinion are not conclusive to the person's own reason, his reason cannot be strengthened, but is likely to be weakened, by his adopting it: and if the inducements to an act are not such as are consentaneous to his own feelings and character (where affection, or the rights of others, are not concerned) it is so much done towards rendering his feelings and character inert and torpid, instead of active and energetic.

He who lets the world, or his own portion of it, choose his plan of life for him, has no need of any other faculty than the ape-like one of imitation. He who chooses his plan for himself, employs all his faculties. He must use observation to see, reasoning and judgement to foresee, activity to gather materials for decision, discrimination to decide, and when he has decided, firmness and self-control to hold to his deliberate decision. And these qualities he requires and exercises exactly in proportion as the part of his conduct which he determines according to his own judgement and feelings is a large one. It is possible that he might be guided in some good path, and kept out of harm's way, without any of these things. But what will be his comparative worth as a human being? It really is of importance, not only what men do, but also what manner of men they are that do it. Among the works of man, which human life is rightly employed in perfecting and beautifying, the first in importance surely is man himself. Supposing it were possible to get houses built, corn grown, battles fought, causes tried, and even churches erected and prayers said, by machinery—by automatons in human form—it would be a considerable loss to exchange for these automatons even the men and women who at present inhabit the more civilized parts of the world, and who assuredly are but starved specimens of what nature can and will produce. Human nature is not a machine to be built after a model, and set to do exactly the work prescribed for it, but a tree, which requires to grow and develop itself on all sides, according to the tendency of the inward forces which make it a living thing.

It will probably be conceded that it is desirable people should exercise their understandings, and that an intelligent following of custom, or even occasionally an intelligent deviation from custom, is better than a blind and simply mechanical adhesion to it. To a certain extent it is admitted, that our understanding should be our own: but there is not the same willingness to admit that our desires and impulses should be our own likewise; or that to possess impulses of our own, and of any strength, is anything but a peril and a snare. Yet desires and impulses are as much a part of a perfect human being, as beliefs and restraints: and strong impulses are only perilous when not properly balanced; when one set of aims and inclinations is developed into strength, while others, which ought to co-exist with them, remain weak and inactive. It is not because men's desires are strong that they act ill; it is because their consciences are weak. There is no natural connexion between strong impulses and a weak conscience. The natural connexion is the other way. To say that one person's desires and feelings are stronger and more various than those of another, is merely to say that he has more of the raw material of human nature, and is therefore capable, perhaps of more evil, but certainly of more good. Strong impulses are but another name for energy. Energy may be turned to bad uses; but more good may always be made of an energetic nature, than of an indolent and impassive one. Those who have most natural feeling, are always those whose cultivated feelings may be made the strongest. The same strong susceptibilities which make the personal impulses vivid and powerful, are also the source from whence are generated the most passionate love of virtue, and the sternest self-control. It is through the cultivation of these, that society both does its duty and protects its interests: not by rejecting the stuff of which heroes are made, because it knows not how to make them. A person whose desires and impulses are his own—are the expression of his own nature, as it has been developed and modified by his own culture—is said to have a character. One whose desires and impulses are not his own, has no character, no more than a steam-engine has a character. If, in addition to being his own, his impulses are strong, and are under the government of a strong will, he has an energetic character. Whoever thinks that individuality of desires and impulses should not be encouraged to unfold itself, must maintain that society has no need of strong natures—is not the better for containing many persons who have much character—and that a high general average of energy is not desirable.

In some early states of society, these forces might be, and were, too much ahead of the power which society then possessed of disciplining and controlling them. There has been a time when the element of spontaneity and individuality was in excess, and the social principle had a hard struggle with it. The difficulty then was, to induce men of strong bodies or minds to pay obedience to any rules which required them to control their impulses. To overcome this difficulty, law and discipline, like the Popes struggling against the Emperors, asserted a power over the whole man, claiming to control all his life in order to control his character—which society had not found any other sufficient means of binding. But society has now fairly got the better of individuality; and the danger which threatens human nature is not the excess, but the deficiency, of personal impulses and preferences. Things are vastly changed, since the passions of those who were strong by station or by

personal endowment were in a state of habitual rebellion against laws
and ordinances, and required to be rigorously chained up to enable the
persons within their reach to enjoy any particle of security. In our times,
from the highest class of society down to the lowest, every one lives as
under the eye of a hostile and dreaded censorship. Not only in what
concerns others, but in what concerns only themselves, the individual or
the family do not ask themselves—what do I prefer? or, what would
suit my character and disposition? or, what would allow the best and
highest in me to have fair play, and enable it to grow and thrive? They
ask themselves, what is suitable to my position? what is usually done by
persons of my station and pecuniary circumstances? or (worse still) what
is usually done by persons of a station and circumstances superior to
mine? I do not mean that they choose what is customary, in preference
to what suits their own inclination. It does not occur to them to have
any inclination, except for what is customary. Thus the mind itself is
bowed to the yoke: even in what people do for pleasure, conformity is
the first thing thought of; they like in crowds; they exercise choice only
among things commonly done: peculiarity of taste, eccentricity of conduct, are shunned equally with crimes: until by dint of not following
their own nature, they have no nature to follow: their human capacities
are withered and starved: they become incapable of any strong wishes
or native pleasures, and are generally without either opinions or feelings
of home growth, or properly their own. Now is this, or is it not, the
desirable condition of human nature?

It is so, on the Calvinistic theory. According to that, the one great
offence of man is self-will. All the good of which humanity is capable
is comprised in obedience. You have no choice; thus you must do, and
no otherwise: "whatever is not a duty, is a sin." Human nature being
radically corrupt, there is no redemption for any one until human
nature is killed within him. To one holding this theory of life, crushing out any of the human faculties, capacities, and susceptibilities,
is no evil: man needs no capacity, but that of surrendering himself
to the will of God: and if he uses any of his faculties for any other
purpose but to do that supposed will more effectually, he is better
without them. This is the theory of Calvinism; and it is held, in a
mitigated form, by many who do not consider themselves Calvinists;

the mitigation consisting in giving a less ascetic interpretation to the alleged will of God; asserting it to be his will that mankind should gratify some of their inclinations; of course not in the manner they themselves prefer, but in the way of obedience, that is, in a way prescribed to them by authority; and, therefore, by the necessary conditions of the case, the same for all.

In some such insidious form there is at present a strong tendency to this narrow theory of life, and to the pinched and hidebound type of human character which it patronises. Many persons, no doubt, sincerely think that human beings thus cramped and dwarfed, are as their Maker designed them to be; just as many have thought that trees are a much finer thing when clipped into pollards, or cut out into figures of animals, than as nature made them. But if it be any part of religion to believe that man was made by a good Being, it is more consistent with that faith to believe, that this Being gave all human faculties that they might be cultivated and unfolded, not rooted out and consumed, and that he takes delight in every nearer approach made by his creatures to the ideal conception embodied in them, every increase in any of their capabilities of comprehension, of action, or of enjoyment. There is a different type of human excellence from the Calvinistic; a conception of humanity as having its nature bestowed on it for other purposes than merely to be abnegated. "Pagan self-assertion" is one of the elements of human worth, as well as "Christian self-denial." [2] There is a Greek ideal of self-development, which the Platonic and Christian ideal of self-government blends with, but does not supersede. It may be better to be a John Knox than an Alcibiades, but it is better to be a Pericles than either; nor would a Pericles, if we had one in these days, be without anything good which belonged to John Knox.

It is not by wearing down into uniformity all that is individual in themselves, but by cultivating it and calling it forth, within the limits imposed by the rights and interests of others, that human beings become a noble and beautiful object of contemplation; and as the works partake the character of those who do them, by the same process

[2] Sterling's *Essays*. [Mill's note.] John Sterling (1806-1844) is best remembered through the charming *Life* (1851), written by his friend Carlyle.

human life also becomes rich, diversified, and animating, furnishing more abundant aliment to high thoughts and elevating feelings, and strengthening the tie which binds every individual to the race, by making the race infinitely better worth belonging to. In proportion to the development of his individuality, each person becomes more valuable to himself, and is therefore capable of being more valuable to others. There is a greater fullness of life about his own existence, and when there is more life in the units there is more in the mass which is composed of them. As much compression as is necessary to prevent the stronger specimens of human nature from encroaching on the rights of others, cannot be dispensed with; but for this there is ample compensation even in the point of view of human development. The means of development which the individual loses by being prevented from gratifying his inclinations to the injury of others, are chiefly obtained at the expense of the development of other people. And even to himself there is a full equivalent in the better development of the social part of his nature, rendered possible by the restraint put upon the selfish part. To be held to rigid rules of justice for the sake of others, develops the feelings and capacities which have the good of others for their object. But to be restrained in things not affecting their good, by their mere displeasure, develops nothing valuable, except such force of character as may unfold itself in resisting the restraint. If acquiesced in, it dulls and blunts the whole nature. To give any fair play to the nature of each, it is essential that different persons should be allowed to lead different lives. In proportion as this latitude has been exercised in any age, has that age been noteworthy to posterity. Even despotism does not produce its worst effects, so long as individuality exists under it; and whatever crushes individuality is despotism, by whatever name it may be called, and whether it professes to be enforcing the will of God or the injunctions of men.

Having said that Individuality is the same thing with development, and that it is only the cultivation of individuality which produces, or can produce, well-developed human beings, I might here close the argument: for what more or better can be said of any condition of human affairs, than that it brings human beings themselves nearer to the best thing they can be? or what worse can be said of any obstruction to good, than that it prevents this? Doubtless, however, these considerations will not suffice to convince those who most need convincing; and it is necessary further to show, that these developed human beings are of some use to the undeveloped—to point out to those who do not desire liberty, and would not avail themselves of it, that they may be in some intelligible manner rewarded for allowing other people to make use of it without hindrance.

In the first place, then, I would suggest that they might possibly learn something from them. It will not be denied by anybody, that originality is a valuable element in human affairs. There is always need of persons not only to discover new truths, and point out when what were once truths are true no longer, but also to commence new practices, and set the example of more enlightened conduct, and better taste and sense in human life. This cannot well be gainsaid by anybody who does not believe that the world has already attained perfection in all its ways and practices. It is true that this benefit is not capable of being rendered by everybody alike: there are but few persons, in comparison with the whole of mankind, whose experiments, if adopted by others, would be likely to be any improvement on established practice. But these few are the salt of the earth; without them, human life would become a stagnant pool. Not only is it they who introduce good things which did not before exist; it is they who keep the life in those which already existed. If there were nothing new to be done, would human intellect cease to be necessary? Would it be a reason why those who do the old things should forget why they are done, and do them like cattle, not like human beings? There is only too great a tendency in the best beliefs and practices to degenerate into the mechanical; and unless there were a succession of persons whose ever-recurring originality prevents the grounds of those beliefs and practices from becoming merely traditional, such dead matter would not resist the smallest shock from anything really alive, and there would be no reason why civilisation should not die out, as in the Byzantine Empire. Persons of genius, it is true, are, and are always likely to be, a small minority; but in order to have them, it is necessary to preserve the soil in which they grow. Genius can only breathe freely in an *atmosphere* of freedom. Persons of genius are, *ex vi termini*,[3] *more* individual than any other people—less capable, consequently, of fitting themselves, without hurtful compression, into any of the small number of moulds which society provides in order to save its members the trouble of forming their own character. If from timidity they consent to be forced into one of these moulds, and to let all that part of themselves which cannot expand under the pressure remain unexpanded, society will be little the better for their genius. If they are of a strong character, and break their fetters, they become a mark for the society which has not succeeded in reducing them to commonplace, to point at with solemn warning as "wild," "erratic," and the like; much as if one should complain of the Niagara river for not flowing smoothly between its banks like a Dutch canal.

I insist thus emphatically on the importance of genius, and the necessity of allowing it to unfold itself freely both in thought and in practice, being well aware that no one will deny the position in theory, but knowing also that almost every one, in reality, is totally indifferent to it. People think genius a fine thing if it enables a man to write an exciting poem, or paint a picture. But in its true sense, that of originality in thought and action, though no one says that it is not a thing to be admired, nearly all, at heart, think that they can do very well without it. Unhappily this is too natural to be wondered at. Originality is the one thing which unoriginal minds cannot feel the use of. They cannot see what it is to do for them: how should they? If they could see what it would do for them, it would not be originality. The first service which originality has to render them, is that of opening their eyes: which being once fully done, they would have a chance of being themselves original. Meanwhile, recollecting that nothing was ever yet done which some one was not the first to do, and that all good things which exist are the fruits of originality, let them be modest enough to believe that there is something still left for it to accomplish, and assure themselves that they are more in need of originality, the less they are conscious of the want.

In sober truth, whatever homage may be professed, or even paid,

---

[3] By force of the term.

to real or supposed mental superiority, the general tendency of things throughout the world is to render mediocrity the ascendant power among mankind. In ancient history, in the middle ages, and in a diminishing degree through the long transition from feudality to the present time, the individual was a power in himself; and if he had either great talents or a high social position, he was a considerable power. At present individuals are lost in the crowd. In politics it is almost a triviality to say that public opinion now rules the world. The only power deserving the name is that of masses, and of governments while they make themselves the organ of the tendencies and instincts of masses. This is as true in the moral and social relations of private life as in public transactions. Those whose opinions go by the name of public opinion are not always the same sort of public: in America they are the whole white population; in England, chiefly the middle class. But they are always a mass, that is to say, collective mediocrity. And what is a still greater novelty, the mass do not now take their opinions from dignitaries in Church or State, from ostensible leaders, or from books. Their thinking is done for them by men much like themselves, addressing them or speaking in their name, on the spur of the moment, through the newspapers. I am not complaining of all this. I do not assert that anything better is compatible, as a general rule, with the present low state of the human mind. But that does not hinder the government of mediocrity from being mediocre government. No government by a democracy or a numerous aristocracy, either in its political acts or in the opinions, qualities, and tone of mind which it fosters, ever did or could rise above mediocrity, except in so far as the sovereign Many have let themselves be guided (which in their best times they always have done) by the counsels and influence of a more highly gifted and instructed One or Few. The initiation of all wise or noble things comes and must come from individuals; generally at first from some one individual. The honour and glory of the average man is that he is capable of following that initiative; that he can respond internally to wise and noble things, and be led to them with his eyes open. I am not countenancing the sort of "hero-worship" which applauds the strong man of genius for forcibly seizing on the government of the world and making it do his bidding in spite of itself. All he can claim is, freedom to point out the way. The power of compelling others into it, is not only inconsistent with the freedom and development of all the rest, but corrupting to the strong man himself. It does seem, however, that when the opinions of masses of merely average men are everywhere become or becoming the dominant power, the counterpoise and corrective to that tendency would be, the more and more pronounced individuality of those who stand on the higher eminences of thought. It is in these circumstances most especially, that exceptional individuals, instead of being deterred, should be encouraged in acting differently from the mass. In other times there was no advantage in their doing so, unless they acted not only differently, but better. In this age, the mere example of non-conformity, the mere refusal to bend the knee to custom, is itself a service. Precisely because the tyranny of opinion is such as to make eccentricity a reproach, it is desirable, in order to break through that tyranny, that people should be eccentric. Eccentricity has always abounded when and where strength of character has abounded; and the amount of eccentricity in a society has generally been proportional to the amount of genius, mental vigour, and moral courage it contained. That so few now dare to be eccentric marks the chief danger of the time.

I have said that it is important to give the freest scope possible to uncustomary things, in order that it may in time appear which of these are fit to be converted into customs. But independence of action, and disregard of custom, are not solely deserving of encouragement for the chance they afford that better modes of action, and customs more worthy of general adoption, may be struck out; nor is it only persons of decided mental superiority who have a just claim to carry on their lives in their own way. There is no reason that all human existence should be constructed on some one or some small number of patterns. If a person possesses any tolerable amount of common sense and experience, his own mode of laying out his existence is the best, not because it is the best in itself, but because it is his own mode. Human beings are not like sheep; and even sheep are not undistinguishably alike. A man cannot get a coat or a pair of boots to fit him, unless they are either made to his measure, or he has a whole warehouseful to choose from: and is it easier to fit him with a life than with a coat, or are human beings more like one another in their whole physical and spiritual conformation than in the shape of their feet? If it were only that people have diversities of taste, that is reason enough for not attempting to shape them all after one model. But different persons also require different conditions for their spiritual development; and can no more exist healthily in the same moral, than all the variety of plants can in the same physical, atmosphere and climate. The same things which are helps to one person towards the cultivation of his higher nature, are hindrances to another. The same mode of life is a healthy excitement to one, keeping all his faculties of action and enjoyment in their best order, while to another it is a distracting burthen, which suspends or crushes all internal life. Such are the differences among human beings in their sources of pleasure, their susceptibilities of pain, and the operation on them of different physical and moral agencies, that unless there is a corresponding diversity in their modes of life, they neither obtain their fair share of happiness, nor grow up to the mental, moral, and aesthetic stature of which their nature is capable. Why then should tolerance, as far as the public sentiment is concerned, extend only to tastes and modes of life which extort acquiescence by the multitude of their adherents? Nowhere (except in some monastic institutions) is diversity of taste entirely unrecognized; a person may, without blame, either like or dislike rowing, or smoking, or music, or athletic exercises, or chess, or cards, or study, because both those who like each of these things, and those who dislike them, are too numerous to be put down. But the man, and still more the woman, who can be accused either of doing "what nobody does," or of not doing "what everybody does," is the subject of as much depreciatory remark as if he or she had committed some grave moral delinquency. Persons require to possess a title, or some other badge of rank, or of the consideration of people of rank, to be able to indulge somewhat in the luxury of doing as they like without detriment to their estimation. To indulge somewhat, I repeat: for whoever allow themselves much of that indulgence, incur the risk of something worse than disparaging speeches—they are in peril of a commission *de lunatico*,[4] and of having their property taken from them and given to their relations.[5]

There is one characteristic of the present direction of public opinion, peculiarly calculated to make it intolerant of any marked demonstration of individuality. The general average of mankind are not only moderate in intellect, but also moderate in inclinations: they have no tastes or wishes strong enough to incline them to do anything unusual, and they consequently do not understand those who have, and class all such with the wild and intemperate whom they are accustomed to look down upon. Now, in addition to this fact which is general, we have only to suppose that a strong movement has set in towards the improvement of morals, and it is evident what we have to expect. In these days such a movement has set in; much has actually been effected in the way of increased regularity of conduct, and discouragement of excesses; and there is a philanthropic spirit abroad, for the exercise of which there is no more inviting field than the moral and prudential improvement of our fellow creatures.

[4] Commission to inquire whether a person is insane.

[5] There is something both contemptible and frightful in the sort of evidence on which, of late years, any person can be judicially declared unfit for the management of his affairs; and after his death, his disposal of his property can be set aside, if there is enough of it to pay the expenses of litigation—which are charged on the property itself. All the minute details of his daily life are pried into, and whatever is found which, seen through the medium of the perceiving and describing faculties of the lowest of the low, bears an appearance unlike absolute commonplace, is laid before the jury as evidence of insanity, and often with success; the jurors being little, if at all, less vulgar and ignorant than the witnesses; while the judges, with that extraordinary want of knowledge of human nature and life which continually astonishes us in English lawyers, often help to mislead them. These trials speak volumes as to the state of feeling and opinion among the vulgar with regard to human liberty. So far from setting any value on individuality—so far from respecting the right of each individual to act in things indifferent, as seems good to his own judgment and inclinations, judges and juries cannot even conceive that a person in a state of sanity can desire such freedom. In former days, when it was proposed to burn atheists, charitable people used to suggest putting them in a mad-house instead: it would be nothing surprising now-a-days were we to see this done, and the doers applauding themselves, because, instead of persecuting for religion, they had adopted so humane and Christian a mode of treating these unfortunates, not without a silent satisfaction at their having thereby obtained their deserts. [Mill's note.]

These tendencies of the times cause the public to be more disposed than at most former periods to prescribe general rules of conduct, and endeavour to make every one conform to the approved standard. And that standard, express or tacit, is to desire nothing strongly. Its ideal of character is to be without any marked character; to maim by compression, like a Chinese lady's foot, every part of human nature which stands out prominently, and tends to make the person markedly dissimilar in outline to commonplace humanity.

As is usually the case with ideals which exclude one-half of what is desirable, the present standard of approbation produces only an inferior imitation of the other half. Instead of great energies guided by vigorous reason, and strong feelings strongly controlled by a conscientious will, its result is weak feelings and weak energies, which therefore can be kept in outward conformity to rule without any strength either of will or of reason. Already energetic characters on any large scale are becoming merely traditional. There is now scarcely any outlet for energy in this country except business. The energy expended in this may still be regarded as considerable. What little is left from that employment, is expended on some hobby; which may be a useful, even a philanthropic hobby, but is always some one thing, and generally a thing of small dimensions. The greatness of England is now all collective: individually small, we only appear capable of anything great by our habit of combining; and with this our moral and religious philanthropists are perfectly contented. But it was men of another stamp than this that made England what it has been; and men of another stamp will be needed to prevent its decline.

The despotism of custom is everywhere the standing hindrance to human advancement, being in unceasing antagonism to that disposition to aim at something better than customary, which is called, according to circumstances, the spirit of liberty, or that of progress or improvement. The spirit of improvement is not always a spirit of liberty, for it may aim at forcing improvements on an unwilling people; and the spirit of liberty, in so far as it resists such attempts, may ally itself locally and temporarily with the opponents of improvement; but the only unfailing and permanent source of improvement is liberty, since by it there are as many possible independent centres of improvement as there are individuals. The progressive principle, however, in either shape, whether as the love of liberty or of improvement, is antagonistic to the sway of Custom, involving at least emancipation from that yoke; and the contest between the two constitutes the chief interest of the history of mankind. The greater part of the world has, properly speaking, no history, because the despotism of Custom is complete. This is the case over the whole East. Custom is there, in all things, the final appeal; justice and right mean conformity to custom; the argument of custom no one, unless some tyrant intoxicated with power, thinks of resisting. And we see the result. Those nations must once have had originality; they did not start out of the ground populous, lettered, and versed in many of the arts of life; they made themselves all this, and were then the greatest and most powerful nations of the world. What are they now? The subjects or dependents of tribes whose forefathers wandered in the forests when theirs had magnificent palaces and gorgeous temples, but over whom custom exercised only a divided rule with liberty and progress. A people, it appears, may be progressive for a certain length of time, and then stop: when does it stop? When it ceases to possess individuality. If a similar change should befall the nations of Europe, it will not be in exactly the same shape: the despotism of custom with which these nations are threatened is not precisely stationariness. It proscribes singularity, but it does not preclude change, provided all change together. We have discarded the fixed costumes of our forefathers; every one must still dress like other people, but the fashion may change once or twice a year. We thus take care that when there is change it shall be for change's sake, and not from any idea of beauty or convenience; for the same idea of beauty or convenience would not strike all the world at the same moment, and be simultaneously thrown aside by all at another moment. But we are progressive as well as changeable: we continually make new inventions in mechanical things, and keep them until they are again superseded by better; we are eager for improvement in politics, in education, even in morals, though in this last our idea of improvement chiefly consists in persuading or forcing other people to be as good as ourselves. It is not progress that we object to; on the contrary, we flatter ourselves that we are the most progressive people who ever lived. It is individuality that we war against: we should think we had done wonders if we had made ourselves all alike; forgetting that the unlikeness of one person to another is generally the first thing which draws the attention of either to the imperfection of his own type, and the superiority of another, or the possibility, by combining the advantages of both, of producing something better than either. We have a warning example in China—a nation of much talent, and, in some respects, even wisdom, owing to the rare good fortune of having been provided at an early period with a particularly good set of customs, the work, in some measure, of men to whom even the most enlightened European must accord, under certain limitations, the title of sages and philosophers. They are remarkable, too, in the excellence of their apparatus for impressing, as far as possible, the best wisdom they possess upon every mind in the community, and securing that those who have appropriated most of it shall occupy the posts of honour and power. Surely the people who did this have discovered the secret of human progressiveness, and must have kept themselves steadily at the head of the movement of the world. On the contrary, they have become stationary—have remained so for thousands of years; and if they are ever to be farther improved, it must be by foreigners. They have succeeded beyond all hope in what English philanthropists are so industriously working at—in making a people all alike, all governing their thoughts and conduct by the same maxims and rules; and these are the fruits. The modern *régime* of public opinion is, in an unorganized form, what the Chinese educational and political systems are in an organized; and unless individuality shall be able successfully to assert itself against this yoke, Europe, notwithstanding its noble antecedents and its professed Christianity, will tend to become another China.

What is it that has hitherto preserved Europe from this lot? What has made the European family of nations an improving, instead of a stationary portion of mankind? Not any superior excellence in them, which, when it exists, exists as the effect, not as the cause; but their remarkable diversity of character and culture. Individuals, classes, nations, have been extremely unlike one another: they have struck out a great variety of paths, each leading to something valuable; and although at every period those who travelled in different paths have been intolerant of one another, and each would have thought it an excellent thing if all the rest could have been compelled to travel his road, their attempts to thwart each other's development have rarely had any permanent success, and each has in time endured to receive the good which the others have offered. Europe is, in my judgement, wholly indebted to this plurality of paths for its progressive and many-sided development. But it already begins to possess this benefit in a considerably less degree. It is decidedly advancing towards the Chinese ideal of making all people alike. M. de Tocqueville, in his last important work,[6] remarks how much more the Frenchmen of the present day resemble one another, than did those even of the last generation. The same remark might be made of Englishmen in a far greater degree. In a passage already quoted from Wilhelm von Humboldt, he points out two things as necessary conditions of human development, because necessary to render people unlike one another; namely, freedom, and variety of situations. The second of these two conditions is in this country every day diminishing. The circumstances which surround different classes and individuals, and shape their characters, are daily becoming more assimilated. Formerly, different ranks, different neighbourhoods, different trades and professions, lived in what might be called different worlds; at present, to a great degree in the same. Comparatively speaking, they now read the same things, listen to the same things, see the same things, go to the same places, have their hopes and fears directed to the same objects, have the same rights and liberties, and the same means of asserting them. Great as are the differences of position which remain, they are nothing to those which have ceased. And the assimilation is still proceeding. All the political changes of the age promote it, since they all tend to raise the low and to lower the high. Every extension of education promotes it, because education brings people under common influences, and gives them access to the general stock of facts and sentiments. Improvements in the means of communication promote it, by

[6] *L'Ancien Régime et la Révolution* (1850).

bringing the inhabitants of distant places into personal contact, and keeping up a rapid flow of changes of residence between one place and another. The increase of commerce and manufactures promotes it, by diffusing more widely the advantages of easy circumstances, and opening all objects of ambition, even the highest, to general competition, whereby the desire of rising becomes no longer the character of a particular class, but of all classes. A more powerful agency than even all these, in bringing about a general similarity among mankind, is the complete establishment, in this and other free countries, of the ascendancy of public opinion in the State. As the various social eminences which enabled persons entrenched on them to disregard the opinion of the multitude gradually become levelled; as the very idea of resisting the will of the public, when it is positively known that they have a will, disappears more and more from the minds of practical politicians; there ceases to be any social support for nonconformity—any substantive power in society, which, itself opposed to the ascendancy of numbers, is interested in taking under its protection opinions and tendencies at variance with those of the public.

The combination of all these causes forms so great a mass of influences hostile to Individuality, that it is not easy to see how it can stand its ground. It will do so with increasing difficulty, unless the intelligent part of the public can be made to feel its value—to see that it is good there should be differences, even though not for the better, even though, as it may appear to them, some should be for the worse. If the claims of Individuality are ever to be asserted, the time is now, while much is still wanting to complete the enforced assimilation. It is only in the earlier stages that any stand can be successfully made against the encroachment. The demand that all other people shall resemble ourselves grows by what it feeds on. If resistance waits till life is reduced *nearly* to one uniform type, all deviations from that type will come to be considered impious, immoral, even monstrous and contrary to nature. Mankind speedily become unable to conceive diversity, when they have been for some time unaccustomed to see it.

Thomas Carlyle

1795-1881

Democracy

❁ The following selection is Chapter Thirteen of Book
Three of *Past and Present* (1843). Because of his
admiration for strong men and autocratic rule,
Carlyle is often treated as a nineteenth-century
prophet of fascism. This view takes insufficient account
of the facts that the Carlylean hero is subject to moral
law and that he acts for the good of humanity in
fulfilling his ordained mission.

If the Serene Highnesses and Majesties do not take
note of that, then, as I perceive, *that* will take note of itself! [1] The time
for levity, insincerity, and idle babble and play-acting, in all kinds, is
gone by; it is a serious, grave time. Old long-vexed questions, not yet
solved in logical words or parliamentary laws, are fast solving themselves in facts, somewhat unblessed to behold! This largest of questions,
this question of Work and Wages, which ought, had we heeded
Heaven's voice, to have begun two generations ago or more, cannot
be delayed longer without hearing Earth's voice. "Labour" will verily
need to be somewhat "organized," as they say,—God knows with
what difficulty. Man will actually need to have his debts and earnings
a little better paid by man; which, let Parliaments speak of them, or be
silent of them, are eternally his due from man, and cannot, without

[1] The preceding chapter of *Past and Present* concludes as follows: "May it please
your Serene Highnesses and Majesties, Lordships and Law-wardships, the proper Epic
of this world is not now 'Arms and the Man'; how much less, 'Shirt-frills and the
Man': no, it is now 'Tools and the Man': that, henceforth to all time, is now our
Epic;—and you, first of all others, I think, were wise to take note of that!"

penalty and at length not without death-penalty, be withheld. How much ought to cease among us straightway; how much ought to begin straightway, while the hours yet are!

Truly they are strange results to which this of leaving all to "Cash"; of quietly shutting up the God's Temple, and gradually opening wide-open the Mammon's Temple, with "Laissez-faire, and Every man for himself,"—have led us in these days! We have Upper, speaking Classes, who indeed do "speak" as never man spake before; the withered flimsiness, godless baseness and barrenness of whose Speech might of itself indicate what kind of Doing and practical Governing went on under it! For Speech is the gaseous element out of which most kinds of Practice and Performance, especially all kinds of moral Performance, condense themselves, and take shape; as the one is, so will the other be. Descending, accordingly, into the Dumb Class in its Stockport Cellars and Poor-Law Bastilles,[2] have we not to announce that they are hitherto unexampled in the History of Adam's Posterity?

Life was never a May-game for men: in all times the lot of the dumb millions born to toil was defaced with manifold sufferings, injustices, heavy burdens, avoidable and unavoidable; not play at all, but hard work that made the sinews sore and the heart sore. As bond-slaves, *villani, bordarii, sochemanni,*[3] nay indeed as dukes, earls and kings, men were oftentimes made weary of their life; and had to say, in the sweat of their brow and of their soul, Behold, it is not sport, it is grim earnest, and our back can bear no more! Who knows not what massacrings and harryings there have been; grinding, long-continuing, unbearable injustices,—till the heart had to rise in madness, and some *"Eu Sachsen, nimith euer sachses,* You Saxons, out with your gully-knives, then!" You Saxons, some "arrestment," partial "arrestment of the Knaves and Dastards" has become indispensable! —The page of Dryasdust is heavy with such details.

And yet I will venture to believe that in no time, since the beginnings of Society, was the lot of those same dumb millions of toilers

[2] Stockport is an industrial town in the north of England about which Carlyle narrates an episode of child-murder in Chapter One, Book One, of *Past and Present.* Poor-Law Bastilles denotes the workhouses created under the New Poor Law of 1834.

[3] Mediaeval names for serfs.

so entirely unbearable as it is even in the days now passing over us. It is not to die, or even to die of hunger, that makes a man wretched; many men have died; all men must die,—the last exit of us all is in a Fire-Chariot of Pain. But it is to live miserable we know not why; to work sore and yet gain nothing; to be heart-worn, weary, yet isolated, unrelated, girt-in with a cold universal Laissez-faire: it is to die slowly all our life long, imprisoned in a deaf, dead, Infinite Injustice, as in the accursed iron belly of a Phalaris Bull![4] This is and remains for ever intolerable to all men whom God has made. Do we wonder at French Revolutions, Chartisms, Revolts of Three Days? The times, if we will consider them, are really unexampled.

Never before did I hear of an Irish Widow reduced to "prove her sisterhood by dying of typhus-fever and infecting seventeen persons," —saying in such undeniable way, "You *see,* I was your sister!"[5] Sisterhood, brotherhood, was often forgotten; but not till the rise of these ultimate Mammon and Shotbelt Gospels did I ever see it so expressly denied. If no pious Lord or *Law-ward* would remember it, always some pious Lady (*"Hlaf dig,"* Benefactress, *"Loaf-giveress,"* they say she is,—blessings on her beautiful heart!) was there, with mild mother-voice and hand, to remember it; some pious thoughtful *Elder,* what we now call "Prester," *Presbyter* or "Priest," was there to put all men in mind of it, in the name of the God who had made all.

---

[4] Phalaris was a tyrannical ruler of ancient Sicily who had criminals roasted alive in a bronze bull.

[5] The reference is to an episode which Carlyle recounts in Chapter Two, Book Three, of *Past and Present:* "A poor Irish Widow, her husband having died in one of the Lanes of Edinburgh, went forth with her three children, bare of all resource, to solicit help from the Charitable Establishments of the City. At this Charitable Establishment and then at that she was refused; referred from one to the other, helped by none;—till she had exhausted them all; till her strength and heart failed her: she sank down in typhus-fever; died, and infected her Lane with fever, so that 'seventeen other persons' died of fever there, in consequence. The humane Physician asks thereupon, as with a heart too full for speaking, Would it not have been *economy* to help this poor Widow? She took typhus-fever, and killed seventeen of you!—Very curious. The forlorn Irish Widow applies to her fellow-creatures, as if saying, 'Behold I am sinking, bare of help: ye must help me! I am your sister, bone of your bone; one God made us: ye must help me!' They answer, 'No, impossible; thou art no sister of ours.' But she proves her sisterhood; her typhus-fever kills *them:* they actually were her brothers, though denying it! Had human creature ever to go lower for a proof?"

Not even in Black Dahomey[6] was it ever, I think, forgotten to the typhus-fever length. Mungo Park,[7] resourceless, had sunk down to die under the Negro Village-Tree, a horrible White object in the eyes of all. But in the poor Black Woman, and her daughter who stood aghast at him, whose earthly wealth and funded capital consisted of one small calabash of rice, there lived a heart richer than *"Laissez-faire"*: they, with a royal munificence, boiled their rice for him; they sang all night to him, spinning assiduous on their cotton distaffs, as he lay to sleep: "Let us pity the poor white man; no mother has he to fetch him milk, no sister to grind him corn!" Thou poor black Noble One,— thou *Lady* too: did not a God make thee too; was there not in thee too something of a God!—

Gurth, born thrall of Cedric the Saxon,[8] has been greatly pitied by Dryasdust[9] and others. Gurth, with the brass collar round his neck, tending Cedric's pigs in the glades of the wood, is not what I call an exemplar of human felicity: but Gurth, with the sky above him, with the free air and tinted boscage and umbrage round him, and in him at least the certainty of supper and social lodging when he came home; Gurth to me seems happy, in comparison with many a Lancashire and Buckinghamshire man, of these days, not born thrall of anybody! Gurth's brass collar did not gall him: Cedric *deserved* to be his Master. The pigs were Cedric's, but Gurth too would get his parings of them. Gurth had the inexpressible satisfaction of feeling himself related indissolubly, though in a rude brass-collar way, to his fellow-mortals in this Earth. He had superiors, inferiors, equals.— Gurth is now "emancipated" long since; has what we call "Liberty." Liberty, I am told, is a Divine thing. Liberty when it becomes the "Liberty to die by starvation" is not so divine!

Liberty? The true liberty of a man, you would say, consisted in his finding out, or being forced to find out the right path, and to walk

[6] A primitive colony in West Africa.

[7] Mungo Park (1771-1806), African explorer, relates this incident in his *Travels in the Interior of Africa* (1799).

[8] Gurth and Cedric are characters in Scott's *Ivanhoe*.

[9] Carlyle habitually uses this satirical name, which he derived from Scott, to designate pedantic historians.

thereon. To learn, or to be taught, what work he actually was able for; and then by permission, persuasion, and even compulsion, to set about doing of the same! That is his true blessedness, honour, "liberty" and maximum of wellbeing: if liberty be not that, I for one have small care about liberty. You do not allow a palpable madman to leap over precipices; you violate his liberty, you that are wise; and keep him, were it in strait-waistcoats, away from the precipices! Every stupid, every cowardly and foolish man is but a less palpable madman: his true liberty were that a wiser man, that any and every wiser man, could, by brass collars, or in whatever milder or sharper way, lay hold of him when he was going wrong, and order and compel him to go a little righter. O, if thou really art my *Senior,* Seigneur, my *Elder,* Presbyter or Priest,—if thou art in very deed my *Wiser,* may a beneficent instinct lead and impel thee to "conquer" me, to command me! If thou do know better than I what is good and right, I conjure thee in the name of God, force me to do it; were it by never such brass collars, whips and handcuffs, leave me not to walk over precipices! That I have been called, by all the Newspapers, a "free man" will avail me little, if my pilgrimage have ended in death and wreck. O that the Newspapers had called me slave, coward, fool, or what it pleased their sweet voices to name me, and I had attained not death, but life!—Liberty requires new definitions.

A conscious abhorrence and intolerance of Folly, of Baseness, Stupidity, Poltroonery and all that brood of things, dwells deep in some men: still deeper in others an *un*conscious abhorrence and intolerance, clothed moreover by the beneficent Supreme Powers in what stout appetites, energies, egoisms so-called, are suitable to it;—these latter are your Conquerors, Romans, Normans, Russians, Indo-English; Founders of what we call Aristocracies. Which indeed have they not the most "divine right" to found;—being themselves very truly Ἄριστοι, BRAVEST, BEST; and conquering generally a confused rabble of WORST, or at lowest, clearly enough, of WORSE? I think their divine right, tried, with affirmatory verdict, in the greatest Law-Court known to me, was good! A class of men who are dreadfully exclaimed against by Dryasdust; of whom nevertheless beneficent Nature has oftentimes had need; and may, alas, again have need.

When, across the hundredfold poor scepticisms, trivialisms, and constitutional cob-webberies of Dryasdust, you catch any glimpse of a William the Conqueror,[10] a Tancred of Hauteville[11] or such like,— do you not discern veritably some rude outline of a true God-made King; whom not the Champion of England cased in tin, but all Nature and the Universe were calling to the throne? It is absolutely necessary that he get thither. Nature does not mean her poor Saxon children to perish, of obesity, stupor or other malady, as yet: a stern Ruler and Line of Rulers therefore is called in,—a stern but most beneficent *perpetual House-Surgeon* is by Nature herself called in, and even the appropriate *fees* are provided for him! Dryasdust talks lamentably about Hereward and the Fen Counties; fate of Earl Waltheof;[12] Yorkshire and the North reduced to ashes; all of which is undoubtedly lamentable. But even Dryasdust apprises me of one fact: "A child, in this William's reign, might have carried a purse of gold from end to end of England." My erudite friend, it is a fact which outweighs a thousand! Sweep away thy constitutional, sentimental, and other cob-webberies; look eye to eye, if thou still have any eye, in the face of this big burly William Bastard: thou wilt see a fellow of most flashing discernment, of most strong lion-heart; —in whom, as it were, within a frame of oak and iron, the gods have planted the soul of "a man of genius"! Dost thou call that nothing? I call it an immense thing!—Rage enough was in this Willelmus Conquæstor, rage enough for his occasions;—and yet the essential element of him, as of all such men, is not scorching *fire,* but shining illuminative *light.* Fire and light are strangely interchangeable; nay, at bottom, I have found them different forms of the same most godlike "elementary substance" in our world: a thing worth stating in these days. The essential element of this Conquæstor is, first of all, the most sun-eyed perception of what *is* really what on this God's-Earth;—

---

[10] William of Normandy (1027-1087), who conquered England in 1066 and ruled there until his death. In calling him William Bastard farther on, Carlyle refers to the fact that he was illegitimate.

[11] A Norman warrior who fought heroically in the First Crusade.

[12] Hereward the Wake was a Saxon outlaw and romantic hero who held out against William the Conqueror; Waltheof, the Saxon Earl of Northumberland, was beheaded by William in 1076 for conspiracy.

which, thou wilt find, does mean at bottom "Justice," and "Virtues" not a few: *Conformity* to what the Maker has seen good to make; that, I suppose, will mean Justice and a Virtue or two?—

Dost thou think Willelmus Conquæstor would have tolerated ten years' jargon, one hour's jargon, on the propriety of killing Cotton-manufactures by partridge Corn-Laws? I fancy, this was not the man to knock out of his night's-rest with nothing but a noisy bedlamism in your mouth! "Assist us still better to bush the partridges; strangle Plugson[13] who spins the shirts?—*"Par la Splendeur de Dieu!"* [14]— Dost thou think Willelmus Conquæstor, in this new time, with Steam-engine Captains of Industry on one hand of him, and Joe-Manton[15] Captains of Idleness on the other, would have doubted which *was* really the BEST; which did deserve strangling, and which not?

I have a certain indestructible regard for Willelmus Conquæstor. A resident House-Surgeon, provided by Nature for her beloved English People, and even furnished with the requisite fees, as I said; for he by no means felt himself doing Nature's work, this Willelmus, but his own work exclusively! And his own work withal it was; informed *"par la Splendeur de Dieu."*—I say, it is necessary to get the work out of such a man, however harsh that be! When a world, not yet doomed for death, is rushing down to ever-deeper Baseness and Confusion, it is a dire necessity of Nature's to bring in her ARISTOCRACIES, her BEST, even by forcible methods. When their descendants or representatives cease entirely to *be* the Best, Nature's poor world will very soon rush down again to Baseness; and it becomes a dire necessity of Nature's to cast them out. Hence French Revolutions, Five-point Charters, Democracies, and a mournful list of *Etceteras,* in these our afflicted times.

To what extent Democracy has now reached, how it advances irresistible with ominous, ever-increasing speed, he that will open his eyes on any province of human affairs may discern. Democracy is every-

---

[13] Plugson of Undershot is Carlyle's name for the typical industrialist of the period.

[14] By God's splendor.

[15] Joseph Manton (1766?-1835) was a well-known London gunsmith whose weapons were much in demand among the sporting aristocracy.

where the inexorable demand of these ages, swiftly fulfilling itself. From the thunder of Napoleon battles, to the jabbering of Open-vestry in St. Mary Axe,[16] all things announce Democracy. A distinguished man, whom some of my readers will hear again with pleasure, thus writes to me what in these days he notes from the Wahngasse of Weissnichtwo, where our London fashions seem to be in full vogue. Let us hear the Herr Teufelsdröckh[17] again, were it but the smallest word!

"Democracy, which means despair of finding any Heroes to govern you, and contented putting up with the want of them,—alas, thou too, *mein Lieber,*[18] seest well how close it is of kin to *Atheism,* and other sad *Isms*: he who discovers no God whatever, how shall he discover Heroes, the visible Temples of God?—Strange enough meanwhile it is, to observe with what thoughtlessness, here in our rigidly Conservative Country, men rush into Democracy with full cry. Beyond doubt, his Excellenz the Titular-Herr Ritter Kauderwälsch von Pferde-fuss-Quacksalber,[19] he our distinguished Conservative Premier[20] himself, and all but the thicker-headed of his Party, discern Democracy to be inevitable as death, and are even desperate of delaying it much!

"You cannot walk the streets without beholding Democracy announce itself: the very Tailor has become, if not properly Sanscullottic, which to him would be ruinous, yet a Tailor unconsciously symbolizing, and prophesying with his scissors, the reign of Equality. What now is our fashionable coat? A thing of superfinest texture, of deeply meditated cut; with Malines-lace cuffs; quilted with gold; so that a man can carry, without difficulty, an estate of land on his back?

[16] A London church. The temporal business of the Church of England was democratically administered by vestries elected annually by the parish.

[17] Diogenes Teufelsdröckh (God-born Devil's-dung) is the name of the German protagonist of Carlyle's semi-autobiographical *Sartor Resartus* (1833-34). The sentiments here attributed to him are, of course, Carlyle's own, couched in a more highflown style. Teufelsdröckh's residence was in Wahngasse (Dream Alley) in the town of Weissnichtwo (I-Know-Not-Where).

[18] My dear friend.

[19] Sir Knight Gibberish von Horsefoot-Quackdoctor.

[20] Sir Robert Peel (1788-1850), who was prime minister when *Past and Present* was published. Although the head of the Tory party, he revealed his democratic sympathies by sponsoring the repeal of the Corn Laws (1846).

Keineswegs, By no manner of means! The Sumptuary Laws[21] have fallen into such a state of desuetude as was never before seen. Our fashionable coat is an amphibium between barn-sack and drayman's doublet. The cloth of it is studiously coarse; the colour a speckled soot-black or rust-brown grey;—the nearest approach to a Peasant's. And for shape,—thou shouldst see it! The last consummation of the year now passing over us is definable as Three Bags; a big bag for the body, two small bags for the arms, and by way of collar a hem! The first Antique Cheruscan[22] who, of felt-cloth or bear's-hide, with bone or metal needle, set about making himself a coat, before Tailors had yet awakened out of Nothing,—did not he make it even so? A loose wide poke for body, with two holes to let out the arms; this was his original coat: to which holes it was soon visible that two small loose pokes, or sleeves, easily appended, would be an improvement.

"Thus has the Tailor-art, so to speak, overset itself, like most other things; changed its centre-of-gravity; whirled suddenly over from zenith to nadir. Your Stulz, with huge somerset, vaults from his high shop-board down to the depths of primal savagery,—carrying much along with him! For I will invite thee to reflect that the Tailor, as topmost ultimate froth of Human Society, is indeed swift-passing, evanescent, slippery to decipher; yet significant of much, nay of all. Topmost evanescent froth, he is churned up from the very lees, and from all intermediate regions of the liquor. The general outcome he, visible to the eye, of what men aimed to do, and were obliged and enabled to do, in this one public department of symbolizing themselves to each other by covering of their skins. A smack of all Human Life lies in the Tailor: its wild struggles towards beauty, dignity, freedom, victory; and how, hemmed in by Sedan and Huddersfield,[23] by Nescience, Dullness, Prurience, and other sad necessities and laws of Nature, it has attained just to this: Grey savagery of Three Sacks with a hem!

"When the very Tailor verges towards Sansculottism, is it not ominous? The last Divinity of poor mankind dethroning himself;

[21] Laws restraining private extravagance.
[22] The Cherusci were an ancient tribe of Germans.
[23] Cloth-manufacturing towns in France and England respectively.

sinking *his* taper too, flame downmost, like the Genius of Sleep or of Death; admonitory that Tailor-time shall be no more!—For, little as one could advise Sumptuary Laws at the present epoch, yet nothing is clearer than that where ranks do actually exist, strict division of costumes will also be enforced; that if we ever have a new Hierarchy and Aristocracy, acknowledged veritably as such, for which I daily pray Heaven, the Tailor will re-awaken; and be, by volunteering and appointment, consciously and unconsciously, a safeguard of that same."
—Certain farther observations, from the same invaluable pen, on our never-ending changes of mode, our "perpetual nomadic and even ape-like appetite for change and mere change" in all the equipments of our existence, and the "fatal revolutionary character" thereby manifested, we suppress for the present. It may be admitted that Democracy, in all meanings of the word, is in full career; irresistible by any Ritter Kauderwälsch or other Son of Adam, as times go. "Liberty" is a thing men are determined to have.

But truly, as I had to remark in the mean while, "the liberty of not being oppressed by your fellow man" is an indispensable, yet one of the most insignificant fractional parts of Human Liberty. No man oppresses thee, can bid thee fetch or carry, come or go, without reason shown. True; from all men thou art emancipated: but from Thyself and from the Devil—? No man, wiser, unwiser, can make thee come or go: but thy own futilities, bewilderments, thy false appetites for Money, Windsor Georges[24] and such like? No man oppresses thee, O free and independent Franchiser: but does not this stupid Porter-pot oppress thee? No Son of Adam can bid thee come or go; but this absurd Pot of Heavy-wet,[25] this can and does! Thou art the thrall not of Cedric the Saxon, but of thy own brutal appetites, and this scoured dish of liquor. And thou pratest of thy "liberty"? Thou entire blockhead!

Heavy-wet and gin: alas, these are not the only kinds of thraldom. Thou who walkest in a vain show, looking out with ornamental dilettante sniff, and serene supremacy, at all Life and all Death; and am-

---

[24] Ceremonial processions showing effigies of St. George, the patron saint of the English.

[25] Slang for strong ale.

blest jauntily; perking up thy poor talk into crotchets, thy poor conduct into fatuous somnambulisms;—and *art* as an "enchanted Ape"
under God's sky, where thou mightest have been a man, had proper
Schoolmasters and Conquerors, and Constables with cat-o'-nine tails,
been vouch-safed thee: dost thou call that "liberty"? Or your un-
reposing Mammon-worshipper, again, driven, as if by Galvanisms,
by Devils and Fixed-Ideas, who rises early and sits late, chasing the
impossible; straining every faculty to "fill himself with the east wind,"
—how merciful were it, could you, by mild persuasion or by the
severest tyranny so-called, check him in his mad path, and turn him
into a wiser one! All painful tyranny, in that case again, were but
mild "surgery"; the pain of it cheap, as health and life, instead of
galvanism and fixed-idea, are cheap at any price.

Sure enough, of all paths a man could strike into, there *is,* at any
given moment, a *best path* for every man; a thing which, here and now,
it were of all things *wisest* for him to do;—which could he be but
led or driven to do, he were then doing "like a man," as we phrase it;
all men and gods agreeing with him, the whole Universe virtually ex-
claiming Well-done to him! His success, in such case, were complete;
his felicity a maximum. This path, to find this path and walk in it, is
the one thing needful for him. Whatsoever forwards him in that, let it
come to him even in the shape of blows and spurnings, is liberty: whatsoever hinders him, were it wardmotes, open-vestries, poll-booths, tremendous cheers, rivers of heavy-wet, is slavery.

The notion that a man's liberty consists in giving his vote at elec-
tion-hustings, and saying, "Behold now I too have my twenty-thou-
sandth part of a Talker in our National Palaver;[26] will not all the gods
be good to me?"—is one of the pleasantest! Nature nevertheless is
kind at present; and puts it into the heads of many, almost of all. The
liberty especially which has to purchase itself by social isolation, and
each man standing separate from the other, having "no business with
him" but a cash-account: this is such a liberty as the Earth seldom
saw;—as the Earth will not long put up with, recommend it how
you may. This liberty turns out, before it have long continued in action, with all men flinging up their caps round it, to be, for the Work-

[26] Parliament.

ing Millions, a liberty to die by want of food; for the Idle Thousands and Units, alas, a still more fatal liberty to live in want of work; to have no earnest duty to do in this God's-World any more. What becomes of a man in such predicament? Earth's Laws are silent; and Heaven's speak in a voice which is not heard. No work, and the ineradicable need of work, give rise to new very wondrous life-philosophies, new very wondrous life-practices! Dilettantism, Pococurantism, Beau-Brummelism,[27] with perhaps an occasional, half-mad, protesting burst of Byronism, establish themselves: at the end of a certain period, —if you go back to "the Dead Sea," there is, say our Moslem friends, a very strange "Sabbath-day" transacting itself there![28]—

[27] Pococurantism—irresponsibility; Beau-Brummelism—dandyism.

[28] The reference is explained by a passage at the end of Chapter Three, Book Three, of *Past and Present:*

"Perhaps few narratives in History or Mythology are more significant than that Moslem one, of Moses and the Dwellers by the Dead Sea. A tribe of men dwelt on the shores of that same Asphaltic Lake; and having forgotten, as we are all prone to do, the inner facts of Nature, and taken up with the falsities and outer semblances of it, were fallen into sad conditions,—verging indeed towards a certain far deeper Lake. Whereupon it pleased kind Heaven to send them the Prophet Moses, with an instructive word of warning, out of which might have sprung 'remedial measures' not a few. But no: the men of the Dead Sea discovered, as the valet-species always does in heroes or prophets, no comeliness in Moses; listened with real tedium to Moses, with light grinning, or with splenetic sniffs and sneers, affecting even to yawn; and signified, in short, that they found him a humbug, and even a bore. Such was the candid theory these men of the Asphalt Lake formed to themselves of Moses, That probably he was a humbug, that certainly he was a bore.

"Moses withdrew; but Nature and her rigorous veracities did not withdraw. The men of the Dead Sea, when we next went to visit them, were 'changed into Apes;' sitting on the trees there, grinning now in the most *un*affected manner; gibbering and chattering very genuine nonsense; finding the whole Universe now a most indisputable Humbug! The Universe has *become* a Humbug to these Apes who thought it one. There they sit and chatter, to this hour: only, I believe, every Sabbath there returns to them a bewildered half-consciousness, half-reminiscence; and they sit with their wizened smoke-dried visages; and such an air of supreme tragicality as Apes may, looking through those blinking smoke-bleared eyes of theirs, into the wonderfulest universal smoky Twilight and undecipherable disordered Dusk of Things; wholly an Uncertainty, Unintelligibility, they and it; and for commentary thereon, here and there an unmusical chatter or mew:—truest, tragicalest Humbug conceivable by the mind of man or ape! They made no use of their souls; and so have lost them. Their worship on the Sabbath now is to roost there with unmusical screeches, and half-remember that they had souls.

"Didst thou never, O Traveller, fall-in with parties of this tribe? Meseems they are grown somewhat numerous in our day."

Brethren, we know but imperfectly yet, after ages of Constitutional Government, what Liberty and Slavery are.

Democracy, the chase of Liberty in that direction, shall go its full course; unrestrained by him of Pferdefuss-Quacksalber, or any of *his* household. The Toiling Millions of Mankind, in most vital need and passionate instinctive desire of Guidance, shall cast away False-Guidance; and hope, for an hour, that No-Guidance will suffice them: but it can be for an hour only. The smallest item of human Slavery is the oppression of man by his Mock-Superiors; the palpablest, but I say at bottom the smallest. Let him shake off such oppression, trample it indignantly under his feet; I blame him not, I pity and commend him. But oppression by your Mock-Superiors well shaken off, the grand problem yet remains to solve: That of finding government by your Real-Superiors! Alas, how shall we ever learn the solution of that, benighted, bewildered, sniffing, sneering, godforgetting unfortunates as we are? It is a work for centuries; to be taught us by tribulations, confusions, insurrections, obstructions; who knows if not by conflagration and despair! It is a lesson inclusive of all other lessons; the hardest of all lessons to learn.

One thing I do know: Those Apes, chattering on the branches by the Dead Sea, never got it learned; but chatter there to this day. To them no Moses need come a second time; a thousand Moseses would be but so many painted Phantasms, interesting Fellow-Apes of new strange aspect,—whom they would "invite to dinner," be glad to meet with in lion-soirées. To them the voice of Prophecy, of heavenly monition, is quite ended. They chatter there, all Heaven shut to them, to the end of the world. The unfortunates! Oh, what is dying of hunger, with honest tools in your hand, with a manful purpose in your heart, and much real labour lying round you done, in comparison? You honestly quit your tools; quit a most muddy confused coil of sore work, short rations, of sorrows, dispiritments and contradictions, having now honestly done with it all;—and await, not entirely in a distracted manner, what the Supreme Powers, and the Silences and the Eternities may have to say to you.

A second thing I know: This lesson will have to be learned,—under penalties! England will either learn it, or England also will cease to exist among Nations. England will either learn to reverence its Heroes, and discriminate them from its Sham-Heroes and Valets and gas-lighted Histrios; and to prize them as the audible God's-voice, amid all inane jargons and temporary market-cries, and say to them with heart-loyalty, "Be ye King and Priest, and Gospel and Guidance for us": or else England will continue to worship new and ever-new forms of Quackhood,—and so, with what resiliences and reboundings matters little, go down to the Father of Quacks! Can I dread such things of England? Wretched, thick-eyed, gross-hearted mortals, why will ye worship lies, and "Stuffed Clothes-suits, created by the ninth-parts of men!" It is not your purses that suffer; your farm-rents, your commerces, your mill-revenues, loud as ye lament over these; no, it is not these alone, but a far deeper than these: it is your souls that lie dead, crushed down under despicable Nightmares, Atheisms, Brain-fumes; and are not souls at all, but mere succedanea for *salt* to keep your bodies and their appetites from putrefying! Your cotton-spinning and thrice-miraculous mechanism, what is this too, by itself, but a larger kind of Animalism? Spiders can spin, Beavers can build and show contrivance: the Ant lays up accumulation of capital, and has, for aught I know, a Bank of Antland. If there is no soul in man higher than all that, did it reach to sailing on the cloud-rack and spinning sea-sand; then I say, man is but an animal, a more cunning kind of brute: he has no soul, but only a succedaneum for salt. Whereupon, seeing himself to be truly of the beasts that perish, he ought to admit it, I think;—and also straightway universally to kill himself; and so, in a manlike manner, at least, *end,* and wave these brute-worlds *his* dignified farewell!—

John Ruskin

1819-1900

The Nature of Gothic

    Presented here is a section of Chapter Six ("The Nature of Gothic") from the second volume of *The Stones of Venice* (1853). Ruskin's writings exhibit a unique fusion of aesthetics and ethics. The leading English art critic of his age, he was a principal instigator of the Gothic Revival in architecture; at the same time, he was perhaps the first to perceive that men were in danger of becoming enslaved to the machines of their own making.

. . . I am not sure when the word "Gothic" was first generally applied to the architecture of the North; but I presume that, whatever the date of its original usage, it was intended to imply reproach, and express the barbaric character of the nations among whom that architecture arose. It never implied that they were literally of Gothic lineage, far less that their architecture had been originally invented by the Goths themselves; but it did imply that they and their buildings together exhibited a degree of sternness and rudeness, which, in contradistinction to the character of southern and eastern nations, appeared like a perpetual reflection of the contrast between the Goth and the Roman in their first encounter. And when that fallen Roman, in the utmost impotence of his luxury, and insolence of his guilt, became the model for the imitation of civilized Europe, at the close of the so-called Dark Ages, the word Gothic became a term of unmitigated contempt, not unmixed with aversion. From that contempt, by the exertion of the antiquaries and architects of this century, Gothic architecture has been sufficiently vindicated; and perhaps some among us, in our admiration of the magnificent science of its structure, and sacredness of its expression, might desire that the term of ancient reproach should be withdrawn, and some other, of more apparent honorableness, adopted in its place. There is no chance, as there is no need, of such a substitution. As far as the epithet was used scornfully, it was used falsely; but there is no reproach in the word, rightly understood; on the contrary, there is a profound truth, which the instinct of mankind almost unconsciously recognizes. It is true, greatly and deeply true, that the architecture of the North is rude and wild; but it is not true, that, for this reason, we are to condemn it, or despise. Far otherwise: I believe it is in this very character that it deserves our profoundest reverence.

The charts of the world which have been drawn up by modern science have thrown into a narrow space the expression of a vast amount of knowledge, but I have never yet seen any one pictorial enough to enable the spectator to imagine the kind of contrast in physical character which exists between Northern and Southern countries. We know the differences in detail, but we have not that broad glance and grasp which would enable us to feel them in their fulness. We know that gentians grow on the Alps, and olives on the Apennines; but we do not enough conceive for ourselves that variegated mosaic of the world's surface which a bird sees in its migration, that difference between the district of the gentian and of the olive which the stork and the swallow see far off, as they lean upon the sirocco wind. Let us, for a moment, try to raise ourselves even above the level of their flight, and imagine the Mediterranean lying beneath us like an irregular lake, and all its ancient promontories sleeping in the sun: here and there an angry spot of thunder, a gray stain of storm, moving upon the burning field; and here and there a fixed wreath of white volcano smoke, surrounded by its circle of ashes; but for the most part a great peacefulness of light, Syria and Greece, Italy and Spain, laid like pieces of a golden pavement into the sea-blue, chased, as we stoop nearer to them, with bossy beaten work of mountain chains, and glowing softly with terraced gardens, and flowers heavy with frankincense, mixed among masses of laurel, and orange, and plumy palm, that abate with their gray-green shadows the burning of the marble rocks, and of the ledges of porphyry sloping under lucent sand. Then let us pass farther toward the north, until we see the orient colors change gradually into a vast belt of rainy green, where the pastures of Switzerland, and poplar valleys of France, and dark forests of the Danube and Carpathians stretch from the mouths of the Loire to those of the Volga, seen through clefts in gray swirls of rain-cloud and flaky veils of the mist of the brooks, spreading low along the pasture lands: and then, farther north still, to see the earth heave into mighty masses of leaden rock and heathy moor, bordering with a broad waste of gloomy purple that belt of field and wood, and splintering into irregular and grisly islands amidst the northern seas, beaten by storm, and chilled by ice-drift, and tormented by furious pulses of contending tide, until the roots of the last forests fail from among the hill ravines, and the hunger of the north wind bites their peaks into barrenness; and, at last, the wall of ice, durable like iron, sets, deathlike, its white teeth against us out of the polar twilight. And, having once traversed in thought this grada- tion of the zoned iris of the earth in all its material vastness, let us go down nearer to it, and watch the parallel change in the belt of animal life; the multitudes of swift and brilliant creatures that glance in the air and sea, or tread the sands of the southern zone; striped zebras and spotted leopards, glistening serpents, and birds arrayed in purple and scarlet. Let us contrast their delicacy and brilliancy of color, and swift- ness of motion, with the frost-cramped strength, and shaggy covering, and dusky plumage of the northern tribes; contrast the Arabian horse with the Shetland, the tiger and leopard with the wolf and bear, the antelope with the elk, the bird of paradise with the osprey; and then, submissively acknowledging the great laws by which the earth and all that it bears are ruled throughout their being, let us not condemn but rejoice in the expression by man of his own rest in the statutes of the lands that gave him birth. Let us watch him with reverence as he sets side by side the burning gems, and smooths with soft sculpture the jasper pillars, that are to reflect a ceaseless sunshine, and rise into a cloudless sky: but not with less reverence let us stand by him, when, with rough strength and hurried stroke, he smites an uncouth anima- tion out of the rocks which he has torn from among the moss of the moorland, and heaves into the darkened air the pile of iron buttress and rugged wall, instinct with work of an imagination as wild and wayward as the northern sea; creatures of ungainly shape and rigid limb, but full of wolfish life; fierce as the winds that beat, and changeful as the clouds that shade them.

There is, I repeat, no degradation, no reproach in this, but all dignity and honorableness: and we should err grievously in refusing either to recognize as an essential character of the existing architecture of the North, or to admit as a desirable character in that which it yet may be, this wildness of thought, and roughness of work; this look of mountain brotherhood between the cathedral and the Alp; this magnificence of sturdy power, put forth only the more energetically because the fine finger-touch was chilled away by the frosty wind, and the eye dimmed by the moor-mist, or blinded by the hail; this outspeaking of the strong spirit of men who may not gather redundant fruitage from the earth, nor bask in dreamy benignity of sunshine, but must break the rock for bread, and cleave the forest for fire, and show, even in what they did for their delight, some of the hard habits of the arm and heart that grew on them as they swung the axe or pressed the plough.

If, however, the savageness of Gothic architecture, merely as an expression of its origin among Northern nations, may be considered, in some sort, a noble character, it possesses a higher nobility still, when considered as an index, not of climate, but of religious principle.

In the 13th and 14th paragraphs of Chapter XXI of the first volume of this work, it was noticed that the systems of architectural ornament, properly so called, might be divided into three:—1. Servile ornament, in which the execution or power of the inferior workman is entirely subjected to the intellect of the higher;—2. Constitutional ornament, in which the executive inferior power is, to a certain point, emancipated and independent, having a will of its own, yet confessing its inferiority and rendering obedience to higher powers;—and 3. Revolutionary ornament, in which no executive inferiority is admitted at all. I must here explain the nature of these divisions at somewhat greater length.

Of Servile ornament, the principal schools are the Greek, Ninevite, and Egyptian; but their servility is of different kinds. The Greek masterworkman was far advanced in knowledge and power above the Assyrian or Egyptian. Neither he nor those for whom he worked could endure the appearance of imperfection in anything; and, therefore, what ornament he appointed to be done by those beneath him was composed of mere geometrical forms,—balls, ridges, and perfectly symmetrical foliage, —which could be executed with absolute precision by line and rule, and were as perfect in their way, when completed, as his own figure sculpture. The Assyrian and Egyptian, on the contrary, less cognizant of accurate form in anything, were content to allow their figure sculpture to be executed by inferior workmen, but lowered the method of its treatment to a standard which every workman could reach, and then trained him by discipline so rigid, that there was no chance of his falling beneath the standard appointed. The Greek gave to the lower workman no subject which he could not perfectly execute. The Assyrian gave him subjects which he could only execute imperfectly, but fixed a legal standard for his imperfection. The workman was, in both systems, a slave.[1]

But in the mediæval, or especially Christian, system of ornament, this slavery is done away with altogether; Christianity having recognized, in small things as well as great, the individual value of every soul. But it not only recognizes its value; it confesses its imperfection, in only bestowing dignity upon the acknowledgment of unworthiness. That admission of lost power and fallen nature, which the Greek or Ninevite felt to be intensely painful, and, as far as might be, altogether refused, the Christian makes daily and hourly, contemplating the fact of it without fear, as tending, in the end, to God's greater glory. Therefore, to every spirit which Christianity summons to her service, her exhortation is: Do what you can, and confess frankly what you are unable to do; neither let your effort be shortened for fear of failure, nor your confession silenced for fear of shame. And it is, perhaps, the principal admirableness of the Gothic schools of architecture, that they thus receive the results of the

---

[1] The third kind of ornament, the Renaissance, is that in which the inferior detail becomes principal, the executor of every minor portion being required to exhibit skill and possess knowledge as great as that which is possessed by the master of the design; and in the endeavour to endow him with this skill and knowledge, his own original power is overwhelmed, and the whole building becomes a wearisome exhibition of well-educated imbecility. We must fully inquire into the nature of this form of error, when we arrive at the examination of the Renaissance schools. [Ruskin's note.]

labor of inferior minds; and out of fragments full of imperfection, and betraying that imperfection in every touch, indulgently raise up a stately and unaccusable whole.

But the modern English mind has this much in common with that of the Greek, that it intensely desires, in all things, the utmost completion or perfection compatible with their nature. This is a noble character in the abstract, but becomes ignoble when it causes us to forget the relative dignities of that nature itself, and to prefer the perfectness of the lower nature to the imperfection of the higher; not considering that as, judged by such a rule, all the brute animals would be preferable to man, because more perfect in their functions and kind, and yet are always held inferior to him, so also in the works of man, those which are more perfect in their kind are always inferior to those which are, in their nature, liable to more faults and shortcomings. For the finer the nature, the more flaws it will show through the clearness of it; and it is a law of this universe, that the best things shall be seldomest seen in their best form. The wild grass grows well and strongly, one year with another; but the wheat is, according to the greater nobleness of its nature, liable to the bitterer blight. And therefore, while in all things that we see or do, we are to desire perfection, and strive for it, we are nevertheless not to set the meaner thing, in its narrow accomplishment, above the nobler thing, in its mighty progress; not to esteem smooth minuteness above shattered majesty; not to prefer mean victory to honorable defeat; not to lower the level of our aim, that we may the more surely enjoy the complacency of success. But, above all, in our dealings with the souls of other men, we are to take care how we check, by severe requirement or narrow caution, efforts which might otherwise lead to a noble issue; and, still more, how we withhold our admiration from great excellencies, because they are mingled with rough faults. Now, in the make and nature of every man, however rude or simple, whom we employ in manual labor, there are some powers for better things; some tardy imagination, torpid capacity of emotion, tottering steps of thought, there are, even at the worst; and in most cases it is all our own fault that they *are* tardy or torpid. But they cannot be strengthened, unless we are content to take them in their feebleness, and unless we prize and honor them in their imperfection above the best and most perfect manual skill. And this is what we have to do with all our laborers; to look for the *thoughtful* part of them, and get that out of them, whatever we lose for it, whatever faults and errors we are obliged to take with it. For the best that is in them cannot manifest itself, but in company with much error. Understand this clearly: You can teach a man to draw a straight line, and to cut one; to strike a curved line, and to carve it; and to copy and carve any number of given lines or forms, with admirable speed and perfect precision; and you find his work perfect of its kind; but if you ask him to think about any of those forms, to consider if he cannot find any better in his own head, he stops: his execution becomes hesitating; he thinks, and ten to one he thinks wrong; ten to one he makes a mistake in the first touch he gives to his work as a thinking being. But you have made a man of him for all that. He was only a machine before, an animated tool.

And observe, you are put to stern choice in this matter. You must either make a tool of the creature, or a man of him. You cannot make both. Men were not intended to work with the accuracy of tools, to be precise and perfect in all their actions. If you will have that precision out of them, and make their fingers measure degrees like cogwheels, and their arms strike curves like compasses, you must unhumanize them. All the energy of their spirits must be given to make cogs and compasses of themselves. All their attention and strength must go to the accomplishment of the mean act. The eye of the soul must be bent upon the finger-point, and the soul's force must fill all the invisible nerves that guide it, ten hours a day, that it may not err from its steely precision, and so soul and sight be worn away, and the whole human being be lost at last—a heap of sawdust, so far as its intellectual work in this world is concerned: saved only by its Heart, which cannot go into the form of cogs and compasses, but expands, after the ten hours are over, into fireside humanity. On the other hand, if you will make a man of the working creature, you cannot make a tool. Let him but begin to imagine, to think, to try to do anything worth doing; and the engine-turned precision is lost at once. Out come all his roughness, all his dulness, all his incapability; shame upon shame, failure upon failure, pause after pause: but out comes the whole majesty of him also; and we know the height of it only when we see the clouds settling upon him. And, whether the clouds be bright or dark, there will be transfiguration behind and within them.

And now, reader, look round this English room of yours, about which you have been proud so often, because the work of it was so good and strong, and the ornaments of it so finished. Examine again all those accurate mouldings, and perfect polishings, and unerring adjustments of the seasoned wood and tempered steel. Many a time you have exulted over them, and thought how great England was, because her slightest work was done so thoroughly. Alas! if read rightly, these perfectnesses are signs of a slavery in our England a thousand times more bitter and more degrading than that of the scourged African, or helot Greek. Men may be beaten, chained, tormented, yoked like cattle, slaughtered like summer flies, and yet remain in one sense, and the best sense, free. But to smother their souls within them, to blight and hew into rotting pollards the suckling branches of their human intelligence, to make the flesh and skin which, after the worm's work on it, is to see God, into leathern thongs to yoke machinery with,—this it is to be slave-masters indeed; and there might be more freedom in England, though her feudal lords' lightest words were worth men's lives, and though the blood of the vexed husbandman dropped in the furrows of her fields, than there is while the animation of her multitudes is sent like fuel to feed the factory smoke, and the strength of them is given daily to be wasted into the fineness of a web, or racked into the exactness of a line.

And, on the other hand, go forth again to gaze upon the old cathedral front, where you have smiled so often at the fantastic ignorance of the old sculptors: examine once more those ugly goblins, and formless monsters, and stern statues, anatomiless and rigid; but do not mock at them, for they are signs of the life and liberty of every workman who struck the stone; a freedom of thought, and rank in scale of being, such as no laws, no charters, no charities can secure; but which it must be the first aim of all Europe at this day to regain for her children.

Let me not be thought to speak wildly or extravagantly. It is verily this degradation of the operative into a machine, which, more than any other evil of the times, is leading the mass of the nations everywhere into vain, incoherent, destructive struggling for a freedom of which they cannot explain the nature to themselves. Their universal outcry against wealth, and against nobility, is not forced from them either by the pressure of famine, or the sting of mortified pride. These do much, and have done much in all ages; but the foundations of society were never yet shaken as they are at this day. It is not that men are ill fed, but that they have no pleasure in the work by which they make their bread, and therefore look to wealth as the only means of pleasure. It is not that men are pained by the scorn of the upper classes, but they cannot endure their own; for they feel that the kind of labor to which they are condemned is verily a degrading one, and makes them less than men. Never had the upper classes so much sympathy with the lower, or charity for them, as they have at this day, and yet never were they so much hated by them: for, of old, the separation between the noble and the poor was merely a wall built by law; now it is a veritable difference in level of standing, a precipice between upper and lower grounds in the field of humanity, and there is pestilential air at the bottom of it. I know not if a day is ever to come when the nature of right freedom will be understood, and when men will see that to obey another man, to labor for him, yield reverence to him or to his place, is not slavery. It is often the best kind of liberty,—liberty from care. The man who says to one, Go, and he goeth, and to another, Come, and he cometh,[2] has, in most cases, more sense of restraint and difficulty than the man who obeys him. The movements of the one are hindered by the burden on his shoulder; of the other, by the bridle on his lips: there is no way by which the burden may be lightened; but we need not suffer from the bridle if we do not champ at it. To yield reverence to another, to hold ourselves and our lives at his disposal, is not slavery; often it is the noblest state in which a man can live in this world. There is, indeed, a reverence which is servile, that is to say, irrational or selfish: but there is also noble reverence, that is to say, reasonable and loving; and a man is never so noble as when he is reverent in this kind; nay, even if the feeling pass the bounds of mere reason, so that it be loving, a man is raised by it. Which had in reality, most of the serf nature in him,—the Irish peasant who was lying in wait yesterday for his landlord, with his musket muzzle thrust through the ragged hedge; or that old mountain servant, who 200 years ago, at Inverkeithing, gave up his own life and the lives of his seven sons for his chief?—as each fell, calling forth his brother to the death, "Another for Rector!"[3] And therefore, in all ages and all countries, reverence has

---

[2] Cf. Matthew viii.9.

[3] *Vide* Preface to *Fair Maid of Perth*. [Ruskin's note.] Walter Scott's novel of this name was published in 1828.

been paid and sacrifice made by men to each other, not only without complaint, but rejoicingly; and famine, and peril, and sword, and all evil, and all shame, have been borne willingly in the causes of masters and kings; for all these gifts of the heart ennobled the men who gave, not less than the men who received them, and nature prompted, and God rewarded the sacrifice. But to feel their souls withering within them, unthanked, to find their whole being sunk into an unrecognized abyss, to be counted off into a heap of mechanism, numbered with its wheels, and weighed with its hammer strokes,—this, nature bade not,—this, God blesses not,—this, humanity for no long time is able to endure.

We have much studied and much perfected, of late, the great civilized invention of the division of labor; only we give it a false name. It is not, truly speaking, the labor that is divided; but the men:—Divided into mere segments of men—broken into small fragments and crumbs of life; so that all the little piece of intelligence that is left in a man is not enough to make a pin, or a nail, but exhausts itself in making the point of a pin or the head of a nail. Now it is a good and desirable thing, truly, to make many pins in a day; but if we could only see with what crystal sand their points were polished,—sand of human soul, much to be magnified before it can be discerned for what it is,—we should think there might be some loss in it also. And the great cry that rises from all our manufacturing cities, louder than their furnace blast, is all in very deed for this,—that we manufacture everything there except men; we blanch cotton, and strengthen steel, and refine sugar, and shape pottery; but to brighten, to strengthen, to refine, or to form a single living spirit, never enters into our estimate of advantages. And all the evil to which that cry is urging our myriads can be met only in one way: not by teaching nor preaching, for to teach them is but to show them their misery, and to preach to them, if we do nothing more than preach, is to mock at it. It can be met only by a right understanding, on the part of all classes, of what kinds of labor are good for men, raising them, and making them happy; by a determined sacrifice of such convenience, or beauty, or cheapness as is to be got only by the degradation of the workman; and by equally determined demand for the products and results of healthy and ennobling labor.

And how, it will be asked, are these products to be recognized, and this demand to be regulated? Easily: by the observance of three broad and simple rules:

1. Never encourage the manufacture of any article not absolutely necessary, in the production of which *Invention* has no share.

2. Never demand an exact finish for its own sake, but only for some practical or noble end.

3. Never encourage imitation or copying of any kind, except for the sake of preserving record of great works.

The second of these principles is the only one which directly rises out of the consideration of our immediate subject; but I shall briefly explain the meaning and extent of the first also, reserving the enforcement of the third for another place.

1. Never encourage the manufacture of anything not necessary, in the production of which invention has no share.

For instance. Glass beads are utterly unnecessary, and there is no design or thought employed in their manufacture. They are formed by first drawing out the glass into rods; these rods are chopped up into fragments of the size of beads by the human hand, and the fragments are then rounded in the furnace. The men who chop up the rods sit at their work all day, their hands vibrating with a perpetual and exquisitely timed palsy, and the beads dropping beneath their vibration like hail. Neither they, nor the men who draw out the rods or fuse the fragments, have the smallest occasion for the use of any single human faculty; and every young lady, therefore, who buys glass beads is engaged in the slave-trade, and in a much more cruel one than that which we have so long been endeavoring to put down.

But glass cups and vessels may become the subjects of exquisite invention; and if in buying these we pay for the invention, that is to say, for the beautiful form, or color, or engraving, and not for mere finish of execution, we are doing good to humanity.

So, again, the cutting of precious stones, in all ordinary cases, requires little exertion of any mental faculty; some tact and judgment in avoiding flaws, and so on, but nothing to bring out the whole mind. Every person who wears cut jewels merely for the sake of their value is, therefore, a slave-driver.

But the working of the goldsmith, and the various designing of grouped jewellery and enamel-work, may become the subject of the most noble human intelligence. Therefore, money spent in the purchase of well-designed plate, of precious engraved vases, cameos, or enamels, does good to humanity; and, in work of this kind, jewels may be employed to heighten its splendor; and their cutting is then a price paid for the attainment of a noble end, and thus perfectly allowable.

I shall perhaps press this law farther elsewhere, but our immediate concern is chiefly with the second, namely, never to demand an exact finish, when it does not lead to a noble end. For observe, I have only dwelt upon the rudeness of Gothic, or any other kind of imperfectness, as admirable, where it was impossible to get design or thought without it. If you are to have the thought of a rough and untaught man, you must have it in a rough and untaught way; but from an educated man, who can without effort express his thoughts in an educated way, take the graceful expression, and be thankful. Only *get* the thought, and do not silence the peasant because he cannot speak good grammar, or until you have taught him his grammar. Grammar and refinement are good things, both, only be sure of the better thing first. And thus in art, delicate finish is desirable from the greatest masters, and is always given by them. In some places Michael Angelo, Leonardo, Phidias, Perugino, Turner, all finished with the most exquisite care; and the finish they give always leads to the fuller accomplishment of their noble purposes. But lower men than these cannot finish, for it requires consummate knowledge to finish consummately, and then we must take their thoughts as they are able to give them. So the rule is simple: Always look for invention first, and after that, for such execution as will help the invention, and as the inventor is capable of without painful effort, and *no more*. Above all, demand no refinement of execution, where there is no thought, for that is slaves' work, unredeemed. Rather choose rough work than smooth work, so only that the practical purpose be answered, and never imagine there is reason to be proud of anything that may be accomplished by patience and sand-paper.

I shall only give one example, which however will show the reader what I mean, from the manufacture already alluded to, that of glass. Our modern glass is exquisitely clear in its substance, true in its form, accurate in its cutting. We are proud of this. We ought to be ashamed of it. The old Venice glass was muddy, inaccurate in all its forms, and clumsily cut, if at all. And the old Venetian was justly proud of it. For there is this difference between the English and Venetian workman, that the former thinks only of accurately matching his patterns, and getting his curves perfectly true and his edges perfectly sharp, and becomes a mere machine for rounding curves and sharpening edges; while the old Venetian cared not a whit whether his edges were sharp or not, but he invented a new design for every glass that he made, and never moulded a handle or a lip without a new fancy in it. And therefore, though some Venetian glass is ugly and clumsy enough when made by clumsy and un-inventive workmen, other Venetian glass is so lovely in its forms that no price is too great for it; and we never see the same form in it twice. Now you cannot have the finish and the varied form too. If the workman is thinking about his edges, he cannot be thinking of his design; if of his design, he cannot think of his edges. Choose whether you will pay for the lovely form or the perfect finish, and choose at the same moment whether you will make the worker a man or a grindstone.

Nay, but the reader interrupts me,—"If the workman can design beautifully, I would not have him kept at the furnace. Let him be taken away and made a gentleman, and have a studio, and design his glass there, and I will have it blown and cut for him by common workmen, and so I will have my design and my finish too."

All ideas of this kind are founded upon two mistaken suppositions: the first, that one man's thoughts can be, or ought to be, executed by another man's hands; the second, that manual labor is a degradation, when it is governed by intellect.

On a large scale, and in work determinable by line and rule, it is indeed both possible and necessary that the thoughts of one man should be carried out by the labor of others; in this sense I have already defined the best architecture to be the expression of the mind of manhood by the hands of childhood. But on a smaller scale, and in a design which cannot be mathematically defined, one man's thoughts can never be expressed by another: and the difference between the spirit of touch of the man who is inventing, and of the man who is obeying directions, is often all the difference between a great and a common work of art. How wide the separation is between original and second-hand execution,

I shall endeavor to show elsewhere; it is not so much to our purpose here as to mark the other and more fatal error of despising manual labor when governed by intellect; for it is no less fatal an error to despise it when thus regulated by intellect, than to value it for its own sake. We are always in these days endeavoring to separate the two; we want one man to be always thinking, and another to be always working, and we call one a gentleman, and the other an operative; whereas the workman ought often to be thinking, and the thinker often to be working, and both should be gentlemen, in the best sense. As it is, we make both ungentle, the one envying, the other despising, his brother; and the mass of society is made up of morbid thinkers, and miserable workers. Now it is only by labor that thought can be made healthy, and only by thought that labor can be made happy, and the two cannot be separated with impunity. It would be well if all of us were good handicraftsmen in some kind, and the dishonor of manual labor done away with altogether; so that though there should still be a trenchant distinction of race between nobles and commoners, there should not, among the latter, be a trenchant distinction of employment, as between idle and working men, or between men of liberal and illiberal professions. All professions should be liberal, and there should be less pride felt in peculiarity of employment, and more in excellence of achievement. And yet more, in each several profession, no master should be too proud to do its hardest work. The painter should grind his own colors; the architect work in the mason's yard with his men; the master-manufacturer be himself a more skilful operative than any man in his mills; and the distinction between one man and another be only in experience and skill, and the authority and wealth which these must naturally and justly obtain.

I should be led far from the matter in hand, if I were to pursue this interesting subject. Enough, I trust, has been said to show the reader that the rudeness or imperfection which at first rendered the term "Gothic" one of reproach is indeed, when rightly understood, one of the most noble characters of Christian architecture, and not only a noble but an *essential* one. It seems a fantastic paradox, but it is nevertheless a most important truth, that no architecture can be truly noble which is *not* imperfect. And this is easily demonstrable. For since the architect, whom we will suppose capable of doing all in perfection, cannot execute

the whole with his own hands, he must either make slaves of his workmen in the old Greek, and present English fashion, and level his work
to a slave's capacities, which is to degrade it; or else he must take his
workmen as he finds them, and let them show their weaknesses together
with their strength, which will involve the Gothic imperfection, but
render the whole work as noble as the intellect of the age can make it.

But the principle may be stated more broadly still. I have confined
the illustration of it to architecture, but I must not leave it as if true of
architecture only. Hitherto I have used the words imperfect and perfect
merely to distinguish between work grossly unskilful, and work executed
with average precision and science; and I have been pleading that any
degree of unskilfulness should be admitted, so only that the laborer's
mind had room for expression. But, accurately speaking, no good work
whatever can be perfect, and *the demand for perfection is always a sign
of a misunderstanding of the ends of art.*

This for two reasons, both based on everlasting laws. The first, that
no great man ever stops working till he has reached his point of failure:
that is to say, his mind is always far in advance of his powers of execution, and the latter will now and then give way in trying to follow it;
besides that he will always give to the inferior portions of his work only
such inferior attention as they require; and according to his greatness he
becomes so accustomed to the feeling of dissatisfaction with the best he
can do, that in moments of lassitude or anger with himself he will not
care though the beholder be dissatisfied also. I believe there has only been
one man who would not acknowledge this necessity, and strove always to
reach perfection, Leonardo; the end of his vain effort being merely that
he would take ten years to a picture and leave it unfinished. And therefore, if we are to have great men working at all, or less men doing their
best, the work will be imperfect, however beautiful. Of human work
none but what is bad can be perfect, in its own bad way.[4]

The second reason is, that imperfection is in some sort essential to

[4] The Elgin marbles are supposed by many persons to be 'perfect.' In the most
important portions they indeed approach perfection, but only there. The draperies
are unfinished, the hair and wool of the animals are unfinished, and the entire
bas-reliefs of the frieze are roughly cut. [Ruskin's note.] The Elgin Marbles, now
in the British Museum, were originally part of the frieze and pediment of the
Parthenon at Athens.

all that we know of life. It is the sign of life in a mortal body, that is to say, of a state of progress and change. Nothing that lives is, or can be, rigidly perfect; part of it is decaying, part nascent. The foxglove blossom, —a third part bud, a third part past, a third part in full bloom,—is a type of the life of this world. And in all things that live there are certain irregularities and deficiencies which are not only signs of life, but sources of beauty. No human face is exactly the same in its lines on each side, no leaf perfect in its lobes, no branch in its symmetry. All admit irregularity as they imply change; and to banish imperfection is to destroy expression, to check exertion, to paralyze vitality. All things are literally better, lovelier, and more beloved for the imperfections which have been divinely appointed, that the law of human life may be Effort, and the law of human judgment, Mercy.

Accept this then for a universal law, that neither architecture nor any other noble work of man can be good unless it be imperfect; and let us be prepared for the otherwise strange fact, which we shall discern clearly as we approach the period of the Renaissance, that the first cause of the fall of the arts of Europe was a relentless requirement of perfection, incapable alike either of being silenced by veneration for greatness, or softened into forgiveness of simplicity. . . .

William Morris

1834-1896

Useful Work versus Useless Toil: The Socialist Platform

> This essay was first published in pamphlet form in 1885 under the auspices of the Socialist League, of which Morris was one of the originators. A master handicraftsman in many fields, Morris established on a co-operative basis a successful firm which revived the decorative arts in England. His message to his age was: "Have nothing in your houses which you do not know to be useful, or believe to be beautiful."

The above title may strike some of my readers as strange. It is assumed by most people nowadays that all work is useful, and by most *well-to-do* people that all work is desirable. Most people, well-to-do or not, believe that, even when a man is doing work which appears to be useless, he is earning his livelihood by it—he is "employed," as the phrase goes; and most of those who are well-to-do cheer on the happy worker with congratulations and praises, if he is only "industrious" enough and deprives himself of all pleasure and holidays in the sacred cause of labour. In short, it has become an article of the creed of modern morality that all labour is good in itself—a convenient belief to those who live on the labour of others. But as to those on whom they live, I recommend them not to take it on trust, but to look into the matter a little deeper.

Let us grant, first, that the race of man must either labour or perish. Nature does not give us our livelihood gratis; we must win it by toil of some sort or degree. Let us see, then, if she does not give us some compensation for this compulsion to labour, since certainly in other matters she takes care to make the acts necessary to the continuance of life in the individual and the race not only endurable, but even pleasurable.

You may be sure that she does so, that it is of the nature of man, when he is not diseased, to take pleasure in his work under certain conditions. And, yet, we must say in the teeth of the hypocritical praise of all labour, whatsoever it may be, of which I have made mention, that there is some labour which is so far from being a blessing that it is a curse; that it would be better for the community and for the worker if the latter were to fold his hands and refuse to work, and either die or let us pack him off to the workhouse or prison—which you will.

Here, you see, are two kinds of work—one good, the other bad; one not far removed from a blessing, a lightening of life; the other a mere curse, a burden to life.

What is the difference between them, then? This: one has hope in it, the other has not. It is manly to do the one kind of work, and manly also to refuse to do the other.

What is the nature of the hope which, when it is present in work, makes it worth doing?

It is threefold, I think—hope of rest, hope of product, hope of pleasure in the work itself; and hope of these also in some abundance and of good quality; rest enough and good enough to be worth having; product worth having by one who is neither a fool nor an ascetic; pleasure enough for all for us to be conscious of it while we are at work; not a mere habit, the loss of which we shall feel as a fidgety man feels the loss of the bit of string he fidgets with.

I have put the hope of rest first because it is the simplest and most natural part of our hope. Whatever pleasure there is in some work, there is certainly some pain in all work, the beast-like pain of stirring up our slumbering energies to action, the beast-like dread of change when things are pretty well with us; and the compensation for this animal pain is animal rest. We must feel while we are working that the time will come when we shall not have to work. Also the rest, when it comes, must be long enough to allow us to enjoy it; it must be longer than is merely necessary for us to recover the strength we have expended in working, and it must be animal rest also in this, that it must not be disturbed by anxiety, else we shall not be able to enjoy it. If we have this amount and kind of rest we shall, so far, be no worse off than the beasts.

As to the hope of product, I have said that Nature compels us to work for that. It remains for *us* to look to it that we *do* really produce something, and not nothing, or at least nothing that we want or are allowed to use. If we look to this and use our wills we shall, so far, be better than machines.

The hope of pleasure in the work itself: how strange that hope must seem to some of my readers—to most of them! Yet I think that to all living things there is a pleasure in the exercise of their energies, and that even beasts rejoice in being lithe and swift and strong. But a man at work, making something which he feels will exist because he is working at it and wills it, is exercising the energies of his mind and soul as well as of his body. Memory and imagination help him as he works. Not only his own thoughts, but the thoughts of the men of past ages guide his hands; and, as a part of the human race, he creates. If we work thus we shall be men, and our days will be happy and eventful.

Thus worthy work carries with it the hope of pleasure in rest, the hope of the pleasure in our using what it makes, and the hope of pleasure in our daily creative skill.

All other work but this is worthless; it is slaves' work—mere toiling to live, that we may live to toil.

Therefore, since we have, as it were, a pair of scales in which to weigh the work now done in the world, let us use them. Let us estimate the worthiness of the work we do, after so many thousand years of toil, so many promises of hope deferred, such boundless exultation over the progress of civilization and the gain of liberty.

Now, the first thing as to the work done in civilization and the easiest to notice is that it is portioned out very unequally amongst the different classes of society. First, there are people—not a few—who do no work, and make no pretence of doing any. Next, there are people, and very many of them, who work fairly hard, though with abundant easements and holidays, claimed and allowed; and lastly, there are people who work so hard that they may be said to do nothing else than work, and are accordingly called "the working classes," as distinguished from the middle classes and the rich, or aristocracy, whom I have mentioned above.

It is clear that this inequality presses heavily upon the "working" class, and must visibly tend to destroy their hope of rest at least, and so, in that particular, make them worse off than mere beasts of the field; but that is not the sum and end of our folly of turning useful work into useless toil, but only the beginning of it.

For first, as to the class of rich people doing no work, we all know that they consume a great deal while they produce nothing. Therefore, clearly, they have to be kept at the expense of those who do work, just as paupers have, and are a mere burden on the community. In these days there are many who have learned to see this, though they can see no further into the evils of our present system, and have formed no idea of any scheme for getting rid of this burden; though perhaps they have a vague hope that changes in the system of voting for members of the House of Commons, may, as if by magic, tend in that direction. With such hopes or superstitions we need not trouble ourselves. Moreover, this class, the aristocracy, once thought most necessary to the State, is scant of numbers, and has now no power of its own, but depends on the support of the class next below it—the middle class. In fact, it is really composed either of the most successful men of that class, or of their immediate descendants.

As to the middle class, including the trading, manufacturing, and professional people of our society, they do, as a rule, seem to work quite hard enough, and so at first sight might be thought to help the community, and not burden it. But by far the greater part of them, though they work, do not produce, and even when they do produce, as in the case of those engaged (wastefully indeed) in the distribution of goods, or doctors, or (genuine) artists and literary men, they consume out of all proportion to their due share. The commercial and manufacturing part of them, the most powerful part, spend their lives and energies in fighting amongst themselves for their respective shares of the wealth which they *force* the genuine workers to provide for them; the others are almost wholly the hangers-on of these; they do not work for the public, but a privileged class: they are the parasites of property, sometimes, as in the case of lawyers, undisguisedly so; sometimes, as the doctors and others above mentioned, professing to be useful, but too often of no use save as supporters of the system of folly, fraud, and tyranny of which they form a part. And all these we must remember have, as a rule, one aim in view; not the production of utilities, but the gaining of a position either for themselves or their children in which they will not have to work at all. It is their ambition and the end of their whole lives to gain, if not for themselves yet at least for their children, the proud position of being obvious burdens on the community. For their work itself, in spite of the sham dignity with which they surround it, they care nothing: save a few enthusiasts, men of science, art or letters, who, if they are not the salt of the earth, are at least (and oh, the pity of it!) the salt of the miserable system of which they are the slaves, which hinders and thwarts them at every turn, and even sometimes corrupts them.

Here then is another class, this time very numerous and all-powerful, which produces very little and consumes enormously, and is therefore in the main supported, as paupers are, by the real producers. The class that remains to be considered produces all that is produced, and supports both itself and the other classes, though it is placed in a position of inferiority to them; real inferiority, mind you, involving a degradation both of mind and body. But it is a necessary consequence of this tyranny and folly that again many of these workers are not producers. A vast number of them once more are merely parasites of property, some of them openly so, as the soldiers by land and sea who are kept on foot for the perpetuating of national rivalries and enmities, and for the purposes of the national struggle for the share of the product of unpaid labour. But besides this obvious burden on the producers and the scarcely less obvious one of domestic servants, there is first the army of clerks, shop-assistants, and so forth, who are engaged in the service of the private war for wealth, which, as above said, is the real occupation of the well-to-do middle class. This is a larger body of workers than might be supposed, for it includes amongst others all those engaged in what I should call competitive salesmanship, or, to use a less dignified word, the puffery of wares, which has now got to such a pitch that there are many things which cost far more to sell than they do to make.

Next there is the mass of people employed in making all those articles of folly and luxury, the demand for which is the outcome of the existence of the rich non-producing classes; things which people leading a manly and uncorrupted life would not ask for or dream of. These things, whoever may gainsay me, I will for ever refuse to call wealth: they are not wealth, but waste. Wealth is what Nature gives us and what a reasonable man can make out of the gifts of Nature for his reasonable use. The sunlight, the fresh air, the unspoiled face of the earth, food, raiment and housing necessary and decent; the storing up of knowledge of all kinds, and the power of disseminating it; means of free communication between man and man; works of art, the beauty which man creates when he is most a man, most aspiring and thoughtful—all things which serve the pleasure of people, free, manly and uncorrupted. This is wealth. Nor can I think of anything worth having which does not come under one or other of these heads. But think, I beseech you, of the product of England, the workshop of the world, and will you not be bewildered, as I am, at the thought of the mass of things which no sane man could desire, but which our useless toil makes—and sells?

Now, further, there is even a sadder industry yet, which is forced on many, very many, of our workers—the making of wares which are necessary to them and their brethren, *because they are an inferior class.* For if many men live without producing, nay, must live lives so empty and foolish that they *force* a great part of the workers to produce wares which no one needs, not even the rich, it follows that most men must be poor; and, living as they do on wages from those whom they support, cannot get for their use the *goods* which men naturally desire, but must put up with miserable makeshifts for them, with coarse food that does not nourish, with rotten raiment which does not shelter, with wretched houses which may well make a town-dweller in civilization look back with regret to the tent of the nomad tribe, or the cave of the pre-historic savage. Nay, the workers must even lend a hand to the great industrial invention of the age—adulteration, and by its help produce for their own use shams and mockeries of the luxury of the rich; for the wage-earners must always live as the wage-payers bid them, and their very habits of life are *forced* on them by their masters.

But it is waste of time to try to express in words due contempt of the production of the much-praised cheapness of our epoch. It must be enough to say that this cheapness is necessary to the system of exploiting on which modern manufacture rests. In other words, our society includes a great mass of slaves, who must be fed, clothed, housed and amused as slaves, and that their daily necessity compels them to make the slave-wares whose use is the perpetuation of their slavery.

To sum up, then, concerning the manner of work in civilized States, these States are composed of three classes—a class which does not even pretend to work, a class which pretends to work but which produces nothing, and a class which works, but is compelled by the other two classes to do work which is often unproductive.

Civilization therefore wastes its own resources, and will do so as long as the present system lasts. These are cold words with which to describe the tyranny under which we suffer; try then to consider what they mean.

There is a certain amount of natural material and of natural forces in the world, and a certain amount of labour-power inherent in the persons of the men that inhabit it. Men urged by their necessities and desires have laboured for many thousands of years at the task of sub-jugating the forces of Nature and of making the natural material useful to them. To our eyes, since we cannot see into the future, that struggle with Nature seems nearly over, and the victory of the human race over her nearly complete. And, looking backwards to the time when history first began, we note that the progress of that victory has been far swifter and more startling within the last two hundred years than ever before. Surely, therefore, we moderns ought to be in all ways vastly better off than any who have gone before us. Surely we ought, one and all of us, to be wealthy, to be well furnished with the good things which our victory over Nature has won for us.

But what is the real fact? Who will dare to deny that the great mass of civilized men are poor? So poor are they that it is mere childishness troubling ourselves to discuss whether perhaps they are in some ways a little better off than their forefathers. They are poor; nor can their poverty be measured by the poverty of a resourceless savage, for he knows of nothing else than his poverty; that he should be cold, hungry, houseless, dirty, ignorant, all that is to him as natural as that he should have a skin. But for us, for the most of us, civilization has bred desires which she forbids us to satisfy, and so is not merely a niggard but a torturer also.

Thus then have the fruits of our victory over Nature been stolen from us, thus has compulsion by Nature to labour in hope of rest, gain, and pleasure been turned into compulsion by man to labour in hope—of living to labour!

What shall we do then, can we mend it?

Well, remember once more that it is not our remote ancestors who achieved the victory over Nature, but our fathers, nay, our very selves. For us to sit hopeless and helpless then would be a strange folly indeed: be sure that we can amend it. What then, is the first thing to be done?

We have seen that modern society is divided into two classes, one of which is *privileged* to be kept by the labour of the other—that is, it forces the other to work for it and takes from this inferior class everything that it *can* take from it, and uses the wealth so taken to keep its own members in a superior position, to make them beings of a higher order than the others: longer lived, more beautiful, more honoured, more refined than those of the other class. I do not say that it troubles itself about its members being *positively* long lived, beautiful or refined, but merely insists that they shall be so *relatively* to the inferior class. As also it cannot use the labour-power of the inferior class fairly in producing real wealth, it wastes it wholesale in the production of rubbish.

It is this robbery and waste on the part of the minority which keeps the majority poor; if it could be shown that it is necessary for the preservation of society that this should be submitted to, little more could be said on the matter, save that the despair of the oppressed majority would probably at some time or other destroy Society. But it has been shown, on the contrary, even by such incomplete experiments, for instance, as Co-operation (so called), that the existence of a privileged class is by no means necessary for the production of wealth, but rather for the "government" of the producers of wealth, or, in other words, for the upholding of privilege.

The first step to be taken then is to abolish a class of men privileged to shirk their duties as men, thus forcing others to do the work which they refuse to do. All must work according to their ability, and so produce what they consume—that is, each man should work as well as he can for his own livelihood, and his livelihood should be assured to him; that is to say, all the advantages which society would provide for each and all of its members.

Thus, at last, would true Society be founded. It would rest on equality of condition. No man would be tormented for the benefit of another— nay, no one man would be tormented for the benefit of Society. Nor, indeed, can that order be called Society which is not upheld for the benefit of every one of its members.

But since men live now, badly as they live, when so many people do not produce at all, and when so much work is wasted, it is clear that, under conditions where all produced and no work was wasted, not only would every one work with the certain hope of gaining a due share of wealth by his work, but also he could not miss his due share of rest. Here, then, are two out of the three kinds of hope mentioned above as an essential part of worthy work assured to the worker. When class robbery is abolished, every man will reap the fruits of his labour, every man will have due rest—leisure, that is. Some Socialists might say we need not go any further than this; it is enough that the worker should get the full produce of his work, and that his rest should be abundant. But though the compulsion of man's tyranny is thus abolished, I yet demand compensation for the compulsion of Nature's necessity. As long as the work is repulsive it will still be a burden which must be taken up daily, and even so would mar our life, even though the hours of labour were short. What we want to do is to add to our wealth without diminishing our pleasure. Nature will not be finally conquered till our work becomes a part of the pleasure of our lives.

That first step of freeing people from the compulsion to labour need-lessly will at least put us on the way towards this happy end; for we shall then have time and opportunities for bringing it about. As things are now, between the waste of labour-power in mere idleness and its waste in unproductive work, it is clear that the world of civilization is supported by a small part of its people; when *all* were working *usefully* for its support, the share of work which each would have to do would be but small, if our standard of life were about on the footing of what well-to-do and refined people now think desirable. We shall have labour-power to spare, and shall in short, be as wealthy as we please. It will be easy to live. If we were to wake up some morning now, under our present system, and find it "easy to live," that system would force us to set to work at once and make it hard to live; we should call that "developing our resources," or some such fine name. The multiplication of labour has become a necessity for us, and as long as that goes on no ingenuity in the invention of machines will be of any real use to us. Each new machine will cause a certain amount of misery among the workers whose special industry it may disturb; so many of them will be reduced from skilled to unskilled workmen, and then gradually matters will slip into their due grooves, and all will work apparently smoothly again; and if it were not that all this is preparing revolution, things would be, for the greater part of men, just as they were before the new wonderful invention.

But when revolution has made it "easy to live," when all are working harmoniously together and there is no one to rob the worker of his time, that is to say, his life; in those coming days there will be no compulsion on us to go on producing things we do not want, no compulsion on us to labour for nothing; we shall be able calmly and thoughtfully to consider what we shall do with our wealth of labour-power. Now, for my part, I think the first use we ought to make of that wealth, of that freedom, should be to make all our labour, even the commonest and most necessary, pleasant to everybody; for thinking over the matter carefully I can see that the one course which will certainly make life happy in the face of all accidents and troubles is to take a pleasurable interest in all the details of life. And lest perchance you think an assertion too universally accepted to be worth making, let me remind you how entirely modern civilization forbids it; with what sordid, and even terrible, details it surrounds the life of the poor, what a mechanical and empty life she forces on the rich; and how rare a holiday it is for any of us to feel ourselves a part of Nature, and unhurriedly, thoughtfully, and happily to note the course of our lives amidst all the little links of events which connect them with the lives of others, and build up the great whole of humanity.

But such a holiday our whole lives might be, if we were resolute to make all our labour reasonable and pleasant. But we must be resolute indeed; for no half measures will help us here. It has been said already that our present joyless labour, and our lives scared and anxious as the life of a hunted beast, are forced upon us by the present system of producing for the profit of the privileged classes. It is necessary to state what this means. Under the present system of wages and capital the "manufacturer" (most absurdly so called, since a manufacturer means a person who makes with his hands) having a monopoly of the means whereby the power to labour inherent in every man's body can be used for production, is the master of those who are not so privileged; he, and he alone, is able to make use of this labour-power, which, on the other hand, is the only commodity by means of which his "capital," that is to say, the accumulated product of past labour, can be made productive to him. He therefore buys the labour-power of those who are bare of capital and can only live by selling it to him; his purpose in this transaction is to increase his capital, to make it breed. It is clear that if he paid those with whom he makes his bargain the full value of their labour, that is to say, all that they produced, he would fail in his purpose. But since he is the monopolist of the means of productive labour, he can *compel* them to make a bargain better for him and worse for them than that; which bargain is that after they have earned their livelihood, estimated according to a standard high enough to ensure their peaceable submission to his mastership, the rest (and by far the larger part as a matter of fact) of what they produce shall belong to him, shall be his *property* to do as he likes with, to use or abuse at his pleasure; which property is, as we all know, jealously guarded by army and navy, police and prison; in short, by that huge mass of physical force which superstition, habit, fear of death by starvation—IGNORANCE, in one word, among the propertyless masses enables the propertied classes to use for the subjection of—their slaves.

Now, at other times, other evils resulting from this system may be put forward. What I want to point out now is the impossibility of our attaining to attractive labour under this system, and to repeat that it is this robbery (there is no other word for it) which wastes the available labour-power of the civilized world, forcing many men to do nothing, and many, very many more to do nothing useful; and forcing those who carry on really useful labour to most burdensome over-work. For understand once for all that the "manufacturer" aims primarily at producing, by means of the labour he has stolen from others, not goods but profits, that is, the "wealth" that is produced over and above the livelihood of his workmen, and the wear and tear of his machinery. Whether that "wealth" is real or sham matters nothing to him. If it sells and yields him a "profit" it is all right. I have said that, owing to there being rich people who have more money than they can spend reasonably, and who therefore buy sham wealth, there is waste on that side; and also that, owing to there being poor people who cannot afford to buy things which are worth making, there is waste on that side. So that the "demand" which the capitalist "supplies" is a false demand. The market in which he sells is "rigged" by the miserable inequalities produced by the robbery of the system of Capital and Wages.

It is this system, therefore, which we must be resolute in getting rid of, if we are to attain to happy and useful work for all. The first step towards making labour attractive is to get the means of making labour fruitful, the Capital, including the land, machinery, factories, etc., into the hands of the community, to be used for the good of all alike, so that we might all work at "supplying" the real "demands" of each and all— that is to say, work for livelihood, instead of working to supply the demand of the profit market—instead of working for profit—*i.e.,* the power of compelling other men to work against their will.

When this first step has been taken and men begin to understand that Nature wills all men either to work or starve, and when they are no longer such fools as to allow some the alternative of stealing, when this happy day is come, we shall then be relieved from the tax of waste, and consequently shall find that we have, as aforesaid, a mass of labour-power available, which will enable us to live as we please within reasonable limits. We shall no longer be hurried and driven by the fear of starvation, which at present presses no less on the greater part of men in civilized communities than it does on mere savages. The first and most obvious necessities will be so easily provided for in a community in which there is no waste of labour, that we shall have time to look round and consider what we really do want, that can be obtained without over-taxing our energies; for the often-expressed fear of mere idleness falling upon us when the force supplied by the present hierarchy of compulsion is withdrawn, is a fear which is but generated by the burden of excessive and repulsive labour, which we most of us have to bear at present.

I say once more that, in my belief, the first thing which we shall think so necessary as to be worth sacrificing some idle time for, will be the attractiveness of labour. No very heavy sacrifice will be required for attaining this object, but some *will* be required. For we may hope that men who have just waded through a period of strife and revolution will be the last to put up long with a life of mere utilitarianism, though Socialists are sometimes accused by ignorant persons of aiming at such a life. On the other hand, the ornamental part of modern life is already rotten to the core, and must be utterly swept away before the new order of things is realized. There is nothing of it—there is nothing which could come of it that could satisfy the aspirations of men set free from the tyranny of commercialism.

We must begin to build up the ornamental part of life—its pleasures, bodily and mental, scientific and artistic, social and individual—on the basis of work undertaken willingly and cheerfully, with the consciousness of benefiting ourselves and our neighbours by it. Such absolutely necessary work as we should have to do would in the first place take up but a small part of each day, and so far would not be burdensome; but it would be a task of daily recurrence, and therefore would spoil our day's pleasure unless it were made at least endurable while it lasted. In other words, all labour, even the commonest, must be made attractive.

How can this be done?—is the question the answer to which will take up the rest of this paper. In giving some hints on this question, I know that, while all Socialists will agree with many of the suggestions made, some of them may seem to some strange and venturesome. These must be considered as being given without any intention of dogmatizing, and as merely expressing my own personal opinion.

From all that has been said already it follows that labour, to be attractive, must be directed towards some obviously useful end, unless in cases where it is undertaken voluntarily by each individual as a pastime. This element of obvious usefulness is all the more to be counted on in sweetening tasks otherwise irksome, since social morality, the responsibility of man towards the life of man, will, in the new order of things, take the place of theological morality, or the responsibility of man to some abstract idea. Next, the day's work will be short. This need not be insisted on. It is clear that with work unwasted it *can* be short. It is clear also that much work which is now a torment, would be easily endurable if it were much shortened.

Variety of work is the next point, and a most important one. To compel a man to do day after day the same task, without any hope of escape or change, means nothing short of turning his life into a prison-torment. Nothing but the tyranny of profit-grinding makes this necessary. A man might easily learn and practise at least three crafts, varying sedentary occupation with outdoor occupation calling for the exercise of strong bodily energy for work in which the mind had more to do. There are few men, for instance, who would not wish to spend part of their lives in the most necessary and pleasantest of all work—cultivating the earth. One thing which will make this variety of employment possible will be the form that education will take in a socially ordered community. At present all education is directed towards the end of fitting people to take their places in the hierarchy of commerce—these as masters, those as workmen. The education of the masters is more ornamental than that of the workmen, but it is commercial still; and even at the ancient universities learning is but little regarded, unless it can in the long run be made *to pay*. Due education is a totally different thing from this, and concerns itself in finding out what different people are fit for, and helping them along the road which they are inclined to take. In a duly ordered society, therefore, young people would be taught such handicrafts as they had a turn for as a part of their education, the discipline of their minds and bodies; and adults would also have opportunities of learning in the same schools, for the development of individual capacities would be of all things chiefly aimed at by education, instead, as now, the subordination of all capacities to the great end of "money-making" for oneself—or one's master. The amount of talent, and even genius, which the present system crushes, and which would be drawn out by such a system, would make our daily work easy and interesting.

Under this head of variety I will note one product of industry which has suffered so much from commercialism that it can scarcely be said to exist, and is, indeed, so foreign from our epoch that I fear there are some who will find it difficult to understand what I have to say on the subject, which I nevertheless must say, since it is really a most important one. I mean that side of art which is, or ought to be, done by the ordinary workman while he is about his ordinary work, and which has got to be called, very properly, Popular Art. This art, I repeat, no longer exists now, having been killed by commercialism. But from the beginning of man's contest with Nature till the rise of the present capitalistic system, it was alive, and generally flourished. While it lasted, everything that was made by man was adorned by man, just as everything made by Nature is adorned by her. The craftsman, as he fashioned the thing he had under his hand, ornamented it so naturally and so entirely without conscious effort, that it is often difficult to distinguish where the mere utilitarian part of his work ended and the ornamental began. Now the origin of this art was the necessity that the workman felt for variety in his work, and though the beauty produced by this desire was a great gift to the world, yet the obtaining variety and pleasure in the work by the workman was a matter of more importance still, for it stamped all labour with the impress of pleasure. All this has now quite disappeared from the work of civilization. If you wish to have ornament, you must pay specially for it, and the workman is compelled to produce ornament, as he is to produce other wares. He is compelled to pretend happiness in his work, so that the beauty produced by man's hand, which was once a solace to his labour, has now become an extra burden to him, and ornament is now but one of the follies of useless toil, and perhaps not the least irksome of its fetters.

Besides the short duration of labour, its conscious usefulness, and the variety which should go with it, there is another thing needed to make it attractive, and that is pleasant surroundings. The misery and squalor which we people of civilization bear with so much complacency as a necessary part of the manufacturing system, is just as necessary to the community at large as a proportionate amount of filth would be in the house of a private rich man. If such a man were to allow the cinders to be raked all over his drawing-room, and a privy to be established in each corner of his dining-room, if he habitually made a dust and refuse heap of his once beautiful garden, never washed his sheets or changed his tablecloth, and made his family sleep five in a bed, he would surely find himself in the claws of a commission *de lunatico*.[1] But such acts of miserly folly are just what our present society is doing daily under the compulsion of a supposed necessity, which is nothing short of madness. I beg you to bring your commission of lunacy against civilization without more delay.

For all our crowded towns and bewildering factories are simply the outcome of the profit system. Capitalistic manufacture, capitalistic land-owning, and capitalistic exchange force men into big cities in order to manipulate them in the interests of capital; the same tyranny contracts the due space of the factory so much that (for instance) the interior of a great weaving-shed is almost as ridiculous a spectacle as it is a horrible one. There is no other necessity for all this, save the necessity for grinding profits out of men's lives, and of producing cheap goods for the use (and subjection) of the slaves who grind. All labour is not yet driven into factories; often where it is there is no necessity for it, save again the profit tyranny. People engaged in all such labour need by no means be compelled to pig together in close city quarters. There is no reason why they should not follow their occupations in quiet country homes, in industrial colleges, in small towns, or, in short, where they find it happiest for them to live.

As to that part of labour which must be associated on a large scale, this very factory system, under a reasonable order of things (though to my mind there might still be drawbacks to it), would at least offer opportunities for a full and eager social life surrounded by many pleas-ures. The factories might be centres of intellectual activity also, and work in them might well be varied very much: the tending of the necessary machinery might to each individual be but a short part of the day's work. The other work might vary from raising food from the surround-ing country to the study and practice of art and science. It is a matter of course that people engaged in such work, and being the masters of their own lives, would not allow any hurry or want of foresight to force them into enduring dirt, disorder, or want of room. Science duly applied would enable them to get rid of refuse, to minimize, if not wholly to

[1] Commission to inquire whether a person is insane.

destroy, all the inconveniences which at present attend the use of elaborate machinery, such as smoke, stench and noise; nor would they endure that the buildings in which they worked or lived should be ugly blots on the fair face of the earth. Beginning by making their factories, buildings, and sheds decent and convenient like their homes, they would infallibly go on to make them not merely negatively good, inoffensive merely, but even beautiful, so that the glorious art of architecture, now for some time slain by commercial greed, would be born again and flourish.

So, you see, I claim that work in a duly ordered community should be made attractive by the consciousness of usefulness, by its being carried on with intelligent interest, by variety, and by its being exercised amidst pleasurable surroundings. But I have also claimed, as we all do, that the day's work should not be wearisomely long. It may be said, "How can you make this last claim square with the others? If the work is to be so refined, will not the goods made be very expensive?"

I do admit, as I have said before, that some sacrifice will be necessary in order to make labour attractive. I mean that, if we *could* be contented in a free community to work in the same hurried, dirty, disorderly, heartless way as we do now, we might shorten our day's labour very much more than I suppose we shall do, taking all kinds of labour into account. But if we did, it would mean that our new-won freedom of condition would leave us listless and wretched, if not anxious, as we are now, which I hold is simply impossible. We should be contented to make the sacrifices necessary for raising our condition to the standard called out for as desirable by the whole community. Nor only so. We should, individually, be emulous to sacrifice quite freely still more of our time and our ease towards the raising of the standard of life. Persons, either by themselves or associated for such purposes, would freely, and for the love of the work and for its results—stimulated by the hope of the pleasure of creation—produce those ornaments of life for the service of all, which they are now bribed to produce (or pretend to produce) for the service of a few rich men. The experiment of a civilized community living wholly without art or literature has not yet been tried. The past degradation and corruption of civilization may force this denial of pleasure upon the society which will arise from its ashes. If that must be, we will accept the passing phase of utilitarianism as a foundation for the art which is to be. If the cripple and the starveling disappear from our streets, if the earth nourish us all alike, if the sun shine for all of us alike, if to one and all of us the glorious drama of the earth— day and night, summer and winter—can be presented as a thing to understand and love, we can afford to wait awhile till we are purified from the shame of the past corruption, and till art arises again amongst people freed from the terror of the slave and the shame of the robber.

Meantime, in any case, the refinement, thoughtfulness, and delibera- tion of labour must indeed be paid for, but not by compulsion to labour long hours. Our epoch has invented machines which would have ap- peared wild dreams to the men of past ages, and of those machines we have as yet *made no use.*

They are called "labour-saving" machines—a commonly used phrase which implies what we expect of them; but we do not get what we expect. What they really do is to reduce the skilled labourer to the ranks of the unskilled, to increase the number of the "reserve army of labour"—that is, to increase the precariousness of life among the workers and to intensify the labour of those who serve the machines (as slaves their masters). All this they do by the way, while they pile up the profits of the employers of labour, or force them to expend those profits in bitter commercial war with each other. In a true society these miracles of ingenuity would be for the first time used for minimizing the amount of time spent in unattractive labour, which by their means might be so reduced as to be but a very light burden on each individual. All the more as these machines would most certainly be very much improved when it was no longer a question as to whether their im- provement would "pay" the individual, but rather whether it would benefit the community.

So much for the ordinary use of machinery, which would probably, after a time, be somewhat restricted when men found out that there was no need for anxiety as to mere subsistence, and learned to take an interest and pleasure in handiwork which, done deliberately and thoughtfully, could be made more attractive than machine work.

Again, as people freed from the daily terror of starvation find out what they really wanted, being no longer compelled by anything but their own needs, they would refuse to produce the mere inanities which are now called luxuries, or the poison and trash now called cheap wares. No one would make plush breeches when there were no flunkies to wear them, nor would anybody waste his time over making oleomargarine when no one was *compelled* to abstain from real butter. Adulteration laws are only needed in a society of thieves—and in such a society they are a dead letter.

Socialists are often asked how work of the rougher and more repulsive kind could be carried out in the new condition of things. To attempt to answer such questions fully or authoritatively would be attempting the impossibility of constructing a scheme of a new society out of the materials of the old, before we knew which of those materials would disappear and which endure through the evolution which is leading us to the great change. Yet it is not difficult to conceive of some arrangement whereby those who did the roughest work should work for the shortest spells. And again, what is said above of the variety of work applies specially here. Once more I say, that for a man to be the whole of his life hopelessly engaged in performing one repulsive and never-ending task, is an arrangement fit enough for the hell imagined by theologians, but scarcely fit for any other form of society. Lastly, if this rougher work were of any special kind, we may suppose that special volunteers would be called on to perform it, who would surely be forthcoming, unless men in a state of freedom should lose the sparks of manliness which they possessed as slaves.

And yet if there be any work which cannot be made other than repulsive, either by the shortness of its duration or the intermittency of its recurrence, or by the sense of special and peculiar usefulness (and therefore honour) in the mind of the man who performs it freely— if there be any work which cannot be but a torment to the worker, what then? Well, then, let us see if the heavens will fall on us if we leave it undone, for it were better that they should. The produce of such work cannot be worth the price of it.

Now we have seen that the semi-theological dogma that all labour, under any circumstances, is a blessing to the labourer, is hypocritical and false; that, on the other hand, labour is good when due hope of rest and pleasure accompanies it. We have weighed the work of civilization in the balance and found it wanting, since hope is mostly lacking to it, and therefore we see that civilization has bred a dire curse for men. But we have seen also that the work of the world might be carried on in hope and with pleasure if it were not wasted by folly and tyranny, by the perpetual strife of opposing classes.

It is Peace, therefore, which we need in order that we may live and work in hope and with pleasure. Peace so much desired, if we may trust men's words, but which has been so continually and steadily rejected by them in deeds. But for us, let us set our hearts on it and win it at whatever cost.

What the cost may be, who can tell? Will it be possible to win peace peaceably? Alas, how can it be? We are so hemmed in by wrong and folly, that in one way or other we must always be fighting against them: our own lives may see no end to the struggle, perhaps no obvious hope of the end. It may be that the best we can hope to see is that struggle getting sharper and bitterer day by day, until it breaks out openly at last into the slaughter of men by actual warfare instead of by the slower and crueller methods of "peaceful" commerce. If we live to see that, we shall live to see much; for it will mean the rich classes grown conscious of their own wrong and robbery, and consciously defending them by open violence; and then the end will be drawing near.

But in any case, and whatever the nature of our strife for peace may be, if we only aim at it steadily and with singleness of heart, and ever keep it in view, a reflection from that peace of the future will illumine the turmoil and trouble of our lives, whether the trouble be seemingly petty, or obviously tragic; and we shall, in our hopes at least, live the lives of men: nor can the present times give us any reward greater than that.

SUGGESTIONS FOR ADDITIONAL READING

To read the great Victorian social novels is to experience at first hand the conditions of life which excited the reforming ardor of such writers as Mill and Carlyle, Ruskin and Morris. Charles Dickens remains the best of all guides through the labyrinthine world of the Victorians, especially in the masterpieces of his later years: *Bleak House* (1852-53), *Hard Times* (1854), *Little Dorrit* (1857-58), *Our Mutual Friend* (1864-65).

The "condition-of-England" question in the mid-nineteenth century called forth a number of works of fiction which portray in realistic detail the sufferings inflicted on individuals by the encroachments of industrialism. The foremost examples of the so-called sociological novel are:

Benjamin Disraeli, *Coningsby, or The New Generation* (1844); *Sybil, or The Two Nations* (1845)

Elizabeth Cleghorn Gaskell, *Mary Barton, A Tale of Manchester Life* (1848); *North and South* (1854-55)

Charles Kingsley, *Yeast, A Problem* (1848); *Alton Locke, Tailor and Poet* (1850)

George Eliot, *Felix Holt, The Radical* (1866)

Two poems famous in their day, Thomas Hood's "Song of the Shirt" (1843) and Elizabeth Barrett Browning's "The Cry of the Children" (1844), significantly contributed to the growth of public indignation over oppressive practices in the labor market.

Later in the century the lot of the lower classes provided material for almost clinical studies of heredity and environment in such naturalistic novels as:

George Moore, *A Mummer's Wife* (1885); *Esther Waters* (1894)

George Robert Gissing, *Demos* (1886); *Thyrza* (1887)

Thomas Hardy, *Jude the Obscure* (1896)

The impact of socialist thinking is apparent in William Morris' enchanting Utopian vision, *News from Nowhere* (1891), as well as in the problem plays of George Bernard Shaw: notably, *Widowers' Houses* (1892), *Mrs. Warren's Profession* (1893), and *Major Barbara* (1905), the last two of which carry important prefaces.

PART THREE

The Search for Faith

Introduction

That the Victorian was a great age of religious speculation will be apparent to even the most casual student of its literature; that it was also a great age of religious faith no one could assert. As the century advanced, more and more of his contemporaries would have been disposed to concur with Matthew Arnold's statement made in 1875: ". . . at the present moment two things about the Christian religion must surely be clear to anybody with eyes in his head. One is, that men cannot do without it; the other, that they cannot do with it as it is." An important early poem of Tennyson is entitled "The Two Voices." The voices are those of faith and doubt; and in their debate we overhear that perplexed "dialogue of the mind with itself" which, according to Arnold, characterizes man's search for spiritual meaning in the modern world. The history of Victorian religious thought is a dialectic expansion of the same debate, become now the dialogue of the age with itself.

The moral seriousness of Victorian England, so conspicuous in every department of its life, was due in no small part, as we have seen, to Evangelical Christianity, which colored the beliefs and practices of so large a segment of the populace. Even when the new historical and scientific knowledge had undermined the orthodox foundations of this faith, there remained the temper of mind which it had instilled, so that no Victorians more earnestly supported ethical standards than the generation of scientific thinkers who embraced Darwin's evolutionary hypothesis. Foremost among these was Thomas Henry Huxley, who invented the term "agnostic" to describe the scientist's sceptical attitude towards traditional religious teachings.[1] A distinguished zoolo-

---

[1] In defining agnosticism, Huxley states that it "is not a creed but a method. . . . Positively the principle may be expressed: In matters of the intellect, follow your reason as far as it will take you, without regard to any other consideration. And negatively: In matters of the intellect do not pretend that conclusions are certain which are not demonstrated or demonstrable. That I take to be the agnostic faith, which if a man keep whole and undefiled, he shall not be ashamed to look the universe in the face, whatever the future may have in store for him."

gist and Darwin's most forthright champion in the controversy over *The Origin of Species,* Huxley yet remained a moral idealist. At the time of his son's death he wrote to Kingsley a moving letter which suggests how fervently the Victorian freethinker sought in other forms of experience compensation for the Christian doctrines which he had rejected:

Kicked into the world as a boy without guide or training, I confess to my shame that few men have drunk deeper of all kinds of sin than I. Happily my course was corrected . . . and for long years I have been slowly and painfully climbing, with many a fall, towards better things. And when I look back what do I find to have been the agents of my redemption? the hope of immortality and future reward? I can honestly say that for these fourteen years such a consideration has never entered my head. No, I can tell you what has been at work. *Sartor Resartus* led me to know that a deep sense of religion was compatible with the entire absence of theology. Secondly, science and her methods gave me a resting place, independent of authority and tradition. Thirdly, love opened up to me a view of the sanctity of human nature, and impressed me with a deep sense of responsibility.

For while Evangelicalism nurtured the need for religious faith in Victorian society, it signally failed to make allowance for the major ideological developments of the age. Widely as its influence was diffused, it based its appeal on emotional rather than intellectual grounds, drawing its evidence from Biblical revelation unsupported by any rigidly defined body of doctrine. When this evidence began to fade away in the cold light of historical inquiry, the better minds in the age turned elsewhere in their quest for certitude. In particular, they turned to movements which, squarely confronting contemporary issues, seemed to offer spiritual grounds for combating the spread of disbelief.

During the early years of Victoria's reign the most formidable opposition to organized Christianity was embodied in that spirit of liberalism which in other ways did so much to raise the cultural tone of the period. Inheritors, as has been said, of the sceptical tradition of British empirical philosophy, the Utilitarians outspokenly condemned all conventional religious observances as superstitious impediments to social progress. Bentham and his followers were the adversaries whom Newman had in mind when he asked: "What must be the face-to-face antagonist, by which to withstand and baffle the fierce energy of passion and the all-corroding, all-dissolving scepticism of the intellect in religious inquiries?"

Within the hierarchy of the official Church of England there was, to start with, notably little disposition to assume the militant role Newman called for. Ecclesiastical power was vested in the so-called High-and-Dry Party (as distinct from the Evangelical and other branches) which controlled the high offices and rich benefices; and church administration was strongly tainted by Erastianism, the doctrine that the state has the final say in religious affairs. Thus, the Establishment offered feeble protest when the first Reform Parliament, filled with Benthamite zeal, introduced in 1833 an Irish Church Bill, which proposed to reduce the number of episcopal sees in that predominantly Catholic country from twenty-two to twelve and to convert the resulting revenue to secular ends. The one voice raised in outrage was that of John Keble, Professor of Poetry at Oxford, who on July 14 delivered a sermon on national apostasy in which he stigmatized the Irish Bill as "a direct disavowal of the sovereignty of God."

To a small group of ardent young clergymen and scholars at Oxford Keble's words seemed to sound the call to a second Reformation. John Henry Newman, who became their guiding spirit, tells the story in his magnificent autobiography, *Apologia pro Vita Sua.* Newman and his associates began in 1833 to issue their famous *Tracts for the Times,* the first of which on the topic of apostolic succession established the keynote of their campaign. As Newman wrote: "The prospect of the loss of state protection . . . made it necessary to look for other reasons for deference to the Church besides obedience to the civil magistrate. In this crisis it was necessary to show that the Anglican priesthood derived its authority, not from the Reform Parliament of 1832, but from the Holy Apostles."

In open repudiation of the secularizing influence of liberal reformers, the Oxford or Tractarian Movement was dedicated to reaffirming the primacy of the Church of England in all religious matters; to do so, it was necessary first to restore the purity of its doctrine and to free it from Erastianism. At the outset all Newman's learning, eloquence, and dialectic skill were directed to showing that the Establishment, deriving its dogma and sacramental system in unbroken line from primitive Christianity, provided a *via media* or middle way be-tween the errors perpetuated by the rigid institutionalism of the Church of Rome and the purely emotional appeal of Dissent, which in his opinion "had no intellectual basis; no internal idea, no principle of unity, no theology." Ultimately his study of the history of the early church, combined with disillusionment over evidences of continuing liberalism in High Anglican circles, led Newman in 1845 to espouse Roman Catholicism. With the secession of its leader the Oxford Move-ment lost its intransigent spirit and subsided back within the Estab-lished Church. Anglo-Catholicism, however, had been aroused from its spiritual torpor and was henceforth to play a central role in the cultural life of the age.

Although so intense, the appeal of the Oxford Movement was too narrow; it was insufficiently concerned with social problems on one hand, and on the other, it was obscurantist in its refusal to take into account the flood of new knowledge threatening traditional belief. Other more or less closely knit groups within the Establishment under-took to supply these deficiencies. The distinguished theologian F. D. Maurice, seconded by Charles Kingsley, formed the Christian Socialists who sought to offset infidelity among the working classes by a closer identification of the Church with their interests. The Broad Church-men or Latitudinarians, of whom Thomas Arnold, the great head-master of Rugby and the poet's father, was a leading representative, were primarily concerned with reinterpreting the Church's theological heritage in the light of historical scholarship. Both tendencies, however, were united in a still more influential intellectual movement which, although anti-Christian in tendency, elicited a profoundly religious re-sponse from a large number of intelligent Victorians. This was the so-called Religion of Humanity. Its origins can be traced to the rise of historical studies during the late eighteenth and early nineteenth centuries. In estimating the general significance of this development, Noel Annan, an English historian of ideas, has written:

The nineteenth century made the mistake of worshipping the Muse of History as a goddess. Truth, they believed, was revealed in History, not in the Bible—but like every revelation it required interpretation. . . . Men began to see the Truth no longer as absolute, philosophically

static, revealed once and for all, but as relative, genetic and evolutionary.
. . . It was not Science itself, but Science interpreted *as History* which
upset the orthodox Cosmology.[2]

As applied to the Bible, the new methods of historical investigation
produced a body of scriptural exegesis known as the Higher Criticism,
of which the most noteworthy example was the *Life of Jesus* (1835),
written by the German scholar D. F. Strauss. In this work the author
argued that Christ was an actual prophet who had died for his beliefs,
but that the story of his life transmitted through the Scriptures is
colored by the Jewish dream of a national hero, still current in early
Christian communities. Strauss, then, represents the Christ figure as a
myth, symbolizing ideal humanity. His followers, principal among
whom were the German philosopher Ludwig Feuerbach and the
French sociologist Auguste Comte, went on from here to apotheosize
humanity itself, identifying man with the godhead. In Feuerbach's
words: "The historical progress of religion consists in this: that what
by an earlier religion was regarded as objective, is now recognized
as subjective; that is, what was formerly contemplated and worshipped
as God is now perceived to be something *human*. . . . The divine being
is nothing else than the human being, or, rather, the human nature
purified, freed from the limits of the individual man. . . . All the
attributes of the divine nature are, therefore, attributes of the human
nature."

Among English advocates of what came to be known as Positivist
philosophy, perhaps the most famous is George Eliot, who translated
Strauss's *Life of Jesus* in 1846 and Feuerbach's *The Essence of Christianity* in 1854. Loss of Christian faith simply redirected this novelist's
deep piety and sense of social responsibility towards the concerns of
mankind at large. Something of her quality of mind emerges in the
following anecdote recounted by a Victorian man of letters, F. W. H.
Myers:

I remember how, at Cambridge, I walked with her once in the
Fellows' Garden of Trinity, on an evening of rainy May; and she,
stirred somewhat beyond her wont, and taking as her text the three

---

[2] Noel Annan, in *Ideas and Beliefs of the Victorians,* p. 151.

words which have been used so often as the inspiring trumpet-calls of men—the words God, Immortality, Duty,—pronounced with terrible earnestness, how inconceivable was the first, how unbelievable the second, and yet how peremptory and absolute the third. Never, perhaps, have sterner accents affirmed the sovereignty of impersonal and unrecompensing Law.

Her own version of the way the religious spirit operated in her occurs in a letter of 1853: ". . . I begin to feel for other people's wants and sorrows a little more than I used to do. Heaven help us! said the old religions—the new one, from its very lack of that faith, will teach us all the more to help one another." The thematic concerns of all George Eliot's fiction testify to the deep sincerity with which she held and practiced this belief. "My books," she once declared, "have for their main bearing a conclusion . . . without which I could not have cared to write any representation of human life—namely, that the fellowship between man and man which has been the principle of development, social and moral, is not dependent on conceptions of what is not man: and that the idea of God, so far as it has been a high spiritual influence, is the ideal of goodness entirely human (*i.e.,* an exaltation of the human)."

Sigmund Freud, the Austrian psychoanalyst, wrote that the ego of modern man has sustained three shattering blows. The first of these was the cosmological blow dealt by Copernicus, after which man could no longer think of himself as occupying a place at the center of the universe; the third was the psychological blow dealt by Freud himself in hypothesizing unconscious regions of being over which man can exercise only the most precarious control. The second and perhaps the most damaging blow to man's dignity and self-esteem was the biological blow under the guise of the evolutionary hypothesis announced by Charles Darwin, first in *The Origin of Species* (1859), and then with specific application to the human species in *The Descent of Man* (1871).

The surmise that higher have developed from lower forms of life by an evolutionary process had been current in European thought for at least a century prior to Darwin. Speculations along these lines appear as early as the mid-eighteenth century in Buffon's *Natural*

History; they are advanced in the poems of Erasmus Darwin, the biologist's grandfather, and find an early Victorian exponent in Robert Chambers, whose *Vestiges of Creation* was anonymously published in 1844. It remained, however, for Darwin to establish evolution as a fact by supplying a satisfactory explanation for how it takes place. This he did in his theory of natural selection; species are gradually modified through a struggle for survival in which favorable variations (those best adapted to the given environment) tend to be reproduced, while others die out.

After the initial outcry of dismay which greeted the imputation that man belongs to the family of primates had begun to subside under the overwhelming mass of evidence which Darwin had gathered in support of his views, the Victorians discovered in Darwinism still more distressing implications for the human situation. These had to do with the total amorality of a biological process which, according to Darwin's account, not only operates extremely slowly but in a perfectly fortuitous way. As Bernard Shaw was to point out, mind is banished from the universe and life left at the mercy of meaningless chance.

But how is one to explain the appearance in man of ethical consciousness unless some teleological purpose underlies life? The search for an answer to such questions encouraged the growth of a school of religious thought which, adopting many of the postulates of Darwinian theory, stressed immanentist rather than transcendentalist concepts. That is to say, the traditional view that the cosmos came into being as the result of an act of creation by a power which remained separate from its handiwork was replaced by the idea that this shaping force inheres in the very scheme of things and is constantly operative there. According to this argument, it is possible to maintain that God's will manifests itself through the evolutionary process which, indeed, evidences his creative method.

A further (and related) optimistic response to Darwinism was an outgrowth of those vitalistic tendencies which, in opposition to empiricism, came to dominate nineteenth-century philosophy, especially through the writings of Hegel, Schopenhauer, and Nietzsche, although we have noted their presence in Carlyle. In terms of vitalism the animating principle at the heart of all existence is what the French philosopher

Henri Bergson called the *élan vital,* the force or energy which informs all organisms and which is creative in the sense that it is constantly seeking to produce more highly organized forms of life. Man responds to, indeed is gripped by this force at the deepest intuitive level of his being, as it seeks to fulfill itself through him. The human faculty which it principally uses for its purpose is the will. In an existential sense man is moved to *impose* meaning on the world. For scientific support of the vitalist view, appeal was frequently made to the theories of the French naturalist Jean Baptiste Lamarck (1744-1829), who was the principal evolutionary thinker before Darwin. In the early years of the nineteenth century Lamarck had expounded an hypothesis of purposive evolution, founded on the belief that acquired characteristics are transmissible through heredity and that, therefore, biological advance is self-perfecting. Among latter-day Victorians both the novelist Samuel Butler (in *The Way of All Flesh* and the satiric *Erewhon*) and the dramatist George Bernard Shaw (in such plays as *Man and Superman* and *Back to Methuselah*) were confirmed neo-Lamarckians, as their religious veneration for the "life force" testifies.

To summarize briefly, the most meaningful expressions of the Victorian search for faith sprang up in response to important intellectual developments of the age. The Oxford Movement, led by Newman, undertook to combat Benthamite liberalism by re-establishing the spiritual sovereignty of the Church of England. The Positivists sought to convert the findings of the historical critics into an argument for their Religion of Humanity. And Darwinism provoked by way of reaction various immanentist and vitalist declarations of faith in man's continuing evolutionary progress.

It is impossible in the available space fully to display the complex gamut of Victorian religious experience, but the following selections illustrate most of the characteristic attitudes which emerged during the period. The authoritarian orthodoxy of John Henry Newman stands in counterpoint to Carlyle's highly intuitive and emotional transcendentalism. Lyric poetry by its subjective nature supplies the best index to the impact on individual minds of the new historical and scientific knowledge. Tennyson's great elegy *In Memoriam* moves through despair to triumphant affirmation, and better than any other single literary work conveys the nature of the religious crisis through which the age was passing. The pessimistic note is carried on by the three poets who follow, ranging from the black nihilism of James Thomson to the brooding stoicism of Thomas Hardy and the slightly cynical epicureanism of A. E. Housman. Balancing their poems are the concluding lyrics by three poets, each of whom takes a hopeful view of human destiny based on vitalist premises: Charles Algernon Swinburne in terms of the Positivist dream of ideal humanity; George Meredith through his trust in a daemonic natural order; and Gerard Manley Hopkins out of the mystic's ecstatic contemplation of a sacramental universe.

John Henry Newman

1801-1890

History of My Religious Opinions to the Year 1833

> Given here, with minor excisions, is the first chapter
> of *Apologia pro Vita Sua* in the edition of 1865,
> slightly revised from the original edition in the
> preceding year, now re-entitled *A History of My
> Religious Opinions*. Newman undertook this work
> to defend himself against Charles Kingsley, the
> influential Anglican clergyman, who had attacked his
> religious position on the grounds of intellectual
> dishonesty. But what began as apologetics grew into
> a spiritual autobiography that rivals the *Confessions*
> of St. Augustine.

It may easily be conceived how great a trial it is to
me to write the following history of myself; but I must not shrink
from the task. The words *"Secretum meum mihi,"* [1] keep ringing in
my ears; but as men draw towards their end, they care less for disclosures. Nor is it the least part of my trial to anticipate that, upon
first reading what I have written, my friends may consider much in it
irrelevant to my purpose; yet I cannot help thinking that, viewed as
a whole, it will effect what I propose to myself in giving it to the
public.

I was brought up from a child to take great delight in reading
the Bible; but I had no formed religious convictions till I was fifteen.
Of course I had a perfect knowledge of my Catechism.

[1] My secret is my own.

After I was grown up, I put on paper my recollections of the thoughts and feelings on religious subjects which I had at the time that I was a child and a boy—such as had remained on my mind with sufficient prominence to make me consider them worth recording. Out of these, written in the Long Vacation of 1820, and transcribed with additions in 1823, I select two, which are at once the most definite among them, and also have a bearing on my later convictions.

1. "I used to wish the *Arabian Tales* were true; my imagination ran on unknown influences, on magical powers, and talismans. . . . I thought life might be a dream, or I an Angel, and all this world a deception, my fellow-angels by a playful device concealing themselves from me, and deceiving me with the semblance of a material world."

Again, "Reading in the Spring of 1816 a sentence from [Dr. Watts's] *Remnants of Time*,[2] entitled 'the Saints unknown to the world,' to the effect, that 'there is nothing in their figure or countenance to distinguish them,' etc., etc., I supposed he spoke of Angels who lived in the world, as it were disguised."

2. The other remark is this: "I was very superstitious, and for some time previous to my conversion [when I was fifteen] used constantly to cross myself on going into the dark."

Of course I must have got this practice from some external source or other; but I can make no sort of conjecture whence; and certainly no one had ever spoken to me on the subject of the Catholic religion, which I only knew by name. The French master was an *émigré*[3] Priest, but he was simply made a butt, as French masters too commonly were in that day, and spoke English very imperfectly. There was a Catholic family in the village, old maiden ladies we used to think; but I knew nothing about them. I have of late years heard that there were one or two Catholic boys in the school; but either we were carefully kept from knowing this, or the knowledge of it made simply no impression on our minds. My brother will bear witness how free the school was from Catholic ideas.

I had once been into Warwick Street Chapel, with my father, who, I believe, wanted to hear some piece of music; all that I bore away

[2] Isaac Watts (1674-1748), the famous writer of hymns.
[3] Royalist refugee from France at the time of the French Revolution.

from it was the recollection of a pulpit and a preacher, and a boy swinging a censer.

When I was at Littlemore,[4] I was looking over old copybooks of my school days, and I found among them my first Latin versebook; and in the first page of it there was a device which almost took my breath away with surprise. I have the book before me now, and have just been showing it to others. I have written in the first page, in my schoolboy hand, "John H. Newman, February 11th, 1811, Verse Book"; then follow my first Verses. Between "Verse" and "Book" I have drawn the figure of a solid cross upright, and next to it is, what may indeed be meant for a necklace, but what I cannot make out to be anything else than a set of beads suspended, with a little cross attached. At this time I was not quite ten years old. I suppose I got these ideas from some romance, Mrs. Radcliffe's or Miss Porter's;[5] or from some religious picture; but the strange thing is, how, among the thousand objects which meet a boy's eyes, these in particular should so have fixed themselves in my mind that I made them thus practically my own. I am certain there was nothing in the churches I attended, or the prayer books I read, to suggest them. It must be recollected that Anglican churches and prayer books were not decorated in those days as I believe they are now.

When I was fourteen, I read Paine's Tracts[6] against the Old Testament, and found pleasure in thinking of the objections which were contained in them. Also, I read some of Hume's Essays; and perhaps that on Miracles.[7] So at least I gave my father to understand; but perhaps it was a brag. Also, I recollect copying out some French verses, perhaps Voltaire's, in denial of the immortality of the soul, and saying to myself something like "How dreadful, but how plausible!"

---

[4] The hamlet near Oxford where Newman lived in virtual seclusion during the years (1842-45) before he joined the Roman Catholic Church.

[5] Ann Radcliffe (1764-1823), author of melodramatic "Gothic" romances, the best known of which is *The Mysteries of Udolpho* (1794); Jane Porter (1776-1850), writer of romances, such as *Thaddeus of Warsaw* (1803) and *The Scottish Chiefs* (1810).

[6] Thomas Paine (1737-1809), revolutionary democrat and freethinker, who wrote *The Age of Reason* (1795).

[7] The essay "Of Miracles" occurs in David Hume's *Enquiry Concerning Human Understanding* (1748).

JOHN HENRY NEWMAN

When I was fifteen (in the autumn of 1816) a great change of thought took place in me. I fell under the influences of a definite Creed, and received into my intellect impressions of dogma, which, through God's mercy, have never been effaced or obscured. Above and beyond the conversations and sermons of the excellent man, long dead, the Rev. Walter Mayers, of Pembroke College, Oxford, who was the human means of this beginning of divine faith in me, was the effect of the books which he put into my hands, all of the school of Calvin. One of the first books I read was a work of Romaine's;[8] I neither recollect the title nor the contents, except one doctrine, which of course I do not include among those which I believe to have come from a divine source, viz., the doctrine of final perseverance. I received it at once, and believed that the inward conversion of which I was conscious (and of which I still am more certain than that I have hands and feet) would last into the next life, and that I was elected to eternal glory. I have no consciousness that this belief had any tendency whatever to lead me to be careless about pleasing God. I retained it till the age of twenty-one, when it gradually faded away; but I believe that it had some influence on my opinions, in the direction of those childish imaginations which I have already mentioned, viz., in isolating me from the objects which surrounded me, in confirming me in my mistrust of the reality of material phenomena, and making me rest in the thought of two and two only absolute and luminously self-evident beings, myself and my Creator—for while I considered myself pre-destined to salvation, my mind did not dwell upon others, as fancying them simply passed over, not predestined to eternal death. I only thought of the mercy to myself.

The detestable doctrine last mentioned is simply denied and abjured, unless my memory strangely deceives me, by the writer who made a deeper impression on my mind than any other, and to whom (humanly speaking) I almost owe my soul—Thomas Scott of Aston Sandford.[9] I so admired and delighted in his writings that, when I was an undergraduate, I thought of making a visit to his Parsonage, in order to

[8] William Romaine (1714-1795), Anglican clergyman and author of religious works.

[9] Thomas Scott (1747-1821), author of a popular commentary on the Bible.

see a man whom I so deeply revered. I hardly think I could have given up the idea of this expedition, even after I had taken my degree; for the news of his death in 1821 came upon me as a disappointment as well as a sorrow. I hung upon the lips of Daniel Wilson,[10] afterwards Bishop of Calcutta, as in two sermons at St. John's Chapel he gave the history of Scott's life and death. I had been possessed of his *Force of Truth* and Essays from a boy; his Commentary I bought when I was an undergraduate.

What, I suppose, will strike any reader of Scott's history and writings is his bold unworldliness and vigorous independence of mind. He followed truth wherever it led him, beginning with Unitarianism, and ending in a zealous faith in the Holy Trinity. It was he who first planted deep in my mind that fundamental truth of religion. With the assistance of Scott's Essays, and the admirable work of Jones of Nayland,[11] I made a collection of Scripture texts in proof of the doctrine, with remarks (I think) of my own upon them, before I was sixteen; and a few months later I drew up a series of texts in support of each verse of the Athanasian Creed. These papers I have still.

Besides his unworldliness, what I also admired in Scott was his resolute opposition to Antinomianism, and the minutely practical character of his writings. They show him to be a true Englishman, and I deeply felt his influence; and for years I used almost as proverbs what I considered to be the scope and issue of his doctrine, "Holiness rather than peace," and "Growth the only evidence of life."

Calvinists make a sharp separation between the elect and the world; there is much in this that is cognate or parallel to the Catholic doctrine; but they go on to say, as I understand them, very differently from Catholicism—that the converted and the unconverted can be discriminated by man, that the justified are conscious of their state of justification, and that the regenerate cannot fall away. Catholics on the other hand shade and soften the awful antagonism between good and evil, which is one of their dogmas, by holding that there are

[10] Daniel Wilson (1778-1858), Evangelical churchman and writer on religious subjects.
[11] William Jones (1726-1800), a High Churchman who wrote *The Catholic Doctrine of the Trinity* (1756).

different degrees of justification, that there is a great difference in point of gravity between sin and sin, that there is the possibility and the danger of falling away, and that there is no certain knowledge given to anyone that he is simply in a state of grace, and much less that he is to persevere to the end. Of the Calvinistic tenets the only one which took root in my mind was the fact of heaven and hell, divine favor and divine wrath, of the justified and the unjustified. The notion that the regenerate and the justified were one and the same, and that the regenerate, as such, had the gift of perseverance, remained with me not many years, as I have said already.

This main Catholic doctrine of the warfare between the city of God and the powers of darkness was also deeply impressed upon my mind by a work of a character very opposite to Calvinism, Law's *Serious Call*.[12]

From this time I held with a full inward assent and belief the doctrine of eternal punishment, as delivered by our Lord Himself, in as true a sense as I hold that of eternal happiness; though I have tried in various ways to make that truth less terrible to the intellect.

Now I come to two other works which produced a deep impression on me in the same autumn of 1816, when I was fifteen years old, each contrary to each, and planting in me the seeds of an intellectual inconsistency which disabled me for a long course of years. I read Joseph Milner's *Church History*,[13] and was nothing short of enamored of the long extracts from St. Augustine, St. Ambrose, and the other Fathers which I found there. I read them as being the religion of the primitive Christians; but simultaneously with Milner I read Newton on the Prophecies,[14] and in consequence became most firmly convinced that the Pope was the Antichrist predicted by Daniel, St. Paul, and St. John. My imagination was stained by the effects of this doctrine up to the year 1843; it had been obliterated from my reason and judg-

---

[12] William Law (1686-1761), Anglican divine, is remembered for his eloquent *Serious Call to a Devout and Holy Life* (1728), which deeply influenced John Wesley.

[13] Joseph Milner (1744-1797), Evangelical clergyman and author of *History of the Church of Christ* (1794-97).

[14] Thomas Newton (1704-1782), Bishop of Bristol, who wrote *Dissertation on the Prophecies* (1754).

ment at an earlier date; but the thought remained upon me as a sort of false conscience. Hence came that conflict of mind, which so many have felt besides myself—leading some men to make a compromise between two ideas, so inconsistent with each other—driving others to beat out the one idea or the other from their minds—and ending in my own case, after many years of intellectual unrest, in the gradual decay and extinction of one of them—I do not say in its violent death, for why should I not have murdered it sooner, if I murdered it at all?

I am obliged to mention, though I do it with great reluctance, another deep imagination, which at this time, the autumn of 1816, took possession of me—there can be no mistake about the fact—viz., that it would be the will of God that I should lead a single life. This anticipation, which has held its ground almost continuously ever since —with the break of a month now and a month then, up to 1829, and, after that date, without any break at all—was more or less connected, in my mind, with the notion that my calling in life would require such a sacrifice as celibacy involved; as, for instance, missionary work among the heathen, to which I had a great drawing for some years. It also strengthened my feeling of separation from the visible world, of which I have spoken above.

In 1822 I came under very different influences from those to which I had hitherto been subjected. At that time, Mr. Whately, as he was then, afterwards Archbishop of Dublin, for the few months he remained in Oxford, which he was leaving for good, showed great kindness to me. He renewed it in 1825, when he became Principal of Alban Hall, making me his Vice-Principal and Tutor. Of Dr. Whately I will speak presently, for from 1822 to 1825 I saw most of the present Provost of Oriel, Dr. Hawkins,[15] at that time Vicar of St. Mary's; and, when I took orders in 1824 and had a curacy in Oxford, then, during the Long Vacations, I was especially thrown into his company. I can say with a full heart that I love him, and have never ceased to love him; and I thus preface what otherwise might sound rude, that in the course of the many years in which we were together afterwards, he provoked me very much from time to time, though I am perfectly certain that I have provoked him a great deal more.

[15] Edward Hawkins (1789-1882).

Moreover, in me such provocation was unbecoming, both because he was the Head of my College, and because, in the first years that I knew him, he had been in many ways of great service to my mind.

He was the first who taught me to weigh my words, and to be cautious in my statements. He led me to that mode of limiting and clearing my sense in discussion and in controversy, and of distinguishing between cognate ideas, and of obviating mistakes by anticipation, which to my surprise has been since considered, even in quarters friendly to me, to savor of the polemics of Rome. He is a man of most exact mind himself, and he used to snub me severely, on reading, as he was kind enough to do, the first sermons that I wrote, and other compositions which I was engaged upon.

Then as to doctrine, he was the means of great additions to my belief. As I have noticed elsewhere, he gave me the *Treatise on Apostolical Preaching,* by Sumner,[16] afterwards Archbishop of Canterbury, from which I was led to give up my remaining Calvinism, and to receive the doctrine of Baptismal Regeneration. In many other ways too he was of use to me, on subjects semireligious and semischolastic.

It was Dr. Hawkins too who taught me to anticipate that, before many years were over, there would be an attack made upon the books and the canon of Scripture. I was brought to the same belief by the conversation of Mr. Blanco White,[17] who also led me to have freer views on the subject of inspiration than were usual in the Church of England at the time.

There is one other principle which I gained from Dr. Hawkins, more directly bearing upon Catholicism than any that I have mentioned; and that is the doctrine of Tradition. When I was an undergraduate, I heard him preach in the University Pulpit his celebrated sermon on the subject, and recollect how long it appeared to me, though he was at that time a very striking preacher; but, when I read it and studied it as his gift, it made a most serious impression upon me. He does not go one step, I think, beyond the high Anglican doctrine, nay he does not reach it; but he does his work thoroughly, and

---

[16] John Bird Sumner (1780-1862); the work mentioned was first published anonymously in 1815.

[17] Joseph Blanco White (1775-1841), writer on theological subjects who forsook the Catholic Church. He took up residence in Oriel College, Oxford, in 1826.

his view was in him original, and his subject was a novel one at the time. He lays down a proposition, self-evident as soon as stated, to those who have at all examined the structure of Scripture, viz., that the sacred text was never intended to teach doctrine, but only to prove it, and that, if we would learn doctrine, we must have recourse to the formularies of the Church; for instance, to the Catechism, and to the Creeds. He considers that, after learning from them the doctrines of Christianity, the inquirer must verify them by Scripture. This view, most true in its outline, most fruitful in its consequences, opened upon me a large field of thought. Dr. Whately held it too. One of its effects was to strike at the root of the principle on which the Bible Society was set up. I belonged to its Oxford Association; it became a matter of time when I should withdraw my name from its subscription-list, though I did not do so at once.

It is with pleasure that I pay here a tribute to the memory of the Rev. William James, then Fellow of Oriel; who, about the year 1823, taught me the doctrine of Apostolical Succession, in the course of a walk, I think, round Christ Church Meadow—I recollect being somewhat impatient of the subject at the time.

It was at about this date, I suppose, that I read Bishop Butler's *Analogy*;[18] the study of which has been to so many, as it was to me, an era in their religious opinions. Its inculcation of a visible Church, the oracle of truth and a pattern of sanctity, of the duties of external religion, and of the historical character of Revelation, are characteristics of this great work which strike the reader at once; for myself, if I may attempt to determine what I most gained from it, it lay in two points, which I shall have an opportunity of dwelling on in the sequel; they are the underlying principles of a great portion of my teaching. First, the very idea of an analogy between the separate works of God leads to the conclusion that the system which is of less importance is economically or sacramentally connected with the more momentous system, and of this conclusion the theory, to which I was inclined as a boy, viz., the unreality of material phenomena, is an ulti-

---

[18] Joseph Butler (1692-1752), Bishop of Bristol and Bishop of Durham in succession. His widely influential *Analogy of Religion* (1736) was directed against the eighteenth-century deists who advocated natural religion.

mate resolution. At this time I did not make the distinction between matter itself and its phenomena, which is so necessary and so obvious in discussing the subject. Secondly, Butler's doctrine that Probability is the guide of life, led me, at least under the teaching to which a few years later I was introduced, to the question of the logical cogency of Faith, on which I have written so much. Thus to Butler I trace those two principles of my teaching which have led to a charge against me both of fancifulness and of skepticism.

And now as to Dr. Whately. I owe him a great deal. He was a man of generous and warm heart. He was particularly loyal to his friends, and to use the common phrase, "all his geese were swans." While I was still awkward and timid in 1822, he took me by the hand, and acted towards me the part of a gentle and encouraging instructor. He, emphatically, opened my mind, and taught me to think and to use my reason. After being first noticed by him in 1822, I became very intimate with him in 1825, when I was his Vice-Principal at Alban Hall. I gave up that office in 1826, when I became Tutor of my College, and his hold upon me gradually relaxed. He had done his work towards me, or nearly so, when he had taught me to see with my own eyes and to walk with my own feet. Not that I had not a good deal to learn from others still, but I influenced them as well as they me, and co-operated rather than merely concurred with them. As to Dr. Whately, his mind was too different from mine for us to remain long on one line. I recollect how dissatisfied he was with an Article of mine in the *London Review*,[19] which Blanco White, good-humoredly, only called Platonic. When I was diverging from him in opinion (which he did not like), I thought of dedicating my first book to him, in words to the effect that he had not only taught me to think, but to think for myself. He left Oxford in 1831; after that, as far as I can recollect, I never saw him but twice—when he visited the University; once in the street in 1834, once in a room in 1838. From the time that he left, I have always felt a real affection for what I must call his memory; for, at least from the year 1834, he made himself dead to me. He had practically indeed given me up from the time that he became Arch-

[19] The first number of the *London Review* (1829), under Blanco White's editorship, carried Newman's essay, "Poetry, with Reference to Aristotle's Poetics."

bishop in 1831; but in 1834 a correspondence took place between us, which, though conducted in the most friendly language on both sides, was the expression of differences of opinion which acted as a final close to our intercourse. My reason told me that it was impossible we could have got on together longer, had he stayed in Oxford; yet I loved him too much to bid him farewell without pain. After a few years had passed, I began to believe that his influence on me in a higher respect than intellectual advance (I will not say through his fault) had not been satisfactory. I believe that he has inserted sharp things in his later works about me. They have never come in my way, and I have not thought it necessary to seek out what would pain me so much in the reading.

What he did for me in point of religious opinion was first to teach me the existence of the Church as a substantive body or corporation; next to fix in me those anti-Erastian views of Church polity which were one of the most prominent features of the Tractarian Movement. On this point, and, as far as I know, on this point alone, he and Hurrell Froude[20] intimately sympathized, though Froude's development of opinion here was of a later date. In the year 1826, in the course of a walk he said much to me about a work then just published, called *Letters on the Church by an Episcopalian*. He said that it would make my blood boil. It was certainly a most powerful composition. One of our common friends told me that, after reading it, he could not keep still, but went on walking up and down his room. It was ascribed at once to Whately; I gave eager expression to the contrary opinion; but I found the belief of Oxford in the affirmative to be too strong for me; rightly or wrongly I yielded to the general voice; and I have never heard, then or since, of any disclaimer of authorship on the part of Dr. Whately.

The main positions of this able essay are these: first, that Church and State should be independent of each other—he speaks of the duty of protesting "against the profanation of Christ's kingdom, by that *double usurpation,* the interference of the Church in temporals, of the

---

[20] Richard Hurrell Froude (1803-1836), fellow of Oriel College and Newman's most intimate friend. He was brother of the historian, James Anthony Froude (1818-1894).

State in spirituals," p. 191; and, secondly, that the Church may justly and by right retain its property, though separated from the State. "The clergy," he says, p. 133, "though they ought not to be the hired servants of the Civil Magistrate, may justly retain their revenues; and the State, though it has no right of interference in spiritual concerns, not only is justly entitled to support from the ministers of religion, and from all other Christians, but would, under the system I am recommending, obtain it much more effectually." The author of this work, whoever he may be, argues out both these points with great force and ingenuity, and with a thoroughgoing vehemence, which perhaps we may refer to the circumstance that he wrote, not *in propria persona*,[21] and as thereby answerable for every sentiment he advanced, but in the professed character of a Scotch Episcopalian. His work had a gradual, but a deep effect on my mind.

I am not aware of any other religious opinion which I owe to Dr. Whately. For his special theological tenets I had no sympathy. In the next year, 1827, he told me he considered that I was Arianizing. The case was this: though at that time I had not read Bishop Bull's *Defensio*[22] nor the Fathers, I was just then very strong for that ante-Nicene view of the Trinitarian doctrine which some writers, both Catholic and non-Catholic, have accused of wearing a sort of Arian exterior. This is the meaning of a passage in Froude's *Remains*,[23] in which he seems to accuse me of speaking against the Athanasian Creed. I had contrasted the two aspects of the Trinitarian doctrine which are respectively presented by the Athanasian Creed and the Nicene. My criticisms were to the effect that some of the verses of the former Creed were unnecessarily scientific. This is a specimen of a certain disdain for Antiquity which had been growing on me now for several years. It showed itself in some flippant language against the Fathers in the *Encyclopaedia Metropolitana*,[24] about whom I knew little at the time, except what I had learned as a boy from Joseph Milner. In writing on the Scripture

[21] In his own person.

[22] George Bull (1634-1710), Bishop of St. David's and author of *Defence of the Nicene Creed* (1685).

[23] Newman wrote the Preface to the *Literary Remains* of Hurrell Froude, published 1838-39.

[24] Newman wrote several articles for this *Encyclopaedia* at Whately's request.

Miracles in 1825-1826, I had read Middleton[25] on the Miracles of the early Church, and had imbibed a portion of his spirit.

The truth is, I was beginning to prefer intellectual excellence to moral; I was drifting in the direction of the liberalism of the day. I was rudely awakened from my dream at the end of 1827 by two great blows—illness and bereavement.[26]

In the beginning of 1829 came the formal break between Dr. Whately and me; the affair of Mr. Peel's re-election[27] was the occasion of it. I think in 1828 or 1827 I had voted in the minority when the Petition to Parliament against the Catholic Claims was brought into Convocation. I did so mainly on the views suggested to me by the theory of the *Letters of an Episcopalian*. Also I disliked the bigoted "two bottle orthodox," as they were invidiously called. Accordingly I took part against Mr. Peel, on a simple academical, not at all an ecclesiastical or a political ground; and this I professed at the time. I considered that Mr. Peel had taken the University by surprise, that his friends had no right to call upon us to turn round on a sudden, and to expose ourselves to the imputation of timeserving, and that a great university ought not to be bullied even by a great Duke of Wellington. Also by this time I was under the influence of Keble[28] and Froude; who, in addition to the reasons I have given, disliked the Duke's change of policy as dictated by liberalism.

Whately was considerably annoyed at me, and he took a humorous revenge, of which he had given me due notice beforehand. As head of a house, he had duties of hospitality to men of all parties; he asked

[25] Conyers Middleton (1683-1750), Latitudinarian divine and author of a controversial treatise on *Miracles* (1748).

[26] The death of Newman's sister Mary.

[27] The bill for Catholic Emancipation was enacted by the Wellington-Peel ministry of 1828-30. Conservative Oxford was opposed to this liberal measure and refused to re-elect Peel as one of its members to Parliament. It will be noticed, however, that in 1827-28 Newman's views had been sufficiently "liberal" for him to vote in favor of the Catholic Claims.

[28] John Keble (1792-1866), clergyman, Professor of Poetry at Oxford (1831-41), and author of an extraordinarily popular volume of religious poetry, *The Christian Year* (1827). His sermon on national apostasy in 1833 inaugurated the Oxford Movement.

a set of the least intellectual men in Oxford to dinner, and men most fond of port; he made me one of this party; placed me between Provost This, and Principal That, and then asked me if I was proud of my friends. However, he had a serious meaning in his act; he saw, more clearly than I could do, that I was separating from his own friends for good and all.

Dr. Whately attributed my leaving his *clientela*[29] to a wish on my part to be the head of a party myself. I do not think that this charge was deserved. My habitual feeling then and since has been that it was not I who sought friends, but friends who sought me. Never man had kinder or more indulgent friends than I have had, but I expressed my own feeling as to the mode in which I gained them, in this very year 1829, in the course of a copy of verses. Speaking of my blessings, I said, "Blessings of friends, which to my door, *unasked, unhoped,* have come." They have come, they have gone; they came to my great joy, they went to my great grief. He who gave, took away. Dr. Whately's impression about me, however, admits of this explanation:

During the first years of my residence at Oriel, though proud of my College, I was not quite at home there. I was very much alone, and I used often to take my daily walk by myself. I recollect once meeting Dr. Copleston,[30] then Provost, with one of the Fellows. He turned round, and with the kind courteousness which sat so well on him, made me a bow and said, *"Nunquam minus solus, quam cum solus."* [31] At that time indeed (from 1823) I had the intimacy of my dear and true friend Dr. Pusey,[32] and could not fail to admire and revere a soul so devoted to the cause of religion, so full of good works, so faithful in his affections; but he left residence when I was getting to know him well. As to Dr. Whately himself, he was too much my superior to allow of my being at my ease with him; and to no one in Oxford at this time did I open my heart fully and familiarly. But things

---

[29] Latin for clientele.
[30] Edward Copleston (1776-1849), Bishop of Llandaff and Dean of St. Paul's.
[31] "Never less alone than when alone" (Cicero, *Republic,* I, 17, 27).
[32] Edward Bouverie Pusey (1800-1882), Regius Professor of Hebrew at Oxford and one of the leaders of the Oxford Movement.

changed in 1826. At that time I became one of the Tutors of my College, and this gave me position; besides, I had written one or two Essays which had been well received. I began to be known. I preached my first University Sermon. Next year I was one of the Public Examiners for the B. A. degree. In 1828 I became Vicar of St. Mary's. It was to me like the feeling of spring weather after winter; and, if I may so speak, I came out of my shell; I remained out of it till 1841.

The two persons who knew me best at that time are still alive, beneficed clergymen, no longer my friends. They could tell better than anyone else what I was in those years. From this time my tongue was, as it were, loosened, and I spoke spontaneously and without effort. One of the two, a shrewd man, said of me, I have been told, "Here is a fellow who, when he is silent, will never begin to speak; and when he once begins to speak, will never stop." It was at this time that I began to have influence, which steadily increased for a course of years. I gained upon my pupils, and was in particular intimate and affectionate with two of our probationer Fellows, Robert Isaac Wilberforce[33] (afterwards Archdeacon) and Richard Hurrell Froude. Whately then, an acute man, perhaps saw around me the signs of an incipient party, of which I was not conscious myself. And thus we discern the first elements of that movement afterwards called Tractarian.

The true and primary author of it, however, as is usual with great motive-powers, was out of sight. Having carried off as a mere boy the highest honors of the University, he had turned from the admiration which haunted his steps, and sought for a better and holier satisfaction in pastoral work in the country. Need I say that I am speaking of John Keble? The first time that I was in a room with him was on occasion of my election to a Fellowship at Oriel, when I was sent for into the Tower, to shake hands with the Provost and Fellows. How is that hour fixed in my memory after the changes of forty-two years, forty-two this very day on which I write! I have lately had a letter in my hands, which I sent at the time to my great friend, John William

---

[33] Robert Isaac Wilberforce (1802-1857), son of the great Evangelical philanthropist, William Wilberforce, and a member of Newman's circle. He was converted to Roman Catholicism in 1854.

Bowden,[34] with whom I passed almost exclusively my undergraduate years. "I had to hasten to the Tower," I say to him, "to receive the congratulations of all the Fellows. I bore it till Keble took my hand, and then felt so abashed and unworthy of the honour done me that I seemed desirous of quite sinking into the ground." His had been the first name which I had heard spoken of, with reverence rather than admiration, when I came up to Oxford. When one day I was walking in High Street with my dear earliest friend just mentioned, with what eagerness did he cry out, "There's Keble!" and with what awe did I look at him! Then at another time I heard a Master of Arts of my college give an account how he had just then had occasion to introduce himself on some business to Keble, and how gentle, courteous, and unaffected Keble had been, so as almost to put him out of countenance. Then too it was reported, truly or falsely, how a rising man of brilliant reputation, the present Dean of St. Paul's, Dr. Milman,[35] admired and loved him, adding that somehow he was strangely unlike anyone else. However, at the time when I was elected Fellow of Oriel he was not in residence, and he was shy of me for years in consequence of the marks which I bore upon me of the evangelical and liberal schools. At least so I have ever thought. Hurrell Froude brought us together about 1828: it is one of the sayings preserved in his *Remains*— "Do you know the story of the murderer who had done one good thing in his life? Well; if I was ever asked what good deed I had ever done, I should say that I had brought Keble and Newman to understand each other."

The Christian Year made its appearance in 1827. It is not necessary, and scarcely becoming, to praise a book which has already become one of the classics of the language. When the general tone of religious literature was so nerveless and impotent, as it was at that time, Keble struck an original note and woke up in the hearts of thousands a new music, the music of a school long unknown in England. Nor can I pretend to analyze, in my own instance, the effect of religious teaching

[34] John William Bowden (1798-1844), an active promoter of the Oxford Movement; author of *Life of Gregory VII* (1840).
[35] Henry Hart Milman (1791-1868), historian and Keble's predecessor as Professor of Poetry at Oxford.

so deep, so pure, so beautiful. I have never till now tried to do so; yet I think I am not wrong in saying that the two main intellectual truths which it brought home to me were the same two which I had learned from Butler, though recast in the creative mind of my new master. The first of these was what may be called, in a large sense of the word, the Sacramental system; that is, the doctrine that material phenomena are both the types and the instruments of real things unseen—a doctrine which embraces in its fullness, not only what Anglicans, as well as Catholics, believe about Sacraments properly so called; but also the article of "the Communion of Saints"; and likewise the Mysteries of the faith. The connection of this philosophy of religion with what is sometimes called "Berkeleyism" has been mentioned above; I knew little of Berkeley[36] at this time except by name; nor have I ever studied him.

On the second intellectual principle which I gained from Mr. Keble, I could say a great deal, if this were the place for it. It runs through very much that I have written, and has gained for me many hard names. Butler teaches us that probability is the guide of life. The danger of this doctrine, in the case of many minds, is its tendency to destroy in them absolute certainty, leading them to consider every conclusion as doubtful, and resolving truth into an opinion, which it is safe indeed to obey or to profess, but not possible to embrace with full internal assent. If this were to be allowed, then the celebrated saying, "O God, if there be a God, save my soul, if I have a soul!" would be the highest measure of devotion—but who can really pray to a Being about whose existence he is seriously in doubt?

I considered that Mr. Keble met this difficulty by ascribing the firmness of assent which we give to religious doctrine, not to the probabilities which introduced it, but to the living power of faith and love which accepted it. In matters of religion, he seemed to say, it is not merely probability which makes us intellectually certain, but probability as it is put to account by faith and love. It is faith and love which give to probability a force which it has not in itself. Faith and love are directed towards an Object; in the vision of that Object they live; it is that Object, received in faith and love, which renders it

[36] George Berkeley (1685-1753), Bishop of Cloyne, whose writings constitute a subtle attack on materialism from the position of philosophic idealism.

reasonable to take probability as sufficient for internal conviction. Thus the argument from Probability, in the matter of religion, became an argument from Personality, which in fact is one form of the argument from Authority.

In illustration, Mr. Keble used to quote the words of the Psalm: "I will guide thee with mine *eye*. Be ye not like to horse and mule, which have no understanding; whose mouths must be held with bit and bridle, lest they fall upon thee." [37] This is the very difference, he used to say, between slaves, and friends or children. Friends do not ask for literal commands; but, from their knowledge of the speaker, they understand his half-words, and from love of him they anticipate his wishes. Hence it is that in his poem for St. Bartholomew's Day, he speaks of the "Eye of God's word"; and in the note quotes Mr. Miller,[38] of Worcester College, who remarks, in his Bampton Lectures, on the special power of Scripture, as having "this Eye, like that of a portrait, uniformly fixed upon us, turn where we will." The view thus suggested by Mr. Keble is brought forward in one of the earliest of the *Tracts for the Times*. In No. 8 I say, "The Gospel is a Law of Liberty. We are treated as sons, not as servants; not subjected to a code of formal commandments, but addressed as those who love God, and wish to please Him."

I did not at all dispute this view of the matter, for I made use of it myself; but I was dissatisfied, because it did not go to the root of the difficulty. It was beautiful and religious, but it did not even profess to be logical; and accordingly I tried to complete it by considerations of my own, which are implied in my *University Sermons, Essay on Ecclesiastical Miracles,* and *Essay on Development of Doctrine.* My argument is in outline as follows: that that absolute certitude which we were able to possess, whether as to the truths of natural theology, or as to the fact of a revelation, was the result of an *assemblage* of concurring and converging probabilities, and that, both according to the constitution of the human mind and the will of its Maker; that certitude was a habit of mind, that certainty was a quality of propositions; that probabilities which did not reach to logical certainty, might suffice for a mental certitude; that the certitude thus brought about might

[37] See Psalms xxxii.8-9.
[38] John Cole Miller (1814-1880), Anglican churchman.

equal in measure and strength the certitude which was created by the strictest scientific demonstration; and that to possess such certitude might in given cases and to given individuals be a plain duty, though not to others in other circumstances.

. . . . .

Hurrell Froude was a pupil of Keble's, formed by him, and in turn reacting upon him. I knew him first in 1826, and was in the closest and most affectionate friendship with him from about 1829 till his death in 1836. He was a man of the highest gifts—so truly many-sided that it would be presumptuous in me to attempt to describe him except under those aspects in which he came before me. Nor have I here to speak of the gentleness and tenderness of nature, the playfulness, the free elastic force and graceful versatility of mind, and the patient winning considerateness in discussion, which endeared him to those to whom he opened his heart; for I am all along engaged upon matters of belief and opinion, and am introducing others into my narrative, not for their own sake, or because I love and have loved them, so much as because, and so far as, they have influenced my theological views. In this respect, then, I speak of Hurrell Froude—in his intellectual aspect—as a man of high genius, brimful and overflowing with ideas and views, in him original, which were too many and strong even for his bodily strength, and which crowded and jostled against each other in their effort after distinct shape and expression. And he had an intellect as critical and logical as it was speculative and bold. Dying prematurely, as he did, and in the conflict and transition-state of opinion, his religious views never reached their ultimate conclusion, by the very reason of their multitude and their depth. His opinions arrested and influenced me, even when they did not gain my assent. He professed openly his admiration of the Church of Rome, and his hatred of the Reformers. He delighted in the notion of an hierarchical system, of sacerdotal power, and of full ecclesiastical liberty. He felt scorn of the maxim, "The Bible and the Bible only is the religion of Protestants"; and he gloried in accepting Tradition as a main instrument of religious teaching. He had a high severe idea of the intrinsic excellence of Virginity; and he considered the Blessed Virgin its great Pattern.

He delighted in thinking of the Saints; he had a vivid appreciation of the idea of sanctity, its possibility and its heights; and he was more than inclined to believe a large amount of miraculous interference as occurring in the early and middle ages. He embraced the principle of penance and mortification. He had a deep devotion to the Real Presence, in which he had a firm faith. He was powerfully drawn to the Medieval Church, but not to the Primitive.

He had a keen insight into abstract truth; but he was an Englishman to the backbone in his severe adherence to the real and the concrete. He had a most classical taste, and a genius for philosophy and art; and he was fond of historical inquiry, and the politics of religion. He had no turn for theology as such. He set no sufficient value on the writings of the Fathers, on the detail or development of doctrine, on the definite traditions of the Church viewed in their matter, on the teaching of the Ecumenical Councils, or on the controversies out of which they arose. He took an eager, courageous view of things on the whole. I should say that his power of entering into the minds of others did not equal his other gifts; he could not believe, for instance, that I really held the Roman Church to be Antichristian. On many points he would not believe but that I agreed with him when I did not. He seemed not to understand my difficulties. His were of a different kind, the contrariety between theory and fact. He was a high Tory of the Cavalier stamp, and was disgusted with the Toryism of the opponents of the Reform Bill. He was smitten with the love of the Theocratic Church; he went abroad and was shocked by the degeneracy which he thought he saw in the Catholics of Italy.

It is difficult to enumerate the precise additions to my theological creed which I derived from a friend to whom I owe so much. He taught me to look with admiration towards the Church of Rome, and in the same degree to dislike the Reformation. He fixed deep in me the idea of devotion to the Blessed Virgin, and he led me gradually to believe in the Real Presence.

There is one remaining source of my opinions to be mentioned, and that far from the least important. In proportion as I moved out of the shadow of that liberalism which had hung over my course, my early devotion towards the Fathers returned; and in the Long Vacation of 1828 I set about to read them chronologically, beginning with St. Ignatius and St. Justin. About 1830 a proposal was made to me by Mr. Hugh Rose, who with Mr. Lyall [39] (afterwards Dean of Canterbury) was providing writers for a Theological Library, to furnish them with a History of the Principal Councils. I accepted it, and at once set to work on the Council of Nicaea. It was to launch myself on an ocean with currents innumerable; and I was drifted back first to the ante-Nicene history, and then to the Church of Alexandria. The work at last appeared under the title of *The Arians of the Fourth Century;* and of its 422 pages, the first 117 consisted of introductory matter, and the Council of Nicaea did not appeal till the 254th, and then occupied at most twenty pages.

I do not know when I first learned to consider that Antiquity was the true exponent of the doctrines of Christianity and the basis of the Church of England; but I take it for granted that the works of Bishop Bull, which at this time I read, were my chief introduction to this principle. The course of reading which I pursued in the composition of my volume was directly adapted to develop it in my mind. What principally attracted me in the ante-Nicene period was the great Church of Alexandria,[40] the historical center of teaching in those times. Of Rome for some centuries comparatively little is known. The battle of Arianism was first fought in Alexandria; Athanasius, the champion of the truth, was Bishop of Alexandria; and in his writings he refers to the great religious names of an earlier date, to Origen, Dionysius, and others who were the glory of its see, or of its school. The broad philosophy of Clement and Origen carried me away; the philosophy, not the theological doctrine; and I have drawn out some features of it in my volume, with the zeal and freshness, but with the partiality of a neophyte. Some portions of their teaching, magnificent in themselves, came like music to my inward ear, as if the response to ideas which, with little external to encourage them, I had cherished so long. These were based on the mystical or sacramental principle, and spoke of the various

---

[39] Hugh James Rose (1795-1838), High Church theologian in whose parsonage at Hadleigh, Suffolk, the program of the Oxford Movement was drawn up; William Rowe Lyall (1788-1857), Anglican divine and editor.

[40] The city of Alexandria was a center of Christian religious activity from the middle of the second century.

Economies or Dispensations of the Eternal. I understood these passages to mean that the exterior world, physical and historical, was but the manifestation to our senses of realities greater than itself. Nature was a parable; Scripture was an allegory; pagan literature, philosophy, and mythology, properly understood, were but a preparation for the Gospel. The Greek poets and sages were in a certain sense prophets; for "thoughts beyond their thought to those high bards were given." There had been a directly divine dispensation granted to the Jews; but there had been in some sense a dispensation carried on in favor of the Gentiles. He who had taken the seed of Jacob for His elect people had not therefore cast the rest of mankind out of His sight. In the fullness of time both Judaism and Paganism had come to naught; the outward framework, which concealed yet suggested the Living Truth, had never been intended to last, and it was dissolving under the beams of the Sun of Justice which shone behind it and through it. The process of change had been slow; it had been done not rashly, but by rule and measure, "at sundry times and in divers manners," first one disclosure and then another, till the whole evangelical doctrine was brought into full manifestation. And thus room was made for the anticipation of further and deeper disclosures, of truths still under the veil of the letter, and in their season to be revealed. The visible world still remains without its divine interpretation; Holy Church in her sacraments and her hierarchical appointments, will remain, even to the end of the world, after all but a symbol of those heavenly facts which fill eternity. Her mysteries are but the expressions in human language of truths to which the human mind is unequal. It is evident how much there was in all this in correspondence with the thoughts which had attracted me when I was young, and with the doctrine which I have already associated with the *Analogy* and the *Christian Year*.

．　　．　　．　　．　　．

While I was engaged in writing my work upon the Arians, great events were happening at home and abroad, which brought out into form and passionate expression the various beliefs which had so gradually been winning their way into my mind. Shortly before, there had been a Revolution in France;[41] the Bourbons had been dismissed; and I held

[41] The "July Revolution" of 1830 in France, when the Bourbon King Charles X was dethroned and replaced by the "Citizen King" Louis Philippe.

that it was unchristian for nations to cast off their governors, and, much more, sovereigns who had the divine right of inheritance. Again, the great Reform Agitation[42] was going on around me as I wrote. The Whigs had come into power; Lord Grey had told the Bishops to set their house in order, and some of the Prelates had been insulted and threatened in the streets of London. The vital question was how were we to keep the Church from being liberalized? there was such apathy on the subject in some quarters, such imbecile alarm in others; the true principles of Churchmanship seemed so radically decayed, and there was such distraction in the councils of the Clergy. Blomfield,[43] the Bishop of London of the day, an active and open-hearted man, had been for years engaged in diluting the high orthodoxy of the Church by the introduction of members of the Evangelical body into places of influence and trust. He had deeply offended men who agreed in opinion with myself, by an offhand saying (as it was reported) to the effect that belief in the Apostolical succession had gone out with the Non-jurors.[44] "We can count you," he said to some of the gravest and most venerated persons of the old school. And the Evangelical party itself, with their late successes, seemed to have lost that simplicity and unworldliness which I admired so much in Milner and Scott. It was not that I did not venerate such men as Ryder, the then Bishop of Lichfield, and others of similar sentiments, who were not yet promoted out of the ranks of the Clergy, but I thought little of them as a class. I thought the Evangelicals played into the hands of the Liberals. With the Establishment thus divided and threatened, thus ignorant of its true strength, I compared that fresh vigorous Power of which I was reading in the first centuries. In her triumphant zeal on behalf of that Primeval Mystery to which I had had so great a devotion from my youth, I recognized the movement of my Spiritual Mother, *"Incessu patuit Dea."* [45] The self-conquest of her Ascetics, the patience of her Martyrs, the irresistible determination of her Bishops, the joyous swing of her advance, both exalted and abashed me.

[42] Leading to the Reform Bill of 1832.

[43] Charles James Blomfield (1786-1857).

[44] The name given to the English and Scottish clergymen who refused to take the oath of allegiance to William and Mary, or successive rulers after the Revolution of 1688.

[45] "By her step she appeared a goddess" (*Aeneid* 1.405).

I said to myself, "Look on this picture and on that";[46] I felt affection for my own Church, but not tenderness; I felt dismay at her prospects, anger and scorn at her do-nothing perplexity. I thought that if Liberalism once got a footing within her, it was sure of the victory in the event. I saw that Reformation principles were powerless to rescue her. As to leaving her, the thought never crossed my imagination; still I ever kept before me that there was something greater than the Established Church, and that that was the Church Catholic and Apostolic, set up from the beginning, of which she was but the local presence and the organ. She was nothing, unless she was this. She must be dealt with strongly, or she would be lost. There was need of a second reformation.

At this time I was disengaged from College duties, and my health had suffered from the labor involved in the composition of my Volume. It was ready for the press in July, 1832, though not published till the end of 1833. I was easily persuaded to join Hurrell Froude and his Father, who were going to the south of Europe for the health of the former.

We set out in December, 1832. It was during this expedition that my verses which are in the *Lyra Apostolica*[47] were written—a few indeed before it, but not more than one or two of them after it. Exchanging, as I was, definite Tutorial work, and the literary quiet and pleasant friendships of the last six years, for foreign countries and an unknown future, I naturally was led to think that some inward changes as well as some larger course of action, were coming upon me. At Whitchurch, while waiting for the down mail to Falmouth, I wrote the verses about my Guardian Angel, which begin with these words: "Are these the tracks of some unearthly Friend?" and which go on to speak of "the vision" which haunted me—that vision is more or less brought out in the whole series of these compositions.

I went to various coasts of the Mediterranean, parted with my friends at Rome; went down for the second time to Sicily without companion, at the end of April, and got back to England by Palermo in the early part of July. The strangeness of foreign life threw me back into myself;

---

[46] See *Hamlet* III.iv.53.

[47] The title of a collection of sacred poems written by Keble, Newman, Froude, Robert Isaac Wilberforce, and Isaac Williams; published in 1836.

I found pleasure in historical sites and beautiful scenes, not in men and manners. We kept clear of Catholics throughout our tour. I had a conversation with the Dean of Malta, a most pleasant man, lately dead; but it was about the Fathers, and the Library of the great church. I knew the Abbate Santini, at Rome, who did no more than copy for me the Gregorian tones. Froude and I made two calls upon Monsignore (now Cardinal) Wiseman[48] at the Collegio Inglese, shortly before we left Rome. Once we heard him preach at a church in the Corso. I do not recollect being in a room with any other ecclesiastics, except a priest at Castro-Giovanni in Sicily, who called on me when I was ill, and with whom I wished to hold a controversy. As to Church Services, we attended the Tenebrae, at the Sistine,[49] for the sake of the Miserere;[50] and that was all. My general feeling was, "All, save the spirit of man, is divine." I saw nothing but what was external; of the hidden life of Catholics I knew nothing. I was still more driven back into myself, and felt my isolation. England was in my thoughts solely, and the news from England came rarely and imperfectly. The Bill for the Suppression of the Irish Sees[51] was in progress, and filled my mind. I had fierce thoughts against the Liberals.

It was the success of the Liberal cause which fretted me inwardly. I became fierce against its instruments and its manifestations. A French vessel was at Algiers; I would not even look at the tricolor. On my return, though forced to stop twenty-four hours at Paris, I kept indoors the whole time, and all that I saw of that beautiful city was what I saw from the Diligence. The Bishop of London had already sounded me as to my filling one of the Whitehall preacherships, which he had just then put on a new footing; but I was indignant at the line which he was taking, and from my steamer I had sent home a letter declining the appointment by anticipation, should it be offered to me. At this

[48] Nicholas Patrick Stephen Wiseman (1802-1865), who became Cardinal in 1850.
[49] Religious services held during the last three days of Holy Week to commemorate the sufferings and death of Christ. The Sistine Chapel is in the Vatican.
[50] Musical setting for the 50th Psalm in the Vulgate (51st in the Authorized Version).
[51] The Irish Church Bill of 1833 that instigated the Oxford Movement.

time I was specially annoyed with Dr. Arnold,[52] though it did not last into later years. Someone, I think, asked in conversation at Rome whether a certain interpretation of Scripture was Christian? it was answered that Dr. Arnold took it; I interposed, "But is *he* a Christian?" The subject went out of my head at once; when afterwards I was taxed with it I could say no more in explanation than (what I believe was the fact) that I must have had in mind some free views of Dr. Arnold about the Old Testament—I thought I must have meant, "Arnold answers for the interpretation, but who is to answer for Arnold?" It was at Rome too that we began the *Lyra Apostolica* which appeared monthly in the *British Magazine*. The motto shows the feeling of both Froude and myself at the time; we borrowed from M. Bunsen[53] a Homer, and Froude chose the words in which Achilles, on returning to the battle, says, "You shall know the difference, now that I am back again." [54]

Especially when I was left by myself, the thought came upon me that deliverance is wrought, not by the many but by the few, not by bodies but by persons. Now it was, I think, that I repeated to myself the words, which had ever been dear to me from my school days, *Exoriare aliquis!* [55]—now too, that Southey's beautiful poem of *Thalaba*,[56] for which I had an immense liking, came forcibly to my mind. I began to think that I had a mission. There are sentences of my letters to my friends to this effect, if they are not destroyed. When we took leave of Monsignore Wiseman, he had courteously expressed a wish that we might make a second visit to Rome; I said with great gravity, "We have a work to do in England." I went down at once to Sicily, and the presentiment grew stronger. I struck into the middle of the island, and fell ill of a fever at Leonforte. My servant thought I was dying, and

---

[52] Thomas Arnold (1795-1842), the famous Headmaster of Rugby School and a religious and educational reformer.

[53] Christian Charles Josias, Baron von Bunsen (1791-1860), Prussian diplomat and scholar, envoy to the Papal Court and later ambassador to the Court of St. James.

[54] Cf. *Iliad* xviii.187-238.

[55] "May some (avenger) arise!" (*Aeneid* iv.625).

[56] Robert Southey (1774-1843), Poet Laureate, published his narrative poem *Thalaba the Destroyer* in 1801.

begged for my last directions. I gave them, as he wished; but I said, "I shall not die." I repeated, "I shall not die, for I have not sinned against light, I have not sinned against light." I never have been able to make out at all what I meant.

I got to Castro-Giovanni, and was laid up there for nearly three weeks. Towards the end of May I left for Palermo, taking three days for the journey. Before starting from my inn in the morning of May 26th or 27th, I sat down on my bed, and began to sob bitterly. My servant, who had acted as my nurse, asked what ailed me. I could only answer him, "I have a work to do in England."

I was aching to get home; yet for want of a vessel I was kept at Palermo for three weeks. I began to visit the churches, and they calmed my impatience, though I did not attend any services. I knew nothing of the presence of the Blessed Sacrament there. At last I got off in an orange boat, bound for Marseilles. We were becalmed a whole week in the Straits of Bonifacio. Then it was that I wrote the lines, "Lead, kindly light," which have since become well known. I was writing verses the whole time of my passage. At length I got to Marseilles, and set off for England. The fatigue of traveling was too much for me, and I was laid up for several days at Lyons. At last I got off again, and did not stop night or day (excepting the compulsory delay at Paris) till I reached England, and my mother's house. My brother had arrived from Persia only a few hours before. This was on Tuesday. The following Sunday, July 14th, Mr. Keble preached the Assize Sermon in the University Pulpit. It was published under the title of "National Apostasy." I have ever considered and kept the day as the start of the religious movement of 1833.

Thomas Carlyle

1795-1881

Natural Supernaturalism

The following selection is Chapter Eight of Book
Three of *Sartor Resartus,* originally published in
Fraser's Magazine, 1833-34. It gives the most succinct
account of Carlyle's transcendental philosophy.
In his *Journal* for February 1, 1833, he wrote: "That
the Supernatural differs not from the Natural is a
great Truth, which the last century (especially in
France) has been engaged in demonstrating. The
philosophers went far wrong, however, in this, that
instead of raising the natural to the supernatural, they
strove to sink the supernatural to the natural."

It is in his stupendous Section, headed *Natural Supernaturalism,* that the Professor[1] first becomes a Seer; and, after long
effort, such as we have witnessed, finally subdues under his feet this
refractory Clothes-Philosophy, and takes victorious possession thereof.
Phantasms enough he has had to struggle with; "Cloth-webs and Cobwebs," of Imperial Mantles, Superannuated Symbols, and what not: yet
still did he courageously pierce through. Nay, worst of all, two quite
mysterious, world-embracing Phantasms, TIME, and SPACE, have ever
hovered round him, perplexing and bewildering: but with these also he
now resolutely grapples, these also he victoriously rends asunder. In a

[1] Diogenes Teufelsdröckh, the name given by Carlyle to his *alter ego* in *Sartor
Resartus.* Professor Teufelsdröckh maintains through his Clothes-Philosophy that all
appearances in the phenomenal world are merely the symbols (clothes) for underlying spiritual realities.

word, he has looked fixedly on Existence, till, one after the other, its earthly hulls and garnitures have all melted away; and now, to his rapt vision, the interior celestial Holy of Holies lies disclosed.

Here, therefore, properly it is that the Philosophy of Clothes attains to Transcendentalism; this last leap, can we but clear it, takes us safe into the promised land, where *Palingenesia,*[2] in all senses, may be considered as beginning. "Courage, then!"[3] may our Diogenes exclaim, with better right than Diogenes the First once did. This stupendous Section we, after long painful meditation, have found not to be unintelligible; but, on the contrary, to be clear, nay radiant, and all-illuminating. Let the reader, turning on it what utmost force of speculative intellect is in him, do his part; as we, by judicious selection and adjustment, shall study to do ours:

"Deep has been, and is, the significance of Miracles," thus quietly begins the Professor; "far deeper perhaps than we imagine. Meanwhile, the question of questions were: What specially is a Miracle? To that Dutch King of Siam,[4] an icicle had been a miracle; whoso had carried with him an air-pump and vial of vitriolic ether, might have worked a miracle. To my Horse, again, who unhappily is still more unscientific, do not I work a miracle, and magical *'Open Sesame!'*[5] every time I please to pay twopence, and open for him an impassable *Schlagbaum,* or shut Turnpike?

" 'But is not a real Miracle simply a violation of the Laws of Nature?' ask several. Whom I answer by this new question: What are the Laws of Nature? To me perhaps the rising of one from the dead were no violation of these Laws, but a confirmation; were some far deeper Law, now first penetrated into, and by Spiritual Force, even as the rest have all been, brought to bear on us with its Material Force.

"Here too may some inquire, not without astonishment: On what ground shall one, that can make Iron swim,[6] come and declare that

---

[2] Rebirth.

[3] Laertius in his *Lives of the Philosophers* relates of Diogenes the anecdote that when a dull lecture was almost over he exclaimed: "Courage, friends! I see land!"

[4] The allusion occurs in Hume's *Enquiry Concerning Human Understanding* (Sect X, "Of Miracles").

[5] The magical password that opens the door to the treasure trove in "Ali Baba and the Forty Thieves" in *The Arabian Nights.*

[6] Cf. Kings vi.6.

therefore he can teach Religion? To us, truly, of the Nineteenth Century, such declaration were inept enough; which nevertheless to our fathers, of the First Century, was full of meaning.

" 'But is it not the deepest Law of Nature that she be constant?' cries an illuminated class: 'Is not the Machine of the Universe fixed to move by unalterable rules?' Probable enough, good friends: nay, I too, must believe that the God, whom ancient inspired men assert to be 'without variableness or shadow of turning,' [7] does indeed never change; that Nature, that the Universe, which no one whom it so pleases can be prevented from calling a Machine, does move by the most unalterable rules. And now of you too I make the old inquiry: What those same unalterable rules, forming the complete Statute-Book of Nature, may possibly be?

"They stand written in our Works of Science, say you; in the ac- cumulated records of man's Experience?—Was Man with his Experience present at the Creation, then, to see how it all went on? Have any deepest scientific individuals yet dived down to the foundations of the Universe, and gauged everything there? Did the Maker take them into His counsel; that they read His ground-plan of the incomprehensible All; and can say, This stands marked therein, and no more than this? Alas! not in any wise! These scientific individuals have been nowhere but where we also are; have seen some handbreadths deeper than we see into the Deep that is infinite, without bottom as without shore.[8]

"Laplace's Book on the Stars,[9] wherein he exhibits that certain Planets, with their Satellites, gyrate round our worthy Sun, at a rate and in a course, which, by greatest good fortune, he and the like of him have succeeded in detecting,—is to me as precious as to another. But is this what thou namest "Mechanism of the Heavens," and "System of the World;" this, wherein Sirius and the Pleiades, and all Herschel's[10] Fifteen-thousand Suns per minute, being left out, some paltry handful of Moons, and inert Balls had been—looked at, nicknamed, and marked in the Zodiacal Waybill; so that we can now prate of their Whereabout;

[7] See James 1.17.
[8] Cf. Job xxxviii.4-18.
[9] Reference to the *Traité de Mécanique Céleste* (1799-1825) by the great French astronomer Pierre Simon, Marquis de Laplace (1749-1827).
[10] Sir William Herschel (1738-1822), English astronomer who discovered more than 2,000 nebulae.

their How, their Why, their What, being hid from us, as in the signless Inane?

"System of Nature! To the wisest man, wide as is his vision, Nature remains of quite *infinite* depth, of quite infinite expansion; and all Experience thereof limits itself to some few computed centuries, and measured square-miles. The course of Nature's phases, on this our little fraction of a Planet, is partially known to us: but who knows what deeper courses these depend on; what infinitely larger Cycle (of causes) our little Epicycle revolves on? To the Minnow every cranny and pebble, and quality and accident, of its little native Creek may have become familiar: but does the Minnow understand the Ocean Tides and periodic Currents, the Tradewinds, and Monsoons, and Moon's Eclipses; by all which the condition of its little Creek is regulated, and may, from time to time (*un*miraculously enough), be quite overset and reversed? Such a minnow is Man; his Creek this Planet Earth; his Ocean the immeasurable All; his Monsoons and periodic Currents the mysterious Course of Providence through Æons of Æons.

"We speak of the Volume of Nature: and truly a Volume it is,— whose Author and Writer is God. To read it! Dost thou, does man, so much as well know the Alphabet thereof? With its Words, Sentences, and grand descriptive Pages, poetical and philosophical, spread out through Solar Systems, and Thousands of Years, we shall not try thee. It is a Volume written in celestial hieroglyphs, in the true Sacred-writing; of which even Prophets are happy that they can read here a line and there a line.[11] As for your Institutes, and Academies of Science, they strive bravely; and, from amid the thick-crowded, inextricably inter-twisted hieroglyphic writing, pick out, by dextrous combination, some Letters in the vulgar Character, and therefrom put together this and the other economic Recipe, of high avail in Practice. That Nature is more than some boundless Volume of such Recipes, or huge, well-nigh in-exhaustible Domestic-Cookery Book, of which the whole secret will in this manner one day evolve itself, the fewest dream.

"Custom," continues the Professor, "doth make dotards of us all.[12] Consider well, thou wilt find that Custom is the greatest of Weavers;

---

[11] Cf. Isaiah xxviii.10.
[12] Cf. *Hamlet* iii.i.83: "Thus conscience does make cowards of us all."

and weaves air-raiment for all the Spirits of the Universe: whereby indeed these dwell with us visibly, as ministering servants, in our houses and workshops; but their spiritual nature becomes, to the most, forever hidden. Philosophy complains that Custom has hoodwinked us, from the first; that we do everything by Custom, even Believe by it; that our very Axioms, let us boast of Free-thinking as we may, are oftenest simply such Beliefs as we have never heard questioned. Nay, what is Philosophy throughout but a continual battle against Custom; an ever-renewed effort to *transcend* the sphere of blind Custom, and so become Transcendental?

"Innumerable are the illusions and legerdemain-tricks of Custom: but of all these perhaps the cleverest is her knack of persuading us that the Miraculous, by simple repetition, ceases to be Miraculous. True, it is by this means we live; for man must work as well as wonder: and herein is Custom so far a kind nurse, guiding him to his true benefit. But she is a fond foolish nurse, or rather we are false foolish nurslings, when, in our resting and reflecting hours, we prolong the same deception. Am I to view the Stupendous with stupid indifference, because I have seen it twice, or two-hundred, or two-million times? There is no reason in Nature or in Art why I should: unless, indeed, I am a mere Work-Machine, for whom the divine gift of Thought were no other than the terrestrial gift of Steam is to the Steam-engine; a power whereby cotton might be spun, and money and money's worth realised.

"Notable enough too, here as elsewhere, wilt thou find the potency of Names; which indeed are but one kind of such custom-woven, wonder-hiding Garments. Witchcraft, and all manner of Spectre-work, and Demonology, we have now named Madness, and Diseases of the Nerves. Seldom reflecting that still the new question comes upon us: What is Madness, what are Nerves? Ever, as before, does Madness remain a mysterious-terrific, altogether *infernal* boiling-up of the Nether Chaotic Deep, through this fair-painted Vision of Creation, which swims thereon, which we name the Real. Was Luther's Picture of the Devil [13] less a Reality, whether it were formed within the bodily eye, or without it? In every the wisest Soul lies a whole world of internal Madness, an

[13] Martin Luther threw his inkstand at the Devil, whose apparition appeared to him while he was translating the Bible.

authentic Demon-Empire; out of which, indeed, his world of Wisdom has been creatively built together, and now rests there, as on its dark foundations does a habitable flowery Earth-rind.

"But deepest of all illusory Appearances, for hiding Wonder, as for many other ends, are your two grand fundamental world-enveloping Appearances, SPACE and TIME. These, as spun and woven for us from before Birth itself, to clothe our celestial ME for dwelling here, and yet to blind it,—lie all-embracing, as the universal canvas, or warp and woof, whereby all minor Illusions, in this Phantasm Existence, weave and paint themselves. In vain, while here on Earth, shall you endeavour to strip them off; you can, at best, but rend them asunder for moments, and look through.

"Fortunatus[14] had a wishing Hat, which when he put on, and wished himself Anywhere, behold he was There. By this means had Fortunatus triumphed over Space, he had annihilated Space; for him there was no Where, but all was Here. Were a Hatter to establish himself, in the Wahngasse of Weissnichtwo,[15] and make felts of this sort for all mankind, what a world we should have of it! Still stranger, should, on the opposite side of the street, another Hatter establish himself; and, as his fellow-craftsman made Space-annihilating Hats, make Time-annihilating! Of both would I purchase, were it with my last groschen; but chiefly of this latter. To clap-on your felt, and, simply by wishing that you were Any*where,* straightway to be *There!* Next to clap-on your other felt, and simply by wishing that you were Any*when,* and straightway to be *Then!* This were indeed the grander: shooting at will from the Fire-Creation of the World to its Fire-Consummation; here historically present in the First Century, conversing face to face with Paul and Seneca; there prophetically in the Thirty-first, conversing also face to face with other Pauls and Senecas, who as yet stand hidden in the depth of that late Time!

"Or thinkest thou, it were impossible, unimaginable? Is the Past annihilated, then, or only past; is the Future non-extant or only future? Those mystic faculties of thine, Memory and Hope, already answer: already through those mystic avenues, thou the Earth-blinded summonest

---

[14] The hero of a popular sixteenth-century folk-tale.
[15] Teufelsdröckh's residence in "Dream Alley of I-Know-Not-Where"

both Past and Future, and communest with them, though as yet darkly, and with mute beckonings. The curtains of Yesterday drop down, the curtains of Tomorrow roll up; but Yesterday and Tomorrow both *are*. Pierce through the Time-Element, glance into the Eternal. Believe what thou findest written in the sanctuaries of Man's Soul, even as all Thinkers, in all ages, have devoutly read it there: that Time and Space are not God, but creations of God; that with God as it is a universal HERE, so it is an everlasting NOW.

"And seest thou therein any glimpse of IMMORTALITY?—O Heaven! Is the white Tomb of our Loved One, who died from our arms, and had to be left behind us there, which rises in the distance, like a pale, mournfully receding Milestone, to tell how many toilsome uncheered miles we have journeyed on alone,—but a pale spectral Illusion! Is the lost Friend still mysteriously Here, even as we are Here mysteriously, with God!—Know of a truth that only the Time-shadows have perished, or are perishable; that the real Being of whatever was, and whatever is, and whatever will be, *is* even now and forever. This, should it unhappily seem new, thou mayst ponder at thy leisure; for the next twenty years, or the next twenty centuries: believe it thou must; understand it thou canst not.

"That the Thought-forms, Space and Time, wherein, once for all, we are sent into this Earth to live, should condition and determine our whole Practical reasonings, conceptions, and imagings or imaginings,— seems altogether fit, just, and unavoidable. But that they should, furthermore, usurp such sway over pure spiritual Meditation, and blind us to the wonder everywhere lying close on us, seems nowise so. Admit Space and Time to their due rank as Forms of Thought; nay, even, if thou wilt, to their quite undue rank of Realities: and consider, then, with thyself how their thin disguises hide from us the brightest God-effulgences! Thus, were it not miraculous, could I stretch forth my hand, and clutch the Sun? Yet thou seest me daily stretch forth my hand and therewith clutch many a thing, and swing it hither and thither. Art thou a grown baby, then, to fancy that the Miracle lies in miles of distance, or in pounds avoirdupois of weight; and not to see that the true inexplicable God-revealing Miracle lies in this, that I can stretch forth my hand at all; that I have free Force to clutch aught therewith?

Innumerable other of this sort are the deceptions, and wonder-hiding stupefactions, which Space practises on us.

"Still worse is it with regard to Time. Your grand anti-magician, and universal wonder-hider, is this same lying Time. Had we but the Time-annihilating Hat, to put on for once only, we should see ourselves in a World of Miracles, wherein all fabled or authentic Thaumaturgy, and feats of Magic, were outdone. But unhappily we have not such a Hat; and man, poor fool that he is, can seldom and scantily help himself without one.

"Were it not wonderful, for instance, had Orpheus, or Amphion,[16] built the walls of Thebes by the mere sound of his Lyre? Yet tell me, Who built these walls of Weissnichtwo; summoning out all the sandstone rocks, to dance along from the *Steinbruch*[17] (now a huge Troglodyte Chasm, with frightful green-mantled pools); and shape themselves into Doric and Ionic pillars, squared ashlar houses, and noble streets? Was it not the still higher Orpheus, or Orpheuses, who, in past centuries, by the divine Music of Wisdom, succeeded in civilising man? Our highest Orpheus walked in Judea, eighteen hundred years ago; his sphere-melody, flowing in wild native tones, took captive the ravished souls of men; and, being of a truth sphere-melody, still flows and sounds, though now with thousandfold accompaniments, and rich symphonies, through all our hearts; and modulates, and divinely leads them. Is that a wonder, which happens in two hours; and does it cease to be wonderful if happening in two million? Not only was Thebes built by the music of an Orpheus; but without the music of some inspired Orpheus was no city ever built, no work that man glories in ever done.

"Sweep away the Illusion of Time; glance, if thou have eyes, from the near moving-cause to its far-distant Mover: The stroke that came transmitted through a whole galaxy of elastic balls, was it less a stroke than if the last ball only had been struck, and sent flying? O, could I (with the Time-annihilating Hat) transport thee direct from the Beginnings to the Endings, how were thy eyesight unsealed, and thy heart set flaming in the Light-sea of celestial wonder! Then sawest thou that this

---

[16] The sons of Apollo and Jupiter respectively, famed as musicians. The walls of Thebes were fabled to have built themselves to the music of Amphion's lyre.
[17] Quarry.

fair Universe, were it in the meanest province thereof, is in very deed the star-domed City of God;[18] that through every star, through every grass-blade, and most through every Living Soul, the glory of a present God still beams. But Nature, which is the Time-vesture of God, and reveals Him to the wise, hides Him from the foolish.

"Again, could anything be more miraculous than an actual authentic Ghost? The English Johnson longed, all his life, to see one; but could not, though he went to Cock Lane,[19] and thence to the church-vaults, and tapped on coffins. Foolish Doctor! Did he never, with the mind's eye as well as with the body's, look round him into that full tide of human Life he so loved; did he never so much as look into Himself? The good Doctor was a Ghost, as actual and authentic as heart could wish; well-nigh a million of Ghosts were travelling the streets by his side. Once more I say, sweep away the illusion of Time; compress the threescore years into three minutes: what else was he, what else are we? Are we not Spirits, that are shaped into a body, into an Appearance; and that fade away again into air and Invisibility? This is no metaphor, it is a simple, scientific *fact:* we start out of Nothingness, take figure, and are Apparitions; round us, as round the veriest spectre, is Eternity; and to Eternity minutes are as years and æons. Come there not tones of Love and Faith, as from celestial harp-strings, like the Song of beatified Souls? And again, do not we squeak and gibber[20] (in our discordant, screech-owlish debatings and recriminatings); and glide bodeful and feeble, and fearful; or uproar (*poltern*), and revel in our mad Dance of the Dead,—till the scent of the morning-air[21] summons us to our still Home; and dreamy Night becomes awake and Day? Where now is Alexander of Macedon: does the steel Host, that yelled in fierce battle-shouts at Issus and Arbela,[22] remain behind him; or have they all vanished utterly, even as perturbed Goblins must? Napoleon too, and his Moscow Retreats and Austerlitz Campaigns! Was it all other than

---

[18] The title (*De Civitate Dei*) of St. Augustine's famous work.

[19] The street in London where a ghost was supposed to have appeared. For Samuel Johnson's part in exposing the hoax, see Boswell's *Life* for the year 1763.

[20] Cf. *Hamlet* i.i.116.

[21] Cf. *Hamlet* i.v.58.

[22] Battlefields in Cilicia and Assyria where Alexander defeated the Persians in B.C. 333 and 331.

the veriest Spectre-hunt; which has now, with its howling tumult that made night hideous,[23] flitted away?—Ghosts! There are nigh a thousand-million walking the Earth openly at noontide; some half-hundred have vanished from it, some half-hundred have arisen in it, ere thy watch ticks once.

"O Heaven, it is mysterious, it is awful to consider that we not only carry each a future Ghost within him; but are, in very deed, Ghosts! These Limbs, whence had we them; this stormy Force; this life-blood with its burning Passion? They are dust and shadow;[24] a Shadow-system gathered round our ME; wherein through some moments or years, the Divine Essence is to be revealed in the Flesh. That warrior on his strong war-horse, fire flashes through his eyes; force dwells in his arm and heart: but warrior and war-horse are a vision; a revealed Force, nothing more. Stately they tread the Earth, as if it were a firm substance: fool! the Earth is but a film; it cracks in twain, and warrior and war-horse sink beyond plummet's sounding.[25] Plummet's? Fantasy herself will not follow them. A little while ago they were not; a little while, and they are not, their very ashes are not.

"So it has been from the beginning, so will it be to the end. Generation after generation takes to itself the Form of a Body; and forth-issuing from Cimmerian Night, on Heaven's mission APPEARS. What Force and Fire is in each he expends: one grinding in the mill of Industry; one hunter-like climbing the giddy Alpine heights of Science; one madly dashed in pieces on the rocks of Strife, in war with his fellow:—and then the Heaven-sent is recalled; his earthly Vesture falls away, and soon even to Sense becomes a vanished Shadow. Thus, like some wild-flaming, wild-thundering train of Heaven's Artillery, does this mysterious MANKIND thunder and flame, in long-drawn, quick-succeeding grandeur, through the unknown Deep. Thus, like a God-created, fire-breathing Spirit-host, we emerge from the Inane; haste stormfully across the astonished Earth; then plunge again into the Inane. Earth's mountains are levelled, and her seas filled up, in our passage: can the Earth, which is but dead and a vision, resist Spirits which have reality and are alive?

[23] Cf. *Hamlet* i.iv.54.
[24] Horace's "pulvis et umbra" (*Odes* iv.vii.16).
[25] Cf. *The Tempest* v.i.56.

On the hardest adamant some footprint of us is stamped-in; the last Rear of the host will read traces of the earliest Van. But whence?— O Heaven, whither? Sense knows not; Faith knows not; only that it is through Mystery to Mystery, from God and to God.

> We *are such stuff*
> "As Dreams are made on, and our little Life
> Is rounded with a sleep!" [26]

[26] See *The Tempest* iv.i.156-158.

Alfred Tennyson
1809-1892

In Memoriam

The following lyrics are taken from *In Memoriam* (1850), the elegy which Tennyson composed in memory of the dearest friend of his youth, Arthur Henry Hallam (1811-1833). The entire poem, consisting of 131 numbered lyrics and a Prologue and Epilogue, was not published until the year when Tennyson became Poet Laureate, seventeen years after his friend's death, the author having written the earlier poems to give vent to his grief with no thought of committing to print utterances so private. Most modern criticism concurs with the opinion expressed by T. S. Eliot in his essay on *In Memoriam* (1936): "Its faith is a poor thing, but its doubt is a very intense experience." This view, however, might well be revised in the light of contemporary philosophy; the affirmation to which Tennyson ultimately wins through exemplifies admirably what the American psychologist William James called "the will to believe."

54

O, yet we trust that somehow good
    Will be the final goal of ill,
    To pangs of nature, sins of will,
Defects of doubt, and taints of blood;

That nothing walks with aimless feet;
    That not one life shall be destroy'd,

Or cast as rubbish to the void,
When God hath made the pile complete;

That not a worm is cloven in vain;
    That not a moth with vain desire   10
    Is shrivell'd in a fruitless fire,
Or but subserves another's gain.

Behold, we know not anything;
    I can but trust that good shall fall!
    At last—far off—at last, to all,
And every winter change to spring.

So runs my dream; but what am I?
    An infant crying in the night;
    An infant crying for the light,
And with no language but a cry.   20

55

The wish, that of the living whole
    No life may fail beyond the grave,
    Derives it not from what we have
The likest God within the soul?

Are God and Nature then at strife,
    That Nature lends such evil dreams?
    So careful of the type she seems,
So careless of the single life,

That I, considering everywhere
    Her secret meaning in her deeds,   10
    And finding that of fifty seeds
She often brings but one to bear,

I falter where I firmly trod,
    And falling with my weight of cares
    Upon the great world's altar-stairs
That slope thro' darkness up to God,

I stretch lame hands of faith, and grope,
    And gather dust and chaff, and call
    To what I feel is Lord of all,
And faintly trust the larger hope.[1]   20

56

'So careful of the type?' but no.
    From scarped cliff and quarried stone[2]
    She cries, 'A thousand types are gone;
I care for nothing, all shall go.

'Thou makest thine appeal to me.
    I bring to life, I bring to death;
    The spirit does but mean the breath:
I know no more.' And he, shall he,

Man, her last work, who seem'd so fair,
    Such splendid purpose in his eyes,   10
    Who roll'd the psalm to wintry skies,
Who built him fanes of fruitless prayer,

Who trusted God was love indeed
    And love Creation's final law—
    Tho' Nature, red in tooth and claw
With ravine, shriek'd against his creed—

Who loved, who suffer'd countless ills,
    Who battled for the True, the Just,
    Be blown about the desert dust,
Or seal'd within the iron hills?   20

No more? A monster then, a dream,
    A discord. Dragons of the prime,[3]

[1] In Tennyson's own interpretation, the larger hope is "that the whole human race would through, perhaps, ages of suffering, be at length purified and saved."
[2] Geological formations, containing the fossils of extinct species.
[3] The monsters of prehistoric times.

That tare each other in their slime,
Were mellow music match'd with him.

O life as futile, then, as frail!
     O for thy voice[4] to soothe and bless!
     What hope of answer, or redress?
Behind the veil, behind the veil.

118

Contemplate all this work of Time,
     The giant labouring in his youth;
     Nor dream of human love and truth,
As dying Nature's earth and lime;

But trust that those we call the dead
     Are breathers of an ampler day
     For ever nobler ends. They say,
The solid earth whereon we tread

In tracts of fluent heat began,
     And grew to seeming-random forms,   10
     The seeming prey of cyclic storms,
Till at the last arose the man;

Who throve and branch'd from clime to clime,
     The herald of a higher race,
     And of himself in higher place,
If so he type this work of time

Within himself, from more to more;
     Or, crown'd with attributes of woe
     Like glories, move his course, and show
That life is not as idle ore,   20

But iron dug from central gloom,
     And heated hot with burning fears,
     And dipt in baths of hissing tears,
And batter'd with the shocks of doom

[4] The voice of Hallam.

To shape and use. Arise and fly
    The reeling Faun, the sensual feast;
    Move upward, working out the beast,
And let the ape and tiger die.

120

I trust I have not wasted breath:
    I think we are not wholly brain,
    Magnetic mockeries;[5] not in vain,
Like Paul with beasts,[6] I fought with Death;

Not only cunning casts in clay:
    Let Science prove we are, and then
    What matters Science unto men,
At least to me? I would not stay.

Let him, the wiser man who springs
    Hereafter, up from childhood shape   10
    His action like the greater ape,
But I was *born* to other things.

123

There rolls the deep where grew the tree.
    O earth, what changes hast thou seen!
    There where the long street roars hath been
The stillness of the central sea.

The hills are shadows, and they flow
    From form to form, and nothing stands;
    They melt like mist, the solid lands,
Like clouds they shape themselves and go.

But in my spirit will I dwell,
    And dream my dream, and hold it true;   10
    For tho' my lips may breathe adieu,
I cannot think the thing farewell.

[5] Electrical machines.
[6] Cf. I Corinthians xv.32.

124

That which we dare invoke to bless;
　　Our dearest faith; our ghastliest doubt;
　　He, They, One, All; within, without;
The Power in darkness whom we guess,—

I found Him not in world or sun,
　　Or eagle's wing, or insect's eye,
　　Nor thro' the questions men may try,
The petty cobwebs we have spun.

If e'er when faith had fall'n asleep,
　　I heard a voice, 'believe no more,'　　　　10
　　And heard an ever-breaking shore
That tumbled in the Godless deep,

A warmth within the breast would melt
　　The freezing reason's colder part,
　　And like a man in wrath the heart
Stood up and answer'd, 'I have felt.'

No, like a child in doubt and fear:
　　But that blind clamour made me wise;
　　Then was I as a child that cries,
But, crying, knows his father near;　　　　20

And what I am beheld again
　　What is, and no man understands;
　　And out of darkness came the hands
That reach thro' nature, moulding men.

128

The love that rose on stronger wings,
　　Unpalsied when he met with Death,
　　Is comrade of the lesser faith
That sees the course of human things.

No doubt vast eddies in the flood
　　Of onward time shall yet be made,

And throned races may degrade;[7]
Yet O ye mysteries of good,

Wild Hours that fly with Hope and Fear,
    If all your office had to do   10
    With old results that look like new—
If this were all your mission here,

To draw, to sheathe a useless sword,
    To fool the crowd with glorious lies,
    To cleave a creed in sects and cries,
To change the bearing of a word,

To shift an arbitrary power,
    To cramp the student at his desk,
    To make old bareness picturesque
And tuft with grass a feudal tower,   20

Why, then my scorn might well descend
    On you and yours. I see in part
    That all, as in some piece of art,
Is toil coöperant to an end.

130

Thy voice is on the rolling air;
    I hear thee where the waters run;
    Thou standest in the rising sun,
And in the setting thou art fair.

What art thou then? I cannot guess;
    But tho' I seem in star and flower
    To feel thee some diffusive power,
I do not therefore love thee less.

My love involves the love before;
    My love is vaster passion now;   10
    Tho' mix'd with God and Nature thou,
I seem to love thee more and more.

[7] Degenerate.

Far off thou art, but ever nigh;
    I have thee still, and I rejoice;
    I prosper, circled with thy voice;
I shall not lose thee tho' I die.

James Thomson
1834-1882

The City of Dreadful Night

The following selections are from the long philosophic poem *The City of Dreadful Night* (1874). Thomson doubtless derived his nightmare setting from the streets of London which, as an insomniac, he wandered by night. The use of the city to symbolize the spiritual wasteland of modern life may well bring to mind the similar treatment of urban landscapes in much nineteenth-century writing, notably in the novels of Charles Dickens and the poetry of Charles Baudelaire.

PROEM

Lo, thus, as prostrate, "In the dust I write
  My heart's deep languor and my soul's sad tears."
Yet why evoke the spectres of black night
  To blot the sunshine of exultant years?
Why disinter dead faith from mouldering hidden?
Why break the seals of mute despair unbidden,
  And wail life's discords into careless ears?

Because a cold rage seizes one at whiles
  To show the bitter old and wrinkled truth
Stripped naked of all vesture that beguiles,   10
  False dreams, false hopes, false masks and modes of youth;
Because it gives some sense of power and passion
In helpless impotence to try to fashion
  Our woe in living words howe'er uncouth.

Surely I write not for the hopeful young,
  Or those who deem their happiness of worth,
Or such as pasture and grow fat among
  The shows of life and feel nor doubt nor dearth,
Or pious spirits with a God above them
To sanctify and glorify and love them,   20
  Or sages who foresee a heaven on earth.

For none of these I write, and none of these
  Could read the writing if they deigned to try:
So may they flourish, in their due degrees,
  On our sweet earth and in their unplaced sky.
If any cares for the weak words here written,
It must be someone desolate, Fate-smitten,
  Whose faith and hope are dead, and who would die.

Yes, here and there some weary wanderer
  In that same city of tremendous night,   30
Will understand the speech, and feel a stir
  Of fellowship in all-disastrous fight;
"I suffer mute and lonely, yet another
Uplifts his voice to let me know a brother
  Travels the same wild paths though out of sight."

O sad Fraternity, do I unfold
  Your dolorous mysteries shrouded from of yore?
Nay, be assured; no secret can be told
  To any who divined it not before:
None uninitiate by many a presage   40
Will comprehend the language of the message,
  Although proclaimed aloud for evermore.

I

The City is of Night; perchance of Death,
  But certainly of Night; for never there
Can come the lucid morning's fragrant breath
  After the dewy dawning's cold grey air;

The moon and stars may shine with scorn or pity;
The sun has never visited that city,
   For it dissolveth in the daylight fair.

Dissolveth like a dream of night away;   50
   Though present in distempered gloom of thought
And deadly weariness of heart all day.
   But when a dream night after night is brought
Throughout a week, and such weeks few or many
Recur each year for several years, can any
   Discern that dream from real life in aught?

For life is but a dream whose shapes return,
   Some frequently, some seldom, some by night
And some by day, some night and day: we learn,
   The while all change and many vanish quite,   60
In their recurrence with recurrent changes
A certain seeming order; where this ranges
   We count things real; such is memory's might.

A river girds the city west and south,
   The main north channel of a broad lagoon,
Regurging[1] with the salt tides from the mouth;
   Waste marshes shine and glister to the moon
For leagues, then moorland black, then stony ridges;
Great piers and causeways, many noble bridges,
   Connect the town and islet suburbs strewn.   70

Upon an easy slope it lies at large,
   And scarcely overlaps the long curved crest
Which swells out two leagues, from the river marge.
   A trackless wilderness rolls north and west,
Savannahs, savage woods, enormous mountains,
Bleak uplands, black ravines with torrent fountains;
   And eastward rolls the shipless sea's unrest.

The city is not ruinous, although
   Great ruins of an unremembered past,

[1] Surging back.

With others of a few short years ago   80
　　More sad, are found within its precincts vast.
The street-lamps always burn; but scarce a casement
In house or palace front from roof to basement
　　Doth glow or gleam athwart the mirk air cast.

The street-lamps burn amidst the baleful glooms,
　　Amidst the soundless solitudes immense
Of rangèd mansions dark and still as tombs.
　　The silence which benumbs or strains the sense
Fulfils with awe the soul's despair unweeping:
Myriads of habitants are ever sleeping,   90
　　Or dead, or fled from nameless pestilence!

Yet as in some necropolis you find
　　Perchance one mourner to a thousand dead,
So there; worn faces that look deaf and blind
　　Like tragic masks of stone. With weary tread,
Each wrapped in his own doom, they wander, wander,
Or sit foredone and desolately ponder
　　Through sleepless hours with heavy drooping head.

Mature men chiefly, few in age or youth,
　　A woman rarely, now and then a child: 100
A child! If here the heart turns sick with ruth
　　To see a little one from birth defiled,
Or lame or blind, as preordained to languish
Through youthless life, think how it bleeds with anguish
　　To meet one erring[2] in that homeless wild.

They often murmur to themselves, they speak
　　To one another seldom, for their woe
Broods maddening inwardly and scorns to wreak
　　Itself abroad; and if at whiles it grow
To frenzy which must rave, none heeds the clamour,   110
Unless there waits some victim of like glamour,
　　To rave in turn, who lends attentive show.

[2] Wandering.

225

The City is of Night, but not of Sleep;
   There sweet sleep is not for the weary brain;
The pitiless hours like years and ages creep,
   A night seems termless hell. This dreadful strain
Of thought and consciousness, which never ceases,
Or which some moments' stupor but increases,
   This, worse than woe, makes wretches there insane.

They leave all hope behind who enter there;[3]   120
   One certitude while sane they cannot leave,
One anodyne for torture and despair;
   The certitude of Death, which no reprieve
Can put off long; and which, divinely tender,
But waits the outstretched hand to promptly render
   That draft whose slumber nothing can bereave.[4]

14

Large glooms were gathered in the mighty fane,
   With tinted moongleams slanting here and there;
And all was hush: no swelling organ-strain,
   No chant, no voice or murmuring of prayer;
No priests came forth, no tinkling censers fumed,
And the high altar space was unillumed.

Around the pillars and against the walls
   Leaned men and shadows; others seemed to brood
Bent or recumbent, in secluded stalls.
   Perchance they were not a great multitude   10
Save in that city of so lonely streets
Where one may count up every face he meets.

---

[3] Cf. the inscription over Hell's portal in Dante's *Divine Comedy* (*Inferno* iii.9): "Abandon all hope, ye who enter."

[4] Though the Garden of thy Life be wholly waste, the sweet flowers withered, the fruit-trees barren, over its wall hang ever the rich dark clusters of the Vine of Death, within easy reach of thy hand, which may pluck of them when it will. [Thomson's note.]

All patiently awaited the event
   Without a stir or sound, as if no less
Self-occupied, doomstricken, while attent.
   And then we heard a voice of solemn stress
From the dark pulpit, and our gaze there met
Two eyes which burned as never eyes burned yet:

Two steadfast and intolerable eyes
   Burning beneath a broad and rugged brow;   20
The head behind it of enormous size.
   And as black fir-groves in a large wind bow,
Our rooted congregation, gloom-arrayed,
By that great sad voice deep and full were swayed:—

"O melancholy Brothers, dark, dark, dark!
O battling in black floods without an ark!
   O spectral wanderers of unholy Night!
My soul hath bled for you these sunless years,
With bitter blood-drops running down like tears:
   Oh, dark, dark, dark, withdrawn from joy and light!   30

"My heart is sick with anguish for your bale!
Your woe hath been my anguish; yea, I quail
   And perish in your perishing unblest.
And I have searched the heights and depths, the scope
Of all our universe, with desperate hope
   To find some solace for your wild unrest.

"And now at last authentic word I bring,
Witnessed by every dead and living thing;
   Good tidings of great joy for you, for all;
There is no God; no Fiend with names divine   40
Made us and tortures us; if we must pine,
   It is to satiate no Being's gall.

"It was the dark delusion of a dream,
That living Person conscious and supreme,
   Whom we must curse for cursing us with life;

227

Whom we must curse because the life He gave
Could not be buried in the quiet grave,
   Could not be killed by poison or by knife.

"This little life is all we must endure,
The grave's most holy peace is ever sure,   50
   We fall asleep and never wake again;
Nothing is of us but the mouldering flesh,
Whose elements dissolve and merge afresh
   In earth, air, water, plants, and other men.

"We finish thus; and all our wretched race
Shall finish with its cycle, and give place
   To other beings, with their own time-doom:
Infinite æons ere our kind began;
Infinite æons after the last man
   Has joined the mammoth in earth's tomb and womb.   60

"We bow down to the universal laws,
Which never had for man a special clause
   Of cruelty or kindness, love or hate:
If toads and vultures are obscene to sight,
If tigers burn with beauty and with might,[5]
   Is it by favour or by wrath of fate?

"All substance lives and struggles evermore
Through countless shapes continually at war,
   By countless interactions interknit:
If one is born a certain day on earth,   70
All times and forces tended to that birth,
   Not all the world could change or hinder it.

"I find no hint throughout the Universe
Of good or ill, of blessing or of curse;
   I find alone Necessity Supreme;

[5] Cf. William Blake's well-known poem "Tyger! Tyger! burning bright . . ."

With infinite Mystery, abysmal, dark,
Unlighted ever by the faintest spark
   For us the flitting shadows of a dream.

"O Brothers of sad lives! they are so brief;
A few short years must bring us all relief: 80
   Can we not bear these years of labouring breath?
But if you would not this poor life fulfil,
Lo, you are free to end it when you will,
   Without the fear of waking after death."—

The organ-like vibrations of his voice
   Thrilled through the vaulted aisles and died away;
The yearning of the tones which bade rejoice
   Was sad and tender as a requiem lay:
Our shadowy congregation rested still
As brooding on that "End it when you will."   90

Thomas Hardy
1840-1928

Nature's Questioning
In Tenebris II

🐿 "Nature's Questioning" first appeared in *Wessex Poems and Other Verses* (1898); "In Tenebris II," the second of three poems bearing this title, in *Poems of the Past and the Present* (1902). Although he is today better known for his novels, Hardy devoted the later years of his long life exclusively to poetry; and it is the poems which best express his pessimistic philosophy, with its adjuncts of tender pity and unflinching honesty.

NATURE'S QUESTIONING

When I look forth at dawning, pool,
    Field, flock, and lonely tree,
    All seem to gaze at me
Like chastened children sitting silent in a school;

    Their faces dulled, constrained, and worn,
        As though the master's ways
        Through the long teaching days
Had cowed them till their early zest was overborne.

    Upon them stirs in lippings[1] mere
        (As if once clear in call,   10
        But now scarce breathed at all)—
    "We wonder, ever wonder, why we find us here!

[1] Murmurings.

"Has some Vast Imbecility,
   Mighty to build and blend,
   But impotent to tend,
Framed us in jest, and left us now to hazardry?

"Or come we of an Automaton
   Unconscious of our pains? . . .
   Or are we live remains
Of Godhead dying downwards, brain and eye now gone?   20

"Or is it that some high Plan betides,
   As yet not understood,
   Of Evil stormed by Good,
We the Forlorn Hope over which Achievement strides?"

Thus things around. No answerer I . . .
   Meanwhile the winds, and rains,
   And Earth's old glooms and pains
Are still the same, and Life and Death are neighbours nigh.

IN TENEBRIS

II

"Considerabam ad dexteram, et videbam; et non erat qui cognosceret me. . . .
Non est qui requirat animam meam,"—*Ps.* cxli.[1]

When the clouds' swoln bosoms echo back the shouts of the many and
      strong
That things are all as they best may be, save a few to be right ere long,
And my eyes have not the vision in them to discern what to these is
      so clear,
The blot seems straightway in me alone; one better he were not here.

[1] The motto is taken from the Vulgate, given as follows in the King James Version: "I looked on my right hand, and beheld, but there was no man that would
know me . . . no man cared for my soul" (Psalms cxlii.4).

The stout upstanders say, All's well with us: ruers have nought to
    rue!
And what the potent say so oft, can it fail to be somewhat true?
Breezily go they, breezily come; their dust smokes around their career,
Till I think I am one born out of due time, who has no calling here.

Their dawns bring lusty joys, it seems; their evenings all that is
    sweet;
Our times are blessed times, they cry: Life shapes it as is most meet,   10
And nothing is much the matter; there are many smiles to a tear;
Then what is the matter is I, I say. Why should such an one be
    here? . . .

Let him in whose ears the low-voiced Best is killed by the clash of the
    First,
Who holds that if way to the Better there be, it exacts a full look at
    the Worst,
Who feels that delight is a delicate growth cramped by crookedness,
    custom, and fear,
Get him up and be gone as one shaped awry; he disturbs the order
    here.

Alfred Edward Housman
1859-1936

"Terence, this is stupid stuff . . ."

The following poem is the next to the last (62) in
A Shropshire Lad (1896). The proper name in the
title is explained by the fact that Housman's original
title for his collection was *The Poems of Terence
Hearsay.*

"Terence, this is stupid stuff:
You eat your victuals fast enough;
There can't be much amiss, 'tis clear,
To see the rate you drink your beer.
But, oh, good Lord, the verse you make,
It gives a chap the bellyache.
The cow, the old cow, she is dead;
It sleeps well, the horned head.
We poor lads, 'tis our turn now
To hear such tunes as killed the cow.   **10**
Pretty friendship 'tis to rime
Your friends to death before their time
Moping melancholy mad.
Come, pipe a tune to dance to, lad."

Why, if 'tis dancing you would be,
There's brisker pipes than poetry.
Say, for what were hopyards meant,
Or why was Burton built on Trent? [1]

[1] Burton-upon-Trent in Derbyshire is one of the chief centers for brewing beer in
England. Its brewers were frequently elevated to the peerage.

Oh, many a peer of England brews
Livelier liquor than the Muse,   20
And malt does more than Milton can
To justify God's ways to man.[2]
Ale, man, ale's the stuff to drink
For fellows whom it hurts to think;
Look into the pewter pot
To see the world as the world's not.
And faith, 'tis pleasant till 'tis past;
The mischief is that 'twill not last.
Oh, I have been to Ludlow[3] fair
And left my necktie God knows where,   30
And carried halfway home, or near,
Pints and quarts of Ludlow beer.
Then the world seemed none so bad,
And I myself a sterling lad;
And down in lovely muck I've lain,
Happy till I woke again.
Then I saw the morning sky—
Heigho, the tale was all a lie;
The world, it was the old world yet,
I was I, my things were wet,   40
And nothing now remained to do
But begin the game anew.

    Therefore, since the world has still
Much good, but much less good than ill,
And while the sun and moon endure
Luck's a chance, but trouble's sure,
I'd face it as a wise man would,
And train for ill and not for good.
'Tis true, the stuff I bring for sale
Is not so brisk a brew as ale;   50

[2] Cf. *Paradise Lost* 1.26.
[3] A town in the south of Shropshire.

Out of a stem that scored the hand
I wrung it in a weary land.
But take it—if the smack is sour,
The better for the embittered hour;
It should do good to heart and head
When your soul is in my soul's stead;
And I will friend you, if I may,
In the dark and cloudy day.

There was a king reigned in the East;
There, when kings will sit to feast,   60
They get their fill before they think
With poisoned meat and poisoned drink.
He gathered all that springs to birth
From the many-venomed earth;
First a little, thence to more,
He sampled all her killing store;
And easy, smiling, seasoned sound,
Sate the king when healths went round.
They put arsenic in his meat
And stared aghast to watch him eat;   70
They poured strychnine in his cup
And shook to see him drink it up.
They shook, they stared as white's their shirt;
Them it was their poison hurt.
—I tell the tale that I heard told.
Mithridates, he died old.[4]

[4] Pliny tells this tale of Mithridates VI, king of Pontus (120-63 B.C.), in his *Natural History* xxv.2.

Algernon Charles Swinburne
1837-1909

Prelude to *Songs before Sunrise*

🐚 As the title suggests, the present poem introduces *Songs before Sunrise* (1871). This volume marked a significant thematic shift from Swinburne's *Poems and Ballads* of 1866; the unabashed sensuality of the earlier collection has given way to poetry no less passionately intense, but devoted now to celebrating the emancipation of the human spirit from its agelong subjection to political and theological tyranny. In the following lines the poet traces the psychological progression through which he outgrew the role of Victorian *enfant terrible* to become the zealous prophet of the Religion of Humanity.

Between the green bud and the red
Youth sat and sang by Time, and shed
   From eyes and tresses flowers and tears,
   From heart and spirit hopes and fears,
Upon the hollow stream whose bed
   Is channeled by the foamless years;
And with the white the gold-haired head
   Mixed running locks, and in Time's ears
Youth's dreams hung singing, and Time's truth
Was half not harsh in the ears of Youth.   **10**

Between the bud and the blown flower
Youth talked with joy and grief an hour,

With footless joy and wingless grief
And twin-born faith and disbelief
Who share the seasons to devour;
    And long ere these made up their sheaf
Felt the winds round him shake and shower
    The rose-red and the blood-red leaf,
Delight whose germ grew never grain,
And passion dyed in its own pain.   **20**

Then he stood up, and trod to dust
Fear and desire, mistrust and trust,
    And dreams of bitter sleep and sweet,
    And bound for sandals on his feet
Knowledge and patience of what must
    And what things may be, in the heat
And cold of years that rot and rust
    And alter; and his spirit's meat
Was freedom, and his staff was wrought
Of strength, and his cloak woven of thought.   **30**

For what has he whose will sees clear
To do with doubt and faith and fear,
    Swift hopes and slow despondencies?
    His heart is equal with the sea's
And with the sea-wind's, and his ear
    Is level to the speech of these,
And his soul communes and takes cheer
    With the actual earth's equalities,
Air, light, and night, hills, winds, and streams,
And seeks not strength from strengthless dreams.[1] **40**

His soul is even with the sun
Whose spirit and whose eye are one,
    Who seeks not stars by day, nor light
    And heavy heat of day by night.

[1] Religious beliefs; Swinburne's anti-Christian bias is apparent throughout this poem.

Him can no God cast down, whom none
　Can lift in hope beyond the height
Of fate and nature and things done
　By the calm rule of might and right
That bids men be and bear and do,
And die beneath blind skies or blue.　　　　　50

To him the lights of even and morn
Speak no vain things of love or scorn,
　Fancies and passions miscreate[2]
　By man in things dispassionate.
Nor holds he fellowship forlorn
　With souls that pray and hope and hate,
And doubt they had better not been born,
　And fain would lure or scare off fate
And charm their doomsman from their doom
And make fear dig its own false tomb.　　　　60

He builds not half of doubts and half
Of dreams his own soul's cenotaph,
　Whence hopes and fears with helpless eyes,
　Wrapped loose in cast-off cerecloths,[3] rise
And dance and wring their hands and laugh,
　And weep thin tears and sigh light sighs,
And without living lips would quaff
　The living spring in man that lies,
And drain his soul of faith and strength
It might have lived on a life's length.　　　　70

He hath given himself and hath not sold
To God for heaven or man for gold,
　Or grief for comfort that it gives,
　Or joy for grief's restoratives.
He hath given himself to time, whose fold
　Shuts in the mortal flock that lives

[2] Unnaturally conceived.
[3] Burial garments.

238

On its plain pasture's heat and cold
  And the equal year's alternatives.
Earth, heaven, and time, death, life, and he,
Endure while they shall be to be.   80

"Yet between death and life are hours
To flush with love and hide in flowers;
  What profit save in these?" men cry:
  "Ah, see, between soft earth and sky,
What only good things here are ours!"
  They say, "What better wouldst thou try,
What sweeter sing of? or what powers
  Serve, that will give thee ere thou die
More joy to sing and be less sad,
More heart to play and grow more glad?"   90

Play then and sing; we too have played,
We likewise, in that subtle shade.
  We too have twisted through our hair
  Such tendrils as the wild Loves wear,
And heard what mirth the Mænads[4] made,
  Till the wind blew our garlands bare
And left their roses disarrayed,
  And smote the summer with strange air,
And disengirdled and discrowned
The limbs and locks that vine-wreaths bound.   100

We too have tracked by star-proof trees
The tempest of the Thyiades[5]
  Scare the loud night on hills that hid
  The blood-feasts of the Bassarid,[6]

---

    [4] Orgiastic female worshippers of Dionysus or Bacchus, the Greek god of wine and fertility.
    [5] Literally, "daughters of Thyas," the first devotee of Dionysus. These stanzas describe the frenzied rites with which women celebrated the Dionysian cult.
    [6] A votary of Dionysus, especially in Thrace, where the god was worshipped with animal sacrifices.

Heard their song's iron cadences
  Fright the wolf hungering from the kid,
Outroar the lion-throated seas,
  Outchide the north-wind if it chid,
And hush the torrent-tongued ravines
With thunders of their tambourines.   110

But the fierce flute whose notes acclaim
Dim goddesses of fiery fame,
  Cymbal and clamorous kettledrum,
  Timbrels and tabrets,[7] all are dumb
That turned the high chill air to flame;
  The singing tongues of fire are numb
That called on Cotys[8] by her name
  Edonian, till they felt her come
And maddened, and her mystic face
Lightened along the streams of Thrace.   120

For Pleasure slumberless and pale,
And Passion with rejected veil,
  Pass, and the tempest-footed throng
  Of hours that follow them with song
Till their feet flag and voices fail,
  And lips that were so loud so long
Learn silence, or a wearier wail;
  So keen is change, and time so strong,
To weave the robes of life and rend
And weave again till life have end.   130

But weak is change, but strengthless time,
To take the light from heaven, or climb
  The hills of heaven with wasting feet.
  Songs they can stop that earth found meet,
But the stars keep their ageless rhyme;
  Flowers they can slay that spring thought sweet,

[7] Various kinds of small drums, like tambourines.
[8] Cotytto, a goddess whose licentious cult was associated with Mt. Edon in Thrace.

But the stars keep their spring sublime;
  Passions and pleasures can defeat,
Actions and agonies control,
And life and death, but not the soul.   140

Because man's soul is man's God still,
What wind soever waft his will
  Across the waves of day and night
  To port or shipwreck, left or right,
By shores and shoals of good and ill;
  And still its flame at mainmast height
Through the rent air that foam-flakes fill
  Sustains the indomitable light
Whence only man hath strength to steer
Or helm to handle without fear.   150

Save his own soul's light overhead,
None leads him, and none ever led,
  Across birth's hidden harbor-bar,
  Past youth where shoreward shallows are,
Through age that drives on toward the red
  Vast void of sunset hailed from far,
To the equal waters of the dead;
  Save his own soul he hath no star,
And sinks, except his own soul guide,
Helmless in middle turn of tide.   160

No blast of air or fire of sun
Puts out the light whereby we run
  With girded loins our lamplit race.[9]
  And each from each takes heart of grace
And spirit till his turn be done,
  And light of face from each man's face
In whom the light of trust is one;
  Since only souls that keep their place

[9] Reference to the lampadedromy, a relay race of ancient Greece run in honor of some deity, in which each runner handed on to his successor a lighted torch.

By their own light, and watch things roll,
And stand, have light for any soul.   170

A little time we gain from time
To set our seasons in some chime,
   For harsh or sweet or loud or low,
   With seasons played out long ago
And souls that in their time and prime
   Took part with summer or with snow,
Lived abject lives out or sublime,
   And had their chance of seed to sow
For service or disservice done
To those days dead and this their son.   180

A little time that we may fill
Or with such good works or such ill
   As loose the bonds or make them strong
   Wherein all manhood suffers wrong.
By rose-hung river and light-foot rill
   There are who rest not; who think long
Till they discern as from a hill
   At the sun's hour of morning song,
Known of souls only, and those souls free,
The sacred spaces of the sea.   190

George Meredith

1828-1909

Hard Weather

🕮 This poem was included in the volume entitled *A
Reading of Earth* (1888). A novelist as well as a poet,
Meredith like Hardy found poetry the best medium
for expressing his philosophic ideas. The present
selection illustrates the dynamic interrelationship of
the three orders of being which Meredith called
blood, brain, and spirit. The evolutionary process, as
the poet believed, was leading toward their harmonious
fusion in the noblest types of men and women.

Bursts from a rending East in flaws[1]
The young green leaflet's harrier, sworn
To strew the garden, strip the shaws,[2]
And show our Spring with banner torn.
Was ever such virago morn?
The wind has teeth, the wind has claws.
All the wind's wolves through woods are loose,
The wild wind's falconry aloft.
Shrill underfoot the grassblade shrews,[3]
At gallop, clumped, and down the croft   10
Bestrid by shadows, beaten, tossed;
It seems a scythe, it seems a rod.

[1] Sharp gusts.
[2] Thickets or groves.
[3] Scolds in a shrewish manner.

243

The howl is up at the howl's accost;
The shivers greet and the shivers nod.

Is the land ship? we are rolled, we drive
Tritonly,[4] cleaving hiss and hum;
Whirl with the dead, or mount or dive,
Or down in dregs, or on in scum.
And drums the distant, pipes the near,
And vale and hill are grey in grey,   20
As when the surge is crumbling sheer,
And sea-mews wing the haze of spray.
Clouds—are they bony witches?—swarm,
Darting swift on the robber's flight,
Hurry an infant sky in arms:
It peeps, it becks;[5] 'tis day, 'tis night.
Black while over the loop of blue
The swathe is closed, like shroud on corse.[6]
Lo, as if swift the Furies flew,
The Fates at heel at a cry to horse!   30

Interpret me the savage whirr:
And is it Nature scourged, or she,
Her offspring's executioner,
Reducing land to barren sea?
But is there meaning in a day
When this fierce angel of the air,
Intent to throw, and haply slay,
Can, for what breath of life we bear
Exact the wrestle? Call to mind
The many meanings glistening up   40
When Nature to her nurslings kind,
Hands them the fruitage and the cup!
And seek we rich significance
Not otherwhere than with those tides

4 Like Triton (a sea demigod).
5 Beckons.
6 Corpse.

Of pleasure on the sunned expanse,
Whose flow deludes, whose ebb derides?

Look in the face of men who fare
Lock-mouthed, a match in lungs and thews
For this fierce angel of the air,
To twist with him and take his bruise.   50
That is the face beloved of old
Of Earth, young mother of her brood:
Nor broken for us shows the mould
When muscle is in mind renewed:
Though farther from her nature rude,
Yet nearer to her spirit's hold:
And though of gentler mood serene,
Still forceful of her fountain-jet.
So shall her blows be shrewdly met,
Be luminously read the scene   60
Where Life is at her grindstone set,
That she may give us edgeing keen,
String us for battle, till as play
The common strokes of fortune shower.
Such meaning in a dagger-day[7]
Our wits may clasp to wax in power—
Yea, feel us warmer at her breast,
By spin of blood in lusty drill,
Than when her honeyed hands caressed,
And Pleasure, sapping, seemed to fill.   70

Behold the life at ease; it drifts.
The sharpened life commands its course.
She winnows, winnows roughly; sifts,
To dip her chosen in her source:
Contention is the vital force,
Whence pluck they brain, her prize of gifts,
Sky of the senses! on which height,
Not disconnected, yet released,

[7] A day of threatening weather.

They see how spirit comes to light,
Through conquest of the inner beast,   80
Which Measure tames to movement sane,
In harmony with what is fair.
Never is Earth misread by brain:
That is the welling[8] of her, there
The mirror—with one step beyond,
For likewise is it voice; and more,
Benignest kinship bids respond,
When wail the weak, and then restore
Whom days as fell as this may rive,[9]
While Earth sits ebon in her gloom,   90
Us atomies[10] of life alive
Unheeding, bent on life to come.
Her children of the labouring brain,
These are the champions of the race,
True parents, and the sole humane,
With understanding for their base.
Earth yields the milk, but all her mind
Is vowed to thresh for stouter stock.
Her passion for old giantkind,
That scaled the mount, uphurled the rock,[11] 100
Devolves on them who read aright
Her meaning and devoutly serve;
Nor in her starlessness of night
Peruse her with the craven nerve:
But even as she from grass to corn,
To eagle high from grubbing mole,
Prove in strong brain her noblest born,
The station for the flight of soul.

[8] The meaning is that human intelligence has its source in and wells forth from Earth.

[9] Tear or rend asunder.

[10] Atoms; tiny particles.

[11] Reference to the Giants or Gigantes in Greek myth; they were demigods who rose in rebellion against the tyranny of Zeus.

Gerard Manley Hopkins

1844-1889

God's Grandeur

That Nature is a Heraclitean Fire . . .

   The first collection of Hopkins' poems, prepared by his friend and literary executor, the Poet Laureate Robert Bridges, did not appear until 1918, twenty-nine years after his death. "God's Grandeur" was written in 1877 and "That Nature is a Heraclitean Fire and of the Comfort of the Resurrection" in 1888. The ancient Greek philosopher Heraclitus (c. 535-c. 475 B.C.) maintained that all things originate from fire, the primal material of creation, and that they are constantly in flux as they come into existence and return to their native element. Hopkins converts Heraclitus' materialistic teaching into a Christian celebration of the meaning of the Resurrection.

GOD'S GRANDEUR

The world is charged with the grandeur of God.
It will flame out, like shining from shook foil;[1]
It gathers to a greatness, like the ooze of oil
Crushed.[2] Why do men then now not reck[3] his rod?

---

[1] Hopkins explained this image as follows: "I mean foil in the sense of leaf or tinsel. . . . Shaken goldfoil gives off broad glares like sheet lightning and also, and this is true of nothing else, owing to its zigzag dints and creasings and network of small many-cornered facets, a sort of fork lightning too."

[2] The oil yielded from crushing olives.

[3] Heed or pay attention to.

Generations have trod, have trod, have trod;
  And all is seared with trade; bleared,[4] smeared with toil;
  And wears man's smudge and shares man's smell: the soil
Is bare now, nor can foot feel, being shod.

And for all this, nature is never spent;
  There lives the dearest freshness deep down things;   10
And though the last lights off the black West went
  Oh, morning, at the brown brink eastward, springs—
Because the Holy Ghost over the bent
  World broods with warm breast and with ah! bright wings.

THAT NATURE IS A HERACLITEAN FIRE . . .

Cloud-puffball, torn tufts, tossed pillows | flaunt forth, then
      chevy[1] on an air-
built thoroughfare: heaven-roysterers, in gay-gangs | they
      throng; they glitter in marches.
Down roughcast, down dazzling whitewash, | wherever an
      elm arches,
Shivelights[2] and shadowtackle in long | lashes lace, lance, and
      pair.
Delightfully the bright wind boisterous | ropes, wrestles, beats
      earth bare
Of yestertempest's creases; | in pool and rut peel parches
Squandering ooze to squeezed | dough, crust, dust; stanches,
      starches
Squadroned masks and manmarks | treadmire toil there
Footfretted in it.[3] Million-fuelèd, | nature's bonfire burns on.

[4] Dimmed.

[1] Race or scamper.

[2] Strips of light.

[3] According to W. H. Gardner, editor of *Poems of Gerard Manley Hopkins* (New York and London, 1948), p. 251, the meaning of these difficult lines (6-9) is: ". . . that the wet mud, squeezed into road-ruts and footprints, is dried, pummelled and dust-blown by the boisterous wind, so that the marks of man are obliterated."

But quench her bonniest, dearest | to her, her clearest-selvèd
    spark   10
Man, how fast his firedint,[4] | his mark on mind, is gone!
Both are in an unfathomable, all is in an enormous dark
Drowned. O pity and indig | nation! Manshape, that shone
Sheer off, disseveral,[5] a star, | death blots black out; nor mark
        Is any of him at all so stark
But vastness blurs and time | beats level. Enough! the Resur-
    rection,
A heart's-clarion! Away grief's gasping, | joyless days, dejection.
        Across my foundering deck shone
A beacon, an eternal beam. | Flesh fade, and mortal trash
Fall to the residuary worm; | world's wildfire, leave but ash:
        In a flash, at a trumpet crash,
I am all at once what Christ is, | since he was what I am, and
This Jack, joke, poor potsherd, | patch,[7] matchwood, immortal
    diamond,   20
        Is immortal diamond.

SUGGESTIONS FOR ADDITIONAL READING

The affirmations of Newman's *Apologia* and Carlyle's *Sartor Resartus,*
which will repay study in their entirety, may be profitably compared
with more tentative and sceptical explorations of the spiritual crisis of
the age in the following prose works:

Matthew Arnold, *Literature and Dogma* (1873)
John Stuart Mill, *Three Essays on Religion* (1874)
Thomas Henry Huxley, *Essays on Some Controverted Questions* (1892);

[4] Hopkins' coinage, explained by remainder of line.
[5] Another coinage, meaning, according to W. H. Gardner, "separate and aloof."
[6] A common person.
[7] Fool or clown.

Evolution and Ethics, and Other Essays, Vol. IX of *Collected Essays* (1893-94)

Leslie Stephen, *An Agnostic's Apology, and Other Essays* (1893)

The search for faith provides a recurrent theme in the imaginative literature of the Victorian age. Some of the varieties of religious experience to which this search led are memorably illustrated in the following:

George Eliot, *Adam Bede* (1859); *Middlemarch* (1871-72)

Walter Pater, *Marius the Epicurean* (1885)

Samuel Butler, *The Way of All Flesh* (1903)

George Bernard Shaw, *Man and Superman* (1903), including Preface

The incertitude which shadows Tennyson's *In Memoriam* or such a poem as "The Two Voices" stands in marked contrast to the more hopeful spirit of Robert Browning's great series of poems on religious subjects, including: *Christmas-Eve and Easter-Day* (1850), "Saul," "Rabbi Ben Ezra," and "The Pope" from *The Ring and the Book* (1868-69). Wholly different again is Edward Fitzgerald's exquisitely wrought celebration of hedonistic values, *Rubáiyát of Omar Khayyám,* first published in 1859, and subsequently in altered versions (1868, 1872, 1879).

For a more philosophic definition of the attitudes which inform some of the lyrics presented in this section, the student should read Swinburne's "Hertha," Meredith's "The Woods of Westermain," Hopkins' "The Wreck of the Deutschland," and sections of Hardy's long dramatic epic, *The Dynasts* (1904-8).

PART FOUR

The Role of the Artist

Introduction

In 1940, when Hitler's armored divisions were overrunning Europe, the distinguished poet Archibald MacLeish issued a stern reprimand to American intellectuals for their failure to act in the crisis confronting western culture. His declaration, entitled *The Irresponsibles,* attributed this lack of serious commitment to the fact that scholars and imaginative writers had become divided into separate professions, each of which, engrossed in perfecting its special skills, had lost all concern for the general welfare of humanity. In contrast to the irresponsible attitude of his contemporaries, MacLeish evoked the concept of the artist's role which had prevailed during the nineteenth century:

A century ago the professions of the writer and the scholar were united in the single profession of the man of letters and the man of letters was responsible in everything that touched the mind. He was a man of wholeness of purpose, of singleness of intention—a single intellectual champion, admittedly responsible for the defense of the inherited tradition, avowedly partisan of its practice. . . . Whatever threatened learning or the ends of learning challenged the man of letters. Whatever struck at truth or closed off question or defiled an art or violated decency of thinking struck at him. And he struck back with every weapon masters of the word could find to strike with.[1]

There is hardly a major author of the early and mid-Victorian periods who does not qualify under MacLeish's definition of the man of letters. No Victorian writer influenced the thinking of his time more than Carlyle,[2] and none took a more exalted view of his profession. In

[1] Archibald MacLeish, *The Irresponsibles: A Declaration* (New York, 1940), pp. 21-23.

[2] Of Carlyle's lifelong involvement in the problems of his age, John Morley, another eminent Victorian man of letters, wrote: "One of Mr. Carlyle's chief and just glories is, that for more than forty years he has clearly seen, and kept constantly and conspicuously in his own sight and that of his readers, the profoundly important crisis in the midst of which we are living. The moral and social dissolution in progress about us, and the enormous peril of sailing blindfold and haphazard, without rudder or compass or chart, have always been fully visible to him, and it is no fault of his that they have not become equally plain to his contemporaries. The policy of drifting has had no countenance from him."

1840 when he was at the height of his fame, he delivered six popular lectures *On Heroes, Hero-Worship, and the Heroic in History.* Embodied in the title is the speaker's philosophy of history. "For, as I take it," he asserts,

Universal History . . . is at bottom the History of the Great Men who have worked here. They were the leaders of men, these great ones, the modellers, patterns, and in a wide sense creators, of whatsoever the general mass of men contrived to do or to attain; all things that we see standing accomplished in the world are properly the outer material result, the practical realisation and embodiment, of Thoughts that dwelt in the Great Men sent into the world: the soul of the whole world's history, it may justly be considered, were the history of these.

Among the different categories of heroes whom Carlyle discussed, including great religious and military leaders, lectures were devoted to "The Hero as Poet" (Dante and Shakespeare) and to "The Hero as Man of Letters" (Samuel Johnson, Rousseau, and Robert Burns).

For Carlyle, poet and prophet are equivalent terms. "The true Poet is ever, as of old," he declares, "the Seer; whose eye has been gifted to discern the godlike Mystery of God's Universe, and decipher some new lines of its celestial writing; we can still call him a *Vates* and Seer; for he *sees* into this greatest of secrets 'The open secret;' hidden things become clear; how the Future (both resting on Eternity) is but another phasis of the Present: thereby are his words in very truth prophetic; what he has spoken shall be done." The attributes of the great writer are no different from those which denote the Carlylean hero in other fields of activity. In the first place, his powers of imagination give him inspired insight into ultimate truths. And this grasp of reality carries with it phenomenal intensity of moral commitment. The prophetic vision which he sees, he is in turn impelled to transmit to his age. As a recent study has demonstrated,[3] Carlyle was by no means the only Victorian writer who donned the prophet's mantle in addressing his audience. Nor was that audience reluctant to have its literary spokesmen assume this role. The historian W. E. H. Lecky

---

[3] John Holloway, *The Victorian Sage: Studies in Argument* (London, 1953). The author analyzes the stylistic means through which certain representative "sages," including Carlyle, Newman, Disraeli, Matthew Arnold, and George Eliot, sought to communicate their messages to Victorian England.

remarked that men of letters had taken the place of "the clergy in the direction of the thought of England." "It is our lay writers," he says, "who are moulding the characters and forming the opinions of the age."

The life of almost any eminent Victorian could be cited to illustrate how seriously the artists of the period regarded their public responsibilities. Tennyson's early poems, for example, are the expression of a profoundly melancholy and introspective temperament, most at home in the private world of the imagination. While a student at Cambridge, however, Tennyson joined the "Apostles," an association of brilliant young scholars ardently interested in contemporary problems, much like the group, including Auden, Isherwood, and Spender, which appeared at Oxford exactly a century later. The dawning sense of mission which Tennyson took away from Cambridge can be traced through the lyrics of *In Memoriam*, which beginning as a personal lament grew into a manifesto of faith for Victorian England. Writing in 1894, two years after the laureate's death, James Anthony Froude, the historian and biographer of Carlyle, would say that Tennyson ranked alone beside Shakespeare, "with this relative superiority even to Shakespeare, that he speaks the thoughts and speaks *to* the perplexities and misgivings of his own age." A similar progression is observable in the fiction of Dickens, from *Pickwick Papers,* conceived as pure entertainment, to the burning indignation against institutionalized morality which darkens the pages of the great later novels, such as *Bleak House* and *Little Dorrit.* Of Dickens' achievement in awakening the conscience of his times a Nonconformist preacher made the somber pronouncement: "There have been at work among us three great social agencies: the London City Mission; the novels of Mr. Dickens; the cholera."

But the ways in which the cultural crises of the nineteenth century determined the role of the artist in society can perhaps be best illustrated by a brief résumé of the careers of two of the most influential critics of the period: Ruskin and Arnold. Ruskin, the pampered son of wealthy parents, should by all rights have been a dilettante. When he began at the age of twenty-three to write art criticism, his immediate purpose was to defend the daringly impressionistic later style of the great English landscapist J. M. W. Turner. From this germ grew the five volumes of *Modern Painters* (1843-60), in which the author established the moral aesthetic to which his contemporaries so largely subscribed. In essence, Ruskin argued that the greatness of any work of art depends on its ethical significance, the extent to which it provides "noble grounds for noble emotions." Surface realism is not enough in itself, though it is important; in faithfully transcribing his perceptions, the artist must at the same time educe the ideal truth and beauty which inhere in all phenomena. Ruskin was calling for a fusion of realism and symbolism, such as he thought he recognized in the primitivistic school of Pre-Raphaelite painters, which emerged at the mid-century. A member of this group, George Frederick Watts, spoke of his aims in terms which Ruskin would have fully endorsed: "My intention had been not so much to paint pictures that charm the eye as to suggest great thoughts that will appeal to the imagination and the heart, and kindle all that is noblest and best in humanity."

With this approach to art, it was inevitable that Ruskin should in time turn from painting to architecture. As a moral discipline painting is of limited validity. A picture is the product of a single highly trained talent; and in a period when art galleries were scarce and before modern techniques of reproduction had been developed, there was little opportunity for the populace to benefit from the work of painters and sculptors. Structures such as churches, railroad stations, and post offices, on the other hand, unite many workmen in a communal endeavor; they also serve public purposes and must be erected with these uses in mind. Again, however, just as in his response to painting, Ruskin examined architectural styles primarily for the moral values they exhibited. "Every form of noble architecture," he wrote (and he was among the first to perceive this), "is in some way an embodiment of the Polity, Life, History, and Religious Faith of nations." The principles of social cohesion and corporate responsibility which Ruskin missed in Victorian society, he found most perfectly exemplified in the hierarchic structure of the mediaeval world, where it was symbolically configured in Gothic church-building; and through *The Seven Lamps of Architecture* (1849) and *The Stones of Venice* (1851-53), he lent his vast personal prestige to fostering the revival of that style. That the principal architect of Victorian Gothic, Augustus Welby Pugin, shared Ruskin's vision is apparent from his statement: "The mechanical part of Gothic architecture is pretty well understood, but it is the principles which influenced ancient composition and the soul which appears in all former works, which is so lamentably deficient, nor . . . can anything be regained but by a restoration of the ancient feelings and sentiments."

Despite the frequent incisiveness of his critical judgments, Ruskin had all along, of course, been putting the cart before the horse in recommending art as an agent of social regeneration. The cultural climate of the Middle Ages produced Gothic architecture, not the reverse. The newly rich middle classes might purchase the paintings and erect the kind of buildings that Ruskin praised, but beneath the veneer of culture their commercial attitudes remained unaltered. In time Ruskin came to realize this; here is his saddened admission on the eve of a change in residence:

I have had an indirect influence on nearly every cheap villa-builder between this and Bromley; and there is scarcely a public house near the Crystal Palace but sells its gin and bitters under pseudo-Venetian capitals copied from the Church of the Madonna of Health or of Miracles. And one of my principal notions for leaving my present house is that it is surrounded everywhere by the accursed Frankenstein monsters of, indirectly, my own making.

With the publication of *Unto This Last* in 1862, therefore, Ruskin took up the work of social reform which at incalculable cost to his reputation was henceforth to enlist his best energies. "You will never love art well," he now proclaimed to his age, "till you love what she mirrors better," and

The beginning of all ideal art must be for us in the realistic art of bestowing health and happiness. The first schools of beauty must be the streets of your cities, and the chief of fair designs must be to keep the living creatures round us clean, and in human comfort.

Just as Ruskin's career as man of letters expanded through three successive phases, Arnold's literary life presents no fewer than four aspects, exclusive of his vocation as inspector of government schools.

Along with Tennyson and Browning, he forms the triumvirate of great Victorian poets; but he suffered under the sense of a hostile *Zeitgeist,* convinced that the spirit of the times was unpropitious for artistic creativity. As a result, he had virtually abandoned imaginative writing when he became Professor of Poetry at Oxford in 1857; and in the following years he devoted himself to the literary studies in which are revealed the finest critical intelligence of the age. In essay after essay, many to be gathered in the two series of *Essays in Criticism* (1865 and 1888), he passed authoritative judgment on an astonishing range of authors from all periods and in many languages. As a critic, Arnold shared Ruskin's moral preoccupations. Literature must offer a "criticism of life"; not until modern writers, drawing on the best that had been thought and said in the world, were again prepared to make "noble and profound application of ideas to life" would they be worthy of their high calling. "Modern poetry," he wrote in a letter to his friend, the poet Arthur Hugh Clough, "can only subsist by its *contents:* by becoming a complete magister vitae [guide to life] as the poetry of the ancients did: by including as theirs did, religion with poetry, instead of existing as poetry only. . . ."

Like Ruskin, however, Arnold moved on to social criticism out of the conviction that the loss of artistic vitality in his period was indicative of more deep-seated maladjustments, and that in confining his attention to literature he had been treating symptoms rather than the malady itself. In *Culture and Anarchy* (1869) he subjected Victorian society to an extraordinarily subtle analysis, showing how loss of contact with the great sustaining traditions of western civilization had materialized and vulgarized English habits of mind and ways of life. As a panacea for the anarchy into which the period was drifting, he proposed the ideal of culture. The terms of Arnold's definition of what he means by culture in the Preface to his work clearly suggest the relationship between his social theories and the literary criticism of which they were the logical outgrowth:

The whole scope of the essay is to recommend culture as the great help out of our present difficulties; culture being a pursuit of our total perfection by means of getting to know, on all the matters which most concern us, the best which has been thought and said in the world; and through this knowledge, turning a stream of fresh and free thought upon our stock notions and habits, which we now follow staunchly but mechanically, vainly imagining that there is a virtue in following them staunchly which makes up for the mischief of following them mechanically.

Under existing conditions only a privileged minority could aspire to the intellectual enlightenment which for Arnold was the hallmark of culture; and as he came to realize, its guardians would at best form a small, though influential, elite. His concern for the cultural well-being of society at large led him in due course to propose a more accessible ideal, summarized in the statement: "Religion must provide for the many the guidance literature provides for the few." In the religious writings which now followed, of which *Literature and Dogma* (1873) is the most memorable, Arnold's consistent purpose was to recommend that the Bible, when read as literature rather than as a work of divine revelation, is still the one sure sanction for man's moral nature and the source from which he can best derive satisfaction of his spiritual needs.

The alert student of Victorian life and letters cannot fail to perceive after the mid-century a change in literary climate, symptomatic of a radical shift in aesthetic sensibility. The later writings of nearly all the authors hitherto discussed are gloomy in tendency; their tone is shriller and more petulant; the reader's impression is of deepening disillusionment with the signs of the times. The Victorian prophets, he concludes, had discovered that they were without honor in their country, that they were voices crying in the wilderness of a soulless age that refused to heed their message. At the same time there appears on the scene a new type of artist, altogether different from the typical Victorian man of letters. The poet and painter Dante Gabriel Rossetti may stand for this type. He had early disassociated himself from the original Pre-Raphaelite Brotherhood, whose artistic goals Ruskin sponsored, and gathered around himself a group of younger men who were unfeignedly estranged from the society of their day. To Rossetti it was simply inconceivable that the professional artist should feel any sense of social responsibility. His resistance to such commitment was in the cause of a higher obligation, what Henry James called "the terrible law of the artist—the law of acceptance of *all* experience, of *all* life, of *all* suggestion and sensation and illumination."

Rossetti, however, no controversialist, asked only to be allowed to go his own way, seeking full and uninhibited self-expression in his dreamlike poems and paintings. The role of champion for what became known as "art for art's sake" devolved upon another poet, Algernon Charles Swinburne. Fiery and aggressive by temperament, Swinburne took up the cudgels over the hostile reception of his *Poems and Ballads* (1866), a collection of poems, exquisitely wrought, but outspokenly licentious and blasphemous in theme. In conducting his own defense with consummate boldness and skill, he followed the lead of the great French poet Charles Baudelaire, whose aesthetic theories were an expansion of ideas first expressed by Edgar Allan Poe in "The Poetic Principle" (1848). The modern artist, according to Baudelaire, is menaced by the "heresy of didacticism": "if the poet has set himself a moral goal, he has diminished his poetic force; and it's not a bad bet that his work will be bad. Poetry cannot, under pain of death and failure, associate itself with knowledge or morality; its object is not truth, its object is itself." This was to be the position of Swinburne and of the generation of artistic rebels for whom he spoke. "Art for art's sake first of all," he wrote in his pioneer study of William Blake (1868), "and afterwards we may suppose the rest shall be added (or if not she need hardly be overmuch concerned), but from the man who falls to artistic work with a moral purpose shall be taken away even that which he has—whatever capacity for doing well in either way he may have had at starting."

It remained for a shy Oxford don, Walter Pater, to formulate the theoretical principles of art for art's sake and to assume leadership of the so-called Aesthetic Movement. Distrustful of all absolutes in an age which was discrediting one traditionally received truth after another, Pater based his philosophy on the belief that the mind like all else is in a perpetual state of flux and can know nothing beyond the fleeting impressions which constantly stream through the human consciousness. The fine art of living is to respond to each passing moment with the greatest possible intensity. For Pater the supreme value of art is that through its means this fullness of response is made possible:

For our one chance lies in expanding that interval, in getting as many pulsations as possible into the given time. Great passions may give us this quickened sense of life, ecstasy and sorrow of love, the various forms of enthusiastic activity, disinterested or otherwise, which come naturally to many of us. Only be sure it is passion—that it does yield you this fruit of a quickened, multiplied consciousness. Of such wisdom the poetic passion, the desire of beauty, the love of art for its own sake, has most. For art comes to you proposing frankly to give nothing but the highest quality to your moments as they pass, and simply for those moments' sake.

The artist can know only his own response to any given experience; but the effort to impose form on that experience is his way of arresting the flux, of capturing and perpetuating in ideal aspect one of its manifestations. As Rossetti had written in the introductory poem to his sonnet cycle, *The House of Life:*

> A sonnet is a moment's monument,
> Memorial from the Soul's eternity
> To one dead deathless hour . . . .

In Pater's own words, the artist strives "to realize the unity in variety, to discover *cosmos*—an order that shall satisfy one's reasonable soul—below and within *chaos*." Here is the true meaning of the creative impulse, as it seeks to express itself in works of art that shall be autonomous, a law unto themselves, and enlisting to that end the creator's single-minded allegiance.

From the first Pater had had misgivings lest his young disciples pervert the doctrine to which his own devotion was so austere and pure; lest, for example, his sense of the importance of making refined discriminations between sensations be construed as an invitation to indiscriminate sensationalism. There was the very real danger that some would be attracted by his teachings for the wrong reasons, and that these would be all too inclined to turn, as he phrased it, to "art, or science, to the experience of life itself, not as to portions of human nature's daily food, but as to something that must be, by the circumstances of the case, exceptional; almost as men turn in despair to gambling or narcotics, and in a little while the narcotic, the game of chance or skill, is valued for its own sake. The vocation of the artist, of the student of life or books, will be realized with something—say! of fanaticism, as an end in itself, unrelated, unassociated." And, indeed, certain morbid tendencies within the Aesthetic Movement did come to the surface, so that in its later phase it became known as the Decadent Movement. During his brief heyday Oscar Wilde was the centor of a later generation of aesthetes who, like the protagonist of his novel *The Picture of Dorian Gray* (1891), professed "a new Hedonism"

that was to recreate life, and to save it from that harsh, uncomely Puritanism that is having, in our own day, its curious revival. It was to have its service of the intellect, certainly; yet, it was never to accept any theory or system that would involve the sacrifice of any mode of passionate experience. Its aim, indeed, was to be experience itself, and not the fruits of experience, sweet or bitter as they might be. Of the asceticism that deadens the senses, as of the vulgar profligacy that dulls them, it was to know nothing. But it was to teach each man to concentrate himself upon the moments of a life that is itself but a moment.

The worst excesses of aestheticism came to an end with the Wilde trial in 1895, by which time writers like Henry James, Joseph Conrad, and William Butler Yeats had assimilated the elements of enduring value in the doctrine of art for art's sake. Meanwhile, of course, the opposing doctrine of art for society's sake had never really been in eclipse, but had continued to find its advocates, whether among socialists such as William Morris and Bernard Shaw, or among popular storytellers and poets like Rudyard Kipling, who helped to fan the imperialist spirit in late Victorian England.

John Ruskin, Matthew Arnold, and Walter Horatio Pater are the indisputable authorities on art and literature in their age; and in the prose selections which follow, each sets forth the aesthetic standards which guided his critical practice. The poems by Robert Browning and Dante Gabriel Rossetti deal with artists and concretely illustrate various theories about the role of the artist current in the period.

John Ruskin

1819-1900

Of the Real Nature of Greatness of Style

🍃 The following selection is Chapter Three of the third volume of *Modern Painters* (1856). The texture of the argument is more closely knit than is usually the case in Ruskin's writings, and the reader should heed the author's caution (n. 17) that his four categories are arranged in ascending order of importance.

I doubt not that the reader was ill-satisfied with the conclusion arrived at in the last chapter.[1] That "great art" is art which represents what is beautiful and good, may not seem a very profound discovery; and the main question may be thought to have been all the time lost sight of, namely, "What is beautiful, and what is good?" No; those are not the main, at least not the first questions; on the contrary, our subject becomes at once opened and simplified as soon as we have left those the *only* questions. For observe, our present task, according to our old plan, is merely to investigate the relative degrees of the *beautiful* in the art of different masters; and it is an encouragement to be convinced, first of all, that what is lovely will also be great and what is pleasing, noble. Nor is the conclusion so much a matter of course as it at first appears, for, surprising as the statement may

[1] Entitled "Of Realization"; Ruskin had concluded that "true criticism of art never can consist in the mere application of rules; it can be just only when it is founded on quick sympathy with the innumerable instincts and changeful efforts of human nature, chastened and guided by unchanging love of all things that God has created to be beautiful, and pronounced to be good."

seem, all the confusion into which Reynolds has plunged both himself and his readers, in the essay we have been examining,[2] results primarily from a doubt in his own mind *as to the existence of beauty at all*. In the next paper I alluded to, No. 82 (which needs not, however, to be examined at so great length), he calmly attributes the whole influence of beauty to custom, saying, that "he has no doubt, if we were more used to deformity than to beauty, deformity would then lose the idea now annexed to it, and take that of beauty; as if the whole world shall agree that Yes and No should change their meanings. Yes would then deny, and No would affirm!"

The world does, indeed, succeed—oftener than is, perhaps, altogether well for the world—in making Yes mean No, and No mean Yes. But the world has never succeeded, nor ever will, in making itself delight in black clouds more than in blue sky, or love the dark earth better than the rose that grows from it. Happily for mankind, beauty and ugliness are as positive in their nature as physical pain and pleasure, as light and darkness, or as life and death; and, though they may be denied or misunderstood in many fantastic ways, the most subtle reasoner will at last find that colour and sweetness are still attractive to him, and that no logic will enable him to think the rainbow sombre, or the violet scentless. But the theory that beauty was merely a result of custom was very common in Johnson's time. Goldsmith[3] has, I think, expressed it with more force and wit than any other writer, in various passages of the *Citizen of the World*. And it was indeed a curious retribution of the folly of the world of art, which for some three centuries had given itself recklessly to the pursuit of beauty, that at last it should be led to deny the very existence of what it had so morbidly and passionately sought. It was as if a child should leave its home to pursue the rainbow, and then, breathless and hopeless, declare that it did not exist. Nor is the lesson less useful which may be gained

[2] The essay referred to appeared in *The Idler*, a series of essays contributed by Samuel Johnson, Reynolds, and others to the *Universal Chronicle* (1758-60). Sir Joshua Reynolds (1723-1792), leading English portrait-painter and first president of the Royal Academy of Arts, delivered his influential *Discourses* on art between 1769 and 1790.

[3] Oliver Goldsmith (1730-1774), dramatist and essayist, whose reflections on English manners and morals, *The Citizen of the World,* were published in 1762.

in observing the adoption of such a theory by Reynolds himself. It shows how completely an artist may be unconscious of the principles of his own work, and how he may be led by instinct to *do* all that is right, while he is misled by false logic to *say* all that is wrong. For nearly every word that Reynolds wrote was contrary to his own practice; he seems to have been born to teach all error by his precept, and all excellence by his example; he enforced with his lips generalization and idealism, while with his pencil he was tracing the patterns of the dresses of the belles of his day; he exhorted his pupils to attend only to the invariable, while he himself was occupied in distinguishing every variation of womanly temper; and he denied the existence of the beautiful, at the same instant that he arrested it as it passed, and perpetuated it for ever.

But we must not quit the subject here. However inconsistently or dimly expressed, there is, indeed, some truth in that commonly accepted distinction between high and low art. That a thing should be beautiful is not enough; there is, as we said in the outset, a higher and lower range of beauty, and some ground for separating into various and unequal ranks painters who have, nevertheless, each in his several way, represented something that was beautiful or good.

Nor, if we would, can we get rid of this conviction. We have at all times some instinctive sense that the function of one painter is greater than that of another, even supposing each equally successful in his own way; and we feel that, if it were possible to conquer prejudice, and do away with the iniquities of personal feeling, and the insufficiencies of limited knowledge, we should all agree in this estimate, and be able to place each painter in his right rank, measuring them by a true scale of nobleness. We feel that the men in the higher classes of the scale would be, in the full sense of the word, Great,—men whom one would give much to see the faces of but for an instant; and that those in the lower classes of the scale (though none were admitted but who had true merit of some kind) would be very small men, not greatly exciting either reverence or curiosity. And with this fixed instinct in our minds, we permit our teachers daily to exhort their pupils to the cultivation of "great art"—neither they nor we having any very clear notion as to what the greatness consists in: but sometimes inclining to think it must depend on the space of the canvas, and that art on a scale of 6 feet by 10 is something spiritually separated from that on a scale of 3 feet by 5;— sometimes holding it to consist in painting the nude body, rather than the body decently clothed;—sometimes being convinced that it is connected with the study of past history, and that the art is only great which represents what the painter never saw, and about which he knows nothing;—and sometimes being firmly persuaded that it consists in generally finding fault with, and endeavouring to mend, whatsoever the Divine Wisdom has made. All which various errors, having yet some motes and atoms of truth in the make of each of them, deserve some attentive analysis, for they come under that general law,—that "the corruption of the best is the worst." There are not *worse* errors going than these four; and yet the truth they contain, and the instinct which urges many to preach them, are at the root of all healthy growth in art. We ruin one young painter after another by telling him to follow great art, without knowing, ourselves, what greatness is; and yet the feeling that it verily *is* something, and that there are depths and breadths, shallows and narrows, in the matter, is all that we have to look to, if we would ever make our art serviceable to ourselves or others. To follow art for the sake of being a great man, and therefore to cast about continually for some means of achieving position or attracting admiration, is the surest way of ending in total extinction. And yet it is only by honest reverence for art itself, and by great self-respect in the practice of it, that it can be rescued from dilettantism, raised to approved honourableness, and brought to the proper work it has to accomplish in the service of man.

Let us therefore look into the facts of the thing, not with any metaphysical, or otherwise vain and troublesome effort at acuteness, but in a plain way; for the facts themselves are plain enough, and may be plainly stated, only the difficulty is that out of these facts, right and left, the different forms of misapprehension branch into grievous complexity, and branch so far and wide, that if once we try to follow them, they will lead us quite from our mark into other separate, though not less interesting discussions. The best way will be, therefore, I think, to sketch out at once in this chapter, the different characters which really constitute "greatness" of style, and to indicate the principal directions of the out-branching misapprehensions of them; then, in the succeeding chapters, to take up in succession those which need more talk about them, and follow out at leisure whatever inquiries they may suggest.

I. CHOICE OF NOBLE SUBJECT.—Greatness of style consists, then: first, in the habitual choice of subjects of thought which involve wide interests and profound passions, as opposed to those which involve narrow interests and slight passions. The style is greater or less in exact proportion to the nobleness of the interests and passions involved in the subject. The habitual choice of sacred subjects, such as the Nativity, Transfiguration, Crucifixion (if the choice be sincere), implies that the painter has a natural disposition to dwell on the highest thoughts of which humanity is capable; it constitutes him so far forth a painter of the highest order, as, for instance, Leonardo, in his painting of the Last Supper: he who delights in representing the acts or meditations of great men, as, for instance, Raphael painting the School of Athens, is, so far forth, a painter of the second order: he who represents the passions and events of ordinary life, of the third. And in this ordinary life, he who represents deep thoughts and sorrows, as, for instance, Hunt,[4] in his Claudio and Isabella, and such other works, is of the highest rank in his sphere: and he who represents the slight malignities and passions of the drawing-room, as, for instance, Leslie,[5] of the second rank; he who represents the sports of boys, or simplicities of clowns, as Webster or Teniers,[6] of the third rank; and he who represents brutalities and vices (for delight in them, and not for rebuke of them), of no rank at all, or rather of a negative rank, holding a certain order in the abyss.

The reader will, I hope, understand how much importance is to be attached to the sentence in the first parenthesis, "if the choice be sincere"; for choice of subject is, of course, only available as a criterion of the rank

---

[4] William Holman Hunt (1827-1910), a member of the Pre-Raphaelite school of English artists which Ruskin sponsored. Hunt derived the subject of the painting here cited from Shakespeare's *Measure for Measure*.

[5] Charles Robert Leslie (1794-1859), painter of fashionable life and professor of painting at the Royal Academy.

[6] Thomas Webster (1800-1886), a member of the Royal Academy who specialized in rustic scenes; David Teniers the elder (1582-1649), and David Teniers the younger (1610-1690), both Dutch genre painters whose realistic treatment of scenes of low life displeased Ruskin.

of the painter, when it is made from the heart. Indeed, in the lower orders of painting, the choice is always made from such heart as the painter has; for his selection of the brawls of peasants or sports of children can, of course, proceed only from the fact that he has more sympathy with such brawls or pastimes than with nobler subjects. But the choice of the higher kind of subjects is often insincere; and may, therefore, afford no real criterion of the painter's rank. The greater number of men who have lately painted religious or heroic subjects have done so in mere ambition, because they had been taught that it was a good thing to be a "high-art" painter; and the fact is that, in nine cases out of ten, the so-called historical or "high-art" painter is a person infinitely inferior to the painter of flowers or still life. He is, in modern times, nearly always a man who has great vanity without pictorial capacity, and differs from the landscape or fruit painter merely in misunderstanding and overestimating his own powers. He mistakes his vanity for inspiration, his ambition for greatness of soul, and takes pleasure in what he calls "the ideal," merely because he has neither humility nor capacity enough to comprehend the real.

But also observe, it is not enough even that the choice be sincere. It must also be wise. It happens very often that a man of weak intellect, sincerely desiring to do what is good and useful, will devote himself to high art subjects because he thinks them the only ones on which time and toil can be usefully spent, or, sometimes, because they are really the only ones he has pleasure in contemplating. But not having intellect enough to enter into the minds of truly great men, or to imagine great events as they really happened, he cannot become a great painter; he degrades the subjects he intended to honour, and his work is more utterly thrown away, and his rank as an artist in reality lower, than if he had devoted himself to the imitation of the simplest objects of natural history. The works of Overbeck [7] are a most notable instance of this form of error.

It must also be remembered, that in nearly all the great periods of art the choice of subject has not been left to the painter. His employer,— abbot, baron, or monarch,—determined for him whether he should earn

---

[7] Johann Friedrich Overbeck (1789-1869), leader of the German "Pre-Raphaelite" school, which aspired to false grandeur in its choice of subject matter.

his bread by making cloisters bright with choirs of saints, painting coats of arms on leaves of romances, or decorating presence-chambers with complimentary mythology; and his own personal feelings are ascertainable only by watching, in the themes assigned to him, what are the points in which he seems to take most pleasure. Thus, in the prolonged ranges of varied subjects with which Benozzo Gozzoli[8] decorated the cloisters of Pisa, it is easy to see that love of simple domestic incident, sweet landscape, and glittering ornament, prevails slightly over the solemn elements of religious feeling, which, nevertheless, the spirit of the age instilled into him in such measure as to form a very lovely and noble mind, though still one of the second order. In the work of Orcagna, an intense solemnity and energy in the sublimest groups of his figures, fading away as he touches inferior subjects, indicates that his home was among the archangels, and his rank among the first of the sons of men: while Correggio, in the sidelong grace, artificial smiles, and purple languors of his saints, indicates the inferior instinct which would have guided his choice in quite other directions, had it not been for the fashion of the age, and the need of the day.

It will follow, of course, from the above considerations, that the choice which characterizes the school of high art is seen as much in the treatment of a subject as in its selection, and that the expression of the thoughts of the persons represented will always be the first thing considered by the painter who worthily enters that highest school. For the artist who sincerely chooses the noblest subject will also choose chiefly to represent what makes that subject noble, namely, the various heroism or other noble emotions of the persons represented. If, instead of this, the artist seeks only to make his picture agreeable by the composition of its masses and colours, or by any other merely pictorial merit, as fine drawing of limbs, it is evident, not only that any other subject would have answered his purpose as well, but that he is unfit to approach the subject he has chosen, because he cannot enter into its deepest meaning, and therefore cannot in reality have chosen it for that meaning. Nevertheless, while the expression is always to be the first thing considered, all other merits must be added to the utmost of the painter's power; for

[8] Benozzo Gozzoli (1420-1497), Italian painter whose frescoes are notable for their insistence on realistic detail.

until he can both colour and draw beautifully he has no business to consider himself a painter at all, far less to attempt the noblest subjects of painting; and, when he has once possessed himself of these powers, he will naturally and fitly employ them to deepen and perfect the impression made by the sentiment of his subject.

The perfect unison of expression, as the painter's main purpose, with the full and natural exertion of his pictorial power in the details of the work, is found only in the old Pre-Raphaelite periods, and in the modern Pre-Raphaelite school.[9] In the works of Giotto, Angelico, Orcagna, John Bellini, and one or two more, these two conditions of high art are entirely fulfilled, so far as the knowledge of those days enable them to be fulfilled; and in the modern Pre-Raphaelite school they are fulfilled nearly to the uttermost. Hunt's Light of the World is, I believe, the most perfect instance of expressional purpose with technical power, which the world has yet produced.

Now in the Post-Raphaelite period of ancient art, and in the spurious high art of modern times, two broad forms of error divide the schools; the one consisting in (A) the superseding of expression by technical excellence, and the other in (B) the superseding of technical excellence by expression.

(A). Superseding expression by technical excellence.—This takes place most frankly, and therefore most innocently, in the work of the Venetians.[10] They very nearly ignore expression altogether, directing their aim exclusively to the rendering of external truths of colour and form. Paul Veronese will make the Magdalene wash the feet of Christ with a countenance as absolutely unmoved as that of any ordinary servant bringing a ewer to her master, and will introduce the supper at Emmaus as a background to the portraits of two children playing with a dog. Of the wrongness or rightness of such a proceeding we shall reason in another place; at present we have to note it merely as displacing the

---

[9] The English Pre-Raphaelite painters first exhibited their work in 1848. As the name which they adopted indicates, they were in revolt against existing canons of taste and derived their inspiration from the earlier schools of Italian painting before the High Renaissance. Ruskin's advocacy of their work was enthusiastic, if not always discriminating!

[10] Ruskin has in mind such painters as Giorgione, Titian, Tintoretto, and Veronese, toward whose paintings his attitude vacillated.

Venetian work from the highest or expressional rank of art. But the error is generally made in a more subtle and dangerous way. The artist deceives himself into the idea that he is doing all he can to elevate his subject by treating it under rules of art, introducing into it accurate science, and collecting for it the beauties of (so-called) ideal form; whereas he may, in reality, be all the while sacrificing his subject to his own vanity or pleasure, and losing truth, nobleness, and impressiveness for the sake of delightful lines or creditable pedantries.

(B). Superseding technical excellence by expression.—This is usually done under the influence of another kind of vanity. The artist desires that men should think he has an elevated soul, affects to despise the ordinary excellence of art, contemplates with separated egotism the course of his own imaginations or sensations, and refuses to look at the real facts round about him, in order that he may adore at leisure the shadow of himself. He lives in an element of what he calls tender emotions and lofty aspirations; which are, in fact, nothing more than very ordinary weaknesses or instincts, contemplated through a mist of pride. A large range of modern German art comes under this head.

A more interesting and respectable form of this error is fallen into by some truly earnest men, who, finding their powers not adequate to the attainment of great artistical excellence, but adequate to rendering, up to a certain point, the expression of the human countenance, devote themselves to that object alone, abandoning effort in other directions, and executing the accessories of their pictures feebly or carelessly. With these are associated another group of philosophical painters, who suppose the artistical merits of other parts *adverse* to the expression, as drawing the spectator's attention away from it, and who paint in grey colour, and imperfect light and shade, by way of enforcing the purity of their conceptions. Both these classes of conscientious but narrow-minded artists labour under the same grievous mistake of imagining that wilful fallacy can ever be either pardonable or helpful. They forget that colour, if used at all, must be either true or false, and that what *they* call chastity, dignity, and reserve, is, to the eye of any person accustomed to nature, pure, bold, and impertinent falsehood. It does not, in the eyes of any soundly minded man, exalt the expression of a female face that the cheeks should be painted of the colour of clay, nor does it in the least enhance his reverence for a saint to find the scenery around him deprived, by his presence, of sunshine. It is an important consolation, however, to reflect that no artist ever fell into any of these last three errors (under head B.) who had really the capacity of becoming a great painter. No man ever despised colour who could produce it; and the error of these sentimentalists and philosophers is not so much in the choice of their manner of painting, as in supposing themselves capable of painting at all. Some of them might have made efficient sculptors, but the greater number had their mission in some other sphere than that of art, and would have found, in works of practical charity, better employment for their gentleness and sentimentalism, than in denying to human beauty its colour, and to natural scenery its light; in depriving heaven of its blue, and modesty of its blush.

II. Love of Beauty.—The second characteristic of the great school of art is, that it introduces in the conception of its subject as much beauty as is possible, consistently with truth.[11]

[11] As here, for the first time, I am obliged to use the terms Truth and Beauty in a kind of opposition, I must therefore stop for a moment to state clearly the relation of these two qualities of art; and to protest against the vulgar and foolish habit of confusing truth and beauty with each other. People with shallow powers of thought, desiring to flatter themselves with the sensation of having attained profundity, are continually doing the most serious mischief by introducing confusion into plain matters, and then valuing themselves on being confounded. Nothing is more common than to hear people who desire to be thought philosophical, declare that "beauty is truth," and "truth is beauty." I would most earnestly beg every sensible person who hears such an assertion made to nip the germinating philosopher in his ambiguous bud; and beg him, if he really believes his own assertion, never thenceforward to use two words for the same thing. The fact is, truth and beauty are entirely distinct, though often related, things. One is a property of statements, the other of objects. The statement that "two and two make four" is true, but it is neither beautiful nor ugly, for it is invisible; a rose is lovely, but it is neither true nor false, for it is silent. That which shows nothing cannot be fair, and that which asserts nothing cannot be false. Even the ordinary use of the words false and true as applied to artificial and real things, is inaccurate. An artificial rose is not a "false" rose, it is not a rose at all. The falseness is in the person who states, or induces the belief, that it *is* a rose.

Now, therefore, in things concerning art, the words true and false are only to be rightly used while the picture is considered as a statement of facts. The painter asserts that this which he has painted is the form of a dog, a man, or a tree. If it be *not* the form of a dog, a man, or a tree, the painter's statement is false; and therefore we justly speak of a false line, or false colour; not that any line or colour can in themselves be false, but they become so when they convey a statement that they resemble something which they do *not* resemble. But the beauty of the lines or colours

For instance, in any subject consisting of a number of figures, it will make as many of those figures beautiful as the faithful representation of humanity will admit. It will not deny the facts of ugliness or decrepitude, or relative inferiority and superiority of feature as necessarily manifested in a crowd, but it will, so far as it is in its power, seek for and dwell upon the fairest forms, and in all things insist on the beauty that is in them, not on the ugliness. In this respect, schools of art become higher in exact proportion to the degree in which they apprehend and love the beautiful. Thus, Angelico, intensely loving all spiritual beauty, will be of the highest rank; and Paul Veronese and Correggio, intensely loving physical and corporeal beauty, of the second rank; and Albert Dürer, Rubens, and in general the Northern artists,[12] apparently insensible to beauty, and caring only for truth, whether shapely or not, of the third rank; and Teniers and Salvator, Caravaggio,[13] and other such worshippers of the depraved, of no rank, or, as we said before, of a certain order in the abyss.

The corruptions of the schools of high art, so far as this particular quality is concerned, consists in the sacrifice of truth to beauty. Great art dwells on all that is beautiful; but false art omits or changes all that

---

is wholly independent of any such statement. They may be beautiful lines, though quite inaccurate, and ugly lines, though quite faithful. A picture may be frightfully ugly, which represents with fidelity some base circumstance of daily life; and a painted window may be exquisitely beautiful, which represents men with eagles' faces, and dogs with blue heads and crimson tails (though, by the way, this is not in the strict sense *false* art, as we shall see hereafter, inasmuch as it means no assertion that men ever *had* eagles' faces). If this were not so, it would be impossible to sacrifice truth to beauty; for to attain the one would always be to attain the other. But, unfortunately, this sacrifice is exceedingly possible, and it is chiefly this which characterises the false schools of high art, so far as high art consists in the pursuit of beauty. For although truth and beauty are independent of each other, it does not follow that we are at liberty to pursue whichever we please. They are indeed separable, but it is wrong to separate them; they are to be sought together in the order of their worthiness; that is to say, truth first, and beauty afterwards. High art differs from low art in possessing an excess of beauty in addition to its truth, not in possessing an excess of beauty inconsistent with truth. [Ruskin's note.]

[12] Ruskin was generally insensitive to painters of the northern Renaissance because of their uncompromising realism.

[13] Salvator Rosa (1615-1673), Italian painter of somewhat melodramatic landscapes; Michelangelo da Caravaggio (1565?-1610), Italian realist whose revolutionary technique has received critical recognition only in recent times.

is ugly. Great art accepts Nature as she is, but directs the eyes and thoughts to what is most perfect in her; false art saves itself the trouble of direction by removing or altering whatever it thinks objectionable. The evil results of which proceeding are twofold.

First. That beauty deprived of its proper foils and adjuncts ceases to be enjoyed as beauty, just as light deprived of all shadow ceases to be enjoyed as light. A white canvas cannot produce an effect of sunshine; the painter must darken it in some places before he can make it look luminous in others; nor can an uninterrupted succession of beauty produce the true effect of beauty; it must be foiled by inferiority before its own power can be developed. Nature has for the most part mingled her inferior and nobler elements as she mingles sunshine with shade, giving due use and influence to both, and the painter who chooses to remove the shadow, perishes in the burning desert he has created. The truly high and beautiful art of Angelico is continually refreshed and strengthened by his frank portraiture of the most ordinary features of his brother monks, and of the recorded peculiarities of ungainly sanctity; but the modern German and Raphaelesque schools lose all honour and nobleness in barber-like admiration of handsome faces, and have, in fact, no real faith except in straight noses and curled hair. Paul Veronese opposes the dwarf to the soldier, and the negress to the queen; Shakspeare places Caliban beside Miranda, and Autolycus beside Perdita; but the vulgar idealist withdraws his beauty to the safety of the saloon,[14] and his innocence to the seclusion of the cloister; he pretends that he does this in delicacy of choice and purity of sentiment, while in truth he has neither courage to front the monster, nor wit enough to furnish the knave.

It is only by the habit of representing faithfully all things, that we can truly learn what is beautiful, and what is not. The ugliest objects contain some element of beauty; and in all, it is an element peculiar to themselves, which cannot be separated from their ugliness, but must either be enjoyed together with it, or not at all. The more a painter accepts nature as he finds it, the more unexpected beauty he discovers in what he at first despised; but once let him arrogate the right of rejection, and he will gradually contract his circle of enjoyment, until what he supposed to be nobleness of selection ends in narrowness of perception.

[14] In its original sense of a large reception room.

Dwelling perpetually upon one class of ideas, his art becomes at once monstrous and morbid; until at last he cannot faithfully represent even what he chooses to retain; his discrimination contracts into darkness, and his fastidiousness fades into fatuity.

High art, therefore, consists neither in altering, nor in improving nature; but in seeking throughout nature for "whatsoever things are lovely, and whatsoever things are pure";[15] in loving these, in displaying to the utmost of the painter's power such loveliness as is in them, and directing the thoughts of others to them by winning art, or gentle emphasis. Of the degree in which this can be done, and in which it may be permitted to gather together, without falsifying, the finest forms or thoughts, so as to create a sort of perfect vision, we shall have to speak hereafter; at present, it is enough to remember that art (*cæteris paribus*)[16] is great in exact proportion to the love of beauty shown by the painter, provided that love of beauty forfeit no atom of truth.

III. SINCERITY.—The next [17] characteristic of great art is that it includes the largest possible quantity of Truth in the most perfect possible harmony. If it were possible for art to give all the truths of nature, it ought to do it. But this is not possible. Choice must always be made of some facts which *can* be represented, from among others which must be passed by in silence, or even, in some respects, misrepresented. The inferior artist chooses unimportant and scattered truths; the great artist chooses the most necessary first, and afterwards the most consistent with these, so as to obtain the greatest possible and most harmonious *sum*. For instance, Rembrandt always chooses to represent the exact force with which the light on the most illuminated part of an object is opposed to its obscurer portions. In order to obtain this, in most cases, not very important truth, he sacrifices the light and colour of five sixths of his picture; and the expression of every character of objects which depends on tenderness of shape or tint. But he obtains his single truth, and what picturesque and forcible expression is dependent upon it, with magnificent skill and subtlety. Veronese, on the contrary, chooses to represent the great relations of visible things to each other, to the heaven above,

---

[15] Philippians IV.8.

[16] Other things being equal.

[17] I name them in order of *in*creasing, not decreasing, importance. [Ruskin's note.]

and to the earth beneath them. He holds it more important to show how a figure stands relieved from delicate air, or marble wall; how as a red, or purple, or white figure, it separates itself, in clear discernibility, from things not red, nor purple, nor white; how infinite daylight shines round it; how innumerable veils of faint shadow invest it; how its blackness and darkness are, in the excess of their nature, just as limited and local as its intensity of light: all this, I say, he feels to be more important than showing merely the exact *measure* of the spark of sunshine that gleams on a dagger-hilt, or glows on a jewel. All this, moreover, he feels to be harmonious,—capable of being joined in one great system of spacious truth. And with inevitable watchfulness, inestimable subtlety, he unites all this in tenderest balance, noting in each hair's-breadth of colour, not merely what its rightness or wrongness is in itself, but what its relation is to every other on his canvas; restraining, for truth's sake, his exhaustless energy; reining back, for truth's sake, his fiery strength; veiling, before truth, the vanity of brightness; penetrating, for truth, the discouragement of gloom; ruling his restless invention with a rod of iron; pardoning no error, no thoughtlessness, no forgetfulness; and subduing all his powers, impulses, and imaginations, to the arbitrement of a merciless justice, and the obedience of an incorruptible verity.

I give this instance with respect to colour and shade; but, in the whole field of art, the difference between the great and inferior artists is of the same kind, and may be determined at once by the question, which of them conveys the largest sum of truth? It follows from this principle, that in general all *great* drawing is *distinct* drawing; for truths which are rendered indistinctly might, for the most part, as well not be rendered at all. There are, indeed, certain facts of mystery, and facts of indistinctness, in all objects, which must have their proper place in the general harmony, and the reader will presently find me, when we come to that part of our investigation, telling him that all good drawing must in some sort be *in*distinct. We may, however, understand this apparent contradiction by reflecting that the highest knowledge always involves a more advanced perception of the fields of the unknown; and, therefore, it may most truly be said, that to know anything well involves a profound sensation of ignorance, while yet it is equally true that good and noble knowledge is distinguished from vain and useless knowledge chiefly by its clearness and distinctness, and by the vigorous consciousness of what is known and what is not.

So in art. The best drawing involves a wonderful perception and expression of indistinctness; and yet all noble drawing is separated from the ignoble by its distinctness, by its fine expression and firm assertion of *Something;* whereas the bad drawing, without either firmness or fineness, expresses and asserts *Nothing.* The first thing, therefore, to be looked for as a sign of noble art, is a clear consciousness of what is drawn and what is not; the bold statement, and frank confession—*"This* I know," *"that* I know not"; and, generally speaking, all haste, slurring, obscurity, indecision, are signs of low art, and all calmness, distinctness, luminousness, and positiveness, of high art.

It follows, secondly, from this principle, that as the great painter is always attending to the sum and harmony of his truths rather than to one or the other of any group, a quality of Grasp is visible in his work, like the power of a great reasoner over his subject, or a great poet over his conception, manifesting itself very often in missing out certain details or less truths (which, though good in themselves, he finds are in the way of others), and in a sweeping manner of getting the beginnings and ends of things shown at once, and the squares and depths rather than the surfaces: hence, on the whole, a habit of looking at large masses rather than small ones; and even a physical largeness of handling, and love of working, if possible, on a large scale; and various other qualities, more or less imperfectly expressed by such technical terms as breadth, massing, unity, boldness, &c., all of which are, indeed, great qualities when they mean breadth of truth, weight of truth, unity of truth, and courageous assertion of truth; but which have all their correlative errors and mockeries, almost universally mistaken for them,—the breadth which has no contents, the weight which has no value, the unity which plots deception, and the boldness which faces out fallacy.

And it is to be noted especially respecting largeness of scale, that though for the most part it is characteristic of the more powerful masters, they having both more invention wherewith to fill space (as Ghirlandajo wished that he might paint all the walls of Florence), and, often, an impetuosity of mind which makes them like free play for hand and arm (besides that they usually desire to paint everything in the foreground of their picture of the natural size), yet, as this largeness of scale involves the placing of the picture at a considerable distance from the eye, and this distance involves the loss of many delicate details, and especially of the subtle lines of expression in features, it follows that the masters of refined detail and human expression are apt to prefer a small scale to work upon; so that the chief masterpieces of expression which the world possesses are small pictures by Angelico, in which the figures are rarely more than six or seven inches high; in the best works of Raphael and Leonardo the figures are almost always less than life; and the best works of Turner do not exceed the sizes of 18 inches by 12.

As its greatness depends on the sum of truth, and this sum of truth can always be increased by delicacy of handling, it follows that all great art must have this delicacy to the utmost possible degree. This rule is infallible and inflexible. All coarse work is the sign of low art. Only, it is to be remembered, that coarseness must be estimated by the distance from the eye; it being necessary to consult this distance, when great, by laying on touches which appear coarse when seen near; but which, so far from being coarse, are, in reality, more delicate in a master's work than the finest close handling, for they involve a calculation of result, and are laid on with a subtlety of sense precisely correspondent to that with which a good archer draws his bow; the spectator seeing in the action nothing but the strain of the strong arm, while there is, in reality, in the finger and eye, an ineffably delicate estimate of distance, and touch on the arrow plume. And, indeed, this delicacy is generally quite perceptible to those who know what the truth is, for strokes by Tintoret or Paul Veronese, which were done in an instant, and look to an ignorant spectator merely like a violent dash of loaded colour (and are, as such, imitated by blundering artists), are, in fact, modulated by the brush and finger to that degree of delicacy that no single grain of the colour could be taken from the touch without injury; and little golden particles of it, not the size of a gnat's head, have important share and function in the balances of light in a picture perhaps fifty feet long. Nearly *every* other rule applicable to art has some exception but this. This has absolutely none. All great art is delicate art, and all coarse art is bad art. Nay, even to a certain extent, all *bold* art is bad art; for boldness is not the proper word to apply to the courage and swiftness of a great master, based on knowledge, and coupled with fear and love. There is as much difference between the boldness of the true and the false masters, as there is between the courage of a pure woman and the shamelessness of a lost one.

IV. INVENTION.—The last characteristic of great art is that it must be inventive, that is,—be produced by the imagination. In this respect, it must precisely fulfil the definition already given of poetry; and not only present grounds for noble emotion, but furnish these grounds by *imaginative power*. Hence there is at once a great bar fixed between the two schools of Lower and Higher Art. The lower merely copies what is set before it, whether in portrait, landscape, or still-life; the higher either entirely imagines its subject, or arranges the materials presented to it, so as to manifest the imaginative power in all the three phases which have been already explained in the second volume.

And this was the truth which was confusedly present in Reynolds's mind when he spoke, as above quoted, of the difference between Historical and Poetical painting. *Every relation of the plain facts which the painter saw* is proper *historical* painting. If those facts are unimportant (as that he saw a gambler quarrel with another gambler, or a sot enjoying himself with another sot), then the history is trivial; if the facts are important (as that he saw such and such a great man look thus, or act thus, at such a time), then the history is noble: in each case perfect truth of narrative being supposed, otherwise the whole thing is worthless, being neither history nor poetry, but plain falsehood. And farther, as greater or less elegance and precision are manifested in the relation or painting of the incidents, the merit of the work varies; so that, what with difference of subject, and what with difference of treatment, historical painting falls or rises in changeful eminence, from Dutch trivialities to a Velasquez portrait, just as historical talking or writing varies in eminence, from an old woman's story-telling up to Herodotus. Besides which, certain operations of the imagination come into play inevitably, here and there, so as to touch the history with some light of poetry, that is, with some light shot forth of the narrator's mind, or brought out by the way he has put the accidents together: and wherever the imagination has thus had anything to do with the matter at all (and it must be somewhat cold work where it has not), then, the confines of the lower and higher schools touching each other, the work is coloured by both; but there is no reason why, therefore, we should in the least confuse the historical and poetical characters, any more than that we should confuse blue with crimson, because they may overlap each other, and produce purple.

Now, historical or simply narrative art is very precious in its proper place and way, but it is never *great* art until the poetical or imaginative power touches it; and in proportion to the stronger manifestation of this power, it becomes greater and greater, while the highest art is purely imaginative, all its materials being wrought into their form by invention. . . .

Farther, imaginative art always *includes* historical art; so that, strictly speaking, according to the analogy above used, we meet with the pure blue, and with the crimson ruling the blue and changing it into kingly purple, but not with the pure crimson: for all imagination must deal with the knowledge it has before accumulated; it never produces anything but by combination or contemplation. Creation, in the full sense, is impossible to it. And the mode in which the historical faculties are included by it is often quite simple, and easily seen. Thus, in Hunt's great poetical picture of the Light of the World, the whole thought and arrangement of the picture being imaginative, the several details of it are wrought out with simple portraiture; the ivy, the jewels, the creeping plants, and the moonlight being calmly studied or remembered from the things themselves. But of all these special ways in which the invention works with plain facts, we shall have to treat farther afterwards.

And now, finally, since this poetical power includes the historical, if we glance back to the other qualities required in great art, and put all together, we find that the sum of them is simply the sum of all the powers of man. For as (1) the choice of the high subject involves all conditions of right moral choice, and as (2) the love of beauty involves all conditions of right admiration, and as (3) the grasp of truth involves all strength of sense, evenness of judgment, and honesty of purpose, and as (4) the poetical power involves all swiftness of invention, and accuracy of historical memory, the sum of all these powers is the sum of the human soul. Hence we see why the word "Great" is used of this art. It is literally great. It compasses and calls forth the entire human spirit, whereas any other kind of art, being more or less small or narrow, compasses and calls forth only *part* of the human spirit. Hence the idea of its magnitude is a literal and just one, the art being simply less or greater in proportion to the number of faculties it exercises and addresses. And this is the ultimate meaning of the definition I gave of it long ago, as containing the "greatest number of the greatest ideas."

Such, then, being the characters required in order to constitute high art, if the reader will think over them a little, and over the various ways in which they may be falsely assumed, he will easily perceive how spacious and dangerous a field of discussion they open to the ambitious critic, and of error to the ambitious artist; he will see how difficult it must be, either to distinguish what is truly great art from the mockeries of it, or to rank the real artists in anything like a progressive system of greater and less. For it will have been observed that the various qualities which form greatness are partly inconsistent with each other (as some virtues are, docility and firmness for instance), and partly independent of each other; and the fact is, that artists differ not more by mere capacity, than by the component *elements* of their capacity, each possessing in very different proportions the several attributes of greatness; so that, classed by one kind of merit, as, for instance, purity of expression, Angelico will stand highest; classed by another, sincerity of manner, Veronese will stand highest; classed by another, love of beauty, Leonardo will stand highest; and so on: hence arise continual disputes and misunderstandings among those who think that high art must always be one and the same, and that great artists ought to unite all great attributes in an equal degree.

In one of the exquisitely finished tales of Marmontel, a company of critics are received at dinner by the hero of the story, an old gentleman, somewhat vain of his *acquired* taste, and his niece, by whose incorrigible *natural* taste he is seriously disturbed and tormented. During the entertainment, "On parcourut tous les genres de littérature, et pour donner plus d'essor à l'érudition et à la critique, on mit sur le tapis cette question toute neuve, sçavoir, lequel méritoit la préférence de Corneille ou de Racine. L'on disoit même là-dessus les plus belles choses du monde, lorsque la petite nièce, qui n'avoit pas dit un mot, s'avisa de demander naïvement lequel des deux fruits, de l'orange ou de la pêche, avoit le goût le plus exquis et méritoit le plus d'éloges. Son oncle rougit de sa simplicité, et les convives baissèrent tous les yeux sans daigner répondre à cette bêtise. Ma nièce, dit Fintac, à votre âge, il faut sçavoir écouter, et se tair." [18]

I cannot close this chapter with shorter or better advice to the reader, than merely, whenever he hears discussions about the relative merits of great masters, to remember the young lady's question. It is, indeed, true that there *is* a relative merit, that a peach is nobler than a hawthorn berry, and still more a hawthorn berry than a bead of the nightshade; but in each rank of fruits, as in each rank of masters, one is endowed with one virtue, and another with another; their glory is their dissimilarity, and they who propose to themselves in the training of an artist that he should unite the colouring of Tintoret, the finish of Albert Dürer, and the tenderness of Correggio, are no wiser than a horticulturist would be, who made it the object of his labour to produce a fruit which should unite in itself the lusciousness of the grape, the crispness of the nut, and the fragrance of the pine.

And from these considerations one most important practical corollary is to be deduced, with the good help of Mademoiselle Agathe's simile, namely, that the greatness or smallness of a man is, in the most conclusive sense, determined for him at his birth, as strictly as it is determined for a fruit whether it is to be a currant or an apricot. Education, favourable circumstances, resolution, and industry can do much; in a certain sense they do *everything;* that is to say, they determine whether the poor apricot shall fall in the form of a green bead, blighted by the east wind, and be trodden under foot, or whether it shall expand into tender pride, and sweet brightness of golden velvet. But apricot out of currant,— great man out of small,—did never yet art or effort make; and, in a general way, men have their excellence nearly fixed for them when they

[18] "They ran through all kinds of literature; and in order to give more scope to erudition and criticism, they brought on the carpet this entirely new question, viz. 'Which merited the preference, Corneille or Racine?' They said also on the subject the finest things in the world, when the little niece, who had not spoken a word, took it into her head to ask simply which of the two fruits, the orange or the peach, had the most exquisite taste, and merited the most commendation? Her uncle blushed at her simplicity, and the guests all looked down without deigning to reply to this idle foolery. 'Niece,' said Fintac, 'at your age one should hear and hold one's tongue.' " Jean François Marmontel (1723-1799), French dramatist and author of didactic works. The story is "The Connoisseur" from *Moral Tales.*

are born; a little cramped and frost-bitten on one side, a little sun-burnt and fortune-spotted on the other, they reach, between good and evil chances, such size and taste as generally belong to the men of their calibre, and, the small in their serviceable bunches, the great in their golden isolation, have, these no cause for regret, nor those for disdain.

Therefore it is, that every system of teaching is false which holds forth "great art" as in any wise to be taught to students, or even to be aimed at by them. Great art is precisely that which never was, nor will be taught, it is preeminently and finally the expression of the spirits of great men; so that the only wholesome teaching is that which simply endeavours to fix those characters of nobleness in the pupil's mind, of which it seems easily susceptible; and without holding out to him, as a possible or even probable result, that he should ever paint like Titian, or carve like Michael Angelo, enforces upon him the manifest possibility, and assured duty, of endeavouring to draw in a manner at least honest and intelligible; and cultivates in him those general charities of heart, sincerities of thought, and graces of habit which are likely to lead him, throughout life, to prefer openness to affectation, realities to shadows, and beauty to corruption.

Robert Browning

1812-1889

Fra Lippo Lippi
Andrea del Sarto

The following poems first appeared in the collection entitled *Men and Women* (1855). They represent Browning's full mastery over the technique of the dramatic monologue. In each a vividly realized historical character, caught at a dramatic moment, is made the mouthpiece for some of the author's characteristic views on art and life. The two poems should be read not only in relation to each other, but with the preceding selection from Ruskin in mind. A full account of the historical background of each is given in W. C. DeVane, *A Browning Handbook* (New York, 1955).

FRA LIPPO LIPPI

I am poor brother Lippo, by your leave!
You need not clap your torches to my face.
Zooks,[1] what's to blame? you think you see a monk!
What, 'tis past midnight, and you go the rounds,
And here you catch me at an alley's end
Where sportive ladies leave their doors ajar?
The Carmine's[2] my cloister: hunt it up,

[1] An oath; abbreviated form of "Gadzooks."
[2] The monastery of the Carmelites, of which order Lippo was a member.

Do,—harry out, if you must show your zeal,
Whatever rat, there, haps on his wrong hole,
And nip each softling of a wee white mouse,   10
Weke, weke, that's crept to keep him company!
Aha, you know your betters! Then, you'll take
Your hand away that's fiddling on my throat,
And please to know me likewise. Who am I?
Why, one, sir, who is lodging with a friend
Three streets off—he's a certain . . . how d'ye call?
Master—a . . . Cosimo of the Medici,[3]
I' the house that caps the corner. Boh! you were best!
Remember and tell me, the day you're hanged,
How you affected such a gullet's-gripe   20
But you, sir,[4] it concerns you that your knaves
Pick up a manner nor discredit you:
Zooks, are we pilchards, that they sweep the streets
And count fair prize what comes into their net?
He's Judas to a tittle, that man is!
Just such a face! why, sir, you make amends.
Lord, I'm not angry! Bid your hangdogs go
Drink out this quarter-florin to the health
Of the munificent House that harbours me
(And many more beside, lads! more beside!)   30
And all's come square again. I'd like his face—
His, elbowing on his comrade in the door
With the pike and lantern,—for the slave that holds
John Baptist's head a-dangle by the hair
With one hand ("Look you, now," as who should say)
And his weapon in the other, yet unwiped![5]
It's not your chance to have a bit of chalk,
A wood-coal or the like? or you should see!

---

[3] Duke Cosimo de' Medici (1389-1464), member of the great Florentine banking family and patron of the arts, in whose palace Lippo is living.

[4] Lippo henceforth addresses the constable of the city police, who has apprehended him.

[5] Lippo is imagining a painting of the beheading of John the Baptist.

Yes, I'm the painter, since you style me so.
What, brother Lippo's doings, up and down,   40
You know them and they take you? like enough!
I saw the proper twinkle in your eye—
'Tell you I liked your looks at very first.
Let's sit and set things straight now, hip to haunch.
Here's spring come, and the nights one makes up bands
To roam the town and sing out carnival,
And I've been three weeks shut within my mew,
A-painting for the great man, saints and saints
And saints again. I could not paint all night—
Ouf! I leaned out of window for fresh air.   50
There came a hurry of feet and little feet,
A sweep of lute-strings, laughs, and whifts[6] of song,—
Flower o' the broom,
Take away love, and our earth is a tomb!
Flower o' the quince,
I let Lisa go, and what good in life since?
Flower o' the thyme—and so on. Round they went.
Scarce had they turned the corner when a titter
Like the skipping of rabbits by moonlight,—three slim shapes,
And a face that looked up . . . zooks, sir, flesh and blood,   60
That's all I'm made of! Into shreds it went,
Curtain and counterpane and coverlet,
All the bed-furniture—a dozen knots,
There was a ladder! Down I let myself,
Hands and feet, scrambling somehow, and so dropped,
And after them. I came up with the fun
Hard by Saint Laurence,[7] hail fellow, well met,—
Flowers o' the rose,
If I've been merry, what matter who knows?
And so as I was stealing back again   70
To get to bed and have a bit of sleep

[6] Snatches.
[7] The Church of San Lorenzo.

Ere I rise up to-morrow and go work
On Jerome[8] knocking at his poor old breast
With his great round stone to subdue the flesh,
You snap me of the sudden. Ah, I see!
Though your eye twinkles still, you shake your head—
Mine's shaved,—a monk, you say—the sting's in that!
If Master Cosimo announced himself,
Mum's the word naturally; but a monk!
Come, what am I a beast for? tell us, now!   80
I was a baby when my mother died
And father died and left me in the street.
I starved there, God knows how, a year or two
On fig-skins, melon-parings, rinds and shucks,
Refuse and rubbish. One fine frosty day,
My stomach being empty as your hat,
The wind doubled me up and down I went.
Old Aunt Lapaccia trussed me with one hand,
(Its fellow was a stinger as I knew)
And so along the wall, over the bridge,   90
By the straight cut to the convent. Six words there,
While I stood munching my first bread that month:
"So, boy, you're minded," quoth the good fat father
Wiping his own mouth, 't was refection-time,—
"To quit this very miserable world?
"Will you renounce" . . . "The mouthful of bread?" thought I;
By no means! Brief, they made a monk of me;
I did renounce the world, its pride and greed,
Palace, farm, villa, shop and banking-house,
Trash, such as these poor devils of Medici   100
Have given their hearts to—all at eight years old.
Well, sir, I found in time, you may be sure,
'Twas not for nothing—the good bellyful,
The warm serge and the rope that goes all round,
And day-long blessed idleness beside!

[8] It is recorded that Lippo painted a picture of St. Jerome for Cosimo de' Medici.

"Let's see what the urchin's fit for"—that came next.
Not overmuch their way, I must confess.
Such a to-do! they tried me with their books:
Lord, they'd have taught me Latin in pure waste!
Flower o' the clove,   110
All the Latin I construe is, "amo" I love!
But, mind you, when a boy starves in the streets
Eight years together, as my fortune was,
Watching folk's faces to know who will fling
The bit of half-stripped grape-bunch he desires,
And who will curse or kick him for his pains,—
Which gentleman processional and fine,[9]
Holding a candle to the Sacrament
Will wink and let him lift a plate and catch
The droppings of the wax to sell again,   120
Or holla for the Eight[10] and have him whipped,—
How say I?—nay, which dog bites, which lets drop
His bone from the heap of offal in the street,—
Why, soul and sense of him grow sharp alike,
He learns the look of things, and none the less
For admonition from the hunger-pinch.
I had a store of such remarks, be sure,
Which, after I found leisure, turned to use.
I drew men's faces on my copy-books,
Scrawled them within the antiphonary's marge,   130
Joined legs and arms to the long music-notes,
Found eyes and nose and chin for A's and B's,
And made a string of pictures of the world
Betwixt the ins and outs of verb and noun,
On the wall, the bench, the door. The monks looked black.
"Nay," quoth the Prior, "turn him out, d'ye say?
"In no wise. Lose a crow and catch a lark.
"What if at last we get our man of parts,
"We Carmelites, like those Camaldolese

[9] Walking in procession in fine apparel.
[10] The governing body of Florence.

"And Preaching Friars,[11] to do our church up fine   140
"And put the front on it that ought to be!"
And hereupon he bade me daub away.
Thank you! my head being crammed, the walls a blank,
Never was such prompt disemburdening.
First, every sort of monk, the black and white,
I drew them, fat and lean: then, folk at church,
From good old gossips waiting to confess
Their cribs[12] of barrel-droppings, candle-ends,—
To the breathless fellow at the altar-foot,
Fresh from his murder, safe[13] and sitting there   150
With the little children round him in a row
Of admiration, half for his beard and half
For that white anger of his victim's son
Shaking a fist at him with one fierce arm,
Signing himself with the other because of Christ
(Whose sad face on the cross sees only this
After the passion of a thousand years)
Till some poor girl, her apron o'er her head,
(Which the intense eyes looked through) came at eve
On tip-toe, said a word, dropped in a loaf,   160
Her pair of earrings and a bunch of flowers
(The brute took growling), prayed, and so was gone.
I painted all, then cried " 'Tis ask and have;
"Choose, for more's ready!"—laid the ladder flat,
And showed my covered bit of cloister-wall.
The monks closed in a circle and praised loud
Till checked, taught what to see and not to see,
Being simple bodies,—"That's the very man!
"Look at the boy who stoops to pat the dog!
"That woman's like the Prior's niece who comes   170
"To care about his asthma: it's the life!"

[11] The Camaldolese were monks belonging to the convent of Camaldoli, near Florence; the Preaching Friars were members of the Dominican Order.
[12] Small thefts.
[13] Because he has found sanctuary in a sacred place.

But there my triumph's straw-fire flared and funked;
Their betters took their turn to see and say:
The Prior and the learned pulled a face
And stopped all that in no time. "How? what's here?
"Quite from the mark of painting, bless us all!
"Faces, arms, legs and bodies like the true
"As much as pea and pea! it's devil's game!
"Your business is not to catch men with show,
"With homage to the perishable clay,   180
"But lift them over it, ignore it all,
"Make them forget there's such a thing as flesh.
"Your business is to paint the souls of men—
"Man's soul, and it's a fire, smoke . . . no it's not . . .
"It's vapour done up like a new-born babe—
"(In that shape when you die it leaves your mouth)
"It's . . . well, what matters talking, it's the soul!
"Give us no more of body than shows soul!
"Here's Giotto,[14] with his Saint a-praising God,
"That sets us praising,—why not stop with him?   190
"Why put all thoughts of praise out of our head
"With wonder at lines, colours, and what not?
"Paint the soul, never mind the legs and arms!
"Rub all out, try at it a second time.
"Oh, that white smallish female with the breasts,
"She's just my niece . . . Herodias,[15] I would say,—
"Who went and danced and got men's heads cut off!
"Have it all out!" Now, is this sense, I ask?
A fine way to paint soul, by painting body
So ill, the eye can't stop there, must go further   200
And can't fare worse! Thus, yellow does for white
When what you put for yellow's simply black,

[14] Lippo's reference to Giotto, and subsequently to Fra Angelico and Lorenzo Monaco, dramatizes the contrast between his realistic theory and technique and the unworldly attitude of earlier Italian painters.

[15] Herodias, Herod's sister-in-law who plotted the beheading of John the Baptist. See Matthew xiv.1-12.

And any sort of meaning looks intense
When all beside itself means and looks nought.
Why can't a painter lift each foot in turn,
Left foot and right foot, go a double step,
Make his flesh liker and his soul more like,
Both in their order? Take the prettiest face,
The Prior's niece . . . patron-saint—is it so pretty
You can't discover if it means hope, fear,   210
Sorrow or joy? won't beauty go with these?
Suppose I've made her eyes all right and blue,
Can't I take breath and try to add life's flash
And then add soul and heighten them threefold?
Or say there's beauty with no soul at all—
(I never saw it—put the case the same—)
If you get simple beauty and nought else,
You get about the best thing God invents:
That's somewhat: and you'll find the soul you have missed,
Within yourself when you return him thanks.   220
"Rub all out!" Well, well, there's my life, in short,
And so the thing has gone on ever since.
I'm grown a man no doubt, I've broken bounds:
You should not take a fellow eight years old
And make him swear to never kiss the girls.
I'm my own master, paint now as I please—
Having a friend, you see, in the Corner-house!
Lord, its fast holding by the rings in front—
Those great rings serve more purposes than just
To plant a flag in, or tie up a horse!   230
And yet the old schooling sticks, the old grave eyes
Are peeping o'er my shoulder as I work,
The heads shake still—"It's art's decline, my son!
"You're not of the true painters, great and old;
"Brother Angelico's the man, you'll find:
"Brother Lorenzo[16] stands his single peer:
"Fag on at flesh, you'll never make the third!"

[16] The painters Fra Angelico and Lorenzo Monaco.

Flower o' the pine,
You keep your mistr . . . manners, and I'll stick to mine!
I'm not the third, then: bless us, they must know!   240
Don't you think they're the likeliest to know,
They with their Latin? So I swallow my rage,
Clench my teeth, suck my lips in tight, and paint
To please them—sometimes do and sometimes don't;
For, doing most, there's pretty sure to come
A turn, some warm eve finds me at my saints—
A laugh, a cry, the business of the world—
(*Flower o' the peach,*
Death for us all, and his own life for each!)
And my whole soul revolves, the cup runs over,   250
The world and life's too big to pass for a dream,
And I do these wild things in sheer despite,
And play the fooleries you catch me at,
In pure rage! The old mill-horse, out at grass
After hard years, throws up his stiff heels so,
Although the miller does not preach to him
The only good of grass is to make chaff.
What would men have? Do they like grass or no—
May they or mayn't they? all I want's the thing
Settled for ever one way. As it is,   260
You tell too many lies and hurt yourself:
You don't like what you only like too much,
You do like what, if given you at your word,
You find abundantly detestable.
For me, I think I speak as I was taught;
I always see the garden and God there
A-making man's wife: and, my lesson learned,
The value and significance of flesh,
I can't unlearn ten minutes afterward.

  You understand me: I'm a beast, I know.   270
But see, now—why, I see as certainly
As that the morning-star's about to shine,
What will hap some day. We've a youngster here

Comes to our convent, studies what I do,
Slouches and stares and lets no atom drop:
His name is Guidi[17]—he'll not mind the monks—
They call him Hulking Tom, he lets them talk—
He picks my practice up—he'll paint apace,
I hope so—though I never live so long,
I know what's sure to follow. You be judge!   280
You speak no Latin more than I, belike;
However, you're my man, you've seen the world
—The beauty and the wonder and the power,
The shapes of things, their colours, lights and shades,
Changes, surprises,—and God made it all!
—For what? do you feel thankful, ay or no,
For this fair town's face, yonder river's line,
The mountain round it and the sky above,
Much more the figures of man, woman, child,
These are the frame to? What's it all about?   290
To be passed over, despised? or dwelt upon,
Wondered at? oh, this last of course!—you say.
But why not do as well as say,—paint these
Just as they are, careless what comes of it?
God's works—paint any one, and count it crime
To let a truth slip. Don't object, "His works
"Are here already; nature is complete:
"Suppose you reproduce her—(which you can't)
"There's no advantage! you must beat her, then."
For, don't you mark, we're made so that we love   300
First when we see them painted, things we have passed
Perhaps a hundred times nor cared to see;
And so they are better, painted—better to us,
Which is the same thing. Art was given for that;
God uses us to help each other so,
Lending our minds out. Have you noticed, now,
Your cullion's hanging face? A bit of chalk,

[17] Tommaso Guidi, known as Masaccio (1401-1428), was Lippo's teacher, not his pupil.

And trust me but you should, though! How much more,
If I drew higher things with the same truth!
That were to take the Prior's pulpit-place   310
Interpret God to all of you! Oh, oh,
It makes me mad to see what men shall do
And we in our graves! This world's no blot for us,
Nor blank; it means intensely, and means good:
To find its meaning is my meat and drink.
"Ay, but you don't so instigate to prayer!"
Strikes in the Prior: "when your meaning's plain
"It does not say to folks—remember matins,
"Or, mind you fast next Friday." Why, for this
What need of art at all? A skull and bones,   320
Two bits of stick nailed crosswise, or, what's best,
A bell to chime the hour with, does as well.
I painted a Saint Laurence[18] six months since
At Prato,[19] splashed the fresco in fine style:
"How looks my painting, now the scaffold's down?"
I ask a brother: "Hugely," he returns—
"Already not one phiz of your three slaves
"Who turn the Deacon off his toasted side,
"But's scratched and prodded to our heart's content,
"The pious people have so eased their own   330
"With coming to say prayers there in a rage:
"We get on fast to see the bricks beneath.
"Expect another job this time next year,
"For pity and religion grow i' the crowd—
"Your painting serves its purpose!" Hang the fools!

    —That is—you'll not mistake an idle word
Spoke in a huff by a poor monk, God wot,
Tasting the air this spicy night which turns
The unaccustomed head like Chianti wine!
Oh, the church knows! don't misreport me, now!   340

---

[18] St. Laurence was martyred in 258 A.D. by being roasted to death on a gridiron.
[19] Lippo did some of his best work in the Cathedral of Prato, near Florence.

It's natural a poor monk out of bounds
Should have his apt word to excuse himself:
And hearken how I plot to make amends.
I have bethought me: I shall paint a piece[20]
. . . There's for you! Give me six months, then go, see
Something in Sant' Ambrogio's! [21] Bless the nuns!
They want a cast o' my office.[22] I shall paint
God in the midst, Madonna and her babe,
Ringed by a bowery flowery angel-brood,
Lilies and vestments and white faces, sweet   350
As puff on puff of grated orris-root
When ladies crowd to Church at midsummer.
And then i' the front, of course a saint or two—
Saint John,[23] because he saves the Florentines,
Saint Ambrose, who puts down in black and white
The convent's friends and gives them a long day.
And Job, I must have him there past mistake,
The man of Uz, (and Us without the z,
Painters who need his patience). Well, all these
Secured at their devotion, up shall come   360
Out of a corner when you least expect,
As one by a dark stair into a great light,
Music and talking, who but Lippo! [24] I!—
Mazed, motionless and moonstruck—I'm the man!
Back I shrink—what is this I see and hear?
I, caught up with my monk's things by mistake,
My old serge gown and rope that goes all round,
I, in this presence, this pure company!
Where's a hole, where's a corner for escape?
Then steps a sweet angelic slip of a thing   370

[20] In the following lines Lippo describes his famous painting of *The Coronation of the Virgin,* now in the Academy of Fine Arts, Florence.

[21] The Church of Sant' Ambrogio in Florence, named for the patron saint of the convent.

[22] An example of my work.

[23] John the Baptist, patron saint of Florence.

[24] Lippo put a portrait of himself in the lower right-hand corner of the painting.

Forward, puts out a soft palm—"Not so fast!"
—Addresses the celestial presence, "nay—
"He made you and devised you, after all,
"Though he's none of you! Could Saint John there draw—
"His camel-hair make up a painting-brush? [25]
"We come to brother Lippo for all that,
"*Iste perfecit opus!*" [26] So, all smile—
I shuffle sideways with my blushing face
Under the cover of a hundred wings
Thrown like a spread of kirtles when you're gay   380
And play hot cockles,[27] all the doors being shut,
Till, wholly unexpected, in there pops
The hothead husband! Thus I scuttle off
To some safe bench behind, not letting go
The palm of her, the little lily thing
That spoke the good word for me in the nick,
Like the Prior's niece . . . Saint Lucy, I would say.
And so all's saved for me, and for the church
A pretty picture gained. Go, six months hence!
Your hand, sir, and good-bye: no lights, no lights!   390
The street's hushed, and I know my own way back,
Don't fear me! there's the grey beginning. Zooks!

ANDREA DEL SARTO
(*Called "The Faultless Painter"*)

But do not let us quarrel any more,
No, my Lucrezia;[1] bear with me for once:
Sit down and all shall happen as you wish.
You turn your face, but does it bring your heart?

---

[25] Cf. Mark 1.6.
[26] "This one performed the work."
[27] A game like blindman's buff.

[1] Andrea is addressing Lucrezia del Fede, his wife, who was the original for the type of feminine beauty in most of his paintings.

I'll work then for your friend's friend, never fear,
Treat his own subject after his own way,
Fix his own time, accept too his own price,
And shut the money into this small hand
When next it takes mine. Will it? tenderly?
Oh, I'll content him,—but to-morrow, Love!   10
I often am much wearier than you think,
This evening more than usual, and it seems
As if—forgive now—should you let me sit
Here by the window with your hand in mine
And look a half-hour forth on Fiesole,[2]
Both of one mind, as married people use,
Quietly, quietly, the evening through,
I might get up to-morrow to my work
Cheerful and fresh as ever. Let us try.
To-morrow, how you shall be glad for this!   20
Your soft hand is a woman of itself,
And mine the man's bared breast she curls inside.
Don't count the time lost, neither; you must serve
For each of the five pictures we require:
It saves a model. So! keep looking so—
My serpentining beauty, rounds on rounds!
—How could you ever prick those perfect ears,
Even to put the pearl there! oh, so sweet—
My face, my moon, my everybody's moon,
Which everybody looks on and calls his,   30
And, I suppose, is looked on by in turn,
While she looks—no one's: very dear, no less.
You smile? why, there's my picture ready made,
There's what we painters call our harmony!
A common greyness silvers everything,—
All in a twilight, you and I alike
—You, at the point of your first pride in me
(That's gone, you know),—but I, at every point;
My youth, my hope, my art, being all toned down

[2] A suburb of Florence.

To yonder sober pleasant Fiesole.   40
There's the bell clinking from the chapel-top;
That length of convent-wall across the way
Holds the trees safer, huddled more inside;
The last monk leaves the garden; days decrease,
And autumn grows, autumn in everything.
Eh? the whole seems to fall into a shape
As if I saw alike my work and self
And all that I was born to be and do,
A twilight-piece. Love, we are in God's hand.
How strange now, looks the life he makes us lead!   50
So free we seem, so fettered fast we are!
I feel he laid the fetter: let it lie!
This chamber for example—turn your head—
All that's behind us! you don't understand
Nor care to understand about my art,
But you can hear at least when people speak:
And that cartoon,[3] the second from the door
—It is the thing, Love! so such things should be—
Behold Madonna!—I am bold to say.
I can do with my pencil what I know,   60
What I see, what at bottom of my heart
I wish for, if I ever wish so deep—
Do easily, too—when I say, perfectly,
I do not boast, perhaps: yourself are judge
Who listened to the Legate's[4] talk last week,
And just as much they used to say in France.[5]
At any rate 'tis easy, all of it!
No sketches first, no studies, that's long past:
I do what many dream of all their lives,
—Dream? strive to do, and agonize to do,   70

[3] A preliminary sketch for an oil painting.
[4] Papal envoy.
[5] In 1518 Andrea had gone to live in Fontainebleau, France, under the patronage of King Francis I; but at his wife's persuasion he is said to have forsaken the French court, appropriating for his own purposes funds the king had given him to purchase paintings.

And fail in doing. I could count twenty such
On twice your fingers, and not leave this town,
Who strive—you don't know how the others strive
To paint a little thing like that you smeared
Carelessly passing with your robes afloat,—
Yet do much less, so much less, Someone[6] says,
(I know his name, no matter)—so much less!
Well, less is more, Lucrezia: I am judged.
There burns a truer light of God in them,
In their vexed beating stuffed and stopped-up brain,   80
Heart, or whate'er else, than goes on to prompt
This low-pulsed forthright craftsman's hand of mine.
Their works drop groundward, but themselves, I know,
Reach many a time a heaven that's shut to me,
Enter and take their place there sure enough,
Though they come back and cannot tell the world.
My works are nearer heaven, but I sit here.
The sudden blood of these men! at a word—
Praise them, it boils, or blame them, it boils too.
I, painting from myself and to myself,   90
Know what I do, am unmoved by men's blame
Or their praise either. Somebody remarks
Morello's[7] outline there is wrongly traced,
His hue mistaken; what of that? or else,
Rightly traced and well ordered; what of that?
Speak as they please, what does the mountain care?
Ah, but a man's reach should exceed his grasp,
Or what's a heaven for? all is silver-grey
Placid and perfect with my art: the worse!
I know both what I want and what might gain   100
And yet how profitless to know, to sigh
"Had I been two, another and myself.
"Our head would have o'erlooked the world!" No doubt.
Yonder's a work now, of that famous youth

[6] Michelangelo, see l. 199.
[7] A peak in the Apennines, north of Florence.

The Urbinate[8] who died five years ago.
('Tis copied, George Vasari[9] sent it me.)
Well, I can fancy how he did it all,
Pouring his soul, with kings and popes to see,
Reaching, that heaven might so replenish him,
Above and through his art—for it gives way;   110
That arm is wrongly put—and there again—
A fault to pardon in the drawing's lines,
Its body, so to speak: its soul is right,
He means right—that, a child may understand.
Still, what an arm! and I could alter it:
But all the play, the insight and the stretch—
Out of me, out of me! And wherefore out?
Had you enjoined them on me, given me soul,
We might have risen to Rafael, I and you!
Nay, Love, you did give all I asked, I think—   120
More than I merit, yes, by many times.
But had you—oh, with the same perfect brow,
And perfect eyes, and more than perfect mouth,
And the low voice my soul hears, as a bird
The fowler's pipe, and follows to the snare—
Had you, with these the same, but brought a mind!
Some women do so. Had the mouth there urged
"God and the glory! never care for gain.
"The present by the future, what is that?
"Live for fame, side by side with Agnolo! [10]   130
"Rafael is waiting: up to God all three!"
I might have done it for you. So it seems:
Perhaps not. All is as God over-rules.
Beside, incentives come from the soul's self;
The rest avail not. Why do I need you?

---

[8] Reference to Raphael, who was born at Urbino.
[9] Giorgio Vasari (1511-1574), originally a pupil of Andrea, and author of *The Lives of the Most Eminent Painters, Sculptors, and Architects* (1568), which was Browning's principal literary source for his knowledge of Renaissance art history.
[10] Michelangelo.

What wife had Rafael, or has Agnolo?
In this world, who can do a thing, will not;
And who would do it, cannot, I perceive:
Yet the will's somewhat—somewhat, too, the power—
And thus we half-men struggle. At the end,   140
God, I conclude, compensates, punishes.
'Tis safer for me, if the award be strict,
That I am something underrated here,
Poor this long while, despised, to speak the truth.
I dared not, do you know, leave home all day,
For fear of chancing on the Paris lords.
The best is when they pass and look aside;
But they speak sometimes; I must bear it all.
Well may they speak! That Francis, that first time,
And that long festal year at Fontainebleau!   150
I surely then could sometimes leave the ground,
Put on the glory, Rafael's daily wear,
In that humane great monarch's golden look,—
One finger in his beard or twisted curl
Over his mouth's good mark that made the smile,
One arm about my shoulder, round my neck,
The jingle of his gold chain in my ear,
I painting proudly with his breath on me,
All his court round him, seeing with his eyes,
Such frank French eyes, and such a fire of souls   160
Profuse, my hand kept plying by those hearts,—
And, best of all, this, this, this face beyond,
This in the background, waiting on my work,
To crown the issue with a last reward!
A good time, was it not, my kingly days?
And had you not grown restless . . . but I know—
'Tis done and past; 'twas right, my instinct said;
Too live the life grew, golden and not grey,
And I'm the weak-eyed bat no sun should tempt
Out of the grange whose four walls make his world.   170
How could it end in any other way?

You called me, and I came home to your heart.
The triumph was—to reach and stay there; since
I reached it ere the triumph, what is lost?
Let my hands frame your face in your hair's gold,
You beautiful Lucrezia that are mine!
"Rafael did this, Andrea painted that;
"The Roman's[11] is the better when you pray,
"But still the other's Virgin was his wife—"
Men will excuse me. I am glad to judge   180
Both pictures in your presence; clearer grows
My better fortune, I resolve to think.
For, do you know, Lucrezia, as God lives,
Said one day Agnolo, his very self,
To Rafael . . . I have known it all these years . . .
(When the young man was flaming out his thoughts
Upon a palace-wall for Rome to see,
Too lifted up in heart because of it)
"Friend, there's a certain sorry little scrub
"Goes up and down our Florence, none cares how,   190
"Who, were he set to plan and execute
"As you are, pricked on by your popes and kings,
"Would bring the sweat into that brow of yours!"
To Rafael's!—And indeed the arm is wrong.
I hardly dare . . . yet, only you to see,
Give the chalk here—quick, thus the line should go!
Ay, but the soul! he's Rafael! rub it out!
Still, all I care for, if he spoke the truth,
(What he? why, who but Michel Agnolo?
Do you forget already words like those?)   200
If really there was such a chance, so lost,—
Is, whether you're—not grateful—but more pleased.
Well, let me think so. And you smile indeed!
This hour has been an hour! Another smile?
If you would sit thus by me every night
I should work better, do you comprehend?

[11] Another reference to Raphael, who passed his last years painting in Rome.

I mean that I should earn more, give you more.
See, it is settled dusk now; there's a star;
Morello's gone, the watch-lights show the wall,
The cue-owls[12] speak the name we call them by.   210
Come from the window, love,—come in, at last,
Inside the melancholy little house
We built to be so gay with. God is just.
King Francis may forgive me: oft at nights
When I look up from painting, eyes tired out,
The walls become illumined, brick from brick
Distinct, instead of mortar, fierce bright gold,
That gold of his I did cement them with!
Let us but love each other. Must you go?
That Cousin[13] here again? he waits outside?   220
Must see you—you, and not with me? Those loans?
More gaming debts to pay? you smiled for that?
Well, let smiles buy me! have you more to spend?
While hand and eye and something of a heart
Are left me, work's my ware, and what's it worth?
I'll pay my fancy. Only let me sit
The grey remainder of the evening out,
Idle, you call it, and muse perfectly
How I could paint, were I but back in France,
One picture, just one more—the Virgin's face,   230
Not yours this time! I want you at my side
To hear them—that is, Michel Agnolo—
Judge all I do and tell you of its worth.
Will you? To-morrow, satisfy your friend.
I take the subjects for his corridor,
Finish the portrait out of hand—there, there,
And throw him in another thing or two
If he demurs; the whole should prove enough
To pay for this same Cousin's freak. Beside,
What's better and what's all I care about,   240

[12] Diminutive European owls.
[13] "That Cousin" is, of course, Lucrezia's lover.

303

Get you the thirteen scudi for the ruff!
Love, does that please you? Ah, but what does he,
The Cousin! what does he to please you more?

    I am grown peaceful as old age to-night.
I regret little, I would change still less.
Since there my past life lies, why alter it?
The very wrong to Francis!—it is true
I took his coin, was tempted and complied,
And built this house and sinned, and all is said.
My father and my mother died of want.   250
Well, had I riches of my own? you see
How one gets rich! Let each one bear his lot.
They were born poor, lived poor, and poor they died:
And I have laboured somewhat in my time
And not been paid profusely. Some good son
Paint my two hundred pictures—let him try!
No doubt, there's something strikes a balance. Yes,
You loved me quite enough, it seems to-night.
This must suffice me here. What would one have?
In heaven, perhaps, new chances, one more chance— 260
Four great walls in the New Jerusalem,[14]
Meted on each side by the angel's reed,
For Leonard,[15] Rafael, Agnolo and me
To cover—the three first without a wife,
While I have mine! So—still they overcome
Because there's still Lucrezia,—as I choose.

    Again the Cousin's whistle! Go, my Love.

[14] Cf. Revelation xxi.10-21.
[15] Leonardo da Vinci.

Matthew Arnold

1822-1888

The Study of Poetry

🎜 Originally written as the general introduction to
T. H. Ward's *The English Poets* (1880), this essay
was reprinted at the beginning of *Essays in Criticism,
Second Series* (1888). Arnold's use of poetic "touch-
stones" has regularly provided a stumbling block for
students of his critical theories. It seems safe to assume
that Arnold selected these short passages not solely
for their intrinsic poetic merit, but also with the
intention that they should evoke in the reader's mind
the full majesty of the epic and dramatic works
in which they occur. Only the first part of the essay
is given here.

"The future of poetry is immense, because in poetry,
where it is worthy of its high destinies, our race, as time goes on, will
find an ever surer and surer stay. There is not a creed which is not
shaken, not an accredited dogma which is not shown to be question-
able, not a received tradition which does not threaten to dissolve.
Our religion has materialized itself in the fact, in the supposed fact;
it has attached its emotion to the fact, and now the fact is failing it.
But for poetry the idea is everything; the rest is a world of illusion, of
divine illusion. Poetry attaches its emotion to the idea; the idea *is* the
fact. The strongest part of our religion today is its unconscious poetry." [1]

[1] This quotation is a slightly shortened version of the final paragraph of Arnold's
brief introduction to a collection entitled *The Hundred Greatest Men* (London, 1879).

Let me be permitted to quote these words of my own, as uttering the thought which should, in my opinion, go with us and govern us in all our study of poetry. In the present work it is the course of one great contributory stream to the world-river of poetry that we are invited to follow. We are here invited to trace the stream of English poetry. But whether we set ourselves, as here, to follow only one of the several streams that make the mighty river of poetry, or whether we seek to know them all, our governing thought should be the same. We should conceive of poetry worthily, and more highly than it has been the custom to conceive of it. We should conceive of it as capable of higher uses, and called to higher destinies, than those which in general men have assigned to it hitherto. More and more mankind will discover that we have to turn to poetry to interpret life for us, to console us, to sustain us. Without poetry, our science will appear incomplete; and most of what now passes with us for religion and philosophy will be replaced by poetry. Science, I say, will appear incomplete without it. For finely and truly does Wordsworth call poetry "the impassioned expression which is in the countenance of all science";[2] and what is a countenance without its expression? Again, Wordsworth finely and truly calls poetry "the breath and finer spirit of all knowledge": our religion, parading evidences such as those on which the popular mind relies now; our philosophy, pluming itself on its reasonings about causation and finite and infinite being; what are they but the shadows and dreams and false shows of knowledge? The day will come when we shall wonder at ourselves for having trusted to them, for having taken them seriously; and the more we perceive their hollowness, the more we shall prize "the breath and finer spirit of knowledge" offered to us by poetry.

But if we conceive thus highly of the destinies of poetry, we must also set our standard for poetry high, since poetry, to be capable of fulfilling such high destinies, must be poetry of a high order of excellence. We must accustom ourselves to a high standard and to a strict judgment. Sainte-Beuve[3] relates that Napoleon one day said, when

---

[2] See Preface to *Lyrical Ballads*, 2nd ed. (1800).

[3] See Sainte-Beuve, *Les Cahiers* (Paris, 1876), p. 51. Arnold referred to his French contemporary as "the finest critical spirit of our times" and "one of my chief benefactors."

somebody was spoken of in his presence as a charlatan: "Charlatan as much as you please; but where is there *not* charlatanism?"—"Yes," answers Sainte-Beuve, "in politics, in the art of governing mankind, that is perhaps true. But in the order of thought, in art, the glory, the eternal honor is that charlatanism shall find no entrance; herein lies the inviolableness of that noble portion of man's being." It is admirably said, and let us hold fast to it. In poetry, which is thought and art in one, it is the glory, the eternal honor, that charlatanism shall find no entrance; that this noble sphere be kept inviolate and inviolable. Charlatanism is for confusing or obliterating the distinctions between excellent and inferior, sound and unsound or only half-sound, true and untrue or only half-true. It is charlatanism, conscious or unconscious, whenever we confuse or obliterate these. And in poetry, more than anywhere else, it is unpermissible to confuse or obliterate them. For in poetry the distinction between excellent and inferior, sound and unsound or only half-sound, true and untrue or only half-true, is of paramount importance. It is of paramount importance because of the high destinies of poetry. In poetry, as a criticism of life under the conditions fixed for such a criticism by the laws of poetic truth and poetic beauty, the spirit of our race will find, we have said, as time goes on and as other helps fail, its consolation and stay. But the consolation and stay will be of power in proportion to the power of the criticism of life. And the criticism of life will be of power in proportion as the poetry conveying it is excellent rather than inferior, sound rather than unsound or half-sound, true rather than untrue or half-true.

The best poetry is what we want; the best poetry will be found to have a power of forming, sustaining, and delighting us, as nothing else can. A clearer, deeper sense of the best in poetry, and of the strength and joy to be drawn from it, is the most precious benefit which we can gather from a poetical collection such as the present. And yet in the very nature and conduct of such a collection there is inevitably something which tends to obscure in us the consciousness of what our benefit should be, and to distract us from the pursuit of it. We should therefore steadily set it before our minds at the outset, and should compel ourselves to revert constantly to the thought of it as we proceed.

Yes; constantly in reading poetry, a sense for the best, the really excellent, and of the strength and joy to be drawn from it, should be present in our minds and should govern our estimate of what we read. But this real estimate, the only true one, is liable to be superseded, if we are not watchful, by two other kinds of estimate, the historic estimate and the personal estimate, both of which are fallacious. A poet or a poem may count to us historically, they may count to us on grounds personal to ourselves, and they may count to us really. They may count to us historically. The course of development of a nation's language, thought, and poetry, is profoundly interesting; and by regarding a poet's work as a stage in this course of development we may easily bring ourselves to make it of more importance as poetry than in itself it really is, we may come to use a language of quite exaggerated praise in criticizing it; in short, to over-rate it. So arises in our poetic judgments the fallacy caused by the estimate which we may call historic. Then, again, a poet or a poem may count to us on grounds personal to ourselves. Our personal affinities, likings, and circumstances, have great power to sway our estimate of this or that poet's work, and to make us attach more importance to it as poetry than in itself it really possesses, because to us it is, or has been, of high importance. Here also we over-rate the object of our interest, and apply to it a language of praise which is quite exaggerated. And thus we get the source of a second fallacy in our poetic judgments—the fallacy caused by an estimate which we may call personal.

Both fallacies are natural. It is evident how naturally the study of the history and development of a poetry may incline a man to pause over reputations and works once conspicuous but now obscure, and to quarrel with a careless public for skipping, in obedience to mere tradition and habit, from one famous name or work in its national poetry to another, ignorant of what it misses, and of the reason for keeping what it keeps, and of the whole process of growth in its poetry. The French have become diligent students of their own early poetry, which they long neglected; the study makes many of them dissatisfied with their so-called classical poetry, the court-tragedy of the seventeenth century, a poetry which Pellisson[4] long ago reproached with its want

[4] Paul Pellisson (1624-1693), French critic and historiographer to Louis XIV.

of the true poetic stamp, with its *politesse stérile et rampante*[5] but which nevertheless has reigned in France as absolutely as if it had been the perfection of classical poetry indeed. The dissatisfaction is natural; yet a lively and accomplished critic, M. Charles d'Héricault,[6] the editor of Clément Marot, goes too far when he says that "the cloud of glory playing round a classic is a mist as dangerous to the future of a literature as it is intolerable for the purposes of history." "It hinders," he goes on, "it hinders us from seeing more than one single point, the culminating and exceptional point; the summary, fictitious and arbitrary, of a thought and of a work. It substitutes a halo for a physiognomy, it puts a statue where there was once a man, and hiding from us all trace of the labor, the attempts, the weaknesses, the failures, it claims not study but veneration; it does not show us how the thing is done, it imposes upon us a model. Above all, for the historian this creation of classic personages is inadmissible; for it withdraws the poet from his time, from his proper life, it breaks historical relationships, it blinds criticism by conventional admiration, and renders the investigation of literary origins unacceptable. It gives us a human personage no longer, but a God seated immovable amidst His perfect work, like Jupiter on Olympus: and hardly will it be possible for the young student, to whom such work is exhibited at such a distance from him, to believe that it did not issue ready made from that divine head."

All this is brilliantly and tellingly said, but we must plead for a distinction. Everything depends on the reality of a poet's classic character. If he is a dubious classic, let us sift him; if he is a false classic, let us explode him. But if he is a real classic, if his work belongs to the class of the very best (for this is the true and right meaning of the word *classic, classical*), then the great thing for us is to feel and enjoy his work as deeply as ever we can, and to appreciate the wide difference between it and all work which has not the same high character. This is what is salutary, this is what is formative; this is the great benefit to be got from the study of poetry. Everything which interferes with it, which hinders it, is injurious. True, we must read our classic with open eyes, and not with eyes blinded with superstition; we must per-

[5] Barren and servile civility.
[6] Charles-Joseph de Ricault (1823-1899), French historian and novelist.

ceive when his work comes short, when it drops out of the class of
the very best, and we must rate it, in such cases, at its proper value.
But the use of this negative criticism is not in itself, it is entirely in its
enabling us to have a clearer sense and a deeper enjoyment of what is
truly excellent. To trace the labor, the attempts, the weaknesses, the
failures of a genuine classic, to acquaint oneself with his time and his
life and his historical relationships, is mere literary dilettantism unless
it has that clear sense and deeper enjoyment for its end. It may be
said that the more we know about a classic the better we shall enjoy
him; and, if we lived as long as Methuselah and had all of us heads
of perfect clearness and wills of perfect steadfastness, this might be
true in fact as it is plausible in theory. But the case here is much the
same as the case with the Greek and Latin studies of our schoolboys.
The elaborate philological groundwork which we require them to lay
is in theory an admirable preparation for appreciating the Greek and
Latin authors worthily. The more thoroughly we lay the groundwork,
the better we shall be able, it may be said, to enjoy the authors. True,
if time were not so short, and schoolboys' wits not so soon tired and
their power of attention exhausted; only, as it is, the elaborate philological
preparation goes on, but the authors are little known and less enjoyed. So with the investigator of "historic origins" in poetry. He ought
to enjoy the true classic all the better for his investigations; he often is
distracted from the enjoyment of the best, and with the less good he
overbusies himself, and is prone to over-rate it in proportion to the
trouble which it has cost him.

The idea of tracing historic origins and historical relationships cannot be absent from a compilation like the present. And naturally the
poets to be exhibited in it will be assigned to those persons for exhibition who are known to prize them highly, rather than to those
who have no special inclination towards them. Moreover the very
occupation with an author, and the business of exhibiting him, disposes
us to affirm and amplify his importance. In the present work, therefore, we are sure of frequent temptation to adopt the historic estimate,
or the personal estimate, and to forget the real estimate; which latter,
nevertheless, we must employ if we are to make poetry yield us its
full benefit. So high is that benefit, the benefit of clearly feeling and

of deeply enjoying the really excellent, the truly classic in poetry, that we do well, I say, to set it fixedly before our minds as our object in studying poets and poetry, and to make the desire of attaining it the one principle to which, as the "Imitation" says, whatever we may read or come to know, we always return. *Cum multa legeris et cognoveris, ad unum semper oportet redire principium.*[7]

The historic estimate is likely in especial to affect our judgment and our language when we are dealing with ancient poets; the personal estimate when we are dealing with poets our contemporaries, or at any rate modern. The exaggerations due to the historic estimate are not in themselves, perhaps, of very much gravity. Their report hardly enters the general ear; probably they do not always impose even on the literary men who adopt them. But they lead to a dangerous abuse of language. So we hear Cædmon,[8] among our own poets, compared to Milton. I have already noticed the enthusiasm of one accomplished French critic for "historic origins." Another eminent French critic, M. Vitet,[9] comments upon that famous document of the early poetry of his nation, the *Chanson de Roland.*[10] It is indeed a most interesting document. The *joculator* or *jongleur,* Taillefer, who was with William the Conqueror's army at Hastings,[11] marched before the Norman troops, so said the tradition, singing "of Charlemagne and of Roland and of Oliver, and of the vassals who died at Roncevaux";[12] and it is suggested that in the *Chanson de Roland* by one Turoldus or Théroulde,[13] a poem preserved in a manuscript of the twelfth century

---

[7] "When you have read and learned many things, you ought always to return to the one principle." The quotation is from Thomas à Kempis, *Imitation of Christ,* III, xliii, 2.

[8] Cædmon is sometimes called the "father of English poetry."

[9] Ludovic Vitet (1802-1873), French politician and man of letters.

[10] The national epic of France, dating from the eleventh century.

[11] *Jongleur* (Latin *joculator*), literally, jester, the name given to wandering minstrels in mediaeval France. As a result of the Battle of Hastings in 1066, the Norman William the Conqueror subdued England to his rule. For the story of Taillefer, see Edward Augustus Freeman, *History of the Norman Conquest* (New York, 1873), III, 319-320.

[12] The *Chanson de Roland* recounts how Charlemagne's troops were overthrown by the Saracens at Roncevaux in the Pyrenees.

[13] Turoldus' connection with the manuscript, on which his name appears, has not been determined.

in the Bodleian Library at Oxford, we have certainly the matter, perhaps even some of the words, of the chant which Taillefer sang. The poem has vigor and freshness; it is not without pathos. But M. Vitet is not satisfied with seeing in it a document of some poetic value, and of very high historic and linguistic value; he sees in it a grand and beautiful work, a monument of epic genius. In its general design he finds the grandiose conception, in its details he finds the constant union of simplicity with greatness, which are the marks, he truly says, of the genuine epic, and distinguish it from the artificial epic of literary ages. One thinks of Homer; this is the sort of praise which is given to Homer, and justly given. Higher praise there cannot well be, and it is the praise due to epic poetry of the highest order only, and to no other. Let us try, then, the *Chanson de Roland* at its best. Roland, mortally wounded, lays himself down under a pine-tree, with his face turned towards Spain and the enemy—

> De plusurs choses à remembrer li prist,
> De tantes teres cume li bers cunquist,
> De dulce France, des humes de sun lign,
> De Carlemagne sun seignor ki l'nurrit.[14]

That is primitive work, I repeat, with an undeniable poetic quality of its own. It deserves such praise, and such praise is sufficient for it. But now turn to Homer—

> Ὣς φάτο, τοὺς δ' ἤδη κάτεχεν φυσίζοος αἶα
> ἐν Λακεδαίμονι αὖθι, φίλῃ ἐν πατρίδι γαίῃ.[15]

We are here in another world, another order of poetry altogether; here is rightly due such supreme praise as that which M. Vitet gives to the *Chanson de Roland.* If our words are to have any meaning, if our judgments are to have any solidity, we must not heap that supreme praise upon poetry of an order immeasurably inferior.

---

[14] "Then began he to call many things to remembrance,—all the lands which his valour conquered, and pleasant France, and the men of his lineage, and Charlemagne his liege lord who nourished him."—*Chanson de Roland,* III, 939-942. [Arnold's note.]

[15] "So said she; they long since in Earth's soft arms were reposing,
There, in their own dear land, their fatherland, Lacedæmon."—*Iliad,* III, 243-4 (translated by Dr. Hawtrey). [Arnold's note.]

Indeed there can be no more useful help for discovering what poetry belongs to the class of the truly excellent, and can therefore do us most good, than to have always in one's mind lines and expressions of the great masters, and to apply them as a touchstone to other poetry. Of course we are not to require this other poetry to resemble them; it may be very dissimilar. But if we have any tact we shall find them, when we have lodged them well in our minds, an infallible touchstone for detecting the presence or absence of high poetic quality, and also the degree of this quality, in all other poetry which we may place beside them. Short passages, even single lines, will serve our turn quite sufficiently. Take the two lines which I have just quoted from Homer, the poet's comment on Helen's mention of her brothers;[16]—or take his

$$\text{ἆ δειλώ, τί σφῶϊ δόμεν Πηλῆϊ ἄνακτι}$$
$$\text{θνητῷ, ὑμεῖς δ' ἐστὸν ἀγήρω τ' ἀθανάτω τε;}$$
$$\text{ἢ ἵνα δυστήνοισι μετ' ἀνδράσιν ἄλγε' ἔχητον;}^{17}$$

the address of Zeus to the horses of Peleus;—or take finally his

$$\text{καὶ σέ, γέρον, τὸ πρὶν μὲν ἀκούομεν ὄλβιον}$$
$$\text{εἶναι·}^{18}$$

the words of Achilles to Priam, a suppliant before him. Take that incomparable line and a half of Dante, Ugolino's tremendous words—

Io no piangeva; sì dentro impietrai.
Piangevan elli . . .[19]

[16] Castor and Pollux were the brothers of Helen of Troy.

[17] "Ah, unhappy pair, why gave we you to King Peleus, to a mortal? but ye are without old age, and immortal. Was it that with men born to misery ye might have sorrow?"—*Iliad*, XVII, 443-445. [Arnold's note.]

[18] "Nay, and thou too, old man, in former days wast, as we hear, happy."—*Iliad*, XXIV, 543. [Arnold's note.] Achilles, the Greek hero, slew Hector, son of Priam the Trojan king.

[19] "I wailed not, so of stone grew I within;—*they* wailed."—*Inferno*, XXXIII, 39-40. [Arnold's note.] Actually the lines are 49-50. During his visit to Hell Dante met the shade of Ugolino, a political leader who had been imprisoned in 1288, along with his two sons and two small grandsons. Dante describes their death by starvation. The wailing is that of the little boys.

take the lovely words of Beatrice to Virgil—

> Io son fatta da Dio, sua mercè, tale,
> Che la vostra miseria non mi tange,
> Nè fiamma d'esto incendio non m'assale . . .[20]

take the simple, but perfect, single line—

> In la sua volontade è nostra pace.[21]

Take of Shakespeare a line or two of Henry the Fourth's expostulation with sleep—

> Wilt thou upon the high and giddy mast
> Seal up the ship-boy's eyes, and rock his brains
> In cradle of the rude imperious surge . . .[22]

and take, as well, Hamlet's dying request to Horatio—

> If thou didst ever hold me in thy heart,
> Absent thee from felicity awhile,
> And in this harsh world draw thy breath in pain
> To tell my story . . .[23]

Take of Milton that Miltonic passage—

> Darken'd so, yet shone
> Above them all the archangel; but his face
> Deep scars of thunder had intrench'd, and care
> Sat on his faded cheek . . .[24]

add two such lines as—

> And courage never to submit or yield
> And what is else not to be overcome . . .[25]

---

[20] "Of such sort hath God, thanked be His mercy, made me, that your misery toucheth me not, neither doth the flame of this fire strike me."—*Inferno*, II, 91-93. [Arnold's note.] Beatrice was Dante's early love, to whose memory he remained faithful after her death. The Roman poet Virgil guided Dante on his visit to Hell.

[21] "In His will is our peace."—*Paradiso*, III, 85. [Arnold's note.]

[22] *Henry IV*, Part Two, III, i, 18-20.

[23] *Hamlet* v.ii.357-360.

[24] *Paradise Lost* I.599-602.

[25] *Paradise Lost* I.108-109.

and finish with the exquisite close to the loss of Proserpine, the loss

> . . . which cost Ceres all that pain
> To seek her through the world.[26]

These few lines, if we have tact and can use them, are enough even of themselves to keep clear and sound our judgments about poetry, to save us from fallacious estimates of it, to conduct us to a real estimate.

The specimens I have quoted differ widely from one another, but they have in common this: the possession of the very highest poetical quality. If we are thoroughly penetrated by their power, we shall find that we have acquired a sense enabling us, whatever poetry may be laid before us, to feel the degree in which a high poetical quality is present or wanting there. Critics give themselves great labor to draw out what in the abstract constitutes the characters of a high quality of poetry. It is much better simply to have recourse to concrete examples;—to take specimens of poetry of the high, the very highest quality, and to say: The characters of a high quality of poetry are what is expressed *there*. They are far better recognized by being felt in the verse of the master, than by being perused in the prose of the critic. Nevertheless if we are urgently pressed to give some critical account of them, we may safely, perhaps, venture on laying down, not indeed how and why the characters arise, but where and in what they arise. They are in the matter and substance of the poetry, and they are in its manner and style. Both of these, the substance and matter on the one hand, the style and manner on the other, have a mark, an accent, of high beauty, worth, and power. But if we are asked to define this mark and accent in the abstract, our answer must be: No, for we should thereby be darkening the question, not clearing it. The mark and accent are as given by the substance and matter of that poetry, by the style and manner of that poetry, and of all other poetry which is akin to it in quality.

Only one thing we may add as to the substance and matter of poetry, guiding ourselves by Aristotle's profound observation that the superiority of poetry over history consists in its possessing a higher truth and a

[26] *Paradise Lost* iv.271-272.

higher seriousness (φιλοσοφώτερον καὶ σπουδαιότερον).[27] Let us add, therefore, to what we have said, this: that the substance and matter of the best poetry acquire their special character from possessing, in an eminent degree, truth and seriousness. We may add yet further, what is in itself evident, that to the style and manner of the best poetry their special character, their accent, is given by their diction, and, even yet more, by their movement. And though we distinguish between the two characters, the two accents, of superiority, yet they are nevertheless vitally connected one with the other. The superior character of truth and seriousness, in the matter and substance of the best poetry, is inseparable from the superiority of diction and movement marking its style and manner. The two superiorities are closely related, and are in steadfast proportion one to the other. So far as high poetic truth and seriousness are wanting to a poet's matter and substance, so far also, we may be sure, will a high poetic stamp of diction and movement be wanting to his style and manner. In proportion as this high stamp of diction and movement, again, is absent from a poet's style and manner, we shall find, also, that high poetic truth and seriousness are absent from his substance and matter. . . .

[27] Arnold refers to Aristotle's statement in *Poetics* IX: "They [the historian and the poet] are distinguished by this—that the one relates what has been, the other what might be. On this account Poetry is a more philosophical and a more serious thing than History: for Poetry is chiefly conversant about general truth, History about particular."

Walter Horatio Pater
1839-1894

Preface

La Gioconda

Conclusion

The first of the following selections Pater wrote to
preface his *Studies in the History of the Renaissance*
(1873), the title being changed in subsequent editions
to *The Renaissance: Studies in Art and Poetry*. The
famous description of the painting *La Gioconda,*
better known as *Mona Lisa,* occurs in an essay
on Leonardo da Vinci, first published in the
Fortnightly Review (November 1869), and then in
somewhat revised form as the sixth essay of *The
Renaissance.* The Conclusion, written as early as 1868,
was printed in the first edition of *The Renaissance,*
withdrawn from the second (1877), and then re-
instated in the third edition (1888) with an accompanying note by Pater: "This brief 'Conclusion' was
omitted in the second edition of this book, as I
conceived it might possibly mislead some of those
young men into whose hands it might fall. On the
whole, I have thought it best to reprint it here, with
some slight changes which bring it closer to my
original meaning. I have dealt more fully in *Marius
the Epicurean* with the thoughts suggested by it."

THE ROLE OF THE ARTIST

PREFACE

Many attempts have been made by writers on art and poetry to define beauty in the abstract, to express it in the most general terms, to find a universal formula for it. The value of these attempts has most often been in the suggestive and penetrating things said by the way. Such discussions help us very little to enjoy what has been well done in art or poetry, to discriminate between what is more and what is less excellent in them, or to use words like beauty, excellence, art, poetry, with a more precise meaning than they would otherwise have. Beauty, like all other qualities presented to human experience, is relative; and the definition of it becomes unmeaning and useless in proportion to its abstractness. To define beauty, not in the most abstract, but in the most concrete terms possible, to find, not a universal formula for it, but the formula which expresses most adequately this or that special manifestation of it, is the aim of the true student of æsthetics.

"To see the object as in itself it really is," [1] has been justly said to be the aim of all true criticism whatever; and in æsthetic criticism the first step towards seeing one's object as it really is, is to know one's own impression as it really is, to discriminate it, to realise it distinctly. The objects with which æsthetic criticism deals—music, poetry, artistic and accomplished forms of human life—are indeed receptacles of so many powers or forces: they possess, like the products of nature, so many virtues or qualities. What is this song or picture, this engaging personality presented in life or in a book, to *me*? What effect does it really produce on me? Does it give me pleasure? and if so, what sort or degree of pleasure? How is my nature modified by its presence, and under its influence? The answers to these questions are the original facts with which the æsthetic critic has to do; and, as in the study of light, of morals, of number, one must realise such primary data for oneself, or not at all. And he who experiences these impressions strongly, and drives directly at the analysis and discrimination of them, has no need to trouble himself with the abstract question what beauty is in itself, or what its exact relation to truth or experience—meta-

---

[1] The phrase occurs in the concluding paragraph of the second of Arnold's lectures *On Translating Homer* (1861).

physical questions, as unprofitable as metaphysical questions elsewhere. He may pass them all by as being, answerable or not, of no interest to him.

The æsthetic critic, then, regards all the objects with which he has to do, all works of art, and the fairer forms of nature and human life, as powers or forces producing pleasurable sensations, each of a more or less peculiar or unique kind. This influence he feels, and wishes to explain, analysing it, and reducing it to its elements. To him, the picture, the landscape, the engaging personality in life or in a book, *La Gioconda,* the hills of Carrara, Pico of Mirandola,[2] are valuable for their virtues, as we say, in speaking of a herb, a wine, a gem; for the property each has of affecting one with a special, a unique, impression of pleasure. Our education becomes complete in proportion as our susceptibility to these impressions increases in depth and variety. And the function of the æsthetic critic is to distinguish, analyse, and separate from its adjuncts, the virtue by which a picture, a landscape, a fair personality in life or in a book, produces this special impression of beauty or pleasure, to indicate what the source of that impression is, and under what conditions it is experienced. His end is reached when he has disengaged that virtue, and noted it, as a chemist notes some natural element, for himself and others; and the rule for those who would reach this end is stated with great exactness in the words of a recent critic of Sainte-Beuve: *De se borner à connaître de près les belles choses, et à s'en nourrir en exquis amateurs, en humanistes accomplis.*[3]

What is important, then, is not that the critic should possess a correct abstract definition of beauty for the intellect, but a certain kind of temperament, the power of being deeply moved by the presence of beautiful objects. He will remember always that beauty exists in many forms. To him all periods, types, schools of taste, are in themselves equal. In all ages there have been some excellent workmen, and some excellent work done. The question he asks is always:—In whom did

[2] Leonardo's renowned portrait, which hangs in the Louvre Gallery in Paris; the mountains near Carrara in northern Italy from which the famous marble of that name is quarried; Giovanni Pico, Count of Mirandola (1463-1494), brilliant Italian humanist to whom Pater devoted an essay in *The Renaissance.*

[3] "To confine themselves to knowing beautiful objects at first hand, and to nourish themselves on these as refined amateurs and accomplished humanists."

the stir, the genius, the sentiment of the period find itself? where was the receptacle of its refinement, its elevation, its taste? "The ages are all equal," says William Blake, "but genius is always above its age." [4]

Often it will require great nicety to disengage this virtue from the commoner elements with which it may be found in combination. Few artists, not Goethe or Byron even, work quite cleanly, casting off all *débris,* and leaving us only what the heat of their imagination has wholly fused and transformed. Take, for instance, the writings of Wordsworth. The heat of his genius, entering into the substance of his work, has crystallised a part, but only a part, of it; and in that great mass of verse there is much which might well be forgotten. But scattered up and down it, sometimes fusing and transforming entire compositions, like the stanzas on *Resolution and Independence,* and the Ode on the *Recollections of Childhood,*[5] sometimes, as if at random, depositing a fine crystal here or there, in a matter it does not wholly search through and transform, we trace the action of his unique, incommunicable faculty, that strange, mystical sense of a life in natural things, and of man's life as a part of nature, drawing strength and colour and character from local influences, from the hills and streams, and from natural sights and sounds. Well! that is the *virtue,* the active principle in Wordsworth's poetry; and then the function of the critic of Wordsworth is to follow up that active principle, to disengage it, to mark the degree in which it penetrates his verse.

The subjects of the following studies are taken from the history of the Renaissance, and touch what I think the chief points in that complex, many-sided movement. I have explained in the first of them what I understand by the word, giving it a much wider scope than was intended by those who originally used it to denote only that revival of classical antiquity in the fifteenth century which was but one of many results of a general excitement and enlightening of the human mind, but of which the great aim and achievements of what, as Christian art, is often falsely opposed to the Renaissance, were another result. This outbreak of the

---

[4] Pater has in mind Blake's comment on his painting of the Canterbury Pilgrims from Chaucer; see *Poems,* ed. W. B. Yeats (London, 1893), p. 216.

[5] The title of Wordsworth's poem is "Ode: Intimations of Immortality from Recollections of Early Childhood."

human spirit may be traced far into the Middle Age itself, with its qualities already clearly pronounced, the care for physical beauty, the worship of the body, the breaking down of those limits which the religious system of the Middle Age imposed on the heart and the imagination. I have taken as an example of this movement, this earlier Renaissance within the Middle Age itself, and as an expression of its qualities, two little compositions in early French; not because they constitute the best possible expression of them, but because they help the unity of my series, inasmuch as the Renaissance ends also in France, in French poetry, in a phase of which the writings of Joachim du Bellay are in many ways the most perfect illustration; the Renaissance thus putting forth in France an aftermath, a wonderful later growth, the products of which have to the full that subtle and delicate sweetness which belongs to a refined and comely decadence; just as its earliest phases have the freshness which belongs to all periods of growth in art, the charm of *ascêsis,*[6] of the austere and serious girding of the loins in youth.

But it is in Italy, in the fifteenth century, that the interest of the Renaissance mainly lies,—in that solemn fifteenth century which can hardly be studied too much, not merely for its positive results in the things of the intellect and the imagination, its concrete works of art, its special and prominent personalities, with their profound æsthetic charm, but for its general spirit and character, for the ethical qualities of which it is a consummate type.

The various forms of intellectual activity which together make up the culture of an age, move for the most part from different starting-points, and by unconnected roads. As products of the same generation they partake, indeed, of a common character, and unconsciously illustrate each other; but of the producers themselves, each group is solitary, gaining what advantage or disadvantage there may be in intellectual isolation. Art and poetry, philosophy and the religious life, and that other life of refined pleasure and action in the open places of the world, are each of them confined to its own circle of ideas, and those who prosecute either of them are generally little curious of the thoughts of others. There come, however, from time to time, eras of more favourable conditions,

---

[6] In his essay on "Style" Pater defines this term, in his usage, as "self-restraint, a skilful economy of means."

in which the thoughts of men draw nearer together than is their wont, and the many interests of the intellectual world combine in one complete type of general culture. The fifteenth century in Italy is one of these happier eras; and what is sometimes said of the age of Pericles is true of that of Lorenzo:[7]—it is an age productive in personalities, many-sided, centralised, complete. Here, artists and philosophers and those whom the action of the world has elevated and made keen, do not live in isolation, but breathe a common air, and catch light and heat from each other's thoughts. There is a spirit of general elevation and enlightenment in which all alike communicate. It is the unity of this spirit which gives unity to all the various products of the Renaissance; and it is to this intimate alliance with mind, this participation in the best thoughts which that age produced, that the art of Italy in the fifteenth century owes much of its grave dignity and influence.

I have added an essay on Winckelmann,[8] as not incongruous with the studies which precede it, because Winckelmann, coming in the eighteenth century, really belongs in spirit to an earlier age. By his enthusiasm for the things of the intellect and the imagination for their own sake, by his Hellenism, his life-long struggle to attain to the Greek spirit, he is in sympathy with the humanists of an earlier century. He is the last fruit of the Renaissance, and explains in a striking way its motive and tendencies.

[7] Pericles, the Athenian statesman of the fifth century B.C.; Lorenzo de' Medici, called The Magnificent, the great Renaissance prince and patron of the arts.

[8] Johann Joachim Winckelmann (1717-1768), the great German archaeologist and historian of classical art.

WALTER HORATIO PATER

LA GIOCONDA

La Gioconda[9] is, in the truest sense, Leonardo's masterpiece, the revealing instance of his mode of thought and work. In suggestiveness, only the *Melancholia*[10] of Dürer is comparable to it; and no crude symbolism disturbs the effect of its subdued and graceful mystery. We all know the face and hands of the figure, set in its marble chair, in that cirque of fantastic rocks, as in some faint light under the sea. Perhaps of all ancient pictures time has chilled it least.[11] As often happens with works in which invention seems to reach its limit, there is an element in it given to, not invented by, the master. In that inestimable folio of drawings, once in the possession of Vasari,[12] were certain designs by Verrocchio, faces of such impressive beauty that Leonardo in his boyhood copied them many times. It is hard not to connect with these designs of the elder, by-past master, as with its germinal principle, the unfathomable smile, always with a touch of something sinister in it, which plays over all Leonardo's work. Besides, the picture is a portrait. From childhood we see this image defining itself on the fabric of his dreams; and but for express historical testimony, we might fancy that this was but his ideal lady, embodied and beheld at last. What was the relationship of a living Florentine to this creature of his thought? By means of what strange affinities had the person and the dream grown up thus apart, and yet so closely together? Present from the first incorporeally in Leonardo's thought, dimly traced in the designs of Verrocchio, she is found present at last in Il Giocondo's house. That there is much of mere portraiture in the picture is attested by the legend that by artificial means, the presence of mimes and flute-players, that subtle expression was protracted on the face. Again, was it in four years and by renewed labor never really completed, or in four months and as by stroke of magic, that the image was projected?

The presence that thus rose so strangely beside the waters, is expressive of what in the ways of a thousand years men had come to desire. Hers

---

[9] See note 2, p. 319.

[10] One of Dürer's most famous engravings bears this title.

[11] "Yet for Vasari there was some further magic of crimson in the lips and cheeks, lost to us." [Pater's note.]

[12] Giorgio Vasari (1511-1574), Italian painter and writer of the lives of artists.

is the head upon which all "the ends of the world are come," [13] and the eyelids are a little weary. It is a beauty wrought out from within upon the flesh, the deposit, little cell by cell, of strange thoughts and fantastic reveries and exquisite passions. Set it for a moment beside one of those white Greek goddesses or beautiful women of antiquity, and how would they be troubled by this beauty, into which the soul with all its maladies has passed! All the thoughts and experience of the world have etched and moulded there, in that which they have of power to refine and make expressive the outward form, the animalism of Greece, the lust of Rome, the reverie of the Middle Age with its spiritual ambition and imaginative loves, the return of the Pagan world, the sins of the Borgias.[14] She is older than the rocks among which she sits; like the vampire, she has been dead many times, and learned the secrets of the grave; and has been a diver in deep seas, and keeps their fallen day about her; and trafficked for strange webs with Eastern merchants; and, as Leda, was the mother of Helen of Troy, and, as Saint Anne, the mother of Mary; and all this has been to her but as the sound of lyres and flutes, and lives only in the delicacy with which it has moulded the changing lineaments, and tinged the eyelids and the hands. The fancy of a perpetual life, sweeping together ten thousand experiences, is an old one; and modern thought has conceived the idea of humanity as wrought upon by, and summing up in itself, all modes of thought and life. Certainly Lady Lisa might stand as the embodiment of the old fancy, the symbol of the modern idea.

[13] See I Corinthians x.11.

[14] A powerful family of Renaissance nobles, whose members were notorious for their debauchery and crimes.

WALTER HORATIO PATER

CONCLUSION

Λέγει που Ἡράκλειτος ὅτι πάντα χωρεῖ καὶ οὐδὲν μένει [15]

To regard all things and principles of things as inconstant modes or fashions has more and more become the tendency of modern thought. Let us begin with that which is without—our physical life. Fix upon it in one of its more exquisite intervals, the moment, for instance, of delicious recoil from the flood of water in summer heat. What is the whole physical life in that moment but a combination of natural elements to which science gives their names? But these elements, phosphorus and lime and delicate fibres, are present not in the human body alone: we detect them in places most remote from it. Our physical life is a perpetual motion of them—the passage of the blood, the wasting and repairing of the lenses of the eye, the modification of the tissues of the brain by every ray of light and sound—processes which science reduces to simpler and more elementary forces. Like the elements of which we are composed, the action of these forces extends beyond us; it rusts iron and ripens corn. Far out on every side of us those elements are broadcast, driven by many forces; and birth and gesture [16] and death and the springing of violets from the grave are but a few out of ten thousand resultant combinations. That clear, perpetual outline of face and limb is but an image of ours, under which we group them—a design in a web, the actual threads of which pass out beyond it. This at least of flame-like our life has, that it is but the concurrence, renewed from moment to moment, of forces parting sooner or later on their ways.

Or if we begin with the inward world of thought and feeling, the whirlpool is still more rapid, the flame more eager and devouring. There it is no longer the gradual darkening of the eye and fading of colour from the wall,—the movement of the shore-side, where the water flows down indeed, though in apparent rest,—but the race of the mid-stream, a drift of momentary acts of sight and passion and thought. At first sight experience seems to bury us under a flood of external objects, pressing

[15] "Heraclitus says, 'All things give way; nothing remaineth.' " Pater's translation occurs in his *Plato and Platonism*, Chapter I.
[16] In the original meaning of "activity."

325

upon us with a sharp and importunate reality, calling us out of ourselves in a thousand forms of action. But when reflexion begins to act upon those objects they are dissipated under its influence; the cohesive force seems suspended like a trick of magic; each object is loosed into a group of impressions—colour, odour, texture—in the mind of the observer. And if we continue to dwell in thought on this world, not of objects in the solidity with which language invests them, but of impressions unstable, flickering, inconsistent, which burn and are extinguished with our consciousness of them, it contracts still further; the whole scope of observation is dwarfed to the narrow chamber of the individual mind. Experience, already reduced to a swarm of impressions, is ringed round for each one of us by that thick wall of personality through which no real voice has ever pierced on its way to us, or from us to that which we can only conjecture to be without. Every one of those impressions is the impression of the individual in his isolation, each mind keeping as a solitary prisoner its own dream of a world. Analysis goes a step farther still, and assures us that those impressions of the individual mind to which, for each one of us, experience dwindles down, are in perpetual flight; that each of them is limited by time, and that as time is infinitely divisible, each of them is infinitely divisible also; all that is actual in it being a single moment, gone while we try to apprehend it, of which it may ever be more truly said that it has ceased to be than that it is. To such a tremulous wisp constantly reforming itself on the stream, to a single sharp impression, with a sense in it, a relic more or less fleeting, of such moments gone by, what is real in our life fines itself down. It is with this movement, with the passage and dissolution of impressions, images, sensations, that analysis leaves off—that continual vanishing away, that strange, perpetual weaving and unweaving of ourselves.

Philosophiren, says Novalis, *ist dephlegmatisiren, vivificiren.*[17] The service of philosophy, of speculative culture, towards the human spirit is to rouse, to startle it into sharp and eager observation. Every moment some form grows perfect in hand or face; some tone on the hills or the sea is choicer than the rest; some mood of passion or insight or intel-

---

[17] "To philosophize is to throw off inertia, to come to life." Novalis was the pseudonym of Friedrich von Hardenberg (1772-1801), German Romantic poet and philosopher.

lectual excitement is irresistibly real and attractive for us,—for that moment only. Not the fruit of experience, but experience itself, is the end. A counted number of pulses only is given to us of a variegated, dramatic life. How may we see in them all that is to be seen in them by the finest senses? How shall we pass most swiftly from point to point, and be present always at the focus where the greatest number of vital forces unite in their purest energy?

To burn always with this hard, gemlike flame, to maintain this ecstasy, is success in life. In a sense it might even be said that our failure is to form habits: for, after all, habit is relative to a stereotyped world, and meantime it is only the roughness of the eye that makes any two persons, things, situations, seem alike. While all melts under our feet, we may well catch at any exquisite passion, or any contribution to knowledge that seems by a lifted horizon to set the spirit free for a moment, or any stirring of the senses, strange dyes, strange colours, and curious odours, or work of the artist's hands, or the face of one's friend. Not to discriminate every moment some passionate attitude in those about us, and in the brilliancy of their gifts some tragic dividing of forces on their ways, is, on this short day of frost and sun, to sleep before evening. With this sense of the splendour of our experience and of its awful brevity, gathering all we are into one desperate effort to see and touch, we shall hardly have time to make theories about the things we see and touch. What we have to do is to be for ever curiously testing new opinions and courting new impressions, never acquiescing in a facile orthodoxy of Comte, or of Hegel, or of our own. Philosophical theories or ideas, as points of view, instruments of criticism, may help us to gather up what might otherwise pass unregarded by us. "Philosophy is the microscope of thought." The theory or idea or system which requires of us the sacrifice of any part of this experience, in consideration of some interest into which we cannot enter, or some abstract theory we have not identified with ourselves, or what is only conventional, has no real claim upon us.

One of the most beautiful passages in the writings of Rousseau is that in the sixth book of the *Confessions,* where he describes the awakening in him of the literary sense. An undefinable taint of death had always clung about him, and now in early manhood he believed himself smitten by mortal disease. He asked himself how he might make as much as possible of the interval that remained; and he was not biassed by anything in his previous life when he decided that it must be by intellectual excitement, which he found just then in the clear, fresh writings of Voltaire. Well! we are all *condamnés,* as Victor Hugo says: we are all under sentence of death but with a sort of indefinite reprieve —*les hommes sont tous condamnés à mort avec des sursis indéfinis:*[18] we have an interval, and then our place knows us no more. Some spend this interval in listlessness, some in high passions, the wisest, at least among "the children of this world," [19] in art and song. For our one chance lies in expanding that interval, in getting as many pulsations as possible into the given time. Great passions may give us this quickened sense of life, ecstasy and sorrow of love, the various forms of enthusiastic activity, disinterested or otherwise, which come naturally to many of us. Only be sure it is passion—that it does yield you this fruit of a quickened, multiplied consciousness. Of this wisdom, the poetic passion, the desire of beauty, the love of art for art's sake, has most. For art comes to you professing frankly to give nothing but the highest quality to your moments as they pass, and simply for those moments' sake.

[18] "All men are condemned to death with indefinite reprieves."
[19] Cf. Luke xvi.8: ". . . the children of this world are wiser in their generation than the children of light."

Dante Gabriel Rossetti
1828-1882

The Portrait

> ⚘ The following selection was first published in *Poems*
> (1870). In a perceptive essay on Rossetti, Pater wrote:
> "Like Dante, he knows no region of spirit which
> shall not be sensuous also, or material. The shadowy
> world, which he realizes so powerfully, has still the
> ways and houses, the land and water, the light and
> darkness, the fire and flowers, that had so much
> to do in the moulding of those bodily powers and
> aspects which counted for so large a part of the soul,
> here." It should be remembered that Rossetti was
> an accomplished and successful painter as well as poet.

This is her picture as she was:
    It seems a thing to wonder on,[1]
As though mine image in the glass
    Should tarry when myself am gone.
I gaze until she seems to stir,—
Until mine eyes almost aver
    That now, even now, the sweet lips part
    To breathe the words of the sweet heart:—
And yet the earth is over her.

[1] Cf. the opening lines of Browning's celebrated dramatic monologue, "My Last
Duchess":
> That's my last Duchess painted on the wall,
> Looking as if she were alive. I call
> That piece a wonder, now . . .

Rossetti passionately admired Browning's poetry.

Alas! even such the thin-drawn ray   10
   That makes the prison-depths more rude,—
The drip of water night and day
   Giving a tongue to solitude.
Yet only this, of love's whole prize,
Remains; save what in mournful guise
   Takes counsel with my soul alone,—
   Save what is secret and unknown,
Below the earth, above the skies.

In painting her I shrined her face
   Mid mystic trees, where light falls in   20
Hardly at all; a covert place
   Where you might think to find a din
Of doubtful talk, and a live flame
Wandering, and many a shape whose name
   Not itself knoweth, and old dew,
   And your own footsteps meeting you,
And all things going as they came.

A deep dim wood; and there she stands
   As in that wood that day: for so
Was the still movement of her hands   30
   And such the pure line's gracious flow.
And passing fair the type must seem,
Unknown the presence and the dream.
   'Tis she: though of herself, alas!
   Less than her shadow on the grass
Or than her image in the stream.

That day we met there, I and she
   One with the other all alone;
And we were blithe; yet memory
   Saddens those hours, as when the moon   40
Looks upon daylight. And with her
I stooped to drink the spring-water,
   Athirst where other waters sprang:

And where the echo is, she sang,—
My soul another echo there.

But when that hour my soul won strength
    For words whose silence wastes and kills,
Dull raindrops smote us, and at length
    Thundered the heat within the hills.
That eve I spoke those words again   50
Beside the pelted window-pane;
    And there she hearkened what I said,
    With under-glances that surveyed
The empty pastures blind with rain.

Next day the memories of these things,
    Like leaves through which a bird has flown,
Still vibrated with Love's warm wings;
    Till I must make them all my own
And paint this picture. So, 'twixt ease
Of talk and sweet long silences,   60
    She stood among the plants in bloom
    At windows of a summer room,
To feign the shadow of the trees.

And as I wrought, while all above
    And all around was fragrant air,
In the sick burthen of my love
    It seemed each sun-thrilled blossom there
Beat like a heart among the leaves.
O heart that never beats nor heaves,
    In that one darkness lying still,   70
    What now to thee my love's great will
Or the fine web the sunshine weaves?

For now doth daylight disavow
    Those days—nought left to see or hear.
Only in solemn whispers now
    At night-time these things reach mine ear,

When the leaf-shadows at a breath
Shrink in the road, and all the heath,
   Forest and water, far and wide,
   In limpid starlight glorified,   80
Lie like the mystery of death.

Last night at last I could have slept,
   And yet delayed my sleep till dawn,
Still wandering. Then it was I wept:
   For unawares I came upon
Those glades where once she walked with me:
And as I stood there suddenly,
   All wan with traversing the night,
   Upon the desolate verge of light
Yearned loud the iron-bosomed sea.   90

Even so, where Heaven holds breath and hears
   The beating heart of Love's own breast,—
Where round the secret of all spheres
   All angels lay their wings to rest,—
How shall my soul stand rapt and awed,
When, by the new birth borne abroad
   Throughout the music of the suns,
   It enters in her soul at once
And knows the silence there for God!

Here with her face doth memory sit   100
   Meanwhile, and wait the day's decline,
Till other eyes shall look from it,
   Eyes of the spirit's Palestine,
Even than the old gaze tenderer:
While hopes and aims long lost with her
   Stand round her image side by side,
   Like tombs of pilgrims that have died
About the Holy Sepulchre.

SUGGESTIONS FOR ADDITIONAL READING

For the student of Victorian aesthetic theory, the following writings will illuminate the principal critical positions of the age with regard to literature and the arts:

Thomas Carlyle, *On Heroes, Hero-Worship, and the Heroic in History* (1841): Lecture III, "The Hero as Poet. Dante; Shakespeare"; Lecture V, "The Hero as Man of Letters. Johnson; Rousseau; Burns"

Dante Gabriel Rossetti, "Hand and Soul," published in *The Germ* (1850)

Matthew Arnold, "Preface to the First Edition of *Poems* (1853)"; *Essays in Criticism, First Series* (1865), including "The Function of Criticism at the Present Time"; *Essays in Criticism, Second Series* (1888), including "The Study of Poetry"

John Ruskin, *Modern Painters*, Vol. III (1856), including "Of the Pathetic Fallacy"

Algernon Charles Swinburne, *Notes on Poems and Reviews* (1866)

Walter Pater, *The Renaissance: Studies in Art and Poetry* (1873; 1888); *Appreciations, with an Essay on Style* (1889)

William Morris, *Hopes and Fears for Art: Five Lectures* (1882)

James Abbot McNeill Whistler, "The Ten O'clock" lecture (1885), published in *The Gentle Art of Making Enemies* (1890)

Oscar Wilde, "The Critic as Artist," in *Intentions* (1891); *The Picture of Dorian Gray* (1891)

The nature of the creative process and the dual role of the artist, divided in allegiance between his responsibilities to society and to the private life of the imagination, are central motifs in the work of all major Victorian poets. Among poems bearing in whole or in part on these concerns, account should be taken of the following:

Alfred Tennyson, "The Palace of Art"; "The Lady of Shalott"; "Tithonus"; *In Memoriam;* "Tiresias"

Robert Browning, "Pictor Ignotus"; "Old Pictures in Florence"; "The Statue and the Bust"; "A Toccata of Galuppi's"; "Abt Vogler"; "How It Strikes a Contemporary"; "Transcendentalism: A Poem in Twelve Books"

Matthew Arnold, "Resignation"; "The Strayed Reveller"; "Memorial Verses"; "The Scholar-Gipsy"; "Thyrsis"

Dante Gabriel Rossetti, *The House of Life*

PART FIVE

The Ends of Education

Introduction

Victorians were united, as in no other way, by their common faith in the efficacy of education to provide solutions for the problems confronting the age. Benthamites and Evangelicals alike wholeheartedly encouraged the spread of literacy, though for different reasons: the former as a means of promoting social welfare by training a responsible electorate; the latter for the purpose of ministering to the individual's spiritual well-being by Bible study. Among the initial activities of the first Reform parliament was the appointment of a committee to inquire into the state of education. The appalling amount of illiteracy which its members uncovered, especially in industrial regions, led in 1833 to a government grant of £20,000 to help in the erection of school buildings. This was the first step toward the system of national education established by Forster's Bill of 1870. In 1880 primary education was made compulsory; in 1891 it became available to all without expense. Between 1870 and 1890 school attendance rose from one and one-quarter to four and one-half millions.

The support for adult education was no less persistent. Henry Brougham had founded the first Mechanics' Institute in 1823. Within twenty-five years there were 610 vocational schools of this kind, with a membership of more than one hundred thousand laboring men. At the mid-century F. D. Maurice established, as part of his Christian Socialist movement, a Working Men's College, designed to offer something more than technical training. Ruskin lectured on art and taught classes in drawing there, and encouraged other artists to do likewise. Toward the end of the period William Morris' Socialist League and the Fabian Society, with Bernard Shaw as a leading member, based their appeal to the working classes on programs of popular education, conducted through pamphlets, lectures, and public discussions.

There is scarcely a figure represented in this volume who was not at some time in his career engaged in educational activities. The most notable contributions, however, were made by Arnold and Huxley, both of whom served as government inspectors of schools. On three occasions

337

Arnold visited the Continent to look into systems of state education, especially in France and Germany; and his resulting reports exercised considerable influence in shaping English educational policy. Huxley, who for thirty-one years held the chair of natural history at the Royal School of Mines, revolutionized methods of teaching scientific subjects. When he became inspector of science schools in 1873, there were only six instructional laboratories in Great Britain; thirty years later there were more than one thousand.

It is no exaggeration to say that education, more even than the reform agitation of the period, smoothed Victorian England's peaceful transition through the successive stages of the Industrial Revolution. If by the end of the century the sharpest divisions between Disraeli's Two Nations had been obliterated, the credit must largely go to the various dedicated individuals and groups who had by unrelenting pressure kept before the country the idea that men must be taught to help themselves. At the same time, Victorian educational theorists had early foreseen the crisis which has become so acute in the twentieth century. This is the situation ably presented by C. P. Snow in his Rede Lecture (1959), published under the title: *The Two Cultures and the Scientific Revolution*. Snow's argument, by now familiar, is that the Industrial Revolution of the nineteenth century has entered a more purely scientific phase, of which society at large remains woefully ignorant because humanists and scientists no longer share a common language.

From the very outset of the period, farseeing Victorians had recognized the importance of technology as an agent in social change. One of these was Henry Brougham, already cited as the progenitor of the Mechanics' Institutes. In 1825 he helped originate plans for London University, the first nonsectarian seat of higher learning in England; and two years later he founded the Society for the Diffusion of Useful Knowledge, for which he wrote the first pamphlet, significantly entitled "Pleasures and Advantages of Science." Perhaps the clearest evidence of the Victorians' receptivity to new knowledge, however, is the wide and immediate impact on their thinking of the single most important scientific event of the century: the publication of *The Origin of Species*. Something has already been said, in the introductory essay to Part Three, of the emergence of immanentist doctrine as a religious response to evolution. More generally diffused in its effects was the phenomenon known as social Darwinism. No sooner had Darwin announced his hypothesis than political economists, such as Walter Bagehot and Herbert Spencer, began to explore its significance for the social sciences.[1]

In general, Oxford and Cambridge stood somewhat apart from the main streams of Victorian life. Of the intellectual movements represented in this collection, almost none was at home in the milieu of the two great universities. Although traditionally strong in mathematics, Cambridge did not institute its triposes in the natural and moral sciences until 1848; and Oxford's honours schools of natural science, law, and history date from 1850. Dissenters were not eligible to take degrees at either place until the passage of the University Tests Act in 1871. Yet, if Oxford and Cambridge in their conservatism originated no revolutionary tendencies in the thought of the age, they to a surprising extent did educate the individuals who were to guide such tendencies and to reconcile them within the dominant patterns of Victorian culture.

To understand the Cambridge of the "Apostles" and the Oxford to which Arnold of Rugby sent his pupils in the eighteen-thirties and forties is to gain insight into much that is most typical and most admirable in the Victorian temper of mind. In the introduction to the preceding section attention was drawn to the Cambridge "Apostles," that society of brilliant and public-spirited young scholars founded by F. D. Maurice and John Sterling, which continued throughout the century to supply intellectual leaders in all walks of life. Just as Tennyson was the poetic voice of this group, so Matthew Arnold spoke for the equally idealistic and dedicated band who matriculated at Oxford from Rugby School, of which his father, Thomas Arnold, was headmaster from 1828 to 1842. During his tenure, Dr. Arnold, an eminent Broad Church divine, modernized secondary education in line with the best liberal thought of the period. It was an article of his educational philosophy to stress the formation of character even above mental discipline to the end of turning out serious, selfless, and above all, responsible servants of humanity. In his own words: "What we must look for is first, religious and moral principle; secondly, gentlemanly conduct; thirdly, intellectual ability."

Such were the ideals which Matthew Arnold took with him to the

[1] See Walter Bagehot's *Physics and Politics* (1872) and Herbert Spencer's *The Man versus the State* (1884).

university, ideals that were to inform all of his writings. They are inscribed on "Rugby Chapel," his fine elegy to Dr. Arnold; and they sound throughout *Culture and Anarchy,* notably in the tribute to Newman, whose stand against the materialistic bias of the age symbolized for Arnold the fine flower of the Oxford spirit:

And who will estimate how much the currents of feeling created by Dr. Newman's movement, the keen desire for beauty and sweetness which it nourished, the deep aversion it manifested to the hardness and vulgarity of middle-class liberalism, the strong light it turned on the hideous and grotesque illusions of middle-class Protestantism,—who will estimate how much all these contributed to swell the tide of secret dissatisfaction which has mined the ground under self-confident liberalism of the last thirty years, and has prepared the way for its sudden collapse and supersession? It is in this manner that the sentiment of Oxford for beauty and sweetness conquers, and in this manner long may it continue to conquer!

Indeed, Newman himself was to give most eloquent expression to the values which were nurtured at Oxford and Cambridge in the series of nine lectures, *The Idea of a University,* which he prepared for delivery in Dublin in 1852. At the conclusion of the eighth discourse the speaker summarized his views about the goals of university education as follows:

But a University training is the great ordinary means to a great but ordinary end; it aims at raising the intellectual tone of society, at cultivating the public mind, at purifying the national taste, at supplying true principles to popular enthusiasm and fixed aims to popular aspiration, and giving enlargement and sobriety to the ideas of the age, at facilitating the exercise of political power, and refining the intercourse of private life.

One of Newman's arguments for higher education, commonly misapprehended, is that it tends to form gentlemen. For the Victorians believed that gentlemen are made, not born, and that the making of a gentleman is an educational matter. As every reader of Victorian novels knows, this belief is a central theme in the fiction of the time, whether in Dickens or Thackeray, Trollope or Meredith. Rank does not necessarily denote gentlemanliness, still less does wealth do so; rather, the true gentleman is to be known by the use which he makes of these privileges in all his social relationships, the extent to which he has learned, often at great sacrifice of personal inclination, to devote them to altruistic ends.

In the introductory essay to this volume the statement was made that Victorian society is principally remarkable for its achievement of a public morality. To this accomplishment no agency contributed more directly than the habit of mind instilled by the kind of liberal education provided at Oxford and Cambridge, to which church and state, as well as the learned professions, had traditionally looked for their leaders. "If we imagine Victorian England without Oxford and Cambridge," writes G. M. Young, "what barrier can we see against an all-encroaching materialism and professionalism?"[2] To a much greater degree than he appears to have realized, Arnold's call for an intellectual elite who should cherish and promulgate the gospel of culture was answered by the ranks of finely trained and humanely disposed graduates who emerged from the great sister universities during the latter half of the century. Their role in the life of the age has gained for them from one historian of Victorian ideas the title of "The Intellectual Aristocracy"; and of the influence, at once progressive and stabilizing, which they exerted, this writer remarks:

Thus they gradually spread over the length and breadth of English intellectual life criticising the assumptions of the ruling class above them and forming the opinions of the upper middle class to which they belonged. They were the leaders of the new intelligentsia. Stability is not a quality usually associated with an intelligentsia, a term which, Russian in origin, suggests the shifting, shiftless members of revolutionary or literary cliques who have cut themselves adrift from the moorings of family. Yet the English intelligentsia, wedded to gradual reform of accepted institutions and able to move between the world's of speculation and government, was stable.[3]

[2] G. M. Young, *Victorian England: Portrait of an Age* (London, 1944), pp. 95-96. This slim volume remains the best study of Victorianism for anyone who has some background knowledge of nineteenth-century English history. It is an expansion of the concluding chapter in *Early Victorian England, 1830-1865,* ed. G. M. Young, 2 vols. (London, 1934).

[3] Noel Annan, "The Intellectual Aristocracy," in *Studies in Social History: A Tribute to G. M. Trevelyan,* ed. J. H. Plumb (London and New York, 1955), p. 244. See also the same author's fine critical biography of one of the leaders of the "intellectual aristocracy," *Leslie Stephen: His Thought and Character in Relation to His Time* (Cambridge, Mass., 1952).

THE ENDS OF EDUCATION

Any discussion of educational procedures in nineteenth-century England must take into account the influence of that most unassailable of Victorian social institutions, the family. In an era which brought about revolutionary changes in most departments of the nation's life, there was no disposition to question the age-old creed that "an Englishman's home is his castle." On the sanctity of the family circle, that last refuge of individualism, the state dare not intrude. The point was presented with telling emphasis by William Cooke-Taylor, an early authority on the factory system, in a debate over government regulation of employment for working-class mothers:

> We have hitherto prided ourselves in this country—and prided ourselves justly—on the liberty of the subject, on the sanctity of the domestic hearth, and on the decency and privacy of our family life. That unit, the Family, is the unit upon which a constitutional Government has been raised which is the admiration and envy of mankind. Hitherto, whatever else the laws have touched, they have not dared to invade this sacred precinct.

As the literature of the age attests, the significance of childhood and youthful experience was a discovery of the nineteenth century. "The Child is father of the Man," wrote Wordsworth, whose major work, *The Prelude,* traces back to the writer's earliest memories the crucial influences on the growth of his poetic imagination. Involved here once more is that insistence on organic process which shaped so many of the intellectual movements in Victorian England. The rise of autobiographical writing in the period is directly related to the new interest in origins and the consequent importance attached to heredity and environment as factors in determining the outcome of an individual's life. A catalogue of Victorian writings which give accounts of the authors' formative years, either under fictional guise or as straight memoirs, would include virtually every important literary figure of the time.

Other reasons help to explain the deliberate glorification of the child in Victorian literature, much of it written for younger readers. In his celebrated "Ode: Intimations of Immortality" Wordsworth had mourned the passing with youth of those intuitions, as yet unsullied by contact with the world, which yield evidences of spiritual truths beyond adult cognition. The widespread belief that a kind of saintly wisdom accompanies the innocence of childhood became fused with a pervasive sense of guilt over the sufferings of children, who too often seemed the principal victims of the hardship brought about by the Industrial Revolution. As a result, the representations of early life in the writing of the period are often nostalgic in tone, the writers looking back on the pure hopes and glad expectancy of bygone years as to a lost Eden. A typical expression of this mood occurs in *The Nemesis of Faith* (1849), the autobiographical novel in which the historian James Anthony Froude recounted his own loss of orthodox faith:

I would gladly give away all I am, and all I ever may become, all the years, every one of them, which may be given me to live, but for one week of my old child's faith, to go back to calm and peace again, and then to die in hope. Oh, for one look of the blue sky, as it looked then when we called it Heaven!

Victorians liked to assume that it was the responsibility of the family to encourage the sympathies and cultivate the affections of the young. The home was also the stronghold of Evangelical Christianity, a form of religious faith which, in stressing the education of the feelings, further strengthened the emotional ties which bound children to their parents in unquestioning loyalty and obedience. James Mill's failure to temper the intellectual rigors of the training he imposed on his son with any appeal to the heart precipitated the nervous breakdown which John Stuart Mill so poignantly describes in the fifth chapter of his *Autobiography*. Looking back after his recovery upon the prolonged crisis through which he had passed, Mill wrote: "I had now learnt by experience that the passive susceptibilities needed to be cultivated as well as the active capacities, and required to be nourished and enriched as well as guided. . . . The cultivation of the feelings became one of the cardinal points in my ethical and philosophic creed."

Too often, indeed, Victorian parents abused their authority, converting the home into a grotesquely cruel parody of those kindly and gentle virtues which it was supposed to safeguard. One turns to the novel for the most memorable descriptions of what it was like to grow up in Victorian England. Immediately there springs to mind a long list of works of fiction which have as their common theme the education of the principal character for life: Charlotte Brontë's *Jane Eyre,*

THE ENDS OF EDUCATION

Dickens' *David Copperfield*, Thackeray's *Pendennis*, George Eliot's *The Mill on the Floss*, Meredith's *The Ordeal of Richard Feverel*, Hardy's *Jude the Obscure*, Samuel Butler's *The Way of All Flesh*. In virtually every one of these stories the protagonist, mishandled as a child, enters on his active career by impulsively rebelling against parental oppression. This initial act of rebellion provides the pattern for all the conflicts that follow, as he seeks to discover his own identity under constant social pressure to conform; for society has now taken over the parent's tyrannical role. The process of self-education is complete only when he has learned to follow the dictates of the heart, purified of egoism by suffering. In *Hard Times* Dickens tells of the educational experiment which the Benthamite Thomas Gradgrind performs on his two children, Tom and Louisa. Brought up on a regimen of unadorned facts, with no opportunity to indulge the play of fancy or to give vent to spontaneous feelings, Tom turns into a thief and Louisa contracts a loveless marriage. When his daughter comes home to confront him with her ruined life, Gradgrind haltingly voices sentiments which may well epitomize the best thought of the age about the ends of education:

Some persons hold that there is a wisdom of the Head, and that there is a wisdom of the Heart. I have not supposed so; but, as I have said, I mistrust myself now. I have supposed the head to be all-sufficient. It may not be all-sufficient; how can I venture this morning to say it is! If that other kind of wisdom should be what I have neglected, and should be the instinct that is wanted . . .

The ensuing selections are arranged in complementary pairs. The addresses by Thomas Henry Huxley and Matthew Arnold inaugurate at a very high level the debate between the Two Cultures, here engaged in by one of the most eminent scientists of the period and the leading Victorian humanist, each of whom reveals full understanding of and respect for the other's position. In the two specimens of autobiographical writing which follow, the delightfully factual narrative of his early years by Charles Robert Darwin is set over against Walter Pater's Proustian remembrance of things past.

Thomas Henry Huxley

1825-1895

Science and Culture

The following address, from which the introductory paragraphs have been omitted, was delivered at the opening of Sir Josiah Mason's Science College, Birmingham, on October 1, 1880. It was first published in *Science and Culture, and Other Essays* (1881). In a famous passage from an earlier address, "A Liberal Education; and Where to Find It" (1868), Huxley defined the goals of liberal education as follows: "That man, I think, has had a liberal education who has been so trained in youth that his body is the ready servant of his will, and does with ease and pleasure all the work that, as a mechanism, it is capable of; whose intellect is a clear, cold, logic engine, with all its parts of equal strength, and in smooth working order; ready, like a steam engine, to be turned to any kind of work, and spin the gossamers as well as forge the anchors of the mind; whose mind is stored with a knowledge of the great and fundamental truths of Nature and of the laws of her operations; one who, no stunted ascetic, is full of life and fire, but whose passions are trained to come to heel by a vigorous will, the servant of a tender conscience; who has learned to love all beauty, whether of Nature or of art, to hate all vileness, and to respect others as himself."

. . . From the time that the first suggestion to introduce physical science into ordinary education was timidly whispered, until now, the advocates of scientific education have met with opposition of two kinds. On the one hand, they have been pooh-poohed by the men of business who pride themselves on being the representatives of practicality; while, on the other hand, they have been excommunicated by the classical scholars, in their capacity of Levites[1] in charge of the ark of culture and monopolists of liberal education.

The practical men believed that the idol whom they worship—rule of thumb—has been the source of the past prosperity, and will suffice for the future welfare of the arts and manufactures. They are of opinion that science is speculative rubbish; that theory and practice have nothing to do with one another; and that the scientific habit of mind is an impediment, rather than an aid, in the conduct of ordinary affairs.

I have used the past tense in speaking of the practical men—for although they were very formidable thirty years ago, I am not sure that the pure species has not been extirpated. In fact, so far as mere argument goes, they have been subjected to such a *feu d'enfer*[2] that it is a miracle if any have escaped. But I have remarked that your typical practical man has an unexpected resemblance to one of Milton's angels. His spiritual wounds, such as are inflicted by logical weapons, may be as deep as a well and as wide as a church door, but beyond shedding a few drops of ichor, celestial or otherwise, he is no whit the worse. So, if any of these opponents be left, I will not waste time in vain repetition of the demonstrative evidence of the practical value of science; but knowing that a parable will sometimes penetrate where syllogisms fail to effect an entrance, I will offer a story for their consideration.

Once upon a time, a boy,[3] with nothing to depend upon but his own vigorous nature, was thrown into the thick of the struggle for existence in the midst of a great manufacturing population. He seems to have had

---

[1] Cf. Numbers 1.48-53; and I Chronicles xxiii.24.

[2] Hell-fire.

[3] Sir Josiah Mason (1795-1881) had a remarkable career. Beginning as a street pedlar, he tried his hand at many trades before he made a large fortune in the manufacture of steel pens and in the electro-plating business. His chief benefaction was the endowment of the scientific college in Birmingham, to which he gave £180,000.

a hard fight, inasmuch as, by the time he was thirty years of age, his total disposable funds amounted to twenty pounds. Nevertheless, middle life found him giving proof of his comprehension of the practical problems he had been roughly called upon to solve, by a career of remarkable prosperity.

Finally, having reached old age with its well-earned surroundings of "honour, troops of friends," [4] the hero of my story bethought himself of those who were making a like start in life, and how he could stretch out a helping hand to them.

After long and anxious reflection this successful practical man of business could devise nothing better than to provide them with the means of obtaining "sound, extensive, and practical scientific knowledge." And he devoted a large part of his wealth and five years of incessant work to this end.

I need not point the moral of a tale which, as the solid and spacious fabric of the Scientific College assures us, is no fable, nor can anything which I could say intensify the force of this practical answer to practical objections.

We may take it for granted then, that, in the opinion of those best qualified to judge, the diffusion of thorough scientific education is an absolutely essential condition of industrial progress; and that the College which has been opened today will confer an inestimable boon upon those whose livelihood is to be gained by the practise of the arts and manufactures of the district.

The only question worth discussion is, whether the conditions, under which the work of the College is to be carried out, are such as to give it the best possible chance of achieving permanent success.

Sir Josiah Mason, without doubt most wisely, has left very large freedom of action to the trustees, to whom he proposes ultimately to commit the administration of the College, so that they may be able to adjust its arrangements in accordance with the changing conditions of the future. But, with respect to three points, he has laid most explicit injunctions upon both administrators and teachers.

[4] See *Macbeth* v.iii.25.

Party politics are forbidden to enter into the minds of either, so far as the work of the College is concerned; theology is as sternly banished from its precincts; and finally, it is especially declared that the College shall make no provision for "mere literary instruction and education."

It does not concern me at present to dwell upon the first two injunctions any longer than may be needful to express my full conviction of their wisdom. But the third prohibition brings us face to face with those other opponents of scientific education, who are by no means in the moribund condition of the practical man, but alive, alert, and formidable.

It is not impossible that we shall hear this express exclusion of "literary instruction and education" from a College which, nevertheless, professes to give a high and efficient education, sharply criticised. Certainly the time was that the Levites of culture would have sounded their trumpets against its walls as against an educational Jericho.[5]

How often have we not been told that the study of physical science is incompetent to confer culture; that it touches none of the higher problems of life; and, what is worse, that the continual devotion to scientific studies tends to generate a narrow and bigoted belief in the applicability of scientific methods to the search after truth of all kinds? How frequently one has reason to observe that no reply to a troublesome argument tells so well as calling its author a "mere scientific specialist." And, as I am afraid it is not permissible to speak of this form of opposition to scientific education in the past tense; may we not expect to be told that this, not only omission, but prohibition, of "mere literary instruction and education" is a patent example of scientific narrow-mindedness?

I am not acquainted with Sir Josiah Mason's reasons for the action which he has taken; but if, as I apprehend is the case, he refers to the ordinary classical course of our schools and universities by the name of "mere literary instruction and education," I venture to offer sundry reasons of my own in support of that action.

For I hold very strongly by two convictions: The first is, that neither the discipline nor the subject-matter of classical education is of such direct value to the student of physical science as to justify the expenditure of valuable time upon either; and the second is, that for the purpose of

[5] Cf. Joshua VI.

attaining real culture, an exclusively scientific education is at least as effectual as an exclusively literary education.

I need hardly point out to you that these opinions, especially the latter, are diametrically opposed to those of the great majority of educated Englishmen, influenced as they are by school and university traditions. In their belief, culture is obtainable only by a liberal education; and a liberal education is synonymous, not merely with education and instruction in literature, but in one particular form of literature, namely, that of Greek and Roman antiquity. They hold that the man who has learned Latin and Greek, however little, is educated; while he who is versed in other branches of knowledge, however deeply, is a more or less respectable specialist, not admissible into the cultured caste. The stamp of the educated man, the University degree, is not for him.

I am too well acquainted with the generous catholicity of spirit, the true sympathy with scientific thought, which pervades the writings of our chief apostle of culture[6] to identify him with these opinions; and yet one may cull from one and another of those epistles to the Philistines, which so much delight all who do not answer to that name, sentences which lend them some support.

Mr. Arnold tells us that the meaning of culture is "to know the best that has been thought and said in the world." It is the criticism of life contained in literature. That criticism regards "Europe as being, for intellectual and spiritual purposes, one great confederation, bound to a joint action and working to a common result; and whose members have, for their common outfit, a knowledge of Greek, Roman, and Eastern antiquity, and of one another. Special, local, and temporary advantages being put out of account, that modern nation will in the intellectual and spiritual sphere make most progress, which most thoroughly carries out this programme. And what is that but saying that we too, all of us, as individuals, the more thoroughly we carry it out, shall make the more progress?"[7]

[6] Matthew Arnold; see paragraph following. The "epistles to the Philistines" are, of course, Arnold's essays, criticizing the materialistic complacency of the Victorian middle classes.

[7] These quotations are from Arnold's essay, "The Function of Criticism at the Present Time."

We have here to deal with two distinct propositions. The first, that a criticism of life is the essence of culture; the second, that literature contains the materials which suffice for the construction of such criticism.

I think that we must all assent to the first proposition. For culture certainly means something quite different from learning or technical skill. It implies the possession of an ideal, and the habit of critically estimating the value of things by comparison with a theoretic standard. Perfect culture should supply a complete theory of life, based upon a clear knowledge alike of its possibilities and of its limitations.

But we may agree to all this, and yet strongly dissent from the assumption that literature alone is competent to supply this knowledge. After having learnt all that Greek, Roman, and Eastern antiquity have thought and said, and all that modern literature have to tell us, it is not self-evident that we have laid a sufficiently broad and deep foundation for that criticism of life, which constitutes culture.

Indeed, to any one acquainted with the scope of physical science, it is not at all evident. Considering progress only in the "intellectual and spiritual sphere," I find myself wholly unable to admit that either nations or individuals will really advance, if their common outfit draws nothing from the stores of physical science. I should say that an army, without weapons of precision and with no particular base of operations, might more hopefully enter upon a campaign on the Rhine, than a man, devoid of a knowledge of what physical science has done in the last century, upon a criticism of life.

When a biologist meets with an anomaly, he instinctively turns to the study of development to clear it up. The rationale of contradictory opinions may with equal confidence be sought in history.

It is, happily, no new thing that Englishmen should employ their wealth in building and endowing institutions for educational purposes. But, five or six hundred years ago, deeds of foundation expressed or implied conditions as nearly as possible contrary to those which have been thought expedient by Sir Josiah Mason. That is to say, physical science was practically ignored, while a certain literary training was enjoined as a means to the acquirement of knowledge which was essentially theological.

The reason of this singular contradiction between the actions of men alike animated by a strong and disinterested desire to promote the welfare of their fellows is easily discovered.

At that time, in fact, if any one desired knowledge beyond such as could be obtained by his own observation, or by common conversation, his first necessity was to learn the Latin language, inasmuch as all the higher knowledge of the western world was contained in works written in that language. Hence, Latin grammar, with logic and rhetoric, studied through Latin, were the fundamentals of education. With respect to the substance of the knowledge imparted through this channel, the Jewish and Christian Scriptures, as interpreted and supplemented by the Romish Church, were held to contain a complete and infallibly true body of information.

Theological dicta were, to the thinkers of those days, that which the axioms and definitions of Euclid are to the geometers of these. The business of the philosophers of the middle ages was to deduce from the data furnished by the theologians, conclusions in accordance with ecclesiastical decrees. They were allowed the high privilege of showing, by logical process, how and why that which the Church said was true, must be true. And if their demonstrations fell short of or exceeded this limit, the Church was materially ready to check their aberrations; if need were, by the help of the secular arm.

Between the two, our ancestors were furnished with a compact and complete criticism of life. They were told how the world began and how it would end; they learned that all material existence was but a base and insignificant blot upon the fair face of the spiritual world, and that nature was, to all intents and purposes, the playground of the devil; they learned that the earth is the centre of the visible universe, and that man is the cynosure of things terrestrial, and more especially was it inculcated that the course of nature had no fixed order, but that it could be, and constantly was, altered by the agency of innumerable spiritual beings, good and bad, according as they were moved by the deeds and prayers of men. The sum and substance of the whole doctrine was to produce the conviction that the only thing really worth knowing in this world was how to secure that place in a better which, under certain conditions, the Church promised.

Our ancestors had a living belief in this theory of life, and acted upon it in their dealings with education, as in all other matters. Culture meant saintliness—after the fashion of the saints of those days; the education that led to it was, of necessity, theological; and the way to theology lay through Latin.

That the study of nature—further than was requisite for the satisfaction of everyday wants—should have any bearing on human life was far from the thoughts of men thus trained. Indeed, as nature had been cursed for man's sake,[8] it was an obvious conclusion that those who meddled with nature were likely to come into pretty close contact with Satan. And, if any born scientific investigator followed his instincts, he might safely reckon upon earning the reputation, and probably upon suffering the fate, of a sorcerer.

Had the western world been left to itself in Chinese isolation, there is no saying how long this state of things might have endured. But, happily, it was not left to itself. Even earlier than the thirteenth century, the development of Moorish civilisation in Spain and the great movement of the Crusades had introduced the leaven which, from that day to this, has never ceased to work. At first, through the intermediation of Arabic translations, afterwards by the study of the originals, the western nations of Europe became acquainted with the writings of the ancient philosophers and poets, and, in time, with the whole of the vast literature of antiquity.

Whatever there was of high intellectual aspiration or dominant capacity in Italy, France, Germany, and England, spent itself for centuries in taking possession of the rich inheritance left by the dead civilisations of Greece and Rome. Marvelously aided by the invention of printing, classical learning spread and flourished. Those who possessed it prided themselves on having attained the highest culture then within the reach of mankind.

And justly. For, saving Dante on his solitary pinnacle, there was no figure in modern literature at the time of the Renascence to compare with the men of antiquity; there was no art to compete with their sculpture; there was no physical science but that which Greece had created.

[8] Cf. Genesis III.17.

Above all, there was no other example of perfect intellectual freedom—of the unhesitating acceptance of reason as the sole guide to truth and the supreme arbiter of conduct.

The new learning necessarily soon exerted a profound influence upon education. The language of the monks and schoolmen seemed little better than gibberish to scholars fresh from Virgil and Cicero, and the study of Latin was placed upon a new foundation. Moreover, Latin itself ceased to afford the sole key to knowledge. The student who sought the highest thought of antiquity, found only a second-hand reflection of it in Roman literature, and turned his face to the full light of the Greeks. And after a battle, not altogether dissimilar to that which is at present being fought over the teaching of physical science, the study of Greek was recognised as an essential element of all higher education.

Then the Humanists, as they were called, won the day; and the great reform which they effected was of incalculable service to mankind. But the Nemesis of all reformers is finality; and the reformers of education, like those of religion, fell into the profound, however common, error of mistaking the beginning for the end of the work of reformation.

The representatives of the Humanists, in the nineteenth century, take their stand upon classical education as the sole avenue to culture, as firmly as if we were still in the age of Renascence. Yet, surely, the present intellectual relations of the modern and the ancient worlds are profoundly different from those which obtained three centuries ago. Leaving aside the existence of a great and characteristically modern literature, of modern painting, and especially, of modern music, there is one feature of the present state of the civilised world which separates it more widely from the Renascence, than the Renascence was separated from the middle ages.

This distinctive character of our own times lies in the vast and constantly increasing part which is played by natural knowledge. Not only is our daily life shaped by it; not only does the prosperity of millions of men depend upon it, but our whole theory of life has long been influenced, consciously or unconsciously, by the general conceptions of the universe, which have been forced upon us by physical science.

In fact, the most elementary acquaintance with the results of scientific investigation shows us that they offer a broad and striking contradiction to the opinion so implicitly credited and taught in the middle ages.

The notions of the beginning and the end of the world entertained by our forefathers are no longer credible. It is very certain that the earth is not the chief body in the material universe, and that the world is not subordinated to man's use. It is even more certain that nature is the expression of a definite order with which nothing interferes, and that the chief business of mankind is to learn that order and govern themselves accordingly. Moreover this scientific "criticism of life" presents itself to us with different credentials from any other. It appeals not to authority, nor to what anybody may have thought or said, but to nature. It admits that all our interpretations of natural fact are more or less imperfect and symbolic, and bids the learner seek for truth not among words but among things. It warns us that the assertion which outstrips evidence is not only a blunder but a crime.

The purely classical education advocated by the representatives of the Humanists in our day, gives no inkling of all this. A man may be a better scholar than Erasmus, and know no more of the chief causes of the present intellectual fermentation than Erasmus did. Scholarly and pious persons, worthy of all respect, favour us with allocutions upon the sadness of the antagonism of science to their mediæval way of thinking, which betray an ignorance of the first principles of scientific investigation, an incapacity for understanding what a man of science means by veracity, and an unconsciousness of the weight of established scientific truths, which is almost comical.

There is no great force in the *tu quoque*[9] argument, or else the advocates of scientific education might fairly enough retort upon the modern Humanists that they may be learned specialists, but that they possess no such sound foundation for a criticism of life as deserves the name of culture. And, indeed, if we were disposed to be cruel, we might urge that the Humanists have brought this reproach upon themselves, not because they are too full of the spirit of the ancient Greek, but because they lack it.

The period of the Renascence is commonly called that of the "Revival of Letters," as if the influences then brought to bear upon the mind of

[9] You also.

Western Europe had been wholly exhausted in the field of literature. I think it is very commonly forgotten that the revival of science, effected by the same agency, although less conspicuous, was not less momentous.

In fact, the few and scattered students of nature of that day picked up the clue to her secrets exactly as it fell from the hands of the Greeks a thousand years before. The foundations of mathematics were so well laid by them, that our children learn their geometry from a book[10] written for the schools of Alexandria two thousand years ago. Modern astronomy is the natural continuation and development of the work of Hipparchus and of Ptolemy; modern physics of that of Democritus and of Archimedes; it was long before modern biological science outgrew the knowledge bequeathed to us by Aristotle, by Theophrastus, and by Galen.

We cannot know all the best thoughts and sayings of the Greeks unless we know what they thought about natural phenomena. We cannot fully apprehend their criticism of life unless we understand the extent to which that criticism was affected by scientific conceptions. We falsely pretend to be the inheritors of their culture, unless we are penetrated, as the best minds among them were, with an unhesitating faith that the free employment of reason, in accordance with scientific method, is the sole method of reaching truth.

Thus I venture to think that the pretensions of our modern Humanists to the possession of the monopoly of culture and to the exclusive inheritance of the spirit of antiquity must be abated, if not abandoned. But I should be very sorry that anything I have said should be taken to imply a desire on my part to depreciate the value of classical education, as it might be and as it sometimes is. The native capacities of mankind vary no less than their opportunities; and while culture is one, the road by which one man may best reach it is widely different from that which is most advantageous to another. Again, while scientific education is yet inchoate and tentative, classical education is thoroughly well organised upon the practical experience of generations of teachers. So that, given ample time for learning and estimation for ordinary life, or for a literary

[10] Euclid's *Elements*.

career, I do not think that a young Englishman in search of culture can do better than follow the course usually marked out for him, supplementing its deficiencies by his own efforts.

But for those who mean to make science their serious occupation; or who intend to follow the profession of medicine; or who have to enter early upon the business of life; for all these, in my opinion, classical education is a mistake; and it is for this reason that I am glad to see "mere literary education and instruction" shut out from the curriculum of Sir Josiah Mason's College, seeing that its inclusion would probably lead to the introduction of the ordinary smattering of Latin and Greek.

Nevertheless, I am the last person to question the importance of genuine literary education, or to suppose that intellectual culture can be complete without it. An exclusively scientific training will bring about a mental twist as surely as an exclusively literary training. The value of the cargo does not compensate for a ship's being out of trim; and I should be very sorry to think that the Scientific College would turn out none but lopsided men.

There is no need, however, that such a catastrophe should happen. Instruction in English, French, and German is provided, and thus the three greatest literatures of the modern world are made accessible to the student.

French and German, and especially the latter language, are absolutely indispensable to those who desire full knowledge in any department of science. But even supposing that the knowledge of these languages acquired is not more than sufficient for purely scientific purposes, every Englishman has, in his native tongue, an almost perfect instrument of literary expression; and, in his own literature, models of every kind of literary excellence. If an Englishman cannot get literary culture out of his Bible, his Shakespeare, his Milton, neither, in my belief, will the profoundest study of Homer and Sophocles, Virgil and Horace, give it to him.

Thus, since the constitution of the College makes sufficient provision for literary as well as for scientific education, and since artistic instruction is also contemplated, it seems to me that a fairly complete culture is offered to all who are willing to take advantage of it.

But I am not sure that at this point the "practical" man, scotched but not slain, may ask what all this talk about culture has to do with an Institution, the object of which is defined to be "to promote the prosperity of the manufactures and the industry of the country." He may suggest that what is wanted for this end is not culture, nor even a purely scientific discipline, but simply a knowledge of applied science.

I often wish that this phrase, "applied science," had never been invented. For it suggests that there is a sort of scientific knowledge of direct practical use, which can be studied apart from another sort of scientific knowledge, which is of no practical utility, and which is termed "pure science." But there is no more complete fallacy than this. What people call applied science is nothing but the application of pure science to particular classes of problems. It consists of deductions from those general principles, established by reasoning and observation, which constitute pure science. No one can safely make these deductions until he has a firm grasp of the principles; and he can obtain that grasp only by personal experience of the operations of observation and of reasoning on which they are founded.

Almost all the processes employed in the arts and manufactures fall within the range either of physics or of chemistry. In order to improve them, one must thoroughly understand them; and no one has a chance of really understanding them, unless he has obtained that mastery of principles and that habit of dealing with facts, which is given by long-continued and well-directed purely scientific training in the physical and the chemical laboratory. So that there really is no question as to the necessity of purely scientific discipline, even if the work of the College were limited by the narrowest interpretation of its stated aims.

And, as to the desirableness of a wider culture than that yielded by science alone, it is to be recollected that the improvement of manufacturing processes is only one of the conditions which contribute to the prosperity of industry. Industry is a means and not an end; and mankind work only to get something which they want. What that something is depends partly on their innate, and partly on their acquired, desires.

If the wealth resulting from prosperous industry is to be spent upon the gratification of unworthy desires, if the increasing perfection of manufacturing processes is to be accompanied by an increasing debasement of those who carry them on, I do not see the good of industry and prosperity.

Now it is perfectly true that men's views of what is desirable depend upon their characters; and that the innate proclivities to which we give that name are not touched by any amount of instruction. But it does not follow that even mere intellectual education may not, to an indefinite extent, modify the practical manifestation of the characters of men in their actions, by supplying them with motives unknown to the ignorant. A pleasure-loving character will have pleasure of some sort; but, if you give him the choice, he may prefer pleasures which do not degrade him to those which do. And this choice is offered to every man, who possesses in literary or artistic culture a never-failing source of pleasures, which are neither withered by age, nor staled by custom,[11] nor embittered in the recollection by the pangs of self-reproach.

If the Institution opened today fulfils the intention of its founder, the picked intelligences among all classes of the population of this district will pass through it. No child born in Birmingham, henceforward, if he have the capacity to profit by the opportunities offered to him, first in the primary and other schools, and afterwards in the Scientific College, need fail to obtain, not merely the instruction, but the culture most appropriate to the conditions of his life.

Within these walls, the future employer and the future artisan may sojourn together for a while, and carry, through all their lives, the stamp of the influences then brought to bear upon them. Hence, it is not beside the mark to remind you, that the prosperity of industry depends not merely upon the improvement of manufacturing processes, not merely upon the ennobling of the individual character, but upon a third condition, namely, a clear understanding of the conditions of social life, on the part of both the capitalist and the operative, and their agreement upon common principles of social action. They must learn that social phenomena are as much the expression of natural laws as any others; that no social arrangements can be permanent unless they harmonise with the requirements of social statics and dynamics; and that, in the nature of things, there is an arbiter whose decisions execute themselves.

[11] Cf. *Antony and Cleopatra* ii.ii.240-241.

But this knowledge is only to be obtained by the application of the methods of investigation adopted in physical researches to the investigation of the phenomena of society. Hence, I confess, I should like to see one addition made to the excellent scheme of education propounded for the College, in the shape of provision for the teaching of Sociology. For though we are all agreed that party politics are to have no place in the instruction of the College; yet in this country, practically governed as it is now by universal suffrage, every man who does his duty must exercise political functions. And, if the evils which are inseparable from the good of political liberty are to be checked, if the perpetual oscillation of nations between anarchy and despotism is to be replaced by the steady march of self-restraining freedom; it will be because men will gradually bring themselves to deal with political, as they now deal with scientific questions; to be as ashamed of undue haste and partisan prejudice in the one case as in the other; and to believe that the machinery of society is at least as delicate as that of a spinning-jenny, and as little likely to be improved by the meddling of those who have not taken the trouble to master the principles of its action.

In conclusion, I am sure that I make myself the mouthpiece of all present in offering to the venerable founder of the Institution, which now commences its beneficent career, our congratulations on the completion of his work; and in expressing the conviction, that the remotest posterity will point to it as a crucial instance of the wisdom which natural piety leads all men to ascribe to their ancestors.

Matthew Arnold

1822-1888

Literature and Science

🕮 "Literature and Science" was delivered as the Rede Lecture at Cambridge University in 1882. With the opening paragraphs revised to their present form, it then became one of the three lectures in Arnold's repertoire during his visit to the United States (1883-84), to be published later in the collection entitled *Discourses in America* (1885). Although Arnold's defense of the humanist position was prepared with Huxley's "Science and Culture" in mind, the argument looks forward seventy-seven years to C. P. Snow's *The Two Cultures and the Scientific Revolution,* also first presented as a Rede Lecture.

Practical people talk with a smile of Plato and of his absolute ideas;[1] and it is impossible to deny that Plato's ideas do often seem unpractical and impracticable, and especially when one views them in connection with the life of a great work-a-day world like the United States. The necessary staple of the life of such a world Plato regards with disdain; handicraft and trade and the working professions he regards with disdain; but what becomes of the life of an industrial modern community if you take handicraft and trade and the working professions out of it? The base mechanic arts and handicrafts, says Plato, bring about a natural weakness in the principle of excellence in a man, so that he cannot govern the ignoble growths in him, but nurses them, and cannot understand fostering any other. Those who exercise such arts and

---

[1] See especially Plato, *Republic,* x, 596-597.

trades, as they have their bodies, he says, marred by their vulgar businesses, so they have their souls, too, bowed and broken by them. And if one of these uncomely people has a mind to seek self-culture and philosophy, Plato compares him to a bald little tinker, who has scraped together money, and has got his release from service, and has had a bath, and bought a new coat, and is rigged out like a bridegroom about to marry the daughter of his master who has fallen into poor and helpless estate.[2]

Nor do the working professions fare any better than trade at the hands of Plato. He draws for us an inimitable picture of the working lawyer, and of his life of bondage; he shows how this bondage from his youth up has stunted and warped him, and made him small and crooked of soul, encompassing him with difficulties which he is not man enough to rely on justice and truth as means to encounter, but has recourse, for help out of them, to falsehood and wrong. And so, says Plato, this poor creature is bent and broken, and grows up from boy to man without a particle of soundness in him, although exceedingly smart and clever in his own esteem.[3]

One cannot refuse to admire the artist who draws these pictures. But we say to ourselves that his ideas show the influence of a primitive and obsolete order of things, when the warrior caste and the priestly caste were alone in honor, and the humble work of the world was done by slaves. We have now changed all that; the modern majesty consists in work, as Emerson declares;[4] and in work, we may add, principally of such plain and dusty kind as the work of cultivators of the ground, handicraftsmen, men of trade and business, men of the working professions. Above all is this true in a great industrious community such as that of the United States.

Now education, many people go on to say, is still mainly governed by the ideas of men like Plato, who lived when the warrior caste and the priestly or philosophical class were alone in honor, and the really useful part of the community were slaves. It is an education fitted for persons of leisure in such a community. This education passed from Greece and Rome to the feudal communities of Europe, where also the warrior caste

[2] *Republic* vi.495.
[3] Cf. Plato, *Theaetetus,* 172-173.
[4] Ralph Waldo Emerson, "Literary Ethics," *Works,* Centenary ed. (Boston, 1903-4) I, 179.

and the priestly caste were alone held in honor, and where the really useful and working part of the community, though not nominally slaves as in the pagan world, were practically not much better off than slaves, and not more seriously regarded. And how absurd it is, people end by saying, to inflict this education upon an industrious modern community, where very few indeed are persons of leisure, and the mass to be considered has not leisure, but is bound, for its own great good, and for the great good of the world at large, to plain labor and to industrial pursuits, and the education in question tends necessarily to make men dissatisfied with these pursuits and unfitted for them!

That is what is said. So far I must defend Plato, as to plead that his view of education and studies is in the general, as it seems to me, sound enough, and fitted for all sorts and conditions of men, whatever their pursuits may be. "An intelligent man," says Plato, "will prize those studies which result in his soul getting soberness, righteousness, and wisdom, and will less value the others." [5] I cannot consider *that* a bad description of the aim of education, and of the motives which should govern us in the choice of studies, whether we are preparing ourselves for a hereditary seat in the English House of Lords or for the pork trade in Chicago.

Still I admit that Plato's world was not ours, that his scorn of trade and handicraft is fantastic, that he had no conception of a great industrial community such as that of the United States, and that such a community must and will shape its education to suit its own needs. If the usual education handed down to it from the past does not suit it, it will certainly before long drop this and try another. The usual education in the past has been mainly literary. The question is whether the studies which were long supposed to be the best for all of us are practically the best now; whether others are not better. The tyranny of the past, many think, weighs on us injuriously in the predominance given to letters in education. The question is raised whether, to meet the needs of our modern life, the predominance ought not now to pass from letters to science; and naturally the question is nowhere raised with more energy than here in the United States. The design of abasing what is called "mere literary

[5] See *Republic* IX.591.

instruction and education," and of exalting what is called "sound, extensive, and practical scientific knowledge," is, in this intensely modern world of the United States, even more perhaps than in Europe, a very popular design, and makes great and rapid progress.

I am going to ask whether the present movement for ousting letters from their old predominance in education, and for transferring the predominance in education to the natural sciences, whether this brisk and flourishing movement ought to prevail, and whether it is likely that in the end it really will prevail. An objection may be raised which I will anticipate. My own studies have been almost wholly in letters, and my visits to the field of the natural sciences have been very slight and inadequate, although those sciences have always strongly moved my curiosity. A man of letters, it will perhaps be said, is not competent to discuss the comparative merits of letters and natural science as means of education. To this objection I reply, first of all, that his incompetence, if he attempts the discussion but is really incompetent for it, will be abundantly visible; nobody will be taken in; he will have plenty of sharp observers and critics to save mankind from that danger. But the line I am going to follow is, as you will soon discover, so extremely simple, that perhaps it may be followed without failure even by one who for a more ambitious line of discussion would be quite incompetent.

Some of you may possibly remember a phrase of mine which has been the object of a good deal of comment; an observation to the effect that in our culture, the aim being *to know ourselves and the world,* we have, as the means to this end, *to know the best which has been thought and said in the world.*[6] A man of science, who is also an excellent writer and the very prince of debaters, Professor Huxley, in a discourse at the opening of Sir Josiah Mason's college at Birmingham,[7] laying hold of this phrase, expanded it by quoting some more words of mine, which are these: "The civilized world is to be regarded as now being, for intellectual and spiritual purposes, one great confederation, bound to a joint action and working to a common result; and whose members have for their proper outfit a knowledge of Greek, Roman, and Eastern antiquity, and

[6] These words occur near the end of "The Function of Criticism at the Present Time."

[7] See preceding selection.

of one another. Special local and temporary advantages being put out of account, that modern nation will in the intellectual and spiritual sphere make most progress, which most thoroughly carries out this programme." [8]

Now on my phrase, thus enlarged, Professor Huxley remarks that when I speak of the above-mentioned knowledge as enabling us to know ourselves and the world, I assert *literature* to contain the materials which suffice for thus making us know ourselves and the world. But it is not by any means clear, says he, that after having learnt all which ancient and modern literatures have to tell us, we have laid a sufficiently broad and deep foundation for that criticism of life, that knowledge of ourselves and the world, which constitutes culture. On the contrary, Professor Huxley declares that he finds himself "wholly unable to admit that either nations or individuals will really advance, if their outfit draws nothing from the stores of physical science. An army without weapons of precision, and with no particular base of operations, might more hopefully enter upon a campaign on the Rhine, than a man, devoid of a knowledge of what physical science has done in the last century, upon a criticism of life."

This shows how needful it is for those who are to discuss any matter together, to have a common understanding as to the sense of the terms they employ—how needful, and how difficult. What Professor Huxley says, implies just the reproach which is so often brought against the study of *belles lettres,* as they are called: that the study is an elegant one, but slight and ineffectual; a smattering of Greek and Latin and other ornamental things, of little use for any one whose object is to get at truth, and to be a practical man. So, too, M. Renan talks of the "superficial humanism" [9] of a school-course which treats us as if we were all going to be poets, writers, preachers, orators, and he opposes this humanism to positive science, or the critical search after truth. And there is always a tendency in those who are remonstrating against the predominance of letters in education, to understand by letters *belles lettres,* and by *belles lettres* a superficial humanism the opposite of science or true knowledge.

[8] See note 6.
[9] The phrase appears in Ernest Renan, "L'Instruction Supérieur en France," *Questions Contemporaines* (Paris, 1868), end of Section Two.

MATTHEW ARNOLD

But when we talk of knowing Greek and Roman antiquity, for instance, which is the knowledge people have called the humanities, I for my part mean a knowledge which is something more than a superficial humanism, mainly decorative. "I call all teaching *scientific*," says Wolf,[10] the critic of Homer, "which is systematically laid out and followed up to its original sources. For example: a knowledge of classical antiquity is scientific when the remains of classical antiquity are correctly studied in the original languages." There can be no doubt that Wolf is perfectly right; that all learning is scientific which is systematically laid out and followed up to its original sources, and that a genuine humanism is scientific.

When I speak of knowing Greek and Roman antiquity, therefore, as a help to knowing ourselves and the world, I mean more than a knowledge of so much vocabulary, so much grammar, so many portions of authors in the Greek and Latin languages, I mean knowing the Greeks and Romans, and their life and genius, and what they were and did in the world; what we get from them, and what is its value. That, at least, is the ideal; and when we talk of endeavoring to know Greek and Roman antiquity, as a help to knowing ourselves and the world, we mean endeavoring so to know them as to satisfy this ideal, however much we may still fall short of it.

The same also as to knowing our own and other modern nations, with the like aim of getting to understand ourselves and the world. To know the best that has been thought and said by the modern nations, is to know, says Professor Huxley, "only what modern *literatures* have to tell us; it is the criticism of life contained in modern literature." And yet "the distinctive character of our times," he urges, "lies in the vast and constantly increasing part which is played by natural knowledge." And how, therefore, can a man, devoid of knowledge of what physical science has done in the last century, enter hopefully upon a criticism of modern life?

Let us, I say, be agreed about the meaning of the terms we are using. I talk of knowing the best which has been thought and uttered in the world; Professor Huxley says this means knowing *literature*. Literature

[10] Friedrich August Wolf (1759-1824), German classical scholar.

365

is a large word; it may mean everything written with letters or printed in a book. Euclid's "Elements" and Newton's "Principia" are thus literature. All knowledge that reaches us through books is literature. But by literature Professor Huxley means *belles lettres*. He means to make me say, that knowing the best which has been thought and said by the modern nations is knowing their *belles lettres* and no more. And this is no sufficient equipment, he argues, for a criticism of modern life. But as I do not mean, by knowing ancient Rome, knowing merely more or less of Latin *belles lettres*, and taking no account of Rome's military, and political, and legal, and administrative work in the world; and as, by knowing ancient Greece, I understand knowing her as the giver of Greek art, and the guide to a free and right use of reason and to scientific method, and the founder of our mathematics and physics and astronomy and biology—I understand knowing her as all this, and not merely knowing certain Greek poems, and histories, and treatises, and speeches—so as to the knowledge of modern nations also. By knowing modern nations, I mean not merely knowing their *belles lettres,* but knowing also what has been done by such men as Copernicus, Galileo, Newton, Darwin. "Our ancestors learned," says Professor Huxley, "that the earth is the centre of the visible universe, and that man is the cynosure of things terrestrial; and more especially was it inculcated that the course of nature had no fixed order, but that it could be, and constantly was, altered." But for us now, continues Professor Huxley, "the notions of the beginning and the end of the world entertained by our forefathers are no longer credible. It is very certain that the earth is not the chief body in the material universe, and that the world is not subordinated to man's use. It is even more certain that nature is the expression of a definite order, with which nothing interferes." "And yet," he cries, "the purely classical education advocated by the representatives of the humanists in our day gives no inkling of all this!"

In due place and time I will just touch upon that vexed question of classical education; but at present the question is as to what is meant by knowing the best which modern nations have thought and said. It is not knowing their *belles lettres* merely which is meant. To know Italian *belles lettres* is not to know Italy, and to know English *belles lettres* is not to know England. Into knowing Italy and England there comes a great deal more, Galileo and Newton amongst it. The reproach of being a superficial humanism, a tincture of *belles lettres,* may attach rightly enough to some other disciplines; but to the particular discipline recommended when I proposed knowing the best that has been thought and said in the world, it does not apply. In that best I certainly include what in modern times has been thought and said by the great observers and knowers of nature.

There is, therefore, really no question between Professor Huxley and me as to whether knowing the great results of the modern scientific study of nature is not required as a part of our culture, as well as knowing the products of literature and art. But to follow the processes by which those results are reached, ought, say the friends of physical science, to be made the staple of education for the bulk of mankind. And here there does arise a question between those whom Professor Huxley calls with playful sarcasm "the Levites of culture," and those whom the poor humanist is sometimes apt to regard as its Nebuchadnezzars.[11]

The great results of the scientific investigation of nature we are agreed upon knowing, but how much of our study are we bound to give to the processes by which those results are reached? The results have their visible bearing on human life. But all the processes, too, all the items of fact, by which those results are reached and established, are interesting. All knowledge is interesting to a wise man, and the knowledge of nature is interesting to all man. It is very interesting to know, that, from the albuminous white of the egg, the chick in the egg gets the materials for its flesh, bones, blood, and feathers; while from the fatty yolk of the egg, it gets the heat and energy which enable it at length to break its shell and begin the world. It is less interesting, perhaps, but still it is interesting, to know that when a taper burns, the wax is converted into carbonic acid and water. Moreover, it is quite true that the habit of dealing with facts, which is given by the study of nature, is, as the friends of physical science praise it for being, an excellent discipline. The appeal, in the study of nature, is constantly to observation and experiment; not only is it said that the thing is so, but we can be made to see that it is so. Not only does a man tell us that when a taper burns the wax

---

[11] Nebuchadnezzar, Chaldean king of Babylon (c. 605-562 B.C.), was an enemy of the Hebrews, whose priestly class was the Levites.

is converted into carbonic acid and water, as a man may tell us, if he likes, that Charon[12] is punting his ferry-boat on the river Styx, or that Victor Hugo is a sublime poet, or Mr. Gladstone the most admirable of statesmen; but we are made to see that the conversion into carbonic acid and water does actually happen. This reality of natural knowledge it is, which makes the friends of physical science contrast it, as a knowledge of things, with the humanist's knowledge, which is, say they, a knowledge of words. And hence Professor Huxley is moved to lay it down that, "for the purpose of attaining real culture, an exclusively scientific education is at least as effectual as an exclusively literary education." And a certain President of the Section of Mechanical Science in the British Association[13] is, in Scripture phrase, "very bold," and declares that if a man, in his mental training, "has substituted literature and history for natural science, he has chosen the less useful alternative." But whether we go these lengths or not, we must all admit that in natural science the habit gained of dealing with facts is a most valuable discipline, and that every one should have some experience of it.

More than this, however, is demanded by the reformers. It is proposed to make the training in natural science the main part of education, for the great majority of mankind at any rate. And here, I confess, I part company with the friends of physical science, with whom up to this point I have been agreeing. In differing from them, however, I wish to proceed with the utmost caution and diffidence. The smallness of my own acquaintance with the disciplines of natural science is ever before my mind, and I am fearful of doing these disciplines an injustice. The ability and pugnacity of the partisans of natural science make them formidable persons to contradict. The tone of tentative inquiry, which befits a being of dim faculties and bounded knowledge, is the tone I would wish to take and not to depart from. At present it seems to me, that those who are for giving to natural knowledge, as they call it, the chief place in the education of the majority of mankind, leave one important thing out of their account: the constitution of human nature. But I put this forward on the strength of some facts not at all recondite,

---

[12] In Greek mythology the boatman who ferries the souls of the dead across the Styx to Hades.
[13] British Association for the Advancement of Science, established in 1831.

very far from it; facts capable of being stated in the simplest possible fashion, and to which, if I so state them, the man of science will, I am sure, be willing to allow their due weight.

Deny the facts altogether, I think, he hardly can. He can hardly deny, that when we set ourselves to enumerate the powers[14] which go to the building up of human life, and say that they are the power of conduct, the power of intellect and knowledge, the power of beauty, and the power of social life and manners—he can hardly deny that this scheme, though drawn in rough and plain lines enough, and not pretending to scientific exactness, does yet give a fairly true representation of the matter. Human nature is built up by these powers; we have the need for them all. When we have rightly met and adjusted the claims of them all, we shall then be in a fair way for getting soberness, and righteousness with wisdom. This is evident enough, and the friends of physical science would admit it.

But perhaps they may not have sufficiently observed another thing: namely, that the several powers just mentioned are not isolated, but there is, in the generality of mankind, a perpetual tendency to relate them one to another in divers ways. With one such way of relating them I am particularly concerned now. Following our instinct for intellect and knowledge, we acquire pieces of knowledge; and presently in the generality of men, there arises the desire to relate these pieces of knowledge to our sense for conduct, to our sense for beauty—and there is weariness and dissatisfaction if the desire is balked. Now in this desire lies, I think, the strength of that hold which letters have upon us.

All knowledge is, as I said just now, interesting; and even items of knowledge which from the nature of the case cannot well be related, but must stand isolated in our thoughts, have their interest. Even lists of exceptions have their interest. If we are studying Greek accents it is interesting to know that *pais* and *pas,* and some other monosyllables of the same form of declension, do not take the circumflex upon the last syllable of the genitive plural but vary, in this respect, from the common rule. If we are studying physiology, it is interesting to know that the pulmonary artery carries dark blood and the pulmonary vein carries

[14] That is, "capacities" or "potentialities."

bright blood, departing in this respect from the common rule for the division of labor between the veins and the arteries. But every one knows how we seek naturally to combine the pieces of our knowledge together, to bring them under general rules, to relate them to principles; and how unsatisfactory and tiresome it would be to go on forever learning lists of exceptions, or accumulating items of fact which must stand isolated.

Well, that same need of relating our knowledge, which operates here within the sphere of our knowledge itself, we shall find operating, also, outside that sphere. We experience, as we go on learning and knowing —the vast majority of us experience—the need of relating what we have learnt and known to the sense which we have in us for conduct, to the sense which we have in us for beauty.

A certain Greek prophetess of Mantineia in Arcadia, Diotima by name, once explained to the philosopher Socrates that love, and impulse, and bent of all kinds, is, in fact, nothing else but the desire in men that good should forever be present to them.[15] This desire for good, Diotima assured Socrates, is our fundamental desire, of which fundamental desire every impulse in us is only some one particular form. And therefore this fundamental desire it is, I suppose—this desire in men that good should be forever present to them—which acts in us when we feel the impulse for relating our knowledge to our sense for conduct and to our sense for beauty. At any rate, with men in general the instinct exists. Such is human nature. And the instinct, it will be admitted, is innocent, and human nature is preserved by our following the lead of its innocent instincts. Therefore, in seeking to gratify this instinct in question, we are following the instinct of self-preservation in humanity.

But, no doubt, some kinds of knowledge cannot be made to directly serve the instinct in question, cannot be directly related to the sense for beauty, to the sense for conduct. These are instrument-knowledges; they lead on to other knowledges, which can. A man who passes his life in instrument-knowledges is a specialist. They may be invaluable as instruments to something beyond, for those who have the gift thus to employ them; and they may be disciplines in themselves wherein it is useful for every one to have some schooling. But it is inconceivable that the gen-

---

[15] Cf. Plato, *Symposium*, 201-207.

erality of men should pass all their mental life with Greek accents or with formal logic. My friend Professor Sylvester,[16] who is one of the first mathematicians in the world, holds transcendental doctrines as to the virtue of mathematics, but those doctrines are not for common men. In the very Senate House and heart of our English Cambridge[17] I once ventured, though not without an apology for my profaneness, to hazard the opinion that for the majority of mankind a little of mathematics, even, goes a long way. Of course this is quite consistent with their being of immense importance as an instrument to something else; but it is the few who have the aptitude for thus using them, not the bulk of mankind.

The natural sciences do not, however, stand on the same footing with these instrument-knowledges. Experience shows us that the generality of men will find more interest in learning that, when a taper burns, the wax is converted into carbonic acid and water, or in learning the explanation of the phenomenon of dew, or in learning how the circulation of the blood is carried on, than they find in learning that the genitive plural of *pais* and *pas* does not take the circumflex on the termination. And one piece of natural knowledge is added to another, and others are added to that, and at last we come to propositions so interesting as Mr. Darwin's famous proposition that "our ancestor was a hairy quadruped furnished with a tail and pointed ears, probably arboreal in his habits." [18] Or we come to propositions of such reach and magnitude as those which Professor Huxley delivers, when he says that the notions of our forefathers about the beginning and the end of the world were all wrong, and that nature is the expression of a definite order with which nothing interferes.

Interesting, indeed, these results of science are, important they are, and we should all of us be acquainted with them. But what I now wish you to mark is, that we are still, when they are propounded to us and we receive them, we are still in the sphere of intellect and knowledge. And for the generality of men there will be found, I say, to arise, when

---

[16] James Joseph Sylvester (1814-1897), eminent professor of mathematics at Johns Hopkins University (1877-83) and at Oxford University (1883-97).

[17] Cambridge University was famous as a center for mathematical studies.

[18] See Charles Darwin, *The Descent of Man* (1871), Part Two, Chapter XXI.

they have duly taken in the proposition that their ancestor was "a hairy quadruped furnished with a tail and pointed ears, probably arboreal in his habits," there will be found to arise an invincible desire to relate this proposition to the sense in us for conduct, and to the sense in us for beauty. But this the men of science will not do for us, and will hardly even profess to do. They will give us other pieces of knowledge, other facts, about other animals and their ancestors, or about plants, or about stones, or about stars; and they may finally bring us to those great "general conceptions of the universe, which are forced upon us all," says Professor Huxley, "by the progress of physical science." But still it will be *knowledge* only which they give us; knowledge not put for us into relation with our sense for conduct, our sense for beauty, and touched with emotion by being so put; not thus put for us, and therefore, to the majority of mankind, after a certain while, unsatisfying, wearying.

Not to the born naturalist, I admit. But what do we mean by a born naturalist? We mean a man in whom the zeal for observing nature is so uncommonly strong and eminent, that it marks him off from the bulk of mankind. Such a man will pass his life happily in collecting natural knowledge and reasoning upon it, and will ask for nothing, or hardly anything, more. I have heard it said that the sagacious and admirable naturalist whom we lost not very long ago, Mr. Darwin, once owned to a friend that for his part he did not experience the necessity for two things which most men find so necessary to them—religion and poetry; science and the domestic affections, he thought, were enough. To a born naturalist, I can well understand that this should seem so. So absorbing is his occupation with nature, so strong his love for his occupation, that he goes on acquiring natural knowledge and reasoning upon it, and has little time or inclination for thinking about getting it related to the desire in man for conduct, the desire in man for beauty. He relates it to them for himself as he goes along, so far as he feels the need; and he draws from the domestic affections all the additional solace necessary. But then Darwins are extremely rare. Another great and admirable master of natural knowledge, Faraday, was a Sandemanian.[19] That is to say, he related his knowledge to his instinct for conduct and to his instinct for

[19] The Sandemanians formed a rigid sect of Protestants, whose founder was Robert Sandeman (1718-1771), a Scottish clergyman and manufacturer.

beauty, by the aid of that respectable Scottish sectary, Robert Sandeman. And so strong, in general, is the demand of religion and poetry to have their share in a man, to associate themselves with his knowing, and to relieve and rejoice it, that, probably, for one man amongst us with the disposition to do as Darwin did in this respect, there are at last fifty with the disposition to do as Faraday.

Education lays hold upon us, in fact, by satisfying this demand. Professor Huxley holds up to scorn mediæval education, with its neglect of the knowledge of nature, its poverty even of literary studies, its formal logic devoted to "showing how and why that which the Church said was true must be true." But the great mediæval Universities were not brought into being, we may be sure, by the zeal for giving a jejune and contemptible education. Kings have been their nursing fathers, and queens have been their nursing mothers, but not for this. The mediæval Universities came into being, because the supposed knowledge, delivered by Scripture and the Church, so deeply engaged men's hearts, by so simply, easily, and powerfully relating itself to their desire for conduct, their desire for beauty. All other knowledge was dominated by this supposed knowledge and was subordinated to it, because of the surpassing strength of the hold which it gained upon the affections of men, by allying itself profoundly with their sense for conduct, their sense for beauty.

But now, says Professor Huxley, conceptions of the universe fatal to the notions held by our forefathers have been forced upon us by physical science. Grant to him that they are thus fatal, that the new conceptions must and will soon become current everywhere, and that every one will finally perceive them to be fatal to the beliefs of our forefathers. The need of humane letters, as they are truly called, because they serve the paramount desire in men that good should be forever present to them —the need of humane letters, to establish a relation between the new conceptions, and our instinct for beauty, our instinct for conduct, is only the more visible. The Middle Age could do without humane letters, as it could do without the study of nature, because its supposed knowledge was made to engage its emotions so powerfully. Grant that the supposed knowledge disappears, its power of being made to engage the emotions will of course disappear along with it—but the emotions themselves, and their claim to be engaged and satisfied, will remain. Now if we find by experience that humane letters have an undeniable power of engaging the emotions, the importance of humane letters in a man's training becomes not less, but greater, in proportion to the success of modern science in extirpating what it calls "mediæval thinking."

Have humane letters, then, have poetry and eloquence, the power here attributed to them of engaging the emotions, and do they exercise it? And if they have it and exercise it, *how* do they exercise it, so as to exert an influence upon man's sense for conduct, his sense for beauty? Finally, even if they both can and do exert an influence upon the senses in question, how are they to relate to them the results—the modern results—of natural science? All these questions may be asked. First, have poetry and eloquence the power of calling out the emotions? The appeal is to experience. Experience shows that for the vast majority of men, for mankind in general, they have the power. Next, do they exercise it? They do. But then, *how* do they exercise it so as to affect man's sense for conduct, his sense for beauty? And this is perhaps a case for applying the Preacher's words: "Though a man labor to seek it out, yet he shall not find it; yea, farther, though a wise man think to know it, yet shall he not be able to find it." [20] Why should it be one thing, in its effect upon the emotions, to say, "Patience is a virtue," and quite another thing, in its effect upon the emotions, to say with Homer,

τλητὸν γὰρ Μοῖραι θυμὸν θέσαν ἀνθρώποισιν—[21]

"for an enduring heart have the destinies appointed to the children of men"? Why should it be one thing, in its effect upon the emotions, to say with the philosopher Spinoza, *Felicitas in eo consistit quod homo suum esse conservare potest*—"Man's happiness consists in his being able to preserve his own essence," [22] and quite another thing, in its effect upon the emotions, to say with the Gospel, "What is a man advantaged, if he gain the whole world, and lose himself, forfeit himself?" [23] How does this difference of effect arise? I cannot tell, and I

[20] *Ecclesiastes*, VIII, 17. [Arnold's note.]
[21] *Iliad*, XXIV, 49. [Arnold's note.]
[22] Spinoza, *Ethics*, IV, Proposition XVIII.
[23] Cf. Luke IX.25: "For what is a man advantaged, if he gain the whole world, and lose himself, or be cast away?"

am not much concerned to know; the important thing is that it does arise, and that we can profit by it. But how, finally, are poetry and eloquence to exercise the power of relating the modern results of natural science to man's instinct for conduct, his instinct for beauty? And here again I answer that I do not know *how* they will exercise it, but that they can and will exercise it I am sure. I do not mean that modern philosophical poets and modern philosophical moralists are to come and relate for us, in express terms, the results of modern scientific research to our instinct for conduct, our instinct for beauty. But I mean that we shall find, as a matter of experience, if we know the best that has been thought and uttered in the world, we shall find that the art and poetry and eloquence of men who lived, perhaps long ago, who had the most limited natural knowledge, who had the most erroneous conceptions about many important matters, we shall find that this art, and poetry, and eloquence, have in fact not only the power of refreshing and de-lighting us, they have also the power—such is the strength and worth, in essentials, of their authors' criticism of life—they have a fortifying, and elevating, and quickening, and suggestive power, capable of won-derfully helping us to relate the results of modern science to our need for conduct, our need for beauty. Homer's conceptions of the physical universe were, I imagine, grotesque; but really, under the shock of hear-ing from modern science that "the world is not subordinated to man's use, and that man is not the cynosure of things terrestrial," I could, for my own part, desire no better comfort than Homer's line which I quoted just now,

τλητὸν γὰρ Μοῖραι θυμὸν θέσαν ἀνθρώποισιν—

"for an enduring heart have the destinies appointed to the children of men"!

And the more that men's minds are cleared, the more that the results of science are frankly accepted, the more that poetry and eloquence come to be received and studied as what in truth they really are—the criticism of life by gifted men, alive and active with extraordinary power at an unusual number of points;—so much the more will the value of humane letters, and of art also, which is an utterance having a like kind of power with theirs, be felt and acknowledged, and their place in education be secured.

375

Let us, therefore, all of us, avoid indeed as much as possible any invidious comparison between the merits of humane letters, as means of education, and the merits of natural sciences. But when some President of a Section for Mechanical Science insists on making the comparison, and tells us that "he who in his training has substituted literature and history for natural science has chosen the less useful alternative," let us make answer to him that the student of humane letters only, will, at least, know also the great general conceptions brought in by modern physical science: for science, as Professor Huxley says, forces them upon us all. But the student of the natural sciences only, will, by our very hypothesis, know nothing of humane letters; not to mention that in setting himself to be perpetually accumulating natural knowledge, he sets himself to do what only specialists have in general the gift for doing genially. And so he will probably be unsatisfied, or at any rate incomplete, and even more incomplete than the student of humane letters only.

I once mentioned in a school-report, how a young man in one of our English training colleges having to paraphrase the passage in *Macbeth* beginning,

Can'st thou not minister to a mind diseased? [24]

turned this line into, "Can you not wait upon the lunatic?" And I remarked what a curious state of things it would be, if every pupil of our national schools knew, let us say, that the moon is two thousand one hundred and sixty miles in diameter, and thought at the same time that a good paraphrase for

Can'st thou not minister to a mind diseased?

was, "Can you not wait upon the lunatic?" If one is driven to choose, I think I would rather have a young person ignorant about the moon's diameter, but aware that "Can you not wait upon the lunatic?" is bad, than a young person whose education had been such as to manage things the other way.

Or to go higher than the pupils of our national schools. I have in my mind's eye a member of our British Parliament who comes to travel

[24] See *Macbeth* v.iii.40.

here in America, who afterwards relates his travels, and who shows a really masterly knowledge of the geology of this great country and of its mining capabilities, but who ends by gravely suggesting that the United States should borrow a prince from our Royal Family, and should make him their king, and should create a House of Lords of great landed proprietors after the pattern of ours; and then America, he thinks, would have her future happily and perfectly secured. Surely, in this case, the President of the Section for Mechanical Science would himself hardly say that our member of Parliament, by concentrating himself upon geology and mineralogy, and so on, and not attending to literature and history, had "chosen the more useful alternative."

If then there is to be separation and option between humane letters on the one hand, and the natural sciences on the other, the great majority of mankind, all who have not exceptional and overpowering aptitudes for the study of nature, would do well, I cannot but think, to choose to be educated in humane letters rather than in the natural sciences. Letters will call out their being at more points, will make them live more.

I said that before I ended I would just touch on the question of classical education, and I will keep my word. Even if literature is to retain a large place in our education, yet Latin and Greek, say the friends of progress, will certainly have to go. Greek is the grand offender in the eyes of these gentlemen. The attackers of the established course of study think that against Greek, at any rate, they have irresistible arguments. Literature may perhaps be needed in education, they say; but why on earth should it be Greek literature? Why not French or German? Nay, "has not an Englishman models in his own literature of every kind of excellence?" [25] As before, it is not on any weak pleadings of my own that I rely for convincing the gainsayers; it is on the constitution of human nature itself, and on the instinct of self-preservation in humanity. The instinct for beauty is set in human nature, as surely as the instinct for knowledge is set there, or the instinct for conduct. If the instinct for beauty is served by Greek literature and art as it is served by no other literature and art, we may trust to the instinct of

[25] See Huxley, "Science and Culture," p. 356.

self-preservation in humanity for keeping Greek as part of our culture. We may trust to it for even making the study of Greek more prevalent than it is now. Greek will come, I hope, some day to be studied more rationally than at present; but it will be increasingly studied as men increasingly feel the need in them for beauty, and how powerfully Greek art and Greek literature can serve this need. Women will again study Greek, as Lady Jane Grey did;[26] I believe that in that chain of forts, with which the fair host of the Amazons are now engirdling our English universities,[27] I find that here in America, in colleges like Smith College in Massachusetts, and Vassar College in the State of New York, and in the happy families of the mixed universities out West, they are studying it already.

Defuit una mihi symmetria prisca,—"The antique symmetry was the one thing wanting to me," said Leonardo da Vinci; and he was an Italian. I will not presume to speak for the Americans, but I am sure that, in the Englishman, the want of this admirable symmetry of the Greeks is a thousand times more great and crying than in any Italian. The results of the want show themselves most glaringly, perhaps, in our architecture, but they show themselves, also, in all our art. *Fit details strictly combined, in view of a large general result nobly conceived;* that is just the beautiful *symmetria prisca* of the Greeks, and it is just where we English fail, where all our art fails. Striking ideas we have, and well executed details we have; but that high symmetry which, with satisfying and delightful effect, combines them, we seldom or never have. The glorious beauty of the Acropolis at Athens did not come from single fine things stuck about on that hill, a statue here, a gateway there; —no, it arose from all things being perfectly combined for a supreme total effect. What must not an Englishman feel about our deficiencies in this respect, as the sense for beauty, whereof this symmetry is an essential element, awakens and strengthens within him! what will not one day be his respect and desire for Greece and its *symmetria prisca,* when the scales drop from his eyes as he walks the London streets, and he

[26] Lady Jane Grey (1537-1554), daughter of the Duke of Suffolk, was a Greek scholar. Proclaimed queen by the Duke of Northumberland and his Protestant followers in 1553, she was beheaded the following year.

[27] Arnold here refers to the establishment of women's colleges in England.

sees such a lesson in meanness, as the Strand, for instance, in its true deformity! But here we are coming to our friend Mr. Ruskin's province,[28] and I will not intrude upon it, for he is its very sufficient guardian.

And so we at last find, it seems, we find flowing in favor of the humanities the natural and necessary stream of things, which seemed against them when we started. The "hairy quadruped furnished with a tail and pointed ears, probably arboreal in his habits," this good fellow carried hidden in his nature, apparently, something destined to develop into a necessity for humane letters. Nay, more; we seem finally to be even led to the further conclusion that our hairy ancestor carried in his nature, also, a necessity for Greek.

And, therefore, to say the truth, I cannot really think that humane letters are in much actual danger of being thrust out from their leading place in education, in spite of the array of authorities against them at this moment. So long as human nature is what it is, their attractions will remain irresistible. As with Greek, so with letters generally: they will some day come, we may hope, to be studied more rationally, but they will not lose their place. What will happen will rather be that there will be crowded into education other matters besides, far too many; there will be, perhaps, a period of unsettlement and confusion and false tendency; but letters will not in the end lose their leading place. If they lose it for a time, they will get it back again. We shall be brought back to them by our wants and aspirations. And a poor humanist may possess his soul in patience, neither strive nor cry, admit the energy and brilliancy of the partisans of physical science, and their present favor with the public, to be far greater than his own, and still have a happy faith that the nature of things works silently on behalf of the studies which he loves, and that, while we shall all have to acquaint ourselves with the great results reached by modern science, and to give ourselves as much training in its disciplines as we can conveniently carry, yet the majority of men will always require humane letters; and so much the more, as they have the more and the greater results of science to relate to the need in man for conduct, and to the need in him for beauty.

[28] Ruskin habitually related architectural styles to the cultures which produced them; see, for example, "The Nature of Gothic" in Part Two of the present collection.

Charles Robert Darwin

1809-1882

Autobiography

> 🔖 The manuscript of Darwin's *Autobiography* bears
> the title "Recollections of the Development of my
> Mind and Character"; it concludes as follows: "Aug.
> 3, 1876. This sketch of my life was begun about May
> 28th at Hopedene, and since then I have written
> for nearly an hour on most afternoons." Given here
> are the opening pages of the document as it was
> first published in 1888 in *The Life and Letters of
> Charles Darwin,* edited by his son Francis Darwin,
> who omitted certain passages. A complete text
> has in recent years been edited by the biologist's
> granddaughter, Nora Barlow.

A German Editor having written to me for an account
of the development of my mind and character with some sketch of my
autobiography, I have thought that the attempt would amuse me, and
might possibly interest my children or their children. I know that it would
have interested me greatly to have read even so short and dull a sketch
of the mind of my grandfather,[1] written by himself, and what he
thought and did, and how he worked. I have attempted to write the
following account of myself, as if I were a dead man in another world
looking back at my own life. Nor have I found this difficult, for life is
nearly over with me. I have taken no pains about my style of writing.

I was born at Shrewsbury on February 12th, 1809, and my earliest
recollection goes back only to when I was a few months over four years

[1] Erasmus Darwin (1731-1802), physician, poet, and early exponent of evolutionary theories (see especially the prose work, *Zoonomia* [1794-96]).

old, when we went to near Abergele[2] for sea-bathing, and I recollect some events and places there with some little distinctness.

My mother died in July in 1817, when I was a little over eight years old, and it is odd that I can remember hardly anything about her except her death-bed, her black velvet gown, and her curiously constructed work-table. In the spring of this same year I was sent to a day-school in Shrewsbury,[3] where I stayed a year. I have been told that I was much slower in learning than my younger sister Catherine, and I believe that I was in many ways a naughty boy.

By the time I went to this day-school my taste for natural history, and more especially for collecting, was well developed. I tried to make out the name of plants, and collected all sorts of things, shells, seals, franks, coins, and minerals. The passion for collecting which leads a man to be a systematic naturalist, a virtuoso, or a miser, was very strong in me, and was clearly innate, as none of my sisters or brother ever had this taste.

One little event during this year has fixed itself very firmly in my mind, and I hope that it has done so from my conscience having been afterward sorely troubled by it; it is curious as showing that apparently I was interested at this early age in the variability of plants! I told another little boy (I believe it was Leighton,[4] who afterwards became a well-known lichenologist and botanist), that I could produce variously coloured polyanthuses and primroses by watering them with certain coloured fluids, which was of course a monstrous fable, and had never been tried by me. I may here also confess that as a little boy I was much given to inventing deliberate falsehoods, and this was always done for the sake of causing excitement. For instance, I once gathered much valuable fruit from my father's trees and hid it in the shrubbery, and then ran in breathless haste to spread the news that I had discovered a hoard of stolen fruit.[5]

I must have been a very simple little fellow when I first went to the school. A boy of the name of Garnett took me into a cake shop one day,

<hr>

[2] Located on the coast in northern Wales.
[3] Kept by a Unitarian minister, Rev. G. Case.
[4] William Allport Leighton (1805-1899).
[5] His father wisely treated this tendency not by making crimes of the fibs, but by making light of the discoveries. [Francis Darwin's note.]

and bought some cakes for which he did not pay, as the shopman trusted him. When we came out I asked him why he did not pay for them, and he instantly answered, "Why, do you not know that my uncle left a great sum of money to the town on condition that every tradesman should give whatever was wanted without payment to any one who wore his old hat and moved [it] in a particular manner?" and he then showed me how it was moved. He then went into another shop where he was trusted, and asked for some small article, moving his hat in the proper manner, and of course obtained it without payment. When we came out he said, "Now if you like to go by yourself into that cake-shop (how well I remember its exact position) I will lend you my hat, and you can get whatever you like if you move the hat on your head properly." I gladly accepted the generous offer, and went in and asked for some cakes, moved the old hat and was walking out of the shop, when the shopman made a rush at me, so I dropped the cakes and ran for dear life, and was astonished by being greeted with shouts of laughter by my false friend Garnett.

I can say in my own favour that I was as a boy humane, but I owed this entirely to the instruction and example of my sisters. I doubt indeed whether humanity is a natural or innate quality. I was very fond of collecting eggs, but I never took more than a single egg out of a bird's nest, except on one single occasion, when I took all, not for their value, but from a sort of bravado.

I had a strong taste for angling, and would sit for any number of hours on the bank of a river or pond watching the float; when at Maer[6] I was told that I could kill the worms with salt and water, and from that day I never spitted a living worm, though at the expense probably of some loss of success.

Once as a very little boy whilst at the day school, or before that time, I acted cruelly, for I beat a puppy, I believe, simply from enjoying the sense of power; but the beating could not have been severe, for the puppy did not howl, of which I feel sure, as the spot was near the house. This act lay heavily on my conscience, as is shown by my remembering the exact spot where the crime was committed. It probably lay all the

[6] Maer Hall, near Shrewsbury in Shropshire, the home of Darwin's maternal uncle, Josiah Wedgwood the younger (1808-1896), son of the famous potter.

heavier from my love of dogs being then, and for a long time after-wards, a passion. Dogs seemed to know this, for I was an adept in rob-bing their love from their masters.

I remember clearly only one other incident during this year whilst at Mr. Case's daily school,—namely, the burial of a dragoon soldier; and it is surprising how clearly I can still see the horse with the man's empty boots and carbine suspended to the saddle, and the firing over the grave. This scene deeply stirred whatever poetic fancy there was in me.

In the summer of 1818 I went to Dr. Butler's great school [7] in Shrewsbury, and remained there for seven years till Midsummer 1825, when I was sixteen years old. I boarded at this school, so that I had the great advantage of living the life of a true schoolboy; but as the distance was hardly more than a mile to my home, I very often ran there in the longer intervals between the callings over and before locking up at night. This, I think, was in many ways advantageous to me by keeping up home affections and interests. I remember in the early part of my school life that I often had to run very quickly to be in time, and from being a fleet runner was generally successful; but when in doubt I prayed earnestly to God to help me, and I well remember that I attributed my success to the prayers and not to my quick running, and marvelled how generally I was aided.

I have heard my father and elder sister say that I had, as a very young boy, a strong taste for long solitary walks; but what I thought about I know not. I often became quite absorbed, and once, whilst re-turning to school on the summit of the old fortifications round Shrews-bury, which had been converted into a public foot-path with no parapet on one side, I walked off and fell to the ground, but the height was only seven or eight feet. Nevertheless the number of thoughts which passed through my mind during this very short, but sudden and wholly unexpected fall, was astonishing, and seem hardly compatible with what physiologists have, I believe, proved about each thought requiring quite an appreciable amount of time.

Nothing could have been worse for the development of my mind than

[7] Samuel Butler (1774-1839), bishop of Lichfield and a fine scholar, was head-master of Shrewsbury School (1798-1836).

Dr. Butler's school, as it was strictly classical, nothing else being taught, except a little ancient geography and history. The school as a means of education to me was simply a blank. During my whole life I have been singularly incapable of mastering any language. Especial attention was paid to verse-making, and this I could never do well. I had many friends, and got together a good collection of old verses, which by patching together, sometimes aided by other boys, I could work into any subject. Much attention was paid to learning by heart the lessons of the previous day; this I could effect with great facility, learning forty or fifty lines of Virgil or Homer, whilst I was in morning chapel; but this exercise was utterly useless, for every verse was forgotten in forty-eight hours. I was not idle, and with the exception of versification, generally worked conscientiously at my classics, not using cribs. The sole pleasure I ever received from such studies, was from some of the odes of Horace, which I admired greatly.

When I left the school I was for my age neither high nor low in it; and I believe that I was considered by all my masters and by my father as a very ordinary boy, rather below the common standard in intellect. To my deep mortification my father once said to me, "You care for nothing but shooting, dogs, and rat-catching, and you will be a disgrace to yourself and all your family." But my father, who was the kindest man I ever knew and whose memory I love with all my heart, must have been angry and somewhat unjust when he used such words.[8]

Looking back as well as I can at my character during my school life, the only qualities which at this period promised well for the future, were, that I had strong and diversified tastes, much zeal for whatever interested me, and a keen pleasure in understanding any complex subject or thing. I was taught Euclid by a private tutor, and I distinctly remember the intense satisfaction which the clear geometrical proofs gave me. I remember, with equal distinctness, the delight which my uncle[9] gave me (the father of Francis Galton) by explaining the principle of the vernier of a barometer. With respect to diversified tastes, independently of science, I was fond of reading various books, and I

[8] Francis Darwin here omitted a lengthy section on the author's father, Robert Waring Darwin (1766-1848).

[9] Samuel Tertius Galton (1783-1844), banker.

used to sit for hours reading the historical plays of Shakespeare, generally in an old window in the thick walls of the school. I read also other poetry, such as Thomson's "Seasons," [10] and the recently published poems of Byron and Scott. I mention this because later in life I wholly lost, to my great regret, all pleasure from poetry of any kind, including Shakespeare. In connection with pleasure from poetry, I may add that in 1822 a vivid delight in scenery was first awakened in my mind, during a riding tour on the borders of Wales, and this has lasted longer than any other aesthetic pleasure.

Early in my school days a boy had a copy of the "Wonders of the World," [11] which I often read, and disputed with other boys about the veracity of some of the statements; and I believe that this book first gave me a wish to travel in remote countries, which was ultimately fulfilled by the voyage of the *Beagle*. In the latter part of my school life I became passionately fond of shooting; I do not believe that any one could have shown more zeal for the most holy cause than I did for shooting birds. How well I remember killing my first snipe, and my excitement was so great that I had much difficulty in reloading my gun from the trembling of my hands. This taste long continued, and I became a very good shot. When at Cambridge I used to practise throwing up my gun to my shoulder before a looking-glass to see that I threw it up straight. Another and better plan was to get a friend to wave about a lighted candle, and then to fire at it with a cap on the nipple, and if the aim was accurate the little puff of air would blow out the candle. The explosion of the cap caused a sharp crack, and I was told that the tutor of the college remarked, "What an extraordinary thing it is, Mr. Darwin seems to spend hours in cracking a horse-whip in his room, for I often hear the crack when I pass under his windows."

I had many friends amongst the school boys, whom I loved dearly, and I think that my disposition was then very affectionate.

With respect to science, I continued collecting minerals with much

---

[10] James Thomson (1700-1748), whose long poem *The Seasons* (1726-30) reveals a Romantic attitude towards nature.

[11] Presumably *The Hundred Wonders of the World* (1818) by Rev. C. C. Clarke, the pseudonym of Richard Phillips (1767-1840), who published popular compilations of miscellaneous information.

zeal, but quite unscientifically—all that I cared about was a new-*named* mineral, and I hardly attempted to classify them. I must have observed insects with some little care, for when ten years old (1819) I went for three weeks to Plas Edwards on the sea-coast in Wales, I was very much interested and surprised at seeing a large black and scarlet Hemipterous insect, many moths (*Zygaena*), and a Cicindela which was not found in Shropshire. I almost made up my mind to begin collecting all the insects which I could find dead, for on consulting my sister I concluded that it was not right to kill insects for the sake of making a collection. From reading White's "Selborne," [12] I took much pleasure in watching the habits of birds, and even made notes on the subject. In my simplicity I remember wondering why every gentleman did not become an ornithologist.

Towards the close of my school life, my brother worked hard at chemistry, and made a fair laboratory with proper apparatus in the tool-house in the garden, and I was allowed to aid him as a servant in most of his experiments. He made all the gases and many compounds, and I read with great care several books on chemistry, such as Henry and Parkes' "Chemical Catechism." The subject interested me greatly, and we often used to go on working till rather late at night. This was the best part of my education at school, for it showed me practically the meaning of experimental science. The fact that we worked at chemistry somehow got known at school, and as it was an unprecedented fact, I was nicknamed "Gas." I was also once publicly rebuked by the headmaster, Dr. Butler, for thus wasting my time on such useless subjects; and he called me very unjustly a *"poco curante,"* [13] and as I did not understand what he meant, it seemed to me a fearful reproach.

As I was doing no good at school, my father wisely took me away at a rather earlier age than usual, and sent me (Oct. 1825) to Edinburgh University with my brother, where I stayed for two years or sessions. My brother was completing his medical studies, though I do not believe he ever really intended to practice, and I was sent there to commence

[12] Gilbert White (1720-1793), naturalist and curate of his native village, Selborne in Hampshire, wrote a famous work entitled *Natural History and Antiquities of Selborne* (1789).

[13] An Italian phrase meaning "caring little"; a person lacking in seriousness.

them. But soon after this period I became convinced from various small circumstances that my father would leave me property enough to subsist on with some comfort, though I never imagined that I should be so rich a man as I am; but my belief was sufficient to check any strenuous efforts to learn medicine.

The instruction at Edinburgh was altogether by lectures, and these were intolerably dull, with the exception of those on chemistry by Hope;[14] but to my mind there are no advantages and many disadvantages in lectures compared with reading. Dr. Duncan's[15] lectures on Materia Medica at 8 o'clock on a winter's morning are something fearful to remember. Dr. Monro[16] made his lectures on human anatomy as dull as he was himself, and the subject disgusted me. It has proved one of the greatest evils in my life that I was not urged to practise dissection, for I should soon have got over my disgust; and the practise would have been invaluable for all my future work. This has been an irremediable evil, as well as my incapacity to draw. I also attended regularly the clinical wards in the hospital. Some of the cases distressed me a good deal, and I still have vivid pictures before me of some of them; but I was not so foolish as to allow this to lessen my attendance. I cannot understand why this part of my medical course did not interest me in a greater degree; for during the summer before coming to Edinburgh I began attending some of the poor people, chiefly children and women in Shrewsbury: I wrote down as full an account as I could of the case with all the symptoms, and read them aloud to my father, who suggested further inquiries and advised me what medicines to give, which I made up myself. At one time I had at least a dozen patients, and I felt a keen interest in the work. My father, who was by far the best judge of character whom I ever knew, declared that I should make a successful physician,—meaning by this one who would get many patients. He maintained that the chief element of success was exciting confidence; but what he saw in me which convinced him that I should

[14] Thomas Charles Hope (1766-1844), professor of chemistry at Edinburgh University.

[15] Andrew Duncan the younger (1773-1832), professor of Materia Medica at Edinburgh University.

[16] Alexander Monro the third (1773-1859), professor of anatomy at Edinburgh University.

create confidence I know not. I also attended on two occasions the operating theatre in the hospital at Edinburgh, and saw two very bad operations, one on a child, but I rushed away before they were completed. Nor did I ever attend again, for hardly any inducement would have been strong enough to make me do so; this being long before the blessed days of chloroform. The two cases fairly haunted me for many a long year.

My brother stayed only one year at the University, so that during the second year I was left to my own resources; and this was an advantage, for I became well acquainted with several young men fond of natural science. One of these was Ainsworth,[17] who afterwards published his travels in Assyria; he was a Wernerian geologist,[18] and knew a little about many subjects. Dr. Coldstream[19] was a very different young man, prim, formal, highly religious, and most kind-hearted; he afterwards published some good zoological articles. A third young man was Hardie, who would, I think, have made a good botanist, but died early in India. Lastly, Dr. Grant,[20] my senior by several years, but how I became acquainted with him I cannot remember; he published some first-rate zoological papers, but after coming to London as Professor in University College, he did nothing more in science, a fact which has always been inexplicable to me. I knew him well; he was dry and formal in manner, with much enthusiasm beneath this outer crust. He one day, when we were walking together, burst forth in high admiration of Lamarck and his views on evolution. I listened in silent astonishment, and as far as I can judge without any effect on my mind. I had previously read the "Zoonomia" of my grandfather, in which similar views are maintained, but without producing any effect on me. Nevertheless it is probable that the hearing rather early in life such views maintained and praised may have favoured my upholding them under a different form in my "Ori-

---

[17] William Francis Ainsworth (1807-1896), surgeon and geologist, author of *Researches in Assyria* (1838).

[18] Abraham Gottlieb Werner (1750-1817), German geologist, held the theory that water-deposits had formed the strata of the earth's surface.

[19] John Coldstream (1806-1863), physician and fellow of the Royal College of Surgeons.

[20] Robert Edmund Grant (1793-1874), professor of comparative anatomy and zoology at London University.

gin of Species." At this time I admired greatly the "Zoonomia"; but on reading it a second time after an interval of ten or fifteen years, I was much disappointed; the proportion of speculation being so large to the facts given.

Drs. Grant and Coldstream attended much to marine Zoology, and I often accompanied the former to collect animals in the tidal pools, which I dissected as well as I could. I also became friends with some of the Newhaven[21] fishermen, and sometimes accompanied them when they trawled for oysters, and thus got many specimens. But from not having had any regular practice in dissection, and from possessing only a wretched microscope, my attempts were very poor. Nevertheless I made one interesting little discovery, and read, about the beginning of the year 1826, a short paper on the subject before the Plinian Society. This was that the so-called ova of Flustra had the power of independent movement by means of cilia, and were in fact larvae. In another short paper I showed that the little globular bodies which had been supposed to be the young state of *Fucas Loreus* were the egg-cases of the worm-like *Pontobdella muricata*.

The Plinian Society was encouraged and, I believe, founded by Professor Jameson:[22] it consisted of students and met in an underground room in the University for the sake of reading papers on natural science and discussing them. I used regularly to attend, and the meetings had a good effect on me in stimulating my zeal and giving me new congenial acquaintances. One evening a poor young man got up, and after stammering for a prodigious length of time, blushing crimson, he at last slowly got out the words, "Mr. President, I have forgotten what I was going to say." The poor fellow looked quite overwhelmed, and all the members were so surprised that no one could think of a word to say to cover his confusion. The papers which were read to our little society were not printed, so that I had not the satisfaction of seeing my paper in print; but I believe Dr. Grant noticed my small discovery in his excellent memoir on Flustra.

I was also a member of the Royal Medical Society, and attended

[21] A fishing village near Edinburgh on the Firth of Forth.

[22] Robert Jameson (1774-1854), Regius Professor of natural history at Edinburgh University. The Plinian Society was founded in 1823.

pretty regularly; but as the subjects were exclusively medical, I did not much care about them. Much rubbish was talked there but there were some good speakers, of whom the best was the present Sir J. Kay-Shuttleworth.[23] Dr. Grant took me occasionally to the meetings of the Wernerian Society, where various papers on natural history were read, discussed, and afterwards published in the "Transactions." I heard Audubon deliver there some interesting discourses on the habits of N. American birds, sneering somewhat unjustly at Waterton.[24] By the way, a negro lived in Edinburgh, who had travelled with Waterton, and gained his livelihood by stuffing birds, which he did excellently: he gave me lessons for payment, and I used often to sit with him, for he was a very pleasant and intelligent man.

Mr. Leonard Horner[25] also took me once to a meeting of the Royal Society of Edinburgh, where I saw Sir Walter Scott in the chair as President, and he apologized to the meeting as not feeling fitted for such a position. I looked at him and at the whole scene with some awe and reverence, and I think it was owing to this visit during my youth, and to my having attended the Royal Medical Society, that I felt the honour of being elected a few years ago an honorary member of both these Societies, more than any other similar honour. If I had been told at that time that I should one day have been thus honoured, I declare that I should have thought it as ridiculous and improbable, as if I had been told that I should be elected King of England.

During my second year at Edinburgh I attended Jameson's lectures on Geology and Zoology, but they were incredibly dull. The sole effect they produced on me was the determination never as long as I lived to read a book on Geology, or in any way to study the science. Yet I feel sure that I was prepared for a philosophical treatment of the subject; for an old Mr. Cotton in Shropshire, who knew a good deal about rocks, had pointed out to me two or three years previously a well-known large erratic boulder in the town of Shrewsbury, called the "bell-stone"; he told me that there was no rock of the same kind nearer than Cum-

----

[23] Sir James Phillips Kay-Shuttleworth (1804-1877), liberal statesman, educational leader, and member of scientific commissions.

[24] Charles Waterton (1782-1865), naturalist and writer of travel books.

[25] Leonard Horner (1785-1864), geologist and educator.

berland or Scotland, and he solemnly assured me that the world would come to an end before any one would be able to explain how this stone came where it now lay. This produced a deep impression on me, and I meditated over this wonderful stone. So that I felt the keenest delight when I first read of the action of icebergs in transporting boulders, and I gloried in the progress of Geology. Equally striking is the fact that I, though now only sixty-seven years old, heard the Professor, in a field lecture at Salisbury Craigs,[26] discoursing on a trap-dyke, with amygdaloidal margins and the strata indurated on each side, with volcanic rocks all around us, say that it was a fissure filled with sediment from above, adding with a sneer that there were men who maintained that it had been injected from beneath in a molten condition. When I think of this lecture, I do not wonder that I determined never to attend to Geology.

From attending Jameson's lectures, I became acquainted with the curator of the museum, Mr. Macgillivray,[27] who afterwards published a large and excellent book on the birds of Scotland. I had much interesting natural-history talk with him, and he was very kind to me. He gave me some rare shells, for I at that time collected marine mollusca, but with no great zeal.

My summer vacations during these two years were wholly given up to amusements, though I always had some book in hand, which I read with interest. During the summer of 1826 I took a long walking tour with two friends with knapsacks on our backs through North Wales. We walked thirty miles most days, including one day the ascent of Snowdon. I also went with my sister on a riding tour in North Wales, a servant with saddle-bags carrying our clothes. The autumns were devoted to shooting chiefly at Mr. Owen's, at Woodhouse, and at my Uncle Jos's,[28] at Maer. My zeal was so great that I used to place my shooting-boots open by my bed-side when I went to bed, so as not to lose half a minute in putting them on in the morning; and on one occasion I reached a distant part of the Maer estate, on the 20th of August

[26] A rocky crest to the east of Edinburgh.
[27] William Macgillivray (1796-1852), professor of natural history at Aberdeen University and author of *A History of British Birds* (1837-52).
[28] Josiah Wedgwood.

for black-game shooting, before I could see: I then toiled on with the game-keeper the whole day through thick heath and young Scotch firs.

I kept an exact record of every bird which I shot throughout the whole season. One day when shooting at Woodhouse with Captain Owen, the eldest son, and Major Hill, his cousin, afterwards Lord Berwick, both of whom I liked very much, I thought myself shamefully used, for every time after I had fired and thought that I had killed a bird, one of the two acted as if loading his gun, and cried out, "You must not count that bird, for I fired at the same time," and the game-keeper, perceiving the joke, backed them up. After some hours they told me the joke, but it was no joke to me, for I had shot a large number of birds, but did not know how many, and could not add them to my list, which I used to do by making a knot in a piece of string tied to a button-hole. This my wicked friends had perceived.

How I did enjoy shooting! but I think that I must have been half-consciously ashamed of my zeal, for I tried to persuade myself that shooting was almost an intellectual employment; it required so much skill to judge where to find most game and to hunt the dogs well.

One of my autumnal visits to Maer in 1827 was memorable from meeting there Sir J. Mackintosh,[29] who was the best converser I ever listened to. I heard afterwards with a glow of pride that he had said, "There is something in that young man that interests me." This must have been chiefly due to his perceiving that I listened with much interest to everything which he said, for I was as ignorant as a pig about his subjects of history, politics, and moral philosophy. To hear of praise from an eminent person, though no doubt apt or certain to excite vanity, is, I think, good for a young man, as it helps to keep him in the right course.

My visits to Maer during these two or three succeeding years were quite delightful, independently of the autumnal shooting. Life there was perfectly free; the country was very pleasant for walking or riding; and in the evening there was much very agreeable conversation, not so personal as it generally is in large family parties, together with music. In the summer the whole family used often to sit on the steps of the old

[29] Sir James Mackintosh (1765-1832), eminent Scottish philosopher and historian. He and Josiah Wedgwood were brothers-in-law.

portico, with the flower-garden in front, and with the steep wooded bank opposite the house reflected in the lake, with here and there a fish rising or a water-bird paddling about. Nothing has left a more vivid picture on my mind than these evenings at Maer. I was also attached to and greatly revered my Uncle Jos; he was silent and reserved, so as to be a rather awful man; but he sometimes talked openly with me. He was the very type of an upright man, with the clearest judgment. I do not believe that any power on earth could have made him swerve an inch from what he considered the right course. I used to apply to him in my mind the well-known ode of Horace, now forgotten by me, in which the words "nec vultus tyrrani, &c.," [30] come in.

CAMBRIDGE 1828-1831

After having spent two sessions in Edinburgh, my father perceived, or he heard from my sisters, that I did not like the thought of being a physician, so he proposed that I should become a clergyman. He was very properly vehement against my turning into an idle sporting man, which then seemed my probable destination. I asked for some time to consider, as from what little I had heard or thought on the subject I had scruples about declaring my belief in all the dogmas of the Church of England; though otherwise I liked the thought of being a country clergyman. Accordingly I read with care "Pearson on the Creeds," [31] and a few other books on divinity; and as I did not then in the least doubt the strict and literal truth of every word in the Bible, I soon persuaded myself that our Creed must be fully accepted.

Considering how fiercely I have been attacked by the orthodox, it seems ludicrous that I once intended to be a clergyman. Nor was this intention and my father's wish ever formally given up, but died a natural death when, on leaving Cambridge, I joined the *Beagle* as naturalist. If the phrenologists are to be trusted, I was well fitted in one respect to be a clergyman. A few years ago the secretaries of a German psycho-

[30] See Horace, *Odes,* III, iii, 1-4: "The man tenacious of his purpose in a righteous cause is not shaken from his firm resolve by the frenzy of his fellow citizens bidding what is wrong, *not by the face of threatening tyrant.*" [Loeb trans.]

[31] John Pearson (1613-1686), bishop of Chester and author of *Exposition of the Creed* (1659), a standard work.

logical society asked me earnestly by letter for a photograph of myself; and some time afterwards I received the proceedings of one of the meetings, in which it seemed that the shape of my head had been the subject of a public discussion, and one of the speakers declared that I had the bump of reverence developed enough for ten priests.

As it was decided that I should be a clergyman, it was necessary that I should go to one of the English universities and take a degree; but as I had never opened a classical book since leaving school, I found to my dismay, that in the two intervening years I had actually forgotten, incredible as it may appear, almost everything which I had learnt, even to some few of the Greek letters. I did not therefore proceed to Cambridge at the usual time in October, but worked with a private tutor in Shrewsbury, and went to Cambridge after the Christmas vacation, early in 1828. I soon recovered my school standard of knowledge, and could translate easy Greek books, such as Homer and the Greek Testament, with moderate facility.

During the three years which I spent at Cambridge my time was wasted, as far as the academical studies were concerned, as completely as at Edinburgh and at school. I attempted mathematics, and even went during the summer of 1828 with a private tutor (a very dull man) to Barmouth, but I got on very slowly. The work was repugnant to me, chiefly from my not being able to see any meaning in the early steps of algebra. This impatience was very foolish, and in after years I have deeply regretted that I did not proceed far enough at least to understand something of the great leading principles of mathematics, for men thus endowed seem to have an extra sense. But I do not believe that I should ever have succeeded beyond a very low grade. With respect to Classics I did nothing except attend a few compulsory college lectures, and the attendance was almost nominal. In my second year I had to work for a month or two to pass the Little-Go,[32] which I did easily. Again, in my last year I worked with some earnestness for my final degree of B.A., and brushed up my Classics, together with a little Algebra and Euclid, which latter gave me much pleasure, as it did at school. In order to pass the B.A. examination, it was also necessary to get up

[32] Collegiate slang for the preliminary examination for the B.A. degree.

Paley's "Evidences of Christianity," and his "Moral Philosophy." [33] This was done in a thorough manner, and I am convinced that I could have written out the whole of the "Evidences" with perfect correctness, but not of course in the clear language of Paley. The logic of this book and, as I may add, of his "Natural Theology," gave me as much delight as did Euclid. The careful study of these works, without attempting to learn any part by rote, was the only part of the academical course which, as I then felt and as I still believe, was of the least use to me in the education of my mind. I did not at that time trouble myself about Paley's premises; and taking these on trust, I was charmed and convinced by the long line of argumentation. By answering well the examination questions in Paley, by doing Euclid well, and by not failing miserably in Classics, I gained a good place among the οἱ πολλοὶ or crowd of men who do not go in for honours. Oddly enough, I cannot remember how high I stood, and my memory fluctuates between the fifth, tenth, or twelfth, name on the list.

Public lectures on several branches were given in the University, attendance being quite voluntary; but I was so sickened with lectures at Edinburgh that I did not even attend Sedgwick's[34] eloquent and interesting lectures. Had I done so I should probably have become a geologist earlier than I did. I attended, however, Henslow's[35] lectures on Botany, and liked them much for their extreme clearness, and the admirable illustrations; but I did not study botany. Henslow used to take his pupils, including several of the older members of the University, field excursions, on foot or in coaches, to distant places, or in a barge down the river, and lectured on the rarer plants and animals which were observed. These excursions were delightful.

Although, as we shall presently see, there were some redeeming features in my life at Cambridge, my time was sadly wasted there, and worse than wasted. From my passion for shooting and for hunting, and, when this failed, for riding across country, I got into a sporting set,

---

[33] William Paley (1743-1805), theologian and author of two famous texts prescribed for study at Cambridge University: *Principles of Moral and Political Philosophy* (1785), and *View of the Evidences of Christianity* (1794).

[34] Adam Sedgwick (1785-1873), professor of geology at Cambridge University.

[35] John Stevens Henslow (1796-1861), professor of botany at Cambridge University, who helped Darwin secure his position as naturalist on the *Beagle*.

including some dissipated low-minded young men. We used often to dine together in the evening, though these dinners often included men of a higher stamp, and we sometimes drank too much, with jolly singing and playing of cards afterwards. I know that I ought to feel ashamed of days and evenings thus spent, but as some of my friends were very pleasant, and we were all in the highest spirits, I cannot help looking back to these times with much pleasure.[36]

But I am glad to think that I had many other friends of a widely different nature. I was very intimate with Whitley, who was afterwards Senior Wrangler,[37] and we used continually to take long walks together. He inoculated me with a taste for pictures and good engravings, of which I bought some. I frequently went to the Fitzwilliam Gallery,[38] and my taste must have been fairly good, for I certainly admired the best pictures, which I discussed with the old curator. I read also with much interest Sir Joshua Reynolds' book.[39] This taste, though not natural to me, lasted for several years, and many of the pictures in the National Gallery in London gave me much pleasure; that of Sebastian del Piombo[40] exciting in me a sense of sublimity.

I also got into a musical set, I believe by means of my warm-hearted friend, Herbert,[41] who took a high wrangler's degree. From associating with these men, and hearing them play, I acquired a strong taste for music, and used very often to time my walks so as to hear on week days the anthem in King's College Chapel. This gave me intense pleasure, so that my backbone would sometimes shiver. I am sure that there was no affectation or mere imitation in this taste, for I used generally to go by myself to King's College, and I sometimes hired the chorister boys

---

[36] I gather from some of my father's contemporaries that he has exaggerated the Bacchanalian nature of these parties. [Francis Darwin's note.]

[37] Rev. C. Whitley, Hon. Canon of Durham, formerly Reader in Natural Philosophy in Durham University. [Francis Darwin's note.] At Cambridge University the Senior Wrangler is the top honors scholar in mathematics.

[38] The museum of art at Cambridge.

[39] Reference to Sir Joshua Reynolds' famous *Discourses* on painting (1769-90).

[40] Sebastiano Luciani, called Sebastian del Piombo (1485?-1547), Italian painter of the Venetian school. Darwin probably refers to his picture, *Raising of Lazarus,* in the National Gallery.

[41] The late John Maurice Herbert, County Court Judge of Cardiff and the Monmouth Circuit. [Francis Darwin's note.]

to sing in my rooms. Nevertheless I am so utterly destitute of an ear, that I cannot perceive a discord, or keep time and hum a tune correctly; and it is a mystery how I could possibly have derived pleasure from music.

My musical friends soon perceived my state, and sometimes amused themselves by making me pass an examination, which consisted in ascertaining how many tunes I could recognize when they were played rather more quickly or slowly than usual. "God save the King," when thus played, was a sore puzzle. There was another man with almost as bad an ear as I had, and strange to say he played a little on the flute. Once I had the triumph of beating him in one of our musical examinations.

But no pursuit at Cambridge was followed with nearly so much eagerness or gave me so much pleasure as collecting beetles. It was the mere passion for collecting, for I did not dissect them, and rarely compared their external characters with published descriptions, but got them named anyhow. I will give a proof of my zeal: one day, on tearing off some old bark, I saw two rare beetles, and seized one in each hand; then I saw a third and new kind, which I could not bear to lose, so that I popped the one which I held in my right hand into my mouth. Alas! it ejected some intensely acrid fluid, which burnt my tongue so that I was forced to spit the beetle out, which was lost, as was the third one.

I was very successful in collecting, and invented two new methods; I employed a labourer to scrape, during the winter, moss off old trees and place it in a large bag, and likewise to collect the rubbish at the bottom of the barges in which reeds are brought from the fens, and thus I got some very rare species. No poet ever felt more delighted at seeing his first poem published than I did at seeing, in Stephens' "Illustrations of British Insects," the magic words, "captured by C. Darwin, Esq." I was introduced to entomology by my second cousin, W. Darwin Fox, a clever and most pleasant man, who was then at Christ's College, and with whom I became extremely intimate. Afterwards I became well acquainted, and went out collecting, with Albert Way[42] of Trinity, who

[42] Albert Way (1805-1874), antiquarian and founder of the Archaeological Institute (1845).

in after years became a well-known archaeologist; also with H. Thomson[43] of the same College, afterwards a leading agriculturist, chairman of a great railway, and Member of Parliament. It seems therefore that a taste for collecting beetles is some indication of future success in life!

I am surprised what an indelible impression many of the beetles which I caught at Cambridge have left on my mind. I can remember the exact appearance of certain posts, old trees and banks where I made a good capture. The pretty *Panagaeus cruxmajor* was a treasure in those days, and here at Down[44] I saw a beetle running across a walk, and on picking it up instantly perceived that it differed slightly from *P. cruxmajor,* and it turned out to be *P. quadripunctatus,* which is only a variety or closely allied species, differing from it very slightly in outline. I had never seen in those old days Licinus alive, which to an uneducated eye hardly differs from many of the black Carabidous beetles; but my sons found here a specimen, and I instantly recognized that it was new to me; yet I had not looked at a British beetle for the last twenty years.

I have not as yet mentioned a circumstance which influenced my whole career more than any other. This was my friendship with Professor Henslow. Before coming up to Cambridge, I had heard of him from my brother as a man who knew every branch of science, and I was accordingly prepared to reverence him. He kept open house once every week when all undergraduates, and some older members of the University, who were attached to science, used to meet in the evening. I soon got, through Fox, an invitation, and I went there regularly. Before long I became well acquainted with Henslow, and during the latter half of my time at Cambridge took long walks with him on most days; so that I was called by some of the dons "the man who walks with Henslow"; and in the evening I was very often asked to join his family dinner. His knowledge was great in botany, entomology, chemistry, mineralogy, and geology. His strongest taste was to draw conclusions from long continued minute observations. His judgment was excellent, and his whole mind well balanced; but I do not suppose that any one would say that he possessed much original genius. He was deeply

[43] Sir Harry Stephen Thomson (1809-1874).
[44] The village in Kent where Darwin lived for the last forty years of his life.

religious, and so orthodox that he told me one day he should be grieved if a single word of the Thirty-nine Articles were altered. His moral qualities were in every way admirable. He was free from every tinge of vanity or other petty feeling; and I never saw a man who thought so little about himself or his own concerns. His temper was imperturbably good, with the most winning and courteous manners; yet, as I have seen, he could be roused by any bad action to the warmest indignation and prompt action.

I once saw in his company in the streets of Cambridge almost as horrid a scene as could have been witnessed during the French Revolution. Two body-snatchers had been arrested, and whilst being taken to prison had been torn from the constable by a crowd of the roughest men, who dragged them by their legs along the muddy and stony road. They were covered from head to foot with mud, and their faces were bleeding either from having been kicked or from the stones; they looked like corpses, but the crowd was so dense that I got only a few momentary glimpses of the wretched creatures. Never in my life have I seen such wrath painted on a man's face as was shown by Henslow at this horrid scene. He tried repeatedly to penetrate the mob; but it was simply impossible. He then rushed away to the mayor, telling me not to follow him, but to get more policemen. I forget the issue, except that the two men were got into prison without being killed.

Henslow's benevolence was unbounded, as he proved by his many excellent schemes for his poor parishioners, when in after years he held the living of Hitcham. My intimacy with such a man ought to have been, and I hope was, an inestimable benefit. I cannot resist mentioning a trifling incident, which showed his kind consideration. Whilst examining some pollen-grains on a damp surface, I saw the tubes exserted, and instantly rushed off to communicate my surprising discovery to him. Now I do not suppose any other professor of botany could have helped laughing at my coming in such a hurry to make such a communication. But he agreed how interesting the phenomenon was, and explained its meaning, but made me clearly understand how well it was known; so I left him not in the least mortified, but well pleased at having discovered for myself so remarkable a fact, but determined not to be in such a hurry again to communicate my discoveries.

Dr. Whewell [45] was one of the older and distinguished men who sometimes visited Henslow, and on several occasions I walked home with him at night. Next to Sir J. Mackintosh he was the best converser on grave subjects to whom I ever listened. Leonard Jenyns,[46] who afterwards published some good essays in Natural History, often stayed with Henslow, who was his brother-in-law. I visited him at his parsonage on the borders of the Fens, and had many a good walk and talk with him about Natural History. I became also acquainted with several other men older than me, who did not care much about science, but were friends of Henslow. One was a Scotchman, brother of Sir Alexander Ramsay, and tutor of Jesus College: he was a delightful man, but did not live for many years. Another was Mr. Dawes,[47] afterwards Dean of Hereford, and famous for his success in the education of the poor. These men and others of the same standing, together with Henslow, used sometimes to take distant excursions into the country, which I was allowed to join, and they were most agreeable.

Looking back, I infer that there must have been something in me a little superior to the common run of youths, otherwise the above-mentioned men, so much older than me and higher in academical position, would never have allowed me to associate with them. Certainly I was not aware of any such superiority, and I remember one of my sporting friends, Turner, who saw me at work with my beetles, saying that I should some day be a Fellow of the Royal Society, and the notion seemed to me preposterous.

During my last year at Cambridge, I read with care and profound interest Humboldt's "Personal Narrative." This work, and Sir J. Herschel's "Introduction to the Study of Natural Philosophy," [48] stirred up

[45] William Whewell (1794-1866), philosopher, theologian, mathematician, and Master of Trinity College, Cambridge.

[46] Leonard Jenyns, later Leonard Blomefield (1800-1893), naturalist, who nearly accepted the post on the *Beagle* before it was offered to Darwin.

[47] Richard Dawes (1796-1867), mathematician and writer of educational pamphlets.

[48] Alexander von Humboldt's *Personal Narrative of Travels to the Equinoctial Regions of the New Continent during the Years 1799-1804* was published in France in 1807; Sir John Frederick William Herschel's *Preliminary Discourse on the Study of Natural Philosophy* appeared in 1830.

in me a burning zeal to add even the most humble contribution to the noble structure of Natural Science. No one or a dozen other books influenced me nearly so much as these two. I copied out from Humboldt long passages about Teneriffe, and read them aloud on one of the abovementioned excursions, to (I think) Henslow, Ramsay, and Dawes, for on a previous occasion I had talked about the glories of Teneriffe, and some of the party declared they would endeavour to go there; but I think that they were only half in earnest. I was, however, quite in earnest, and got an introduction to a merchant in London to enquire about ships; but the scheme was, of course, knocked on the head by the voyage of the *Beagle*.

My summer vacations were given up to collecting beetles, to some reading, and short tours. In the autumn my whole time was devoted to shooting, chiefly at Woodhouse and Maer, and sometimes with young Eyton of Eyton.[49] Upon the whole the three years which I spent at Cambridge were the most joyful in my happy life; for I was then in excellent health, and almost always in high spirits.

As I had at first come up to Cambridge at Christmas, I was forced to keep two terms after passing my final examinations, at the commencement of 1831; and Henslow then persuaded me to begin the study of geology. Therefore on my return to Shropshire I examined sections and coloured a map of parts round Shrewsbury. Professor Sedgwick intended to visit North Wales in the beginning of August to pursue his famous geological investigations amongst the older rocks, and Henslow asked him to allow me to accompany him. Accordingly he came and slept at my father's house.

A short conversation with him during this evening produced a strong impression on my mind. Whilst examining an old gravel-pit near Shrewsbury, a labourer told me that he had found in it a large worn tropical Volute shell, such as may be seen on the chimney-pieces of cottages; and as he would not sell the shell, I was convinced that he had really found it in the pit. I told Sedgwick of the fact, and he at once said (no doubt truly) that it must have been thrown away by some one into the pit; but then added, if really embedded there it would be the greatest mis-

---

[49] Thomas Campbell Eyton (1809-1880), who later opposed Darwinism.

fortune to geology, as it would overthrow all that we know about the superficial deposits of the Midland Counties. These gravel-beds belong in fact to the glacial period, and in after years I found in them broken arctic shells. But I was then utterly astonished at Sedgwick not being delighted at so wonderful a fact as a tropical shell being found near the surface in the middle of England. Nothing before had ever made me thoroughly realize, though I had read various scientific books, that science consists in grouping facts so that general laws or conclusions may be drawn from them.

Next morning we started for Llangollen, Conway, Bangor, and Capel Curig. This tour was of decided use in teaching me a little how to make out the geology of a country. Sedgwick often sent me on a line parallel to his, telling me to bring back specimens of the rock and to mark the stratification on a map. I have little doubt that he did this for my good, as I was too ignorant to have aided him. On this tour I had a striking instance of how easy it is to overlook phenomena, however conspicuous, before they have been observed by any one. We spent many hours in Cwm Idwal, examining all the rocks with extreme care, as Sedgwick was anxious to find fossils in them; but neither of us saw a trace of the wonderful glacial phenomena all around us; we did not notice the plainly scored rocks, the perched boulders, the lateral and terminal moraines. Yet these phenomena are so conspicuous that, as I declared in a paper published many years afterwards in the "Philosophical Magazine," [50] a house burnt down by fire did not tell its story more plainly than did this valley. If it had still been filled by a glacier, the phenomena would have been less distinct than they now are.

At Capel Curig I left Sedgwick and went in a straight line by compass and map across the mountains to Barmouth, never following any track unless it coincided with my course. I thus came on some strange wild places, and enjoyed much this matter of travelling. I visited Barmouth to see some Cambridge friends who were reading there, and thence returned to Shrewsbury and to Maer for shooting; for at that time I should have thought myself mad to give up the first days of partridge-shooting for geology or any other science.

[50] *Philosophical Magazine*, 1842. [Francis Darwin's note.]

CHARLES ROBERT DARWIN

VOYAGE OF THE "BEAGLE" FROM DECEMBER 27, 1831, TO OCTOBER 2, 1836

On returning home from my short geological tour in North Wales, I found a letter from Henslow, informing me that Captain Fitz-Roy[51] was willing to give up part of his own cabin to any young man who would volunteer to go with him without pay as naturalist to the Voyage of the *Beagle*. I have given, as I believe, in my MS. Journal an account of all the circumstances which then occurred; I will here only say that I was instantly eager to accept the offer, but my father strongly objected, adding the words, fortunate for me, "If you can find any man of common sense who advises you to go I will give my consent." So I wrote that evening and refused the offer. On the next morning I went to Maer to be ready for September 1st, and, whilst out shooting, my uncle sent for me, offering to drive me over to Shrewsbury and talk with my father, as my uncle thought it would be wise in me to accept the offer. My father always maintained that he was one of the most sensible men in the world, and he at once consented in the kindest manner. I had been rather extravagant at Cambridge, and to console my father, said, "that I should be deuced clever to spend more than my allowance whilst on board the *Beagle*"; but he answered with a smile, "But they tell me you are very clever."

Next day I started for Cambridge to see Henslow, and thence to London to see Fitz-Roy, and all was soon arranged. Afterwards, on becoming very intimate with Fitz-Roy, I heard that I had run a very narrow risk of being rejected, on account of the shape of my nose! He was an ardent disciple of Lavater,[52] and was convinced that he could judge of a man's character by the outline of his features; and he doubted whether any one with my nose could possess sufficient energy and determination for the voyage. But I think he was afterwards well satisfied that my nose had spoken falsely. . . .

[51] Robert Fitzroy (1805-1865), vice-admiral and meteorologist, later governor of New Zealand.

[52] Johann Kaspar Lavater (1741-1801), Swiss poet and mystic who espoused the "science" of physiognomy.

Walter Horatio Pater

1839-1894

The Child in the House

> The following sketch first appeared in *Macmillan's Magazine* (1878) with the title "Imaginary Portrait: The Child in the House." It was later reprinted in the posthumous collection *Miscellaneous Studies* (1895). In the "imaginary portrait" of Florian Deleal, Pater was recapturing his own childhood.

As Florian Deleal walked, one hot afternoon, he overtook by the wayside a poor aged man, and, as he seemed weary with the road, helped him on with the burden which he carried, a certain distance. And as the man told his story, it chanced that he named the place, a little place in the neighbourhood of a great city, where Florian had passed his earliest years, but which he had never since seen, and, the story told, went forward on his journey comforted. And that night, like a reward for his pity, a dream of that place came to Florian, a dream which did for him the office of the finer sort of memory, bringing its object to mind with a great clearness, yet, as sometimes happens in dreams, raised a little above itself, and above ordinary retrospect. The true aspect of the place, especially of the house there in which he had lived as a child, the fashion of its doors, its hearths, its windows, the very scent upon the air of it, was with him in sleep for a season; only, with tints more musically blent on wall and floor, and some finer light and shadow running in and out along its curves and angles, and with all its little carvings daintier. He awoke with a sigh at the thought of almost thirty years which lay between him and that place, yet with a flutter of pleasure still within him at the fair light, as if it were a smile, upon it. And it happened that this accident of his dream was just the thing needed for the beginning of a certain design he then had in view, the noting, namely, of some things in the story of his spirit—in that process of brain-building by which we are, each one of us, what we are. With the image of the place so clear and favourable upon him, he fell to thinking of himself therein, and how his thoughts had grown up to him. In that half-spiritualised house he could watch the better, over again, the gradual expansion of the soul which had come to be there— of which indeed, through the law which makes the material objects about them so large an element in children's lives, it had actually become a part; inward and outward being woven through and through each other into one inextricable texture—half, tint and trace and accident of homely colour and form, from the wood and the bricks; half, mere soul-stuff, floated thither from who knows how far. In the house and garden of his dream he saw a child moving, and could divide the main streams at least of the winds that had played on him, and study so the first stage in that mental journey.

The *old house,* as when Florian talked of it afterwards he always called it (as all children do, who can recollect a change of home, soon enough but not too soon to mark a period in their lives), really was an old house; and an element of French descent in its inmates—descent from Watteau, the old court-painter, one of whose gallant pieces still hung in one of the rooms—might explain, together with some other things, a noticeable trimness and comely whiteness about everything there—the curtains, the couches, the paint on the walls with which the light and shadow played so delicately; might explain also the tolerance of the great poplar in the garden, a tree most often despised by English people, but which French people love, having observed a certain fresh way its leaves have of dealing with the wind, making it sound, in never so slight a stirring of the air, like running water.

The old-fashioned, low wainscoting went round the rooms, and up the staircase with carved balusters and shadowy angles, landing half-way up at a broad window, with a swallow's nest below the sill, and the blossom of an old pear-tree showing across it in late April, against the blue, below which the perfumed juice of the find of fallen fruit in autumn

405

was so fresh. At the next turning came the closet which held on its deep shelves the best china. Little angel faces and reedy flutings stood out round the fireplace of the children's room. And on the top of the house, above the large attic, where the white mice ran in the twilight—an infinite, unexplored wonderland of childish treasures, glass beads, empty scent-bottles still sweet, thrum of coloured silks, among its lumber[1]—a flat space of roof, railed round, gave a view of the neighbouring steeples; for the house, as I said, stood near a great city, which sent up heaven-wards, over the twisting weathervanes, not seldom, its beds of rolling cloud and smoke, touched with storm or sunshine. But the child of whom I am writing did not hate the fog because of the crimson lights which fell from it sometimes upon the chimneys, and the whites which gleamed through its openings, on summer mornings, on turret or pave-ment. For it is false to suppose that a child's sense of beauty is dependent on any choiceness or special fineness, in the objects which present them-selves to it, though this indeed comes to be the rule with most of us in later life; earlier, in some degree, we see inwardly; and the child finds for itself, and with unstinted delight, a difference for the sense, in those whites and reds through the smoke on very homely buildings, and in the gold of the dandelions at the road-side, just beyond the houses, where not a handful of earth is virgin and untouched, in the lack of better ministries to its desire of beauty.

This house then stood not far beyond the gloom and rumours of the town, among high garden-walls, bright all summer-time with Golden-rod, and brown-and-golden Wallflower—*Flos Parietis,* as the children's Latin-reading father taught them to call it, while he was with them. Tracing back the threads of his complex spiritual habit, as he was used in after years to do, Florian found that he owed to the place many tones of sentiment afterwards customary with him, certain inward lights under which things most naturally presented themselves to him. The coming and going of travellers to the town along the way, the shadow of the streets, the sudden breath of the neighbouring gardens, the singular brightness of bright weather there, its singular darknesses which linked themselves in his mind to certain engraved illustrations in the old big

---

[1] Thrum—tufts or fringes; lumber—old household stuff.

Bible at home, the coolness of the dark, cavernous shops round the great church, with its giddy winding stair up to the pigeons and the bells—a citadel of peace in the heart of the trouble—all this acted on his childish fancy, so that ever afterwards the like aspects and incidents never failed to throw him into a well-recognised imaginative mood, seeming actually to have become a part of the texture of his mind. Also, Florian could trace home to this point a pervading preference in himself for a kind of comeliness and dignity, an *urbanity* literally, in modes of life, which he connected with the pale people of towns, and which made him susceptible to a kind of exquisite satisfaction in the trimness and well-considered grace of certain things and persons he afterwards met with, here and there, in his way through the world.

So the child of whom I am writing lived on there quietly; things without thus ministering to him, as he sat daily at the window with the birdcage hanging below it, and his mother taught him to read, wondering at the ease with which he learned, and at the quickness of his memory. The perfume of the little flowers of the lime-tree fell through the air upon them like rain; while time seemed to move ever more slowly to the murmur of the bees in it, till it almost stood still on June afternoons. How insignificant, at the moment, seem the influences of the sensible things which are tossed and fall and lie about us, so, or so, in the environment of early childhood. How indelibly, as we afterwards discover, they affect us; with what capricious attractions and associations they figure themselves on the white paper, the smooth wax, of our ingenuous souls, as "with lead in the rock for ever," [2] giving form and feature, and as it were assigned house-room in our memory, to early experiences of feeling and thought, which abide with us ever afterwards, thus, and not otherwise. The realities and passions, the rumours of the greater world without, steal in upon us, each by its own special little passageway, through the wall of custom about us; and never afterwards quite detach themselves from this or that accident, or trick, in the mode of their first entrance to us. Our susceptibilities, the discovery of our powers, manifold experiences—our various experiences of the coming

[2] Cf. Job xix.23-24: "Oh that my words were now written! oh that they were printed in a book! That they were graven with an iron pen and lead in the rock for ever."

and going of bodily pain, for instance—belong to this or the other well-remembered place in the material habitation—that little white room with the window across which the heavy blossoms could beat so peevishly in the wind, with just that particular catch or throb, such a sense of teasing in it, on gusty mornings; and the early habitation thus gradually becomes a sort of material shrine or sanctuary of sentiment; a system of visible symbolism interweaves itself through all our thoughts and passions; and irresistibly, little shapes, voices, accidents—the angle at which the sun in the morning fell on the pillow—become parts of the great chain wherewith we are bound.

Thus far, for Florian, what all this had determined was a peculiarly strong sense of home—so forcible a motive with all of us—prompting to us our customary love of the earth, and the larger part of our fear of death, that revulsion we have from it, as from something strange, untried, unfriendly; though lifelong imprisonment, they tell you, and final banishment from home is a thing bitterer still; the looking forward to but a short space, a mere childish *goûter*[3] and dessert of it, before the end, being so great a resource of effort to pilgrims and wayfarers, and the soldier in distant quarters, and lending, in lack of that, some power of solace to the thought of sleep in the home churchyard, at least—dead cheek by dead cheek, and with the rain soaking in upon one from above.

So powerful is this instinct, and yet accidents like those I have been speaking of so mechanically determine it; its essence being indeed the early familiar, as constituting our ideal, or typical conception, of rest and security. Out of so many possible conditions, just this for you and that for me, brings ever the unmistakable realisation of the delightful *chez soi;*[4] this for the Englishman, for me and you, with the closely-drawn white curtain and the shaded lamp; that, quite other, for the wandering Arab, who folds his tent every morning, and makes his sleeping-place among haunted ruins, or in old tombs.

With Florian then the sense of home became singularly intense, his good fortune being that the special character of his home was in itself so essentially home-like. As after many wanderings I have come to fancy that some parts of Surrey and Kent are, for Englishmen, the true land-

[3] Afternoon snack.
[4] Being at home.

scape, true home-counties, by right, partly, of a certain earthy warmth in
the yellow of the sand below their gorse-bushes, and of a certain gray-
blue mist after rain, in the hollows of the hills there, welcome to fatigued
eyes, and never seen farther south; so I think that the sort of house I
have described, with precisely those proportions of red-brick and green,
and with a just perceptible monotony in the subdued order of it, for its
distinguishing note, is for Englishmen at least typically home-like. And
so for Florian that general human instinct was reinforced by this special
home-likeness in the place his wandering soul had happened to light on,
as, in the second degree, its body and earthly tabernacle; the sense of
harmony between his soul and its physical environment became, for a
time at least, like perfectly played music, and the life led there singularly
tranquil and filled with a curious sense of self-possession. The love of
security, of an habitually undisputed standing-ground or sleeping-place,
came to count for much in the generation and correcting of his thoughts,
and afterwards as a salutary principle of restraint in all his wanderings of
spirit. The wistful yearning towards home, in absence from it, as the
shadows of evening deepened, and he followed in thought what was
doing there from hour to hour, interpreted to him much of a yearning
and regret he experienced afterwards, towards he knew not what, out
of strange ways of feeling and thought in which, from time to time his
spirit found itself alone; and in the tears shed in such absences there
seemed always to be some soul-subduing foretaste of what his last tears
might be.

And the sense of security could hardly have been deeper, the quiet of
the child's soul being one with the quiet of its home, a place "inclosed"
and "sealed." But upon this assured place, upon the child's assured soul
which resembled it, there came floating in from the larger world without, as at windows left ajar unknowingly, or over the high garden walls,
two streams of impressions, the sentiments of beauty and pain—recog-
nitions of the visible, tangible, audible loveliness of things, as a very real
and somewhat tyrannous element in them—and of the sorrow of the
world, of grown people and children and animals, as a thing not to be
put by in them. From this point he could trace two predominant processes of mental change in him—the growth of an almost diseased sensibility to the spectacle of suffering, and, parallel with this, the rapid

growth of a certain capacity of fascination by bright colour and choice form—the sweet curvings, for instance, of the lips of those who seemed to him comely persons, modulated in such delicate unison to the things they said or sang,—marking early the activity in him of a more than customary sensuousness, "the lust of the eye," [5] as the Preacher says, which might lead him, one day, how far! Could he have foreseen the weariness of the way! In music sometimes the two sorts of impressions came together, and he would weep, to the surprise of older people. Tears of joy too the child knew, also to older people's surprise; real tears, once, or relief from long-strung, childish expectation, when he found returned at evening, with new roses in her cheeks, the little sister who had been to a place where there was a wood, and brought back for him a treasure of fallen acorns, and black crow's feathers, and his peace at finding her again near him mingled all night with some intimate sense of the distant forest, the rumour of its breezes, with the glossy blackbirds aslant and the branches lifted in them, and of the perfect nicety of the little cups that fell. So those two elementary apprehensions of the tenderness and of the colour in things grew apace in him, and were seen by him afterwards to send their roots back into the beginnings of life.

Let me note first some of the occasions of his recognition of the element of pain in things—incidents, now and again, which seemed suddenly to awake in him the whole force of the sentiment which Goethe has called the *Weltschmerz*,[6] and in which the concentrated sorrow of the world seemed suddenly to lie heavy upon him. A book lay in an old bookcase, of which he cared to remember one picture—a woman sitting, with hands bound behind her, the dress, the cap, the hair, folded with a simplicity which touched him strangely, as if not by her own hands, but with some ambiguous care at the hands of others—Queen Marie Antoinette, on her way to execution—we all remember David's drawing, meant merely to make her ridiculous. The face that had been so high had learned to be mute and resistless; but out of its very resistlessness, seemed now to call on men to have pity, and forbear; and he took note of that, as he closed the book, as a thing to look at again, if he should at any time find himself tempted to be cruel. Again he would

[5] See I John ii.16.
[6] World sorrow.

never quite forget the appeal in the small sister's face, in the garden under the lilacs, terrified at a spider lighted on her sleeve. He could trace back to the look then noted a certain mercy he conceived always for people in fear, even of little things, which seemed to make him, though but for a moment, capable of almost any sacrifice of himself. Impressible, susceptible persons, indeed, who had had their sorrows, lived about him; and this sensibility was due in part to the tacit influence of their presence, enforcing upon him habitually the fact that there are those who pass their days, as a matter of course, in a sort of "going quietly." Most poignantly of all he could recall, in unfading minutest circumstance, the cry on the stair, sounding bitterly through the house, and struck into his soul for ever, of an aged woman, his father's sister, come now to announce his death in distant India; how it seemed to make the aged woman like a child again; and, he knew not why, but this fancy was full of pity to him. There were the little sorrows of the dumb animals too—of the white angora, with a dark tail like an ermine's, and a face like a flower, who fell into a lingering sickness, and became quite delicately human in its valetudinarianism, and came to have a hundred different expressions of voice—how it grew worse and worse, till it began to feel the light too much for it, and at last, after one wild morning of pain, the little soul flickered away from the body, quite worn to death already, and now but feebly retaining it.

So he wanted another pet; and as there were starlings about the place, which could be taught to speak, one of them was caught, and he meant to treat it kindly; but in the night its young ones could be heard crying after it, and the responsive cry of the mother-bird towards them; and at last, with the first light, though not till after some debate with himself, he went down and opened the cage, and saw a sharp bound of the prisoner up to her nestlings; and therewith came the sense of remorse,— that he too was become an accomplice in moving, to the limit of his small power, the springs and handles of that great machine in things, constructed so ingeniously to play pain-fugues on the delicate nerve-work of living creatures.

I have remarked how, in the process of our brain-building, as the house of thought in which we live gets itself together, like some airy bird's-nest of floating thistle-down and chance straws, compact at last, little accidents have their consequence; and thus it happened that, as he walked one evening, a garden gate, usually closed, stood open; and lo! within, a great red hawthorn in full flower, embossing heavily the bleached and twisted trunk and branches, so aged that there were but few green leaves thereon—a plumage of tender, crimson fire out of the heart of the dry wood. The perfume of the tree had now and again reached him, in the currents of the wind, over the wall, and he had wondered what might be behind it, and was now allowed to fill his arms with the flowers—flowers enough for all the old blue-china pots along the chimney-piece, making *fête*,[7] in the children's room. Was it some periodic moment in the expansion of soul within him, or mere trick of heat in the heavily-laden summer air? But the beauty of the thing struck home to him feverishly; and in dreams all night he loitered along a magic roadway of crimson flowers, which seemed to open ruddily in thick, fresh masses about his feet, and fill softly all the little hollows in the banks on either side. Always afterwards, summer by summer, as the flowers came on, the blossom of the red hawthorn still seemed to him absolutely the reddest of all things; and the goodly crimson, still alive in the works of old Venetian masters or old Flemish tapestries, called out always from afar the recollection of the flame in those perishing little petals, as it pulsed gradually out of them, kept long in the drawers of an old cabinet. Also then, for the first time, he seemed to experience a passionateness in his relation to fair outward objects, an inexplicable excitement in their presence, which disturbed him, and from which he half longed to be free. A touch of regret or desire mingled all night with the remembered presence of the red flowers, and their perfume in the darkness about him; and the longing for some undivined, entire possession of them was the beginning of a revelation to him, growing ever clearer, with the coming of the gracious summer guise of fields and trees and persons in each succeeding year, of a certain, at times seemingly exclusive, predominance in his interests, of beautiful physical things, a kind of tyranny of the senses over him.

In later years he came upon philosophies which occupied him much in the estimate of the proportion of the sensuous and the ideal elements

[7] Festival.

in human knowledge, the relative parts they bear in it; and, in his intellectual scheme, was led to assign very little to the abstract thought, and much to its sensible vehicle or occasion. Such metaphysical speculation did but reinforce what was instinctive in his way of receiving the world, and for him, everywhere, that sensible vehicle or occasion became, perhaps only too surely, the necessary concomitant of any perception of things, real enough to be of any weight or reckoning, in his house of thought. There were times when he could think of the necessity he was under of associating all thoughts to touch and sight, as a sympathetic link between himself and actual, feeling, living objects; a protest in favour of real men and women against mere gray, unreal abstractions; and he remembered gratefully how the Christian religion, hardly less than the religion of the ancient Greeks, translating so much of its spiritual verity into things that may be seen, condescends in part to sanction this infirmity, if so it be, of our human existence, wherein the world of sense is so much with us, and welcomed this thought as a kind of keeper and sentinel over his soul therein. But certainly, he came more and more to be unable to care for, or think of soul but as in an actual body, or of any world but that wherein are water and trees, and where men and women look, so or so, and press actual hands. It was the trick even his pity learned, fastening those who suffered in anywise to his affections by a kind of sensible attachments. He would think of Julian, fallen into incurable sickness, as spoiled in the sweet blossom of his skin like pale amber, and his honey-like hair; of Cecil, early dead, as cut off from the lilies, from golden summer days, from women's voices; and then what comforted him a little was the thought of the turning of the child's flesh to violets in the turf above him. And thinking of the very poor, it was not the things which most men care most for that he yearned to give them; but fairer roses, perhaps, and power to taste quite as they will, at their ease and not task-burdened, a certain desirable, clear light in the new morning, through which sometimes he had noticed them, quite unconscious of it, on their way to their early toil.

So he yielded himself to these things, to be played upon by them like a musical instrument, and began to note with deepening watchfulness, but always with some puzzled, unutterable longing in his enjoyment, the phases of the seasons and of the growing or waning day, down even to the shadowy changes wrought on bare wall or ceiling—the light cast up from the snow, bringing out their darkest angles; the brown light in the cloud, which meant rain; that almost too austere clearness, in the protracted light of the lengthening day, before warm weather began, as if it lingered but to make a severer workday, with the school-books opened earlier and later; that beam of June sunshine, at last, as he lay awake before the time, a way of gold-dust across the darkness; all the humming, the freshness, the perfume of the garden seemed to lie upon it—and coming in one afternoon in September, along the red gravel walk, to look for a basket of yellow crabapples left in the cool, old parlour, he remembered it the more, and how the colours struck upon him, because a wasp on one bitten apple stung him, and he felt the passion of sudden, severe pain. For this too brought its curious reflexions; and, in relief from it, he would wonder over it—how it had then been with him—puzzled at the depth of the charm or spell over him, which lay, for a little while at least, in the mere absence of pain; once, especially, when an older boy taught him to make flowers of sealing-wax, and he had burnt his hand badly at the lighted taper, and been unable to sleep. He remembered that also afterwards, as a sort of typical thing—a white vision of heat about him, clinging closely, through the languid scent of the ointments put upon the place to make it well.

Also, as he felt this pressure upon him of the sensible world, then, as often afterwards, there would come another sort of curious questioning how the last impressions of eye and ear might happen to him, how they would find him—the scent of the last flower, the soft yellowness of the last morning, the last recognition of some object of affection, hand or voice; it could not be but that the latest look of the eyes, before their final closing, would be strangely vivid; one would go with the hot tears, the cry, the touch of the wistful bystander, impressed how deeply on one! or would it be, perhaps, a mere frail retiring of all things, great or little, away from one, into a level distance?

For with this desire of physical beauty mingled itself early the fear of death—the fear of death intensified by the desire of beauty. Hitherto he had never gazed upon dead faces, as sometimes, afterwards, at the *Morgue* in Paris, or in that fair cemetery at Munich, where all the dead must go and lie in state before burial, behind glass windows, among the flowers and incense and holy candles—the aged clergy with their sacred ornaments, the young men in their dancing shoes and spotless white linen—after which visits, those waxen, resistless faces would always live with him for many days, making the broadest sunshine sickly. The child had heard indeed of the death of his father, and how, in the Indian station, a fever had taken him, so that though not in action he had yet died as a soldier; and hearing of the "resurrection of the just," [8] he could think of him as still abroad in the world, somehow, for his protection—a grand, though perhaps rather terrible figure, in beautiful soldier's things, like the figure in the picture of Joshua's Vision[9] in the Bible—and of that, round which the mourners moved so softly, and afterwards with such solemn singing, as but a worn-out garment left at a deserted lodging. So it was, until on a summer day he walked with his mother through a fair churchyard. In a bright dress he rambled among the graves, in the gay weather, and so came, in one corner, upon an open grave for a child—a dark space on the brilliant grass—the black mould lying heaped up round it, weighing down the little jewelled branches of the dwarf rose-bushes in flower. And therewith came, full-grown, never wholly to leave him, with the certainty that even children do sometimes die, the physical horror of death, with its wholly selfish recoil from the association of lower forms of life, and the suffocating weight above. No benign, grave figure in beautiful soldier's things any longer abroad in the world for his protection! only a few poor, piteous bones; and above them, possibly, a certain sort of figure he hoped not to see. For sitting one day in the garden below an open window, he heard people talking, and could not but listen, how, in a sleepless hour, a sick woman had seen one of the dead sitting beside her, come to call her hence; and from the broken talk evolved with much clearness the notion that not all those dead people had really departed to the churchyard, nor were quite so motionless as they looked, but led a secret, half-fugitive life in their old homes, quite free by night, though sometimes visible in the day, dodging from room to room, with no great goodwill towards those who shared the place with them. All night the figure sat beside him in the reveries of his broken sleep, and was not quite gone in the morning—an odd, irreconcilable new member of the household, making the sweet familiar chambers unfriendly and suspect by its uncertain

[8] See Luke xiv.14.
[9] Cf. Joshua v.13-15.

presence. He could have hated the dead he had pitied so, for being thus. Afterwards he came to think of those poor, home-returning ghosts, which all men have fancied to themselves—the *revenants*[10]—pathetically, as crying, or beating with vain hands at the doors, as the wind came, their cries distinguishable in it as a wilder inner note. But, always making death more unfamiliar still, that old experience would ever, from time to time, return to him; even in the living he sometimes caught its likeness; at any time or place, in a moment, the faint atmosphere of the chamber of death would be breathed around him, and the image with the bound chin, the quaint smile, the straight, stiff feet, shed itself across the air upon the bright carpet, amid the gayest company, or happiest communing with himself.

To most children the sombre questioning to which impressions like these attach themselves, if they come at all, are actually suggested by religious books, which therefore they often regard with much secret distaste, and dismiss, as far as possible, from their habitual thoughts as a too depressing element in life. To Florian such impressions, these misgivings as to the ultimate tendency of the years, of the relationship between life and death, had been suggested spontaneously in the natural course of his mental growth by a strong innate sense for the soberer tones in things, further strengthened by actual circumstances; and religious sentiment, that system of biblical ideas in which he had been brought up, presented itself to him as a thing that might soften and dignify, and light up as with a "lively hope," [11] a melancholy already deeply settled in him. So he yielded himself easily to religious impressions, and with a kind of mystical appetite for sacred things; the more as they came to him through a saintly person who loved him tenderly, and believed that this early preoccupation with them already marked the child out for a saint. He began to love, for their own sakes, church lights, holy days, all that belonged to the comely order of the sanctuary, the secrets of its white linen, and holy vessels, and fonts of pure water; and its hieratic purity and simplicity became the type of something he desired always to have about him in actual life. He pored over the pictures in religious books, and knew by heart the exact mode in which

[10] Returners from the dead, ghosts.
[11] Cf. I Peter i.3.

the wrestling angel grasped Jacob,[12] how Jacob looked in his mysterious sleep,[13] how the bells and pomegranates were attached to the hem of Aaron's vestment, sounding sweetly as he glided over the turf of the holy place.[14] His way of conceiving religion came then to be in effect what it ever afterwards remained—a sacred history indeed, but still more a sacred ideal, a transcendent version or representation, under intenser and more expressive light and shade, of human life and its familiar or exceptional incidents, birth, death, marriage, youth, age, tears, joy, rest, sleep, waking—a mirror, towards which men might turn away their eyes from vanity and dullness, and see themselves therein as angels, with their daily meat and drink, even, become a kind of sacred transaction—a complementary strain or burden,[15] applied to our every-day existence, whereby the stray snatches of music in it re-set themselves, and fall into the scheme of some higher and more consistent harmony. A place adumbrated itself in his thoughts, wherein those sacred personalities, which are at once the reflex and the pattern of our nobler phases of life, housed themselves; and this region in his intellectual scheme all subsequent experience did but tend still further to realise and define. Some ideal, hieratic persons he would always need to occupy it and keep a warmth there. And he could hardly understand those who felt no such need at all, finding themselves quite happy without such heavenly companionship, and sacred double of their life, beside them.

Thus a constant substitution of the typical for the actual took place in his thoughts. Angels might be met by the way, under English elm or beech-tree; mere messengers seemed like angels, bound on celestial errands; a deep mysticity brooded over real meetings and partings; marriages were made in heaven; and deaths also, with hands of angels thereupon, to bear soul and body quietly asunder, each to its appointed rest. All the acts and accidents of daily life borrowed a sacred colour and significance; the very colours of things became themselves weighty with meanings like the sacred stuffs of Moses' tabernacle,[16] full of peni-

[12] Cf. Genesis xxxii.24-30.
[13] Cf. Genesis xxviii.11-16.
[14] Cf. Exodus xxxix.24-25.
[15] In music, the bass underpart.
[16] Cf. Exodus xxv-xxvii.

tence or peace. Sentiment, congruous in the first instance only with those divine transactions, the deep, effusive unction of the House of Bethany,[17] was assumed as the due attitude for the reception of our every-day existence; and for a time he walked through the world in a sustained, not unpleasurable awe, generated by the habitual recognition, beside every circumstance and event of life, of its celestial correspondent.

Sensibility—the desire of physical beauty—a strange biblical awe, which made any reference to the unseen act on him like solemn music —these qualities the child took away with him, when, at about the age of twelve years, he left the old house, and was taken to live in another place. He had never left home before, and anticipating much from this change, had long dreamed over it, jealously counting the days till the time fixed for departure should come; had been a little careless about others even, in his strong desire for it—when Lewis fell sick, for instance, and they must wait still two days longer. At last the morning came, very fine; and all things—the very pavement with its dust, at the roadside—seemed to have a white, pearl-like lustre in them. They were to travel by a favourite road on which he had often walked a certain distance, and on one of those two prisoner days, when Lewis was sick, had walked farther than ever before, in his great desire to reach the new place. They had started and gone a little way when a pet bird was found to have been left behind, and must even now—so it presented itself to him—have already all the appealing fierceness and wild self-pity at heart of one left by others to perish of hunger in a closed house; and he returned to fetch it, himself in hardly less stormy distress. But as he passed in search of it from room to room, lying so pale, with a look of meekness in their denudation, and at last through that little, stripped white room, the aspect of the place touched him like the face of one dead; and a clinging back towards it came over him, so intense that he knew it would last long, and spoiling all his pleasure in the realisation of a thing so eagerly anticipated. And so, with the bird found, but himself in an agony of home-sickness, thus capriciously sprung up within him, he was driven quickly away, far into the rural distance, so fondly speculated on, of that favourite country-road.

[17] Cf. Matthew xxvi.6-13; John xii.1-8.

SUGGESTIONS FOR ADDITIONAL READING

Autobiographical writing constitutes a distinct and important category of Victorian literature. The following notable examples of this genre (supplementing the fictional treatments of childhood and youth listed in the introductory essay) yield profound insight into the educational ideals and procedures of the age:

Thomas Carlyle, *Sartor Resartus* (1833-34)

John Henry Newman, *Apologia pro Vita Sua* (1864)

John Stuart Mill, *Autobiography* (1873)

Anthony Trollope, *Autobiography* (1883)

Mark Pattison, *Memoirs* (1885)

John Ruskin, *Praeterita* (1885-89)

Edmund Gosse, *Father and Son: A Study of Two Temperaments* (1907)

Beatrice Webb, *My Apprenticeship* (1926)

Herbert George Wells, *Experiment in Autobiography* (1934)

Rival theories of higher education are eloquently set forth in John Henry Newman's *The Idea of a University* (1852) and in Thomas Henry Huxley's *Lay Sermons, Addresses and Reviews* (1870) and *Science and Education* (Vol. III of *Collected Essays* [1893-94]). Another instructive comparison, having to do with secondary education, is offered by two stories of school life: Thomas Hughes's *Tom Brown's Schooldays* (1857) and Rudyard Kipling's *Stalky & Co.* (1899).

PART SIX

The Mask of Comedy

Introduction

Anyone who has ever tried to explain the point of a joke knows that humor must be allowed to speak for itself. The following selections have been made with two purposes in mind: to illustrate the copiousness and variety of Victorian comic writing and to suggest its relevance to an understanding of the age. For as G. M. Young has written:

> We may easily forget how deeply our picture of the Victorian age is coloured by its satire, and how much that we call Victorian is known to us only because the Victorians laughed at it; how persistently, in the classes accessible to comedy, defective types and false postures were ridiculed into a sulky self-suppression; worn-out fashions blown away, and new attitudes approved.[1]

Considerations of space have eliminated many names which would otherwise be represented in this section. It has not been possible, for example, to make room for one of Richard Harris Barham's delightfully irreverent *Ingoldsby Legends,* nor for a rowdy exploit from Robert Smith Surtees' sporting novels with John Leech's illustrations, nor for any parodies by that graceful and accomplished versifier, Charles Stuart Calverley. Other reasons explain the absence of greater comic writers who would have seemed to demand inclusion. For all their superlative wit, Thomas Love Peacock's novels are so packed with learned and topical allusions that much of their point is lost on today's readers. Anthony Trollope and George Eliot resist anthologizing; their great passages of humor are imbedded in the narrative and depend on pre-established intimacy with the characters involved. The early comedies of George Bernard Shaw present a still different problem; so tightly are they organized in terms of their controlling themes that no single scene can stand by itself.

The comic spirit is characterized by aloofness, lucidity of intellect, and a keen sense of the incongruity between the actual and the desirable; and the prevalence of comedy in an age denotes its instinct and capacity

[1] G. M. Young, *Victorian England: Portrait of an Age* (London, 1936), p. 163.

for self-criticism. Whether they provoked belly-laughter or the sly smile of irony, whether they directly satirized vice and folly or obliquely mocked the false shows of society, the Victorian humorists were occupied with the same problems which aroused the crusading impulse in the notable prophets of the period. Indeed, there are very few of the following selections which do not comment with astringent wit on issues more soberly explored in the preceding sections. "The Victorians," concludes one of their literary historians, "are still their own severest critics, possessed of an amazing capacity for detachment, and . . . an unequaled talent for parody." [2]

The nineteenth century was the heyday of the illustrated book and magazine; and no survey of Victorian humor could pretend to adequacy which did not reproduce specimens of the graphic art of the time. *Punch,* which began publication in 1841, has come to symbolize Victorianism in motley. Many writers, including Thackeray, Lear, Gilbert, and Beerbohm, made the drawings which enliven their texts. Others, such as Dickens and Carroll, collaborated so closely with their illustrators that it is impossible to imagine Micawber and the White Knight under guises other than those bestowed upon them by "Phiz" (Hablôt Knight Browne) and John Tenniel.

[2] Jerome H. Buckley, *The Victorian Temper: A Study in Literary Culture* (Cambridge, Mass., 1951), p. 5.

1   THE GIN SHOP

2   PIT, BOXES, AND GALLERY

3

DOCTOR BLIMBER'S YOUNG GENTLEMEN
AS THEY APPEARED WHEN ENJOYING THEMSELVES

4   MR. CHADBAND "IMPROVING" A TOUGH SUBJECT

Old Gentleman.   Miss Wiggets.   Two Authors.

5   AUTHORS' MISERIES

OLD GENTLEMAN. *"I am sorry to see you occupied, my dear Miss Wiggets, with that trivial paper 'Punch.' A Railway is not a place, in my opinion, for jokes. I never joke—never."*

MISS W. *"So I should think, Sir."*

OLD GENTLEMAN. *"And besides, are you aware who are the conductors of that paper, and that they are Chartists, Deists, Atheists, Anarchists, and Socialists, to a man? I have it from the best authority, that they meet together once a week in a tavern in Saint Giles's, where they concoct their infamous Print. The chief part of their income is derived from Threatening Letters which they send to the Nobility and Gentry. The principal Writer is a returned Convict. Two have been tried at the Old Bailey; and their Artist—as for their Artist. . . .*

GUARD. *"Swin-dun! Sta-tion!"* [Exeunt two Authors.]

6

THE RAILWAY JUGGERNAUT

OF 1845

7   **BLOOMERISM—AN AMERICAN CUSTOM**

8   **A DELICATE ATTENTION**

An old gentleman, anxious that his wife should possess some trifle from the Great Exhibition, purchases (amongst other things) the stuffed elephant, and the model of the dodo.

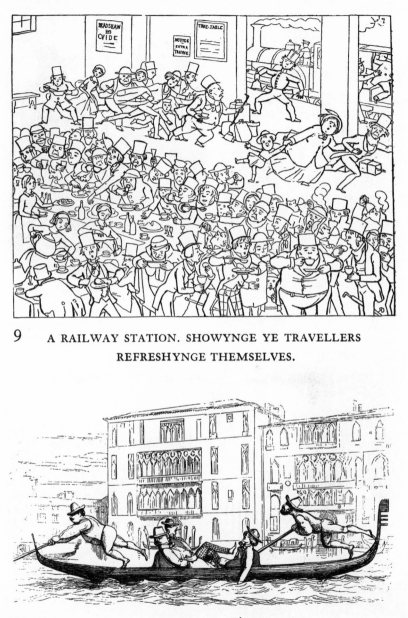

9   A RAILWAY STATION. SHOWYNGE YE TRAVELLERS
REFRESHYNGE THEMSELVES.

10   ENJOYMENT!

A Scene upon the Grand Canal

11

"HIGH" LIFE BELOW STAIRS!

MASTER (sniffing). *"There's a most extraordinary Smell, James. I've noticed it several——"*

HALL PORTER. *"I don't wonder at it, Sir. I've spoke about it Down-Stairs. The Butler, Sir, you see is ''Igh Church,' which he 'as fit up a Horatory in the Pantry, and burns Hincense. We could stand that; but the Cook is the 'Low Church' persuasion, and she burns Brown Paper to hobviate the Hincense. It's perfeckly hawful on Saints' Days, Sir!!!"*

12   MISAPPREHENSION

MARY JANE (indignant). *"Come along, 'Liza. Don't stand looking at that—— Which I call it shameful o' them prefane Darwinites! I don't believe it's a bit like Her!"* [Dedicated to Hanging Committees.]

13 THE HEIGHT OF MAGNIFICENCE

SIR GORGIUS MIDAS. *"Hullo! Where's all the rest of yer gone to?"*

HEAD FOOTMAN. *"If you please, Sir Gorgius, as it was past Two o'Clock, and we didn't know for certain whether you was coming back here, or going to sleep in the City, the hother Footmen thought they might go to bed——"*

SIR GORGIUS. *" 'Thought they might go to Bed,' did they? A pretty State of Things, indeed! So that if I'd a' 'appened to brought 'ome a Friend, there'd a' only been you Four to let us hin, hay!"*

14

THE SIX-MARK TEA-POT

ÆSTHETIC BRIDEGROOM. *"It is quite consummate, is it not?"*

INTENSE BRIDE. *"It is, indeed! Oh, Algernon, let us live up to it!"*

15   MR. TENNYSON, READING "IN MEMORIAM"
TO HIS SOVEREIGN.

16

MR. RUDYARD KIPLING TAKES
A BLOOMIN' DAY AHT, ON THE
BLASTED 'EATH, ALONG WITH
BRITANNIA, 'IS GURL.

Arthur Hugh Clough

1819-1861

The Latest Decalogue

The following lines first appeared in the posthumously published *Poems* of 1862. Like Matthew Arnold, who memorialized their friendship in the beautiful elegy "Thyrsis" (1866), Clough possessed a keenly critical intellect, profound awareness of the cultural crises through which the age was passing, and great spiritual sensitivity—a combination of faculties which made him, again like his brother-poet, suffer very much under the *Zeitgeist*. Had his imagination been less crippled by internal conflict, he might have rivaled Dryden or Byron as a satirist.

Thou shalt have one God only; who
Would be at the expense of two?
No graven images may be
Worshipped, except the currency:
Swear not at all; for for thy curse
Thine enemy is none the worse:
At church on Sunday to attend
Will serve to keep the world thy friend:
Honour thy parents; that is, all
From whom advancement may befall: 10
Thou shalt not kill; but need'st not strive
Officiously to keep alive:
Do not adultery commit;

Advantage rarely comes of it:
Thou shalt not steal; an empty feat,
When it's so lucrative to cheat:
Bear not false witness; let the lie
Have time on its own wings to fly:
Thou shalt not covet; but tradition
Approves all forms of competition.   20

The sum of all is, thou shalt love,
If any body, God above:
At any rate shall never labour
More than thyself to love thy neighbour.

William Makepeace Thackeray

1811-1863

How to Live Well on Nothing a Year

The selection which follows is Chapter Thirty-Six of
Thackeray's great satiric novel of manners, *Vanity
Fair: A Novel without a Hero* (1847-48). This
segment of the narrative recounts how Colonel
Rawdon Crawley and his wife, Becky Sharp (one
of the supreme portraits of an adventuress in
literature), conducted themselves in Paris during the
period immediately following the Battle of Waterloo
(1815). Thackeray's genius for ironic understatement
appears to best advantage in scenes revelatory of
the seamy underside of the lives led by members of
England's privileged classes.

I suppose there is no man in this Vanity Fair of ours
so little observant as not to think sometimes about the worldly affairs of
his acquaintances, or so extremely charitable as not to wonder how his
neighbour Jones, or his neighbour Smith, can make both ends meet at
the end of the year. With the utmost regard for the family, for instance
(for I dine with them twice or thrice in the season), I cannot but own
that the appearance of the Jenkinses in the Park, in the large barouche
with the grenadier footmen, will surprise and mystify me to my dying
day: for though I know the equipage is only jobbed,[1] and all the Jenkins
people are on board-wages,[2] yet those three men and the carriage must

---

[1] Rented.
[2] Wages allowed servants to provide their own food.

represent an expense of six hundred a year at the very least—and then there are the splendid dinners, the two boys at Eton, the prize governess and masters for the girls, the trip abroad, or to Eastbourne or Worthing[3] in the autumn, the annual ball with a supper from Gunter's (who, by the way, supplies most of the *first-rate* dinners which J. gives, as I know very well, having been invited to one of them to fill a vacant place, when I saw at once that these repasts are very superior to the *common* run of entertainments for which the *humbler* sort of J.'s acquaintances get cards) —who, I say, with the most good-natured feelings in the world, can help wondering how the Jenkinses make out matters? What *is* Jenkins?—we all know—Commissioner of the Tape and Sealing-Wax Office, with 1,200£ a year for salary. Had his wife a private fortune? Pooh!—Miss Flint—one of eleven children of a small squire in Buckinghamshire. All she ever gets from her family is a turkey at Christmas, in exchange for which she has to board two or three of her sisters in the off season; and lodge and feed her brothers when they come to town. How does Jenkins balance his income? I say, as every friend of his must say, How is it that he has not been outlawed long since; and that he ever came back (as he did to the surprise of everybody) last year from Boulogne?[4]

"I" is here introduced to personify the world in general—the Mrs. Grundy[5] of each respected reader's private circle—every one of whom can point to some families of his acquaintance who live nobody knows how. Many a glass of wine have we all of us drunk, I have very little doubt, hob-and-nobbing with the hospitable giver, and wondering how the deuce he paid for it.

Some three or four years after his stay in Paris, when Rawdon Crawley and his wife were established in a very small comfortable house in Curzon Street, Mayfair, there was scarcely one of the numerous friends whom they entertained at dinner, that did not ask the above question regarding them. The novelist, it has been said before, knows everything, and as I am in a situation to be able to tell the public how

[3] Fashionable seaside resorts in England.

[4] English bankrupts at this period were in the habit of fleeing to France to escape their creditors.

[5] A character referred to in *Speed the Plough* (1798), a comedy by Thomas Morton (1764?-1838). Mrs. Grundy became for Victorians a symbol of conventional propriety.

Crawley and his wife lived without any income, may I entreat the public newspapers which are in the habit of extracting portions of the various periodical works now published, *not* to reprint the following exact narrative and calculations—of which I ought, as the discoverer (and at some expense, too), to have the benefit. My son, I would say, were I blessed with a child—you may by deep inquiry and constant intercourse with him, learn how a man lives comfortably on nothing a year. But it is best not to be intimate with gentlemen of this profession, and to take the calculations at second-hand, as you do logarithms, for to work them yourself, depend upon it, will cost you something considerable.

On nothing per annum, then, and during a course of some two or three years, of which we can afford to give but a very brief history, Crawley and his wife lived very happily and comfortably at Paris. It was in this period that he quitted the Guards, and sold out of the army.[6] When we find him again, his moustachios and the title of colonel on his card are the only relics of his military profession.

It has been mentioned that Rebecca, soon after her arrival in Paris, took a very smart and leading position in the society of that capital, and was welcomed at some of the most distinguished houses of the restored French nobility.[7] The English men of fashion in Paris courted her, too, to the disgust of the ladies their wives, who could not bear the parvenue. For some months the salons of the Faubourg St. Germain,[8] in which her place was secured, and the splendours of the new Court, where she was received with much distinction, delighted, and perhaps a little intoxicated Mrs. Crawley, who may have been disposed during this period of elation to slight the people—honest young military men mostly—who formed her husband's chief society.

But the colonel yawned sadly among the duchesses and great ladies of the Court. The old women who played écarté[9] made such a noise about a five-franc piece, that it was not worth Colonel Crawley's while

---

[6] The purchase of commissions in the British Army was not abolished until 1871.

[7] With the restoration of the Bourbon King Louis XVIII after Napoleon's downfall, many families of the dispossessed French aristocracy returned to their pre-Revolutionary status.

[8] A street in the most stylish quarter of Paris.

[9] A gambling game of cards.

to sit down at a card-table. The wit of their conversation he could not appreciate, being ignorant of their language. And what good could his wife get, he urged, by making curtsies every night to a whole circle of princesses? He left Rebecca presently to frequent these parties alone; resuming his own simple pursuits and amusements amongst the amiable friends of his own choice.

The truth is, when we say of a gentleman that he lives elegantly on nothing a year, we use the word "nothing" to signify something unknown, meaning, simply, that we don't know how the gentleman in question defrays the expenses of his establishment. Now, our friend the colonel had a great aptitude for all games of chance: and exercising himself, as he continually did, with the cards, the dice-box, or the cue, it is natural to suppose that he attained a much greater skill in the use of these articles than men can possess who only occasionally handle them. To use a cue at billiards well is like using a pencil, or a German flute, or a small-sword [10]—you cannot master any one of these implements at first, and it is only by repeated study and perseverance, joined to a natural taste, that a man can excel in the handling of either. Now, Crawley, from being only a brilliant amateur had grown to be a consummate master of billiards. Like a great general, his genius used to rise with the danger, and when the luck had been unfavourable to him for a whole game, and the bets were consequently against him, he would, with consummate skill and boldness, make some prodigious hits which would restore the battle, and come in a victor at the end, to the astonishment of everybody—of everybody, that is, who was a stranger to his play. Those who were accustomed to see it were cautious how they staked their money against a man of such sudden resources, and brilliant and overpowering skill.

At games of cards he was equally skilful; for though he would constantly lose money at the commencement of an evening, playing so carelessly and making such blunders, that new-comers were often inclined to think meanly of his talent; yet when roused to action, and awakened to caution by repeated small losses, it was remarked that Crawley's play became quite different, and that he was pretty sure of beating his enemy

[10] Duelling-sword.

thoroughly before the night was over. Indeed, very few men could say that they ever had the better of him.

His successes were so repeated that no wonder the envious and the vanquished spoke sometimes with bitterness regarding them. And as the French say of the Duke of Wellington, who never suffered a defeat, that only an astonishing series of lucky accidents enabled him to be an invariable winner; yet even they allow that he cheated at Waterloo, and was enabled to win the last great trick:—so it was hinted at head-quarters in England, that some foul play must have taken place in order to account for the continuous successes of Colonel Crawley.

Though Frascati's and the Salon were open at that time in Paris, the mania for play was so widely spread, that the public gambling-rooms did not suffice for the general ardour, and gambling went on in private houses as much as if there had been no public means for gratifying the passion. At Crawley's charming little *réunions*[11] of an evening this fatal amusement commonly was practised—much to good-natured little Mrs. Crawley's annoyance. She spoke about her husband's passion for dice with the deepest grief; she bewailed it to everybody who came to her house. She besought the young fellows never, never to touch a box; and when young Green, of the Rifles, lost a very considerable sum of money, Rebecca passed a whole night in tears, as the servant told the unfortunate young gentleman, and actually went on her knees to her husband to beseech him to remit the debt, and burn the acknowledgment. How could he? He had lost just as much himself to Blackstone of the Hussars, and Count Punter of the Hanoverian Cavalry. Green might have any decent time; but pay?—of course he must pay;—to talk of burning IOU's was child's play.

Other officers, chiefly young—for the young fellows gathered round Mrs. Crawley—came from her parties with long faces, having dropped more or less money at her fatal card-tables. Her house began to have an unfortunate reputation. The old hands warned the less experienced of their danger. Colonel O'Dowd, of the —th regiment, one of those occu-pying in Paris, warned Lieutenant Spooney of that corps. A loud and violent fracas took place between the infantry-colonel and his lady, who

11 Gatherings.

were dining at the Café de Paris, and Colonel and Mrs. Crawley, who were also taking their meal there. The ladies engaged on both sides. Mrs. O'Dowd snapped her fingers in Mrs. Crawley's face, and called her husband "no better than a blackleg." [12] Colonel Crawley challenged Colonel O'Dowd, C.B. [13] The commander-in-chief hearing of the dispute sent for Colonel Crawley, who was getting ready the same pistols, "which he shot Captain Marker," and had such a conversation with him that no duel took place. If Rebecca had not gone on her knees to General Tufto, Crawley would have been sent back to England; and he did not play, except with civilians, for some weeks after.

But in spite of Rawdon's undoubted skill and constant successes, it became evident to Rebecca, considering these things, that their position was but a precarious one, and that, even although they paid scarcely anybody, their little capital would end one day by dwindling into zero. ' Gambling," she would say, "dear, is good to help your income, but not as an income itself. Some day people may be tired of play, and then where are we?" Rawdon acquiesced in the justice of her opinion; and in truth he had remarked that after a few nights of his little suppers, &c., gentlemen *were* tired of play with him, and, in spite of Rebecca's charms, did not present themselves very eagerly.

Easy and pleasant as their life at Paris was, it was after all only an idle dalliance and amiable trifling, and Rebecca saw that she must push Rawdon's fortune in their own country. She must get him a place or appointment at home or in the colonies; and she determined to make a move upon England as soon as the way could be cleared for her. As a first step she had made Crawley sell out of the Guards, and go on half-pay. His function as aide de camp to General Tufto had ceased previously. Rebecca laughed in all companies at that officer, at his toupee (which he mounted on coming to Paris), at his waistband, at his false teeth, at his pretensions to. be a lady-killer above all, and his absurd vanity in fancying every woman whom he came near was in love with him. It was Mrs. Brent, the beetle-browed wife of Mr. Commissary Brent, to whom the general transferred his attentions now—his bouquets, his dinners at the restaurateurs', his opera-boxes, and his knick-

[12] Swindler.
[13] Companion of the Bath, the lowest order of the knighthood.

knacks. Poor Mrs. Tufto was no more happy than before, and had still to pass long evenings alone with her daughters, knowing that her general was gone off scented and curled to stand behind Mrs. Brent's chair at the play. Becky had a dozen admirers in his place to be sure; and could cut her rival to pieces with her wit. But as we have said, she was growing tired of this idle social life: opera-boxes and restaurateur dinners palled upon her: nosegays could not be laid by as a provision for future years: and she could not live upon knick-knacks, laced handkerchiefs, and kid gloves. She felt the frivolity of pleasure, and longed for more substantial benefits.

At this juncture news arrived which was spread among the many creditors of the colonel at Paris, and which caused them great satisfaction. Miss Crawley, the rich aunt from whom he expected his immense inheritance, was dying; the colonel must haste to her bedside. Mrs. Crawley and her child would remain behind unil he came to reclaim them. He departed for Calais, and having reached that place in safety, it might have been supposed that he went to Dover; but instead he took the diligence to Dunkirk, and thence travelled to Brussels, for which place he had a former predilection. The fact is, he owed more money at London than at Paris; and he preferred the quiet little Belgian city to either of the more noisy capitals.

Her aunt was dead. Mrs. Crawley ordered the most intense mourning for herself and little Rawdon. The colonel was busy arranging the affairs of the inheritance. They could take the premier now, instead of the little entresol [14] of the hotel which they occupied. Mrs. Crawley and the landlord had a consultation about the new hangings, an amicable wrangle about the carpets, and a final adjustment of everything except the bill. She went off in one of his carriages, her French *bonne*[15] with her; the child by her side; the admirable landlord and landlady smiling farewell to her from the gate. General Tufto was furious when he heard she was gone, and Mrs. Brent furious with him for being furious; Lieutenant Spooney was cut to the heart; and the landlord got ready his best apartments previous to the return of the fascinating little woman and her

---

[14] Becky moves to rooms on the first floor (*premier étage*) of the hotel from the less desirable mezzanine or entresol.

[15] Maidservant.

433

husband. He *serré*'d [16] the trunks which she left in his charge with the greatest care. They had been especially recommended to him by Madame Crawley. They were not, however, found to be particularly valuable when opened some time after.

But before she went to join her husband in the Belgic capital, Mrs. Crawley made an expedition into England, leaving behind her her little son upon the Continent, under the care of her French maid.

The parting between Rebecca and the little Rawdon did not cause either party much pain. She had not, to say truth, seen much of the young gentleman since his birth. After the amiable fashion of French mothers, she had placed him out at nurse in a village in the neighbourhood of Paris, where little Rawdon passed the first months of his life, not unhappily, with a numerous family of foster-brothers, in wooden shoes. His father would ride over many a time to see him here, and the elder Rawdon's paternal heart glowed to see him rosy and dirty, shouting lustily, and happy in the making of mud-pies under the superintendence of the gardener's wife, his nurse.

Rebecca did not care much to go and see the son and heir. Once he spoiled a new dove-coloured pelisse of hers. He preferred his nurse's caresses to his mamma's, and when finally he quitted that jolly nurse and almost parent, he cried loudly for hours. He was only consoled by his mother's promise that he should return to his nurse the next day; indeed the nurse herself, who probably would have been pained at the parting too, was told that the child would immediately be restored to her, and for some time awaited quite anxiously his return.

In fact, our friends may be said to have been among the first of that brood of hardy English adventurers who have subsequently invaded the Continent, and swindled in all the capitals of Europe. The respect in those happy days of 1817-18 was very great for the wealth and honour of Britons. They had not then learned, as I am told, to haggle for bargains with the pertinacity which now distinguishes them. The great cities of Europe had not been as yet open to the enterprise of our rascals. And whereas, there is now hardly a town of France or Italy in which you shall not see some noble countryman of our own, with that happy

[16] Corded or tied up.

swagger and insolence of demeanour which we carry everywhere, swindling inn-landlords, passing fictitious cheques upon credulous bankers, robbing coachmakers of their carriages, goldsmiths of their trinkets, easy travellers of their money at cards,—even public libraries of their books: —thirty years ago you needed but to be a Milor Anglais,[17] travelling in a private carriage, and credit was at your hand wherever you chose to seek it, and gentlemen, instead of cheating, were cheated. It was not for some weeks after the Crawleys' departure that the landlord of the hotel which they occupied during their residence at Paris, found out the losses which he had sustained: not until Madame Marabou, the milliner, made repeated visits with her little bill for articles supplied to Madame Crawley; not until Monsieur Didelot from the Boule d'Or in the Palais Royal had asked half a dozen times whether *cette charmante miladi*[18] who had bought watches and bracelets of him was *de retour.*[19] It is a fact that even the poor gardener's wife, who had nursed madame's child, was never paid after the first six months for that supply of the milk of human kindness with which she had furnished the lusty and healthy little Rawdon. No, not even the nurse was paid—the Crawleys were in too great a hurry to remember their trifling debt to her. As for the landlord of the hotel, his curses against the English nation were violent for the rest of his natural life. He asked all travellers whether they knew a certain Colonel Lor Crawley—*avec sa femme—une petite dame, très spirituelle.* *"Ah, monsieur!"* he would add—*"ils m'ont affreusement volé."* [20] It was melancholy to hear his accents as he spoke of that catastrophe.

Rebecca's object in her journey to London was to effect a kind of compromise with her husband's numerous creditors, and by offering them a dividend of ninepence or a shilling in the pound, to secure a return for him into his own country. It does not become us to trace the steps which she took in the conduct of this most difficult negotiation; but, having shown them to their satisfaction, that the sum which she

[17] English nobleman.
[18] This charming lady.
[19] Was coming back.
[20] . . . with his wife—a very witty little woman. "Ah, sir. . . . I have been frightfully robbed by them."

was empowered to offer was all her husband's available capital, and having convinced them that Colonel Crawley would prefer a perpetual retirement on the Continent to a residence in this country with his debts unsettled; having proved to them that there was no possibility of money accruing to him from other quarters, and no earthly chance of their getting a larger dividend than that which she was empowered to offer, she brought the colonel's creditors unanimously to accept her proposals, and purchased with fifteen hundred pounds of ready money, more than ten times that amount of debts.

Mrs. Crawley employed no lawyer in the transaction. The matter was so simple, to have or to leave, as she justly observed, that she made the lawyers of the creditors themselves do the business. And Mr. Lewis representing Mr. Davids, of Red Lion Square, and Mr. Moss acting for Mr. Manasseh of Cursitor Street[21] (chief creditors of the colonel's), complimented his lady upon the brilliant way in which she did business, and declared that there was no professional man who could beat her.

Rebecca received their congratulations with perfect modesty; ordered a bottle of sherry and a bread cake to the little dingy lodgings where she dwelt, while conducting the business, to treat the enemy's lawyers: shook hands with them at parting, in excellent good humour, and returned straightway to the Continent, to rejoin her husband and son, and acquaint the former with the glad news of his entire liberation. As for the latter, he had been considerably neglected during his mother's absence by Mademoiselle Genevieve, her French maid; for that young woman, contracting an attachment for a soldier in the garrison of Calais, forgot her charge in the society of this *militaire,*[22] and little Rawdon very narrowly escaped drowning on Calais sands at this period, where the absent Genevieve had left and lost him.

And so, Colonel and Mrs. Crawley came to London; and it is at their house in Curzon Street, Mayfair, that they really showed the skill which must be possessed by those who would live on the resources above-named.

[21] Mr. Davids and Mr. Manasseh are the names given to Jewish moneylenders from whom Rawdon Crawley has obtained funds.

[22] Military man.

Charles Dickens

1812-1870

Podsnappery

The following passage occurs at the beginning of Chapter Eleven, Book One, of *Our Mutual Friend* (1864-65). In this portrait of the rich insurance broker, John Podsnap, Dickens has permanently etched in acid the lineaments of Arnold's Philistine. The hidebound conventionality, the arrogance and insular prejudices and smug self-satisfaction of the Victorian middle classes are all here, deliberately exaggerated and made grotesque to shock the reader into gusts of wild laughter.

Mr. Podsnap was well to do, and stood very high in Mr. Podsnap's opinion. Beginning with a good inheritance, he had married a good inheritance, and had thriven exceedingly in the Marine Insurance way, and was quite satisfied. He never could make out why everybody was not quite satisfied, and he felt conscious that he set a brilliant social example in being particularly well satisfied with most things, and, above all other things, with himself.

Thus happily acquainted with his own merit and importance, Mr. Podsnap settled that whatever he put behind him he put out of existence. There was a dignified conclusiveness—not to add a grand convenience —in this way of getting rid of disagreeables, which had done much towards establishing Mr. Podsnap in his lofty place in Mr. Podsnap's satisfaction. "I don't want to know about it; I don't choose to discuss it; I don't admit it!" Mr. Podsnap had even acquired a peculiar flourish

437

of his right arm in often clearing the world of its most difficult problems, by sweeping them behind him (and consequently sheer away) with those words and a flushed face. For they affronted him.

Mr. Podsnap's world was not a very large world, morally; no, nor even geographically: seeing that although his business was sustained upon commerce with other countries, he considered other countries, with that important reservation, a mistake, and of their manners and customs would conclusively observe, "Not English!" when, PRESTO! with a flourish of the arm, and a flush of the face, they were swept away. Elsewise, the world got up at eight, shaved close at a quarter-past, breakfasted at nine, went to the City at ten, came home at half-past five, and dined at seven. Mr. Podsnap's notions of the Arts in their integrity might have been stated thus. Literature; large print, respectively descriptive of getting up at eight, shaving close at a quarter-past, breakfasting at nine, going to the City at ten, coming home at half-past five, and dining at seven. Painting and Sculpture; models and portraits representing Professors of getting up at eight, shaving close at a quarter-past, breakfasting at nine, going to the City at ten, coming home at half-past five, and dining at seven. Music; a respectable performance (without variations) on stringed and wind instruments, sedately expressive of getting up at eight, shaving close at a quarter-past, breakfasting at nine, going to the City at ten, coming home at half-past five, and dining at seven. Nothing else to be permitted to those same vagrants the Arts, on pain of excommunication. Nothing else To Be—anywhere!

As a so eminently respectable man, Mr. Podsnap was sensible of its being required of him to take Providence under his protection. Consequently he always knew exactly what Providence meant. Inferior and less respectable men might fall short of that mark, but Mr. Podsnap was always up to it. And it was very remarkable (and must have been very comfortable) that what Providence meant, was invariably what Mr. Podsnap meant.

These may be said to have been the articles of a faith and school which the present chapter takes the liberty of calling, after its representative man, Podsnappery. They were confined within close bounds, as Mr. Podsnap's own head was confined by his shirt-collar; and they were enunciated with a sounding pomp that smacked of the creaking of Mr. Podsnap's own boots.

There was a Miss Podsnap. And this young rocking-horse was being trained in her mother's art of prancing in a stately manner without ever getting on. But the high parental action was not yet imparted to her, and in truth she was but an undersized damsel, with high shoulders, low spirits, chilled elbows, and a rasped surface of nose, who seemed to take occasional frosty peeps out of childhood into womanhood, and to shrink back again, overcome by her mother's head-dress and her father from head to foot—crushed by the mere dead-weight of Podsnappery.

A certain institution in Mr. Podsnap's mind which he called "the young person" may be considered to have been embodied in Miss Podsnap, his daughter. It was an inconvenient and exacting institution, as requiring everything in the universe to be filed down and fitted to it. The question about everything was, would it bring a blush into the cheek of the young person? And the inconvenience of the young person was that, according to Mr. Podsnap, she seemed always liable to burst into blushes when there was no need at all. There appeared to be no line of demarcation between the young person's excessive innocence, and another person's guiltiest knowledge. Take Mr. Podsnap's word for it, and the soberest tints of drab, white, lilac, and grey, were all flaming red to this troublesome Bull of a young person.

The Podsnaps lived in a shady angle adjoining Portman Square. They were a kind of people certain to dwell in the shade, wherever they dwelt. Miss Podsnap's life had been, from her first appearance on this planet, altogether of a shady order; for Mr. Podsnap's young person was likely to get little good out of association with other young persons, and had therefore been restricted to companionship with not very congenial older persons, and with massive furniture. Miss Podsnap's early views of life being principally derived from the reflections of it in her father's boots, and in the walnut and rosewood tables of the dim drawing-room, and in their swarthy giants of looking-glasses, were of a sombre cast; and it was not wonderful that now, when she was on most days solemnly tooled through the Park by the side of her mother in a great tall custard-coloured phaeton, she showed above the apron of that vehicle like a dejected young person sitting up in bed to take a startled look at things in general, and very strongly desiring to get her head under the counterpane again.

Said Mr. Podsnap to Mrs. Podsnap, "Georgiana is almost eighteen."

Said Mrs. Podsnap to Mr. Podsnap, assenting, "Almost eighteen."

Said Mr. Podsnap then to Mrs. Podsnap, "Really I think we should have some people on Georgiana's birthday."

Said Mrs. Podsnap then to Mr. Podsnap, "Which will enable us to clear off all those people who are due."

So it came to pass that Mr. and Mrs. Podsnap requested the honour of the company of seventeen friends of their souls at dinner; and that they substituted other friends of their souls for such of the seventeen original friends of their souls as deeply regretted that a prior engagement prevented their having the honour of dining with Mr. and Mrs. Podsnap, in pursuance of their kind invitation; and that Mrs. Podsnap said of all these inconsolable personages, as she checked them off with a pencil in her list, "Asked, at any rate, and got rid of;" and that they successfully disposed of a good many friends of their souls in this way, and felt their consciences much lightened.

There were still other friends of their souls who were not entitled to be asked to dinner, but had a claim to be invited to come and take a haunch of mutton vapour-bath at half-past nine. For the clearing off of these worthies, Mrs. Podsnap added a small and early evening to the dinner, and looked in at the music-shop to bespeak a well-conducted automaton to come and play quadrilles for a carpet dance.

Mr. and Mrs. Veneering, and Mr. and Mrs. Veneering's brand-new bride and bridegroom, were of the dinner company; but the Podsnap establishment had nothing else in common with the Veneerings. Mr. Podsnap could tolerate taste in a mushroom man[1] who stood in need of that sort of thing, but was far above it himself. Hideous solidity was the characteristic of the Podsnap plate. Everything was made to look as heavy as it could, and to take up as much room as possible. Everything said boastfully, "Here you have as much of me in my ugliness as if I

[1] The Veneerings have sprung into social prominence overnight; see Chapter Two, Book One, of *Our Mutual Friend*.

were only lead; but I am so many ounces of precious metal worth so much an ounce;—wouldn't you like to melt me down?" A corpulent straggling epergne, blotched all over as if it had broken out in an eruption rather than been ornamented, delivered this address from an unsightly silver platform in the centre of the table. Four silver wine-coolers, each furnished with four staring heads, each head obtrusively carrying a big silver ring in each of its ears, conveyed the sentiment up and down the table, and handed it on to the pot-bellied silver salt-cellars. All the big silver spoons and forks widened the mouths of the company expressly for the purpose of thrusting the sentiment down their throats with every morsel they ate.

The majority of the guests were like the plate, and included several heavy articles weighing ever so much. But there was a foreign gentleman among them: whom Mr. Podsnap had invited after much debate with himself—believing the whole European continent to be in mortal alliance against the young person—and there was a droll disposition, not only on the part of Mr. Podsnap, but of everybody else, to treat him as if he were a child who was hard of hearing.

As a delicate concession to this unfortunately-born foreigner, Mr. Podsnap, in receiving him, had presented his wife as "Madame Podsnap"; also his daughter as "Mademoiselle Podsnap," with some inclination to add "ma fille," [2] in which bold venture, however, he checked himself. The Veneerings being at that time the only other arrivals, he had added (in a condescendingly explanatory manner), "Monsieur Veynair-reeng," and had then subsided into English.

"How Do You Like London?" Mr. Podsnap now inquired from his station of host, as if he were administering something in the nature of a powder or potion to the deaf child; "London, Londres, London?"

The foreign gentleman admired it.

"You find it Very Large?" said Mr. Podsnap, spaciously.

The foreign gentleman found it very large.

"And Very Rich?"

The foreign gentleman found it, without doubt, enormément riche.

"Enormously Rich, We say," returned Mr. Podsnap, in a conde-

[2] My daughter.

scending manner. "Our English adverbs do Not terminate in Mong and We Pronounce the 'ch' as if there were a 't' before it. We Say Ritch."

"Reetch," remarked the foreign gentleman.

"And Do You Find, Sir," pursued Mr. Podsnap, with dignity, "Many Evidences that Strike You, of our British Constitution in the Streets Of The World's Metropolis, London, Londres, London?"

The foreign gentleman begged to be pardoned, but did not altogether understand.

"The Constitution Britannique," Mr. Podsnap explained, as if he were teaching in an infant school. "We Say British, But You Say Britannique, You Know" (forgivingly, as if that were not his fault). "The Constitution, Sir."

The foreign gentleman said, "Mais, yees; I know eem."

A youngish sallowish gentleman in spectacles, with a lumpy forehead, seated in a supplementary chair at a corner of the table, here caused a profound sensation by saying, in a raised voice, "ESKER," and then stopping dead.

"Mais oui," said the foreign gentleman, turning towards him. "Est-ce que? Quoi donc?" [3]

But the gentleman with the lumpy forehead having for the time delivered himself of all that he found behind his lumps, spake for the time no more.

"I Was Inquiring," said Mr. Podsnap, resuming the thread of his discourse, "Whether You Have Observed in our Streets as We should say, Upon our Pavvy as You would say, any Tokens——"

The foreign gentleman with patient courtesy entreated pardon; "But what was tokenz?"

"Marks," said Mr. Podsnap; "Signs, you know, Appearances—Traces."

"Ah! Of a Orse?" inquired the foreign gentleman.

"We call it Horse," said Mr. Podsnap, with forbearance. "In England, Angleterre, England, We Aspirate the 'H,' and We Say 'Horse.' Only our Lower Classes Say 'Orse!'"

"Pardon," said the foreign gentleman; "I am alwiz wrong!"

[3] "Yes indeed. . . . Is it so? What then?"

"Our Language," said Mr. Podsnap, with a gracious consciousness of being always right, "is Difficult. Ours is a Copious Language, and Trying to Strangers. I will not Pursue my Question."

But the lumpy gentleman, unwilling to give it up, again madly said, "ESKER," and again spake no more.

"It merely referred," Mr. Podsnap explained, with a sense of meritorious proprietorship, "to Our Constitution, Sir. We Englishmen are Very Proud of our Constitution, Sir. It Was Bestowed Upon Us By Providence. No Other Country is so Favoured as This Country."

"And ozer countries?—" the foreign gentleman was beginning, when Mr. Podsnap put him right again.

"We do not say Ozer; we say Other: the letters are 'T' and 'H'; you say Tay and Aish, You Know;" (still with clemency). "The sound is 'th'—'th!' "

"And *other* countries," said the foreign gentleman. "They do how?"

"They do, Sir," returned Mr. Podsnap, gravely shaking his head; "they do—I am sorry to be obliged to say it—*as* they do."

"It was a little particular of Providence," said the foreign gentleman, laughing; "for the frontier is not large."

"Undoubtedly," assented Mr. Podsnap; "But So it is. It was the Charter of the Land. This island was Blest, Sir, to the Direct Exclusion of such Other Countries as—as there may happen to be. And if we were all Englishmen present, I would say," added Mr. Podsnap, looking round upon his compatriots, and sounding solemnly with his theme, "that there is in the Englishman a combination of qualities, a modesty, an independence, a responsibility, a repose, combined with an absence of everything calculated to call a blush into the cheek of a young person, which one would seek in vain among the Nations of the Earth."

Having delivered this little summary, Mr. Podsnap's face flushed, as he thought of the remote possibility of its being at all qualified by any prejudiced citizen of any other country; and, with his favourite right-arm flourish, he put the rest of Europe and the whole of Asia, Africa, and America nowhere.

The audience was much edified by this passage of words; and Mr. Podsnap, feeling that he was in rather remarkable force to-day, became smiling and conversational. . . .

Algernon Charles Swinburne

1837-1909

The Higher Pantheism in a Nutshell

> This poem was anonymously published in *The Heptalogia; or the Seven against Sense, a Cap with Bells* (1880), a series of seven parodies on Victorian poets, including a delightful self-parody entitled "Nephelidia." For purposes of comparison there is also given Tennyson's "The Higher Pantheism" (1869), the rather cloudy transcendentalism of which called forth Swinburne's mockery. As in all great parodies, the following lines not only felicitously capture the idiom of the original, but reduce its content to absurdity.

One, who is not, we see: but one, whom we see not, is:
Surely this is not that: but that is assuredly this.

What, and wherefore, and whence? for under is over and under:
If thunder could be without lightning, lightning could be without
    thunder.

Doubt is faith, in the main: but faith, on the whole, is doubt:
We cannot believe by proof: but could we believe without?

Why, and whither, and how? for barley and rye are not clover:
Neither are straight lines curves: yet over is under and over.

Two and two may be four: but four and four are not eight:
Fate and God may be twain: but God is the same thing as fate.   10

Ask a man what he thinks, and get from a man what he feels:
God, once caught in the fact, shows you a fair pair of heels.

Body and spirit are twins: God only knows which is which:
The soul squats down in the flesh, like a tinker drunk in a ditch.

More is the whole than a part: but half is more than the whole:
Clearly, the soul is the body: but is not the body the soul?

One and two are not one: but one and nothing is two:
Truth can hardly be false, if falsehood cannot be true.

Once the mastodon was: pterodactyls were common as cocks.
Then the mammoth was God: now is He a prize ox.   20

Parallels all things are: yet many of these are askew:
You are certainly I: but certainly I am not you.

Springs the rock from the plain, shoots the stream from the rock:
Cocks exist for the hen: but hens exist for the cock.

God, whom we see not, is: and God, who is not, we see:
Fiddle, we know, is diddle: and diddle, we take it, is dee.

THE HIGHER PANTHEISM

The sun, the moon, the stars, the seas, the hills and the plains,—
Are not these, O Soul, the Vision of Him who reigns?

Is not the Vision He, tho' He be not that which He seems?
Dreams are true while they last, and do we not live in dreams?

Earth, these solid stars, this weight of body and limb,
Are they not sign and symbol of thy division from Him?

Dark is the world to thee; thyself art the reason why,
For is He not all but thou, that has power to feel 'I am I'?

Glory about thee, without thee; and thou fulfillest thy doom,
Making Him broken gleams and a stifled splendor and gloom.   10

Speak to Him, thou, for He hears, and Spirit with Spirit can meet—
Closer is He than breathing, and nearer than hands and feet.

God is law, say the wise; O Soul, and let us rejoice,
For if He thunder by law the thunder is yet His voice.

Law is God, say some; no God at all, says the fool,
For all we have power to see is a straight staff bent in a pool;

And the ear of man cannot hear, and the eye of man cannot see;
But if we could see and hear, this Vision—were it not He?

Samuel Butler

1835-1902

The Musical Banks

The following selection is taken from the opening of Chapter Fifteen of *Erewhon; or Over the Range* (1872). This work and its equally original and amusing sequel, *Erewhon Revisited* (1901), are, like *Gulliver's Travels,* satiric variations on the Utopian romance. Butler's ferocious, but controlled iconoclasm ranges from Victorian sexual prudery to Darwinism. The grandson of a famous bishop and himself initially destined for holy orders, he here ridicules the outworn traditions and hollow forms of Anglican worship. The story is set in the fabulous land of Erewhon, an anagram for Nowhere.

On my return to the drawing-room, I found that the Mahaina[1] current had expended itself. The ladies were just putting away their work and preparing to go out. I asked them where they were going. They answered with a certain air of reserve that they were going to the bank to get some money.

Now I had already collected that the mercantile affairs of the Erewhonians were conducted on a totally different system from our own; I had, however, gathered little hitherto, except that they had two distinct commercial systems, of which the one appealed more strongly to the imagination than anything to which we are accustomed in Europe, in-

[1] Mahaina is a character who pretends to be a dipsomaniac to dissemble the fact that she is in bad health, physical sickness being punishable as a criminal offense in Erewhon. The narrator is a guest in the home of a successful man of business, Mr. Nosnibor (Robinson), his wife and two daughters, Zulora and Arowhena.

asmuch as the banks that were conducted upon this system were decorated in the most profuse fashion, and all mercantile transactions were accompanied with music, so that they were called Musical Banks, though the music was hideous to a European ear.

As for the system itself I never understood it, neither can I do so now: they have a code in connection with it, which I have not the slightest doubt that they understand, but no foreigner can hope to do so. One rule runs into, and against, another as in a most complicated grammar, or as in Chinese pronunciation, wherein I am told that the slightest change in accentuation or tone of voice alters the meaning of a whole sentence. Whatever is incoherent in my description must be referred to the fact of my never having attained to a full comprehension of the subject.

So far, however, as I could collect anything certain, I gathered that they have two distinct currencies, each under the control of its own banks and mercantile codes. One of these (the one with the Musical Banks) was supposed to be *the* system, and to give out the currency in which all monetary transactions should be carried on; and as far as I could see, all who wished to be considered respectable, kept a larger or smaller balance at these banks. On the other hand, if there is one thing of which I am more sure than another, it is that the amount so kept had no direct commercial value in the outside world; I am sure that the managers and cashiers of the Musical Banks were not paid in their own currency. Mr. Nosnibor used to go to these banks, or rather to the great mother bank of the city, sometimes but not very often. He was a pillar of one of the other kind of banks, though he appeared to hold some minor office also in the musical ones. The ladies generally went alone; as indeed was the case in most families, except on state occasions.

I had long wanted to know more of this strange system, and had the greatest desire to accompany my hostess and her daughters. I had seen them go out almost every morning since my arrival and had noticed that they carried their purses in their hands, not exactly ostentatiously, yet just so as that those who met them should see whither they were going. I had never, however, yet been asked to go with them myself.

It is not easy to convey a person's manner by words, and I can hardly give any idea of the peculiar feeling that came upon me when I saw the ladies on the point of starting for the bank. There was a something of regret, a something as though they would wish to take me with them, but did not like to ask me, and yet as though I were hardly to ask to be taken. I was determined, however, to bring matters to an issue with my hostess about my going with them, and after a little parleying, and many inquiries as to whether I was perfectly sure that I myself wished to go, it was decided that I might do so.

We passed through several streets of more or less considerable houses, and at last turning round a corner we came upon a large piazza, at the end of which was a magnificent building, of a strange but noble architecture and of great antiquity. It did not open directly on to the piazza, there being a screen, through which was an archway, between the piazza and the actual precincts of the bank. On passing under the archway we entered upon a green sward, round which there ran an arcade or cloister, while in front of us uprose the majestic towers of the bank and its venerable front, which was divided into three deep recesses and adorned with all sorts of marbles and many sculptures. On either side there were beautiful old trees wherein the birds were busy by the hundred, and a number of quaint but substantial houses of singularly comfortable appearance; they were situated in the midst of orchards and gardens, and gave me an impression of great peace and plenty.

Indeed it had been no error to say that this building was one that appealed to the imagination; it did more—it carried both imagination and judgment by storm. It was an epic in stone and marble, and so powerful was the effect it produced on me, that as I beheld it I was charmed and melted. I felt more conscious of the existence of a remote past. One knows of this always, but the knowledge is never so living as in the actual presence of some witness to the life of bygone ages. I felt how short a space of human life was the period of our own existence. I was more impressed with my own littleness, and much more inclinable to believe that the people whose sense of the fitness of things was equal to the upraising of so serene a handiwork, were hardly likely to be wrong in the conclusions they might come to upon any subject. My feeling certainly was that the currency of this bank must be the right one.

We crossed the sward and entered the building. If the outside had been impressive the inside was even more so. It was very lofty and divided into several parts by walls which rested upon massive pillars; the windows were filled with stained glass descriptive of the principal commercial incidents of the bank for many ages. In a remote part of the building there were men and boys singing; this was the only disturbing feature, for as the gamut was still unknown, there was no music in the country which could be agreeable to a European ear. The singers seemed to have derived their inspirations from the songs of birds and the wailing of the wind, which last they tried to imitate in melancholy cadences that at times degenerated into a howl. To my thinking the noise was hideous, but it produced a great effect upon my companions, who professed themselves much moved. As soon as the singing was over, the ladies requested me to stay where I was while they went inside the place from which it had seemed to come.

During their absence certain reflections forced themselves upon me.

In the first place, it struck me as strange that the building should be so nearly empty; I was almost alone, and the few besides myself had been led by curiosity, and had no intention of doing business with the bank. But there might be more inside. I stole up to the curtain, and ventured to draw the extreme edge of it on one side. No, there was hardly any one there. I saw a large number of cashiers, all at their desks ready to pay checks, and one or two who seemed to be the managing partners. I also saw my hostess and her daughters and two or three other ladies; also three or four old women and the boys from one of the neighboring Colleges of Unreason;[2] but there was no one else. This did not look as though the bank was doing a very large business; and yet I had always been told that every one in the city dealt with this establishment.

I cannot describe all that took place in these inner precincts, for a sinister-looking person in a black gown came and made unpleasant gestures at me for peeping. I happened to have in my pocket one of the Musical Bank pieces, which had been given me by Mrs. Nosnibor, so I tried to tip him with it; but having seen what it was, he became so

[2] The Colleges of Unreason, the seats of higher learning in Erewhon, stand for the colleges of Oxford and Cambridge Universities.

angry that I had to give him a piece of the other kind of money to pacify him. When I had done this he became civil directly. As soon as he was gone I ventured to take a second look, and saw Zulora in the very act of giving a piece of paper which looked like a check to one of the cashiers. He did not examine it, but putting his hand into an antique coffer hard by, he pulled out a quantity of metal pieces apparently at random, and handed them over without counting them; neither did Zulora count them, but put them into her purse and went back to her seat after dropping a few pieces of the other coinage into an alms box that stood by the cashier's side. Mrs. Nosnibor and Arowhena then did likewise, but a little later they gave all (so far as I could see) that they had received from the cashier back to a verger, who I have no doubt put it back into the coffer from which it had been taken. They then began making towards the curtain; whereon I let it drop and retreated to a reasonable distance.

They soon joined me. For some few minutes we all kept silence, but at last I ventured to remark that the bank was not so busy to-day as it probably often was. On this Mrs. Nosnibor said that it was indeed melancholy to see what little heed people paid to the most precious of all institutions. I could say nothing in reply, but I have ever been of opinion that the greater part of mankind do approximately know where they get that which does them good.

Mrs. Nosnibor went on to say that I must not think there was any want of confidence in the bank because I had seen so few people there; the heart of the country was thoroughly devoted to these establishments, and any sign of their being in danger would bring in support from the most unexpected quarters. It was only because people knew them to be so very safe, that in some cases (as she lamented to say in Mr. Nosnibor's) they felt that their support was unnecessary. Moreover these institutions never departed from the safest and most approved banking principles. Thus they never allowed interest on deposit, a thing now frequently done by certain bubble companies, which by doing an illegitimate trade had drawn many customers away;[3] and even the share-

[3] In reference to the various dissenting bodies whose democratic organization and overt appeal to the religious emotions attracted many Victorians away from the Church of England.

holders were fewer than formerly, owing to the innovations of these unscrupulous persons, for the Musical Banks paid little or no dividend, but divided their profits by way of bonus on the original shares once in every thirty thousand years; and as it was now only two thousand years since there had been one of these distributions, people felt that they could not hope for another in their own time and preferred investments whereby they got some more tangible return; all which, she said, was very melancholy to think of.

Having made these last admissions, she returned to her original statement, namely, that every one in the country really supported these banks. As to the fewness of the people, and the absence of the able-bodied, she pointed out to me with some justice that this was exactly what we ought to expect. The men who were most conversant about the stability of human institutions, such as the lawyers, men of science, doctors, statesmen, painters, and the like, were just those who were most likely to be misled by their own fancied accomplishments, and to be made unduly suspicious by their licentious desire for greater present return, which was at the root of nine-tenths of the opposition; by their vanity, which would prompt them to affect superiority to the prejudices of the vulgar; and by the stings of their own conscience, which was constantly upbraiding them in the most cruel manner on account of their bodies, which were generally diseased.

Let a person's intellect (she continued) be ever so sound, unless his body is in absolute health, he can form no judgment worth having on matters of this kind. The body is everything: it need not perhaps be such a strong body (she said this because she saw that I was thinking of the old and infirm-looking folks whom I had seen in the bank), but it must be in perfect health; in this case, the less active strength it had the more free would be the working of the intellect, and therefore the sounder the conclusion. The people, then, whom I had seen at the bank were in reality the very ones whose opinions were most worth having; they declared its advantages to be incalculable, and even professed to consider the immediate return to be far larger than they were entitled to; and so she ran on, nor did she leave off till we had got back to the house.

She might say what she pleased, but her manner carried no conviction, and later on I saw signs of general indifference to these banks that were not to be mistaken. Their supporters often denied it, but the denial was generally so couched as to add another proof of its existence. In commercial panics, and in times of general distress, the people as a mass did not so much as even think of turning to these banks. A few might do so, some from habit and early training, some from the instinct that prompts us to catch at any straw when we think ourselves drowning, but few from a genuine belief that the Musical Banks could save them from financial ruin, if they were unable to meet their engagements in the other kind of currency.

In conversation with one of the Musical Bank managers I ventured to hint this as plainly as politeness would allow. He said that it had been more or less true till lately; but that now they had put fresh stained glass windows into all the banks in the country, and repaired the buildings, and enlarged the organs; the presidents, moreover, had taken to riding in omnibuses and talking nicely to people in the streets, and to remembering the ages of their children, and giving them things when they were naughty, so that all would henceforth go smoothly.[4]

"But haven't you done anything to the money itself?" said I, timidly.

"It is not necessary," he rejoined; "not in the least necessary, I assure you."

And yet any one could see that the money given out at these banks was not that with which people bought their bread, meat, and clothing. It was like it at a first glance, and was stamped with designs that were often of great beauty; it was not, again, a spurious coinage, made with the intention that it should be mistaken for the money in actual use; it was more like a toy money, or the counters used for certain games at cards; for, notwithstanding the beauty of the designs, the material on which they were stamped was as nearly valueless as possible. Some were covered with tin foil, but the greater part were frankly of a cheap base metal the exact nature of which I was not able to determine. Indeed they were made of a great variety of metals, or, perhaps more accurately, alloys, some of which were hard, while others would bend easily

---

[4] The foregoing references are to the religious awakening brought about within the Established Church by the Oxford Movement on one hand, and Christian Socialism on the other.

and assume almost any form which their possessor might desire at the moment.[5]

Of course every one knew that their commercial value was *nil,* but all those who wished to be considered respectable thought it incumbent upon them to retain a few coins in their possession, and to let them be seen from time to time in their hands and purses. Not only this, but they would stick to it that the current coin of the realm was dross in comparison with the Musical Bank coinage. Perhaps, however, the strangest thing of all was that these very people would at times make fun in small ways of the whole system; indeed, there was hardly any insinuation against it which they would not tolerate and even applaud in their daily newspapers if written anonymously, while if the same thing were said without ambiguity to their faces—nominative case, verb, and accusative being all in their right places, and doubt impossible— they would consider themselves very seriously and justly outraged, and accuse the speaker of being unwell.

I never could understand (neither can I quite do so now, though I begin to see better what they mean) why a single currency should not suffice them; it would seem to me as though all their dealings would have been thus greatly simplified; but I was met with a look of horror if ever I dared to hint at it. Even those who to my certain knowledge kept only just enough money at the Musical Banks to swear by, would call the other banks (where their securities really lay) cold, deadening, paralyzing, and the like. . . .

[5] Butler is here making fun of the doctrinal hairsplitting which divided sect from sect.

George Meredith

1828-1909

Prelude to *The Egoist*

The following selection is the first chapter of *The Egoist* (1879), the novel which most fully embodies Meredith's theories about comedy, first set forth two years earlier in *An Essay on Comedy and the Uses of the Comic Spirit.* After stating that "the test of comedy is that it shall awaken thoughtful laughter," the writer continued in a famous passage:

If you believe that our civilization is founded in common sense (and it is the first condition of sanity to believe it), you will, when contemplating men, discern a Spirit overhead; not more heavenly than the light flashed upward from glassy surfaces, but luminous and watchful; never shooting beyond them, nor lagging in the rear; so closely attached to them that it may be taken for a slavish reflex, until its features are studied. It has the sage's brows, and the sunny malice of a fawn lurks at the corners of the half-closed lips drawn in an idle wariness of half-tension. . . . Men's future upon earth does not attract it; their honesty and shapeliness in the present does; and whenever they wax out of proportion, over-blown, affected, pretentious, bombastical, hypocritical, pedantic, fantastically delicate; whenever it sees them self-deceived or hoodwinked, given to run riot in idolatries, drifting into vanities, congregating in absurdities, planning shortsightedly, plotting dementedly; whenever they are at variance with their professions, and violate the unwritten but perceptible

laws binding them in consideration one to another;
whenever they offend sound reason, fair justice; are
false in humility or mined with conceit, individually,
or in the bulk; the Spirit overhead will look humanely
malign, and cast an oblique light on them, followed
by volleys of silvery laughter. That is the Comic Spirit.

Comedy is a game played to throw reflections upon
social life, and it deals with human nature in the drawing-room of
civilized men and women, where we have no dust of the struggling outer
world, no mire, no violent crashes, to make the correctness of the representation convincing. Credulity is not wooed through the impression-
able senses; nor have we recourse to the small circular glow of the watchmaker's eye to raise in bright relief minutest grains of evidence for the
routing of incredulity. The Comic Spirit conceives a definite situation
for a number of characters, and rejects all accessories in the exclusive
pursuit of them and their speech. For, being a spirit, he hunts the spirit
in men; vision and ardour constitute his merit: he has not a thought of
persuading you to believe in him. Follow and you will see. But there
is a question of the value of a run at his heels.

Now the world is possessed of a certain big book, the biggest book
on earth; that might indeed be called the Book of Earth; whose title
is the Book of Egoism, and it is a book full of the world's wisdom.
So full of it, and of such dimensions is this book, in which the generations have written ever since they took to writing, that to be profitable
to us the Book needs a powerful compression.

Who, says the notable humourist, in allusion to this Book, who can
studiously travel through sheets of leaves now capable of a stretch from
the Lizard [1] to the last few poor pulmonary snips and shreds of leagues
dancing on their toes for cold, explorers tell us, and catching breath by
good luck, like dogs at bones about a table, on the edge of the Pole?
Inordinate unvaried length, sheer longinquity, staggers the heart, ages
the very heart of us at a view. And how if we manage finally to print
one of our pages on the crow-scalp of that solitary majestic outsider?
We may with effort get even him into the Book; yet the knowledge we

[1] Lizard Point or Lizard Head in Cornwall, the southernmost extremity of
Great Britain.

want will not be more present with us than it was when the chapters hung their end over the cliff you ken of at Dover, where sits our great lord and master contemplating the seas without upon the reflex of that within!

In other words, as I venture to translate him (humourists are difficult: it is a piece of their humour to puzzle our wits), the inward mirror, the embracing and condensing spirit, is required to give us those interminable milepost piles of matter (extending well-nigh to the very Pole) in essence, in chosen samples, digestibly. I conceive him to indicate that the realistic method of a conscientious transcription of all the visible, and a repetition of all the audible, is mainly accountable for our present branfulness,[2] and for that prolongation of the vasty and the noisy, out of which, as from an undrained fen, steams the malady of sameness, our modern malady. We have the malady, whatever may be the cure or the cause. We drove in a body to Science the other day for an antidote; which was as if tired pedestrians should mount the engine-box of headlong trains; and Science introduced us to our o'er-hoary ancestry—then in the Oriental posture:[3] whereupon we set up a primaeval chattering to rival the Amazon forest nigh nightfall, cured, we fancied. And before daybreak our disease was hanging on to us again, with the extension of a tail. We had it fore and aft. We were the same, and animals into the bargain. That is all we got from Science.

Art is the specific. We have little to learn of apes, and they may be left. The chief consideration for us is, what particular practice of Art in letters is the best for the perusal of the Book of our common wisdom; so that with clearer minds and livelier manners we may escape, as it were, into daylight and song from a land of fog-horns. Shall we read it by the watchmaker's eye in luminous rings eruptive of the infinitesimal, or pointed with examples and types under the broad Alpine survey of the spirit born of our united social intelligence, which is the Comic Spirit? Wise men say the latter. They tell us that there is a constant tendency in the Book to accumulate excess of substance, and such repleteness, obscuring the glass it holds to mankind, renders us

---

[2] Condition of being full of bran—that is, of unsifted ideas.
[3] Apelike squatting; the implication of this passage is that the Darwinian hypothesis throws no significant light on human nature.

inexact in the recognition of our individual countenances: a perilous thing for civilization. And these wise men are strong in their opinion that we should encourage the Comic Spirit, who is, after all, our own offspring, to relieve the Book. Comedy, they say, is the true diversion, as it is likewise the key of the great Book, the music of the Book. They tell us how it condenses whole sections of the Book in a sentence, volumes in a character; so that a fair part of a book outstripping thousands of leagues when unrolled, may be compassed in one comic sitting.

For verily, say they, we must read what we can of it, at least the page before us, if we would be men. One, with an index on the Book, cries out, in a style pardonable to his fervency: The remedy of your frightful affliction is here, through the stillatory[4] of Comedy, and not in Science, nor yet in Speed, whose name is but another for voracity. Why, to be alive, to be quick in the soul, there should be diversity in the companion throbs of your pulses. Interrogate them. They lump along like the old lob-legs of Dobbin the horse; or do their business like cudgels of carpet-thwackers expelling dust, or the cottage-clock pendulum teaching the infant hour over midnight simple arithmetic. This too in spite of Bacchus.[5] And let them gallop; let them gallop with the God bestriding them, gallop to Hymen,[6] gallop to Hades, they strike the same note. Monstrous monotonousness has enfolded us with the arms of Amphitrite![7] We hear a shout of war for a diversion. —Comedy he pronounces to be our means of reading swiftly and comprehensively. She it is who proposes the correcting of pretentiousness, of inflation, of dulness, and of the vestiges of rawness and grossness to be found among us. She is the ultimate civilizer, the polisher, a sweet cook. If, he says, she watches over sentimentalism with a birch-rod, she is not opposed to romance. You may love, and warmly love, so long as you are honest. Do not offend reason. A lover pretending too much by one foot's length of pretence, will have that foot caught in her trap. In Comedy is the singular scene of charity issuing of disdain under

---

[4] Process of distillation.

[5] Classical god of wine.

[6] Originally a Greek lyric refrain, which came to be synonymous with the god of marriage.

[7] The amorous wife of Poseidon, Greek god of the sea.

the stroke of honourable laughter: an Ariel released by Prospero's wand
from the fetters of the damned witch Sycorax.[8] And this laughter of
reason refreshed is floriferous, like the magical great gale of the shifty
Spring deciding for Summer. You hear it giving the delicate spirit his
liberty. Listen, for comparison, to an unleavened society: a low as of
the udderful cow past milking hour! O for a titled ecclesiastic to curse
to excommunication that unholy thing!—So far an enthusiast perhaps;
but he should have a hearing.

Concerning pathos, no ship can now set sail without pathos; and
we are not totally deficient of pathos; which is, I do not accurately
know what, if not the ballast, reducible to moisture by patent process,
on board our modern vessel; for it can hardly be the cargo, and the
general water-supply has other uses; and ships well charged with it
seem to sail the stiffest:—there is a touch of pathos. The Egoist surely
inspires pity. He who would desire to clothe himself at everybody's
expense, and is of that desire condemned to strip himself stark naked,
he, if pathos ever had a form, might be taken for the actual person.
Only he is not allowed to rush at you, roll you over and squeeze your
body for the briny drops. There is the innovation.

You may as well know him out of hand, as a gentleman of our time
and country, of wealth and station,[9] a not flexile figure, do what we
may with him; the humour of whom scarcely dimples the surface and
is distinguishable but by very penetrative, very wicked imps, whose
fits of roaring below at some generally imperceptible stroke of his
quality have first made the mild literary angels aware of something
comic in him, when they were one and all about to describe the gentleman on the heading of the records baldly (where brevity is most complimentary) as a gentleman of family and property, an idol of a decorous
island that admires the concrete. Imps have their freakish wickedness
in them to kindle detective vision: malignly do they love to uncover
ridiculousness in imposing figures. Wherever they catch sight of Egoism
they pitch their camps, they circle and squat, and forthwith they trim

[8] Cf. *The Tempest* i.ii; through his magical powers Prospero has released Ariel
from the cleft in a pine where he had been imprisoned by the witch Sycorax.

[9] The concluding paragraphs introduce the reader in allusive terms to Sir
Willoughby Patterne of Patterne Hall, the egoist of the novel's title.

their lanterns, confident of the ludicrous to come. So confident that their grip of an English gentleman, in whom they have spied their game, never relaxes until he begins insensibly to frolic and antic, unknown to himself, and comes out in the native steam which is their scent of the chase. Instantly off they scour, Egoist and imps. They will, it is known of them, dog a great House for centuries, and be at the birth of all the new heirs in succession, diligently taking confirmatory notes, to join hands and chime their chorus in one of their merry rings round the tottering pillar of the House, when his turn arrives; as if they had (possibly they had) smelt of old date a doomed colossus of Egoism in that unborn, unconceived inheritor of the stuff of the family. They dare not be chuckling while Egoism is valiant, while sober, while socially valuable, nationally serviceable. They wait.

Aforetime a grand old Egoism built the House. It would appear that ever finer essences of it are demanded to sustain the structure: but especially would it appear that a reversion to the gross original, beneath a mask and in a vein of fineness, is an earthquake at the foundations of the House. Better that it should not have consented to motion, and have held stubbornly to all ancestral ways, than have bred that ana-chronic[10] spectre. The sight, however, is one to make our squatting imps in circle grow restless on their haunches, as they bend eyes instantly, ears at full cock, for the commencement of the comic drama of the suicide. If this line of verse be not yet in our literature,

Through very love of self himself he slew.

let it be admitted for his epitaph.

[10] Anachronistic.

Charles Lutwidge Dodgson

(Lewis Carroll)

1832-1898

A Mad Tea-Party

Here presented is Chapter Seven of *Alice's Adventures in Wonderland* (1865), which, together with *Through the Looking-Glass and What Alice Found There* (1871), should need no introduction. Students, whether of relativity, or semantics, or psychoanalysis, or for that matter, Victorian manners and morals, are perennially fascinated by the layers of implication within Alice's dream-world. The meanings are there, awaiting discovery; but it is unfortunate if the search for them is allowed to diminish the reader's delight in Carroll's brilliant flights of fancy (so well abetted by John Tenniel's illustrations), or to interfere with that "willing suspension of disbelief" with which generations of imaginative children have joyously accepted Alice's adventures on their own terms.

There was a table set out under a tree in front of the house, and the March Hare and the Hatter were having tea at it: a Dormouse[1] was sitting between them, fast asleep, and the other two

---

[1] The dormouse is a squirrel-like European rodent, nocturnal in its habits and therefore torpid during daylight hours. Carroll's Dormouse may have been modeled on the pet wombat kept by the poet Rossetti. Among the author's contemporaries there was a general, though unfounded, belief that the March Hare was a caricature of the great Liberal leader, Gladstone. The original for Tenniel's drawing of the Hatter was an eccentric Oxford furniture dealer named Theophilus Carter, who habitually wore a top hat.

were using it as a cushion, resting their elbows on it, and talking over its head. "Very uncomfortable for the Dormouse," thought Alice; "only as it's asleep, I suppose it doesn't mind."

The table was a large one, but the three were all crowded together at one corner of it. "No room! No room!" they cried out when they saw Alice coming. "There's *plenty* of room!" said Alice indignantly, and she sat down in a large arm-chair at one end of the table.

"Have some wine," the March Hare said in an encouraging tone.

Alice looked all round the table, but there was nothing on it but tea. "I don't see any wine," she remarked.

"There isn't any," said the March Hare.

"Then it wasn't very civil of you to offer it," said Alice angrily.

"It wasn't very civil of you to sit down without being invited," said the March Hare.

"I didn't know it was *your* table," said Alice: "it's laid for a great many more than three."

"Your hair wants cutting," said the Hatter. He had been looking at Alice for some time with great curiosity, and this was his first speech.

"You should learn not to make personal remarks," Alice said with some severity: "It's very rude."

The Hatter opened his eyes very wide on hearing this; but all he *said* was. "Why is a raven like a writing-desk?" [2]

"Come, we shall have some fun now!" thought Alice. "I'm glad they've begun asking riddles—I believe I can guess that," she added aloud.

"Do you mean that you think you can find out the answer to it?" said the March Hare.

"Exactly so," said Alice.

"Then you should say what you mean," the March Hare went on.

"I do," Alice hastily replied; "at least—at least I mean what I say —that's the same thing, you know."

"Not the same thing a bit!" said the Hatter. "Why, you might just as well say that 'I see what I eat' is the same thing as 'I eat what I see'!"

"You might just as well say," added the March Hare, "that 'I like what I get' is the same thing as 'I get what I like'!"

"You might just as well say," added the Dormouse, which seemed to be talking in its sleep, "that 'I breathe when I sleep' is the same thing as 'I sleep when I breathe'!"

"It *is* the same thing with you," said the Hatter, and here the conversation dropped, and the party sat silent for a minute, while Alice thought over all she could remember about ravens and writing-desks, which wasn't much.

The Hatter was the first to break the silence. "What day of the month is it?" he said, turning to Alice: he had taken his watch out of his pocket, and was looking at it uneasily, shaking it every now and then, and holding it to his ear.

Alice considered a little, and then said "The fourth."

"Two days wrong!" sighed the Hatter. "I told you butter wouldn't suit the works!" he added, looking angrily at the March Hare.

"It was the *best* butter," the March Hare meekly replied.

[2] In his Preface to the 1896 edition of *Alice in Wonderland*, Carroll wrote: "Enquiries have been so often addressed to me, as to whether any answer to the Hatter's Riddle can be imagined, that I may as well put on record here what seems to me to be a fairly appropriate answer, viz.: 'Because it can produce a few notes, tho they are *very* flat; and it is never put with the wrong end in front!' This, however, is merely an afterthought; the Riddle, as originally invented, had no answer at all."

"Yes, but some crumbs must have got in as well," the Hatter grumbled: "you shouldn't have put it in with the bread-knife."

The March Hare took the watch and looked at it gloomily: then he dipped it into his cup of tea, and looked at it again: but he could think of nothing better to say than his first remark, "It was the *best* butter, you know."

Alice had been looking over his shoulder with some curiosity. "What a funny watch!" she remarked. "It tells the day of the month, and doesn't tell what o'clock it is!"

"Why should it?" muttered the Hatter. "Does *your* watch tell you what year it is?"

"Of course not," Alice replied very readily: "but that's because it stays the same year for such a long time together."

"Which is just the case with *mine*," said the Hatter.

Alice felt dreadfully puzzled. The Hatter's remark seemed to her to have no sort of meaning in it, and yet it was certainly English. "I don't quite understand you," she said, as politely as she could.

"The Dormouse is asleep again," said the Hatter, and he poured a little hot tea upon its nose.

The Dormouse shook its head impatiently, and said, without opening its eyes, "Of course, of course: just what I was going to remark myself."

"Have you guessed the riddle yet?" the Hatter said, turning to Alice again.

"No, I give it up," Alice replied. "What's the answer?"

"I haven't the slightest idea," said the Hatter.

"Nor I," said the March Hare.

Alice sighed wearily. "I think you might do something better with the time," she said, "than wasting it in asking riddles that have no answers."

"If you knew Time as well as I do," said the Hatter, "you wouldn't talk about wasting *it*. It's *him*."

"I don't know what you mean," said Alice.

"Of course you don't!" the Hatter said, tossing his head contemptuously. "I dare say you never even spoke to Time!"

"Perhaps not," Alice cautiously replied; "but I know I have to beat time when I learn music."

"Ah! That accounts for it," said the Hatter. "He won't stand beating. Now, if you only kept on good terms with him, he'd do almost anything you liked with the clock. For instance, suppose it were nine o'clock in the morning, just time to begin lessons: you'd only have to whisper a hint to Time, and round goes the clock in a twinkling! Half-past one, time for dinner!"

("I only wish it was," the March Hare said to itself in a whisper.)

"That would be grand, certainly," said Alice thoughtfully; "but then —I shouldn't be hungry for it, you know."

"Not at first, perhaps," said the Hatter: "but you could keep it to half-past one as long as you liked."

"Is that the way *you* manage?" Alice asked.

The Hatter shook his head mournfully. "Not I!" he replied. "We quarreled last March——just before *he* went mad, you know——" (pointing with his teaspoon at the March Hare,) "——it was at the great concert given by the Queen of Hearts, and I had to sing

> '*Twinkle, twinkle, little bat!*
> *How I wonder what you're at!*' [3]

You know the song, perhaps?"

[3] The Hatter's song parodies the familiar poem by Jane Taylor (1783-1824), "The Star."

"I've heard something like it," said Alice.

"It goes on, you know," the Hatter continued, "in this way:—

'Up above the world you fly,
Like a tea-tray in the sky.
Twinkle, twinkle——' "

Here the Dormouse shook itself, and began singing in its sleep "Twinkle, twinkle, twinkle, twinkle——" and went on so long that they had to pinch it to make it stop.

"Well, I'd hardly finished the first verse," said the Hatter, "when the Queen bawled out 'He's murdering the time! Off with his head!' "

"How dreadfully savage!" exclaimed Alice.

"And ever since that," the Hatter went on in a mournful tone, "he wo'n't do a thing I ask! It's always six o'clock now."

A bright idea came into Alice's head. "Is that the reason so many tea-things are put out here?" she asked.

"Yes, that's it," said the Hatter with a sigh: "it's always tea-time, and we've no time to wash the things between whiles."

"Then you keep moving round, I suppose?" said Alice.

"Exactly so," said the Hatter: "as the things get used up."

"But what happens when you come to the beginning again?" Alice ventured to ask.

"Suppose we change the subject," the March Hare interrupted, yawning. "I'm getting tired of this. I vote the young lady tells us a story."

"I'm afraid I don't know one," said Alice, rather alarmed at the proposal.

"Then the Dormouse shall!" they both cried. "Wake up, Dormouse!" And they pinched it on both sides at once.

The Dormouse slowly opened its eyes. "I wasn't asleep," it said in a hoarse, feeble voice, "I heard every word you fellows were saying."

"Tell us a story!" said the March Hare.

"Yes, please do!" pleaded Alice.

"And be quick about it," added the Hatter, "or you'll be asleep again before it's done."

"Once upon a time there were three little sisters," the Dormouse began in a great hurry; "and their names were Elsie, Lacie, and Tillie;[4] and they lived at the bottom of a well——"

"What did they live on?" said Alice, who always took a great interest in questions of eating and drinking.

"They lived on treacle," [5] said the Dormouse, after thinking a minute or two.

"They couldn't have done that, you know," Alice gently remarked. "They'd have been ill."

"So they were," said the Dormouse; "*very* ill."

Alice tried a little to fancy to herself what such an extraordinary way of living would be like, but it puzzled her too much: so she went on: "But why did they live at the bottom of a well?"

"Take some more tea," the March Hare said to Alice, very earnestly.

"I've had nothing yet," Alice replied in an offended tone: "so I ca'n't take more."

"You mean you ca'n't take *less*," said the Hatter: "It's very easy to take *more* than nothing."

"Nobody asked *your* opinion," said Alice.

"Who's making personal remarks now?" the Hatter asked triumphantly.

Alice did not quite know what to say to this: so she helped herself to some tea and bread-and-butter, and then turned to the Dormouse, and repeated her question. "Why did they live at the bottom of a well?"

The Dormouse again took a minute or two to think about it, and then said "It was a treacle-well."

"There's no such thing!" Alice was beginning very angrily, but the Hatter and the March Hare went "Sh! Sh!" and the Dormouse sulkily remarked "If you ca'n't be civil, you'd better finish the story for yourself."

"No, please go on!" Alice said very humbly. "I wo'n't interrupt you again. I dare say there may be *one*."

---

[4] A reference to the three small daughters of Henry George Liddell (1811-1898), dean of Christ Church, Oxford, for whom Carroll invented the adventures of Alice. Elsie is L.C. (for Lorina Charlotte); Tillie is Edith (whose family nickname was Matilda); and Lacie is an anagram for Alice, the original of Carroll's heroine.

[5] Molasses.

"One, indeed!" said the Dormouse indignantly. However, he consented to go on. "And so these three little sisters—they were learning to draw, you know——"

"What did they draw?" said Alice, quite forgetting her promise.

"Treacle," said the Dormouse, without considering at all, this time.

"I want a clean cup," interrupted the Hatter: "let's all move one place on."

He moved on as he spoke, and the Dormouse followed him: the March Hare moved into the Dormouse's place, and Alice rather unwillingly took the place of the March Hare. The Hatter was the only one who got any advantage from the change; and Alice was a good deal worse off than before, as the March Hare had just upset the milk-jug into his plate.

Alice did not wish to offend the Dormouse again, so she began very cautiously: "But I don't understand. Where did they draw the treacle from?"

"You can draw water out of a water-well," said the Hatter; "so I should think you could draw treacle out of a treacle-well—eh, stupid?"

"But they were *in* the well," Alice said to the Dormouse, not choosing to notice this last remark.

"Of course they were," said the Dormouse: "well in."

This answer so confused poor Alice, that she let the Dormouse go on for some time without interrupting it.

"They were learning to draw," the Dormouse went on, yawning and rubbing its eyes, for it was getting very sleepy; "and they drew all manner of things—everything that begins with an M——"

"Why with an M?" said Alice.

"Why not?" said the March Hare.

Alice was silent.

The Dormouse had closed its eyes by this time, and was going off into a doze; but, on being pinched by the Hatter, it woke up again with a little shriek, and went on: "——that begins with an M, such as mouse-traps, and the moon, and memory, and muchness—you know you say things are 'much of a muchness'—did you ever see such a thing as a drawing of a muchness!"

"Really, now you ask me," said Alice, very much confused, "I don't think——"

"Then you shouldn't talk," said the Hatter.

This piece of rudeness was more than Alice could bear: she got up in great disgust, and walked off: the Dormouse fell asleep instantly, and neither of the others took the least notice of her going, though she looked back once or twice, half hoping that they would call after her: the last time she saw them, they were trying to put the Dormouse into the teapot.

"At any rate I'll never go *there* again!" said Alice, as she picked her way through the wood. "It's the stupidest tea-party I ever was at in all my life!"

Just as she said this, she noticed that one of the trees had a door leading right into it. "That's very curious!" she thought. "But everything's curious to-day. I think I may as well go in at once." And in she went.

Once more she found herself in the long hall, and close to the little glass table. "Now, I'll manage better this time," she said to herself, and began by taking the little golden key, and unlocking the door that led into the garden. Then she set to work nibbling at the mushroom (she had kept a piece of it in her pocket) till she was about a foot high: then she walked down the little passage: and *then*—she found herself at last in the beautiful garden, among the bright flower-beds and the cool fountains.

Edward Lear

1812-1888

Limericks

The following limericks, a form of comic writing which Lear made peculiarly his own and for which he drew the accompanying illustrations, are taken from *A Book of Nonsense* (1846) and *More Nonsense* (1872). Lear's comic inventiveness, like that of Lewis Carroll, his only rival in this vein of humor, is the product of a "concrete and fastidious" mind. But here there are no ulterior meanings. The reader rejoices in pure nonsense, tinged ever so slightly by the melancholy of all great clowning.

There was an Old Man with a beard,
Who said, 'It is just as I feared!—
Two Owls and a Hen, four Larks and a Wren,
Have all built their nests in my beard!'

There was an Old Man in a tree,
Who was horribly bored by a Bee;
When they said, 'Does it buzz?' he replied, 'Yes, it does!'
'It's a regular brute of a Bee!'

There was an Old Person of Philœ,
Whose conduct was scroobious and wily;
He rushed up a Palm, when the weather was calm,
And observed all the ruins of Philœ.

There was an Old Man of Cape Horn,
Who wished he had never been born;
So he sat on a chair, till he died of despair,
That dolorous Man of Cape Horn.

There was an Old Man on some rocks,
Who shut his wife up in a box,
When she said, 'Let me out,' he exclaimed, 'Without doubt
You will pass all your life in that box.'

There was an Old Man who said, 'Hush!
I perceive a young bird in this bush!'
When they said—'Is it small?' He replied—'Not at all!
It is four times as big as the bush!'

There was an old person of Wick,
Who said, 'Tick-a-Tick, Tick-a-Tick;
Chickabee, Chickabaw,' And he said nothing more,
That laconic old person of Wick.

There is a young lady, whose nose,
Continually prospers and grows;
When it grew out of sight, she exclaimed in a fright,
'Oh! Farewell to the end of my nose!'

There was an old person of Ware,
Who rode on the back of a bear:
When they ask'd,—'Does it trot?'—he said 'Certainly not!
He's a Moppsikon Floppsikon bear!'

There was an old person of Skye,
Who waltz'd with a Bluebottle fly:
They buzz'd a sweet tune, to the light of the moon,
And entranced all the people of Skye.

William Hurrell Mallock

1849-1923

The New Republic

🦢 The ensuing selection is taken from Chapter One,
Book Four, of Mallock's neglected masterpiece of
parody: *The New Republic; or Culture, Faith, and
Philosophy in an English Country House* (1877).
Although Plato's *Republic* lies in the background,
Mallock's principal debt was to the comic novelist
Thomas Love Peacock (1785-1866), from whom he
borrowed the device of gathering a house party of
characters who under thin disguise would "take off"
the sentiments and behavior of well-known figures
in the life of the day. Through Mr. Rose, who here
assumes the leading role, the author offers a brilliant
reductio ad absurdum of Walter Pater's serpentine
style and the somewhat confused values embodied in
his eclectic philosophy.

. . . Mr. Rose had got so dreamy by this time that he felt
himself the necessity of turning a little more matter-of-fact again.

"You will see what I mean, plainly enough," he said, "if you will
just think of our architecture, and consider how that naturally will
be——"

"Yes," said Mr. Luke,[1] "I should be glad to hear about our architecture."

"——How that naturally will be," Mr. Rose went on, "of no style in
particular."

"The deuce it won't!" exclaimed Mr. Luke.

[1] Mr. Luke is Matthew Arnold.

"No," continued Mr. Rose, unmoved; "no style in particular, but a *renaissance* of all styles. It will matter nothing to us whether they be pagan or Catholic, classical or mediaeval. We shall be quite without prejudice or bigotry. To the eye of true taste, an Aquinas in his cell before a crucifix, or a Narcissus gazing at himself in a still fountain,[2] are—in their own ways, you know—equally beautiful."

"Well, really," said Miss Merton,[3] "I can *not* fancy St. Thomas being a very taking object to people who don't believe in him either as a saint or a philosopher. I always think that, except from a Christian point of view, a saint can be hardly better described than by Newman's lines, as—

> A bundle of bones, whose breath
> Infects the world before his death."[4]

"I remember the lines well," said Mr. Rose calmly, "and the writer you mention puts them in the mouth of a yelping devil. But devils, as far as I know, are not generally—except, perhaps, Milton's—conspicuous for taste: indeed, if we may trust Goethe, the very touch of a flower is torture to them."[5]

"Dante's biggest devil," cried Mr. Saunders,[6] to everyone's amazement, "chewed Judas Iscariot like a quid of tobacco, to all eternity.[7] He, at any rate, knew what he liked."

Mr. Rose started, and visited Mr. Saunders with a rapid frown. He then proceeded, turning again to Miss Merton as if nothing had happened.

"Let me rather," he said, "read a nice sonnet to you, which I had sent to me this morning, and which was in my mind just now. These

---

[2] Saint Thomas Aquinas (1225-1274), the great mediaeval scholastic theologian; Narcissus, the beautiful Greek youth whom Aphrodite punished by causing him to become enamored of his own reflection in a fountain.

[3] Miss Merton, a devout young Roman Catholic, was inspired by Mallock's cousin Isey Froude. Like the other women guests at the house party, she provides a leaven of common sense and candor to the discussions.

[4] Miss Merton's couplet is an adaptation of lines 453-457· of John Henry Newman's long dramatic poem, *The Dream of Gerontius* (1865).

[5] Cf. *Faust*, Part II, v, 11, 710 ff.

[6] Mr. Saunders, the atheist, is drawn after William Kingdon Clifford (1845-1879), an eminent mathematician.

[7] Cf. *Inferno* xxxiv.55-63.

lines"—Mr. Rose here produced a paper from his pocket—"were written by a boy of eighteen—a youth of extraordinary promise, I think, whose education I may myself claim to have had some share in directing. "Listen," he said, laying the verses before him, on a clean plate.

> *"Three visions in the watches of one night*
> *Made sweet my sleep—almost too sweet to tell.*
> *One was Narcissus by a woodside well,*
> *And on the moss his limbs and feet were white;*
> *And one, Queen Venus, blown for my delight*
> *Across the blue sea in a rosy shell;*[8]
> *And one, a lean Aquinas in his cell,*
> *Kneeling, his pen in hand, with aching sight*
> *Strained towards a carven Christ; and of these three*
> *I knew not which was fairest. First I turned*
> *Towards that soft boy, who laughed and fled from me;*
> *Towards Venus then; and she smiled once, and she*
> *Fled also. Then with teeming heart I yearned,*
> *O Angel of the Schools,*[9] *towards Christ with thee!"*

"Yes," murmured Mr. Rose to himself, folding up the paper; "they are dear lines. Now, there," he said, "we have a true and tender expression of the really Catholic spirit of modern aestheticism which holds nothing common or unclean. It is in this spirit, I say, that the architects of our state will set to work. And thus for our houses, for our picture-galleries, for our churches—I trust we shall have many churches—they will select and combine——"

"Do you seriously mean," broke in Allen,[10] a little impatiently, "that it is a thing to wish for and to look forward to, that we should abandon all attempts at original architecture, and content ourselves with simply sponging on the past?"

"I do," replied Mr. Rose suavely; "and for this reason, if for no other, that the world can now successfully do nothing else. Nor, indeed, is it to be expected or even wished that it should."

---

[8] According to Hesiod, Venus, or Aphrodite, sprang from the foam of the sea; cf. Botticelli's famous painting of *The Birth of Venus*.

[9] The reference is, of course, to Aquinas.

[10] Lord Allen, who represents the best type of English aristocrat, was modeled on George Robert Charles Herbert, thirteenth earl of Pembroke (1850-1895).

"You say we have no good architecture now!" exclaimed Lady Ambrose;[11] "but, Mr. Rose, have you forgotten our modern churches? Don't you think them beautiful? Perhaps you never go to All Saints'?"[12]

"I every now and then," said Mr. Rose, "when I am in the weary mood for it, attend the services of our English Ritualists, and I admire their churches very much indeed. In some places the whole thing is really managed with surprising skill. The dim religious twilight, fragrant with the smoke of incense; the tangled roofs that the music seems to cling to; the tapers, the high altar, and the strange intonation of the priests, all produce a curious old-world effect, and seem to unite one with things that have been long dead. Indeed, it all seems to me far more a part of the past than the services of the Catholics."

Lady Ambrose did not express her approbation of the last part of this sentiment, out of regard for Miss Merton; but she gave a smile and a nod of pleased intelligence to Mr. Rose.

"Yes," Mr. Rose went on, "there is a regretful insincerity about it all, that is very nice, and that at once appeals to me, '*Gleich einer alten halbverklungen Sage.*'[13] The priests are only half in earnest; the congregations, even——"

"Then I am quite sure," interrupted Lady Ambrose with vigour, "that you can never have heard Mr. Cope preach."

"I don't know," said Mr. Rose languidly. "I never enquired, nor have I ever heard anyone so much as mention, the names of any of them. Now all that, Lady Ambrose, were life really in the state it should be, you would be able to keep."

"Do you seriously, and in sober earnest, mean," Allen again broke in, "that you think it a good thing that all our art and architecture should be borrowed and insincere, and that our very religion should be nothing but a dilettante memory?"

"The opinion," said Mr. Rose, "which by the way you slightly misrepresent, is not mine only, but that of all those of our own day who

---

[11] Mallock identified the worldly and urbane Lady Ambrose as a portrait of his friend, Lady Heathcoat-Amory.

[12] The modern Gothic Church of All Saints, Margaret Street, London, whose High Anglican services attracted a fashionable congregation.

[13] "Like an old, half-forgotten tale," Goethe, Dedication to *Faust,* 11.

are really devoting themselves to art for its own sake. I will try to explain the reason of this. In the world's life, just as in the life of a man, there are certain periods of eager and all-absorbing action, and these are followed by periods of memory and reflection. We then look back upon our past, and become for the first time conscious of what we are, and of what we have done. We then see the dignity of toil, and the grand results of it, the beauty and the strength of faith, and the fervent power of patriotism; which, whilst we laboured, and believed, and loved, we were quite blind to. Upon such a reflective period has the world now entered. It has acted and believed already; its task now is to learn to value action and belief—to feel and to be thrilled at the beauty of them. And the chief means by which it can learn this is art—the art of a *renaissance*. For by the power of such art, all that was beautiful, strong, heroic, or tender in the past—all the actions, passions, faiths, aspirations of the world, that lie so many fathom deep in the years— float upwards to the tranquil surface of the present, and make our lives like what seems to me one of the loveliest things in nature, the iridescent film on the face of a stagnant water. Yes; the past is not dead unless we choose that it shall be so. Christianity itself is not dead. There is 'nothing of it that doth fade,' but turns 'into something rich and strange,' [14] for us to give a new tone to our lives with. And, believe me," Mr. Rose went on, gathering earnestness, "that the happiness possible in such conscious periods is the only true happiness. Indeed, the active periods of the world were not really happy at all. We only fancy them to have been so by a pathetic fallacy. Is the hero happy during his heroism? No, but after it, when he sees what his heroism was, and reads the glory of it in the eyes of youth or maiden."

"All this is very poor stuff—*very* poor stuff," murmured Dr. Jenkinson,[15] whose face had become gradually the very picture of crossness.

"Do you mean, Mr. Rose," said Miss Merton, with a half humorous, half incredulous smile, "that we never value religion till we have come to think it nonsense?"

[14] See Ariel's song in *The Tempest* i.ii.399-401.
[15] Dr. Jenkinson is a masterly caricature of Benjamin Jowett (1817-1893), the famous Master of Balliol College, Oxford, and translator of Plato. Jowett detested Pater's brand of aestheticism.

"Not nonsense—no," exclaimed Mr. Rose in gentle horror; "I only mean that it never lights our lives so beautifully as when it is leaving them like the evening sun. It is in such periods of the world's life that art springs into being in its greatest splendour. Your Raphael, Miss Merton, who painted you your 'dear Madonnas,' was a luminous cloud in the sunset sky of the Renaissance,—a cloud that took its fire from a faith that was sunk or sinking."

"I'm afraid that the faith is not quite sunk yet," said Miss Merton, with a slight sudden flush in her cheeks, and with just the faintest touch of suppressed anger.

Mr. Saunders, Mr. Stockton, Mr. Storks,[16] and Mr. Luke all raised their eyebrows.

"No," said Mr. Rose, "such cyclic sunsets are happily apt to linger."

"Mr. Rose," exclaimed Lady Ambrose, with her most gracious of smiles, "of course everyone who has ears must know that all this is very beautiful, but I am positively so stupid that I haven't been quite able to follow it all."

"I will try to make my meaning clearer," he said, in a brisker tone. "I often figure to myself an unconscious period and a conscious one, as two women—one an untamed creature with embrowned limbs native to the air and the sea; the other marble-white and swan-soft, couched delicately on cushions before a mirror, and watching her own supple reflection gleaming in the depths of it. On the one is the sunshine and the sea-spray. The wind of Heaven and her unbound hair are playmates. The light of the sky is in her eyes; on her lips is a free laughter. *We* know it, mark me; but *she* knows it not. Turn, however, to the other, and all is changed. Outwardly, there is no gladness there. Her dark, gleaming eyes open depth within depth upon us, like the circles of a new Inferno. There is a clear, shadowy pallor on her cheek. Only her lips are scarlet. There is a sadness—a languor, even in the grave tendrils of her heavy hair, and in each changing curve of her bosom as she breathes or sighs."

"What a very odd man Mr. Rose is!" said Lady Ambrose in a loud

[16] Mr. Stockton—John Tyndall (1820-1893), professor of natural history at the Royal Institution and popular writer on scientific subjects; Mr. Storks—Thomas Henry Huxley.

whisper. "He always seems to talk of everybody as if they had no clothes on. And does he mean by this that we ought to be always in the dumps?"

"Yes," Mr. Rose was meanwhile proceeding, his voice again growing visionary, "there is no eagerness, no action there; and yet all eagerness, all action is known to her as the writing on an open scroll; only, as she reads, even in the reading of it, action turns into emotion, and eagerness into a sighing memory. Yet such a woman really may stand symbolically for us as the patroness and the lady of all gladness, who makes us glad in the only way now left us. And not only in the only way, but in the best way—the way of ways. Her secret is self-consciousness. She knows that she is fair; she knows, too, that she is sad; but she sees that sadness is lovely, and so sadness turns to joy. Such a woman may be taken as a symbol, not of our architecture only, but of all the aesthetic surroundings with which we shall shelter and express our life. Such a woman do I see whenever I enter a ritualistic church——"

"I know," said Mrs. Sinclair,[17] "that very peculiar people do go to such places; but, Mr. Rose," she said with a look of appealing enquiry, "I thought they were generally rather over-dressed than otherwise?"

"The imagination," said Mr. Rose, opening his eyes in grave wonder at Mrs. Sinclair, "may give her what garb it chooses. Our whole city, then—the city of our new Republic—will be in keeping with this spirit. It will be the architectural and decorative embodiment of the most educated longings of our own times after order and loveliness and delight, whether of the senses or the imagination. It will be, as it were, a resurrection of the past, in response to the longing and the passionate regret of the present. It will be such a resurrection as took place in Italy during its greatest epoch, only with this difference——"

"You seem to have forgotten trade and business altogether," said Dr. Jenkinson. "I think, however rich you intend to be, you will find that they are necessary."

"Yes, Mr. Rose, you're not going to deprive us of all our shops, I hope?" said Lady Ambrose.

[17] The original of the beautiful and witty Mrs. Sinclair was Mary Montgomerie, Lady Currie (1843-1905), who under the *nom de plume* of Violet Fane was an esteemed poet and novelist. Mallock dedicated *The New Republic* to her.

"Because, you know," said Mrs. Sinclair, with a soft maliciousness, "we can't go without dresses altogether, Mr. Rose. And if I were there," she continued plaintively, "I should want a book-seller to publish the scraps of verse—poetry, as I am pleased to call it—that I am always writing."

"Pooh!" said Mr. Rose, a little annoyed, "we shall have all that somewhere, of course; but it will be out of the way, in a sort of Piraeus, where the necessary χαπήλοι——" [18]

"A sort of what?" said Lady Ambrose.

"Mr. Rose merely means," said Donald Gordon, "that there must be good folding-doors between the offices and the house of life; and that the servants are not to be seen walking about in the pleasure-grounds."

"Yes," said Mr. Rose, "exactly so."

"Well, then," said Lady Ambrose, "I quite agree with you, Mr. Rose; and if wishing were only having, I've not the least doubt that we should all of us be going back to Mr. Rose's city to-morrow, instead of to London, with its carts, and cabs, and smoke, and all its thousand-and-one drawbacks. I'm sure," she said, turning to Miss Merton, "you would, my dear, with all your taste."

"It certainly," said Miss Merton, smiling, "all sounds very beautiful. All I am afraid of is that we should not be quite worthy of it.". . .

[18] Hucksters. Piraeus is the seaport and business center of Athens.

William Schwenk Gilbert
1836-1911

Etiquette
Patience; or Bunthorne's Bride

> "Etiquette," illustrated by the author, first appeared in the Christmas number of the weekly *Graphic* in 1869. It was included in the collected edition of *Bab Ballads* (1869), the volume of light verse through which Gilbert first made his reputation as a comic writer. The second selection is from Act One of the phenomenally successful comic opera *Patience; or Bunthorne's Bride* (1881), for which Arthur Sullivan provided the musical accompaniment to Gilbert's libretto. The sense of fun which had dictated the *Bab Ballads* had by now acquired a biting edge; and in the character of his protagonist, Reginald Bunthorne, who vainly woos the dairymaid Patience, the author was burlesquing the posturings of the young aesthetes of the day, and of Oscar Wilde in particular.

ETIQUETTE

The *Ballyshannon* foundered off the coast of Cariboo,
And down in fathoms many went the captain and the crew;
Down went the owners—greedy men whom hope of gain allured:
Oh, dry the starting tear, for they were heavily insured.

Besides the captain and the mate, the owners and the crew,
The passengers were also drowned excepting only two:

Young PETER GRAY, who tasted teas for BAKER, CROOP, AND CO.,
And SOMERS, who from Eastern shores imported indigo.

These passengers, by reason of their clinging to a mast,
Upon a desert island were eventually cast.
They hunted for their meals, as ALEXANDER SELKIRK[1] used,
But they couldn't chat together—they had not been introduced.

For PETER GRAY, and SOMERS too, though certainly in trade,
Were properly particular about the friends they made;
And somehow thus they settled it without a word of mouth—
That GRAY should take the northern half, while SOMERS took the south.

On PETER's portion oysters grew—a delicacy rare,
But oysters were a delicacy PETER couldn't bear.
On SOMERS' side was turtle, on the shingle lying thick,
Which SOMERS couldn't eat, because it always made him sick.

GRAY gnashed his teeth with envy as he saw a mighty store
Of turtle unmolested on his fellow-creature's shore:
The oysters at his feet aside impatiently he shoved,
For turtle and his mother were the only things he loved.

And SOMERS sighed in sorrow as he settled in the south,
For the thought of PETER's oysters brought the water to his mouth.
He longed to lay him down upon the shelly bed, and stuff:
He had often eaten oysters, but had never had enough.

[1] Alexander Selkirk (1676-1721), the original of Defoe's Robinson Crusoe, was
a shoemaker who ran away to sea, and who was marooned for five years (1704-9)
on the desert island of Juan Fernandez after he had quarreled with his captain.

How they wished an introduction to each other they had had
When on board the *Ballyshannon!* And it drove them nearly mad
To think how very friendly with each other they might get,
If it wasn't for the arbitrary rule of etiquette!

One day, when out a-hunting for the *mus ridiculus,*[2]
GRAY overheard his fellow-man soliloquizing thus:
'I wonder how the playmates of my youth are getting on,
M'CONNELL, S. B. WALTERS, PADDY BYLES, and ROBINSON?'

These simple words made PETER as delighted as could be,
Old chummies at the Charterhouse[3] were ROBINSON and he!
He walked straight up to SOMERS, then he turned extremely red,
Hesitated, hummed and hawed a bit, then cleared his throat, and said:

'I beg your pardon—pray forgive me if I seem too bold,
But you have breathed a name I knew familiarly of old.

[2] See Horace, *Ars Poetica,* 139; "funny little mouse" (with a play on the word *mus* (mouse), from which "mussel" is derived.
[3] One of the great English boarding schools.

You spoke of ROBINSON—I happened to be by—
You know him?' 'Yes, extremely well.' 'Allow me—so do I!'

It was enough: they felt they could more sociably get on,
For (ah, the magic of the fact!) they each knew ROBINSON!
And MR SOMERS' turtle was at PETER's service quite,
And MR SOMERS punished PETER's oyster-beds all night.

They soon became like brothers from community of wrongs:
They wrote each other little odes and sang each other songs;
They told each other anecdotes disparaging their wives;
On several occasions, too, they saved each other's lives.

They felt quite melancholy when they parted for the night,
And got up in the morning soon as ever it was light;
Each other's pleasant company they reckoned so upon,
And all because it happened that they both knew ROBINSON!

They lived for many years on that inhospitable shore,
And day by day they learned to love each other more and more.
At last, to their astonishment, on getting up one day,
They saw a vessel anchored in the offing of the bay!

To PETER an idea occurred. 'Suppose we cross the main?
So good an opportunity may not occur again.'
And SOMERS thought a minute, then ejaculated, 'Done!
I wonder how my business in the City's[4] getting on?'

[4] The business center of London.

'But stay,' said MR PETER: 'when in England, as you know,
I earned a living tasting teas for BAKER, CROOP, AND CO.,
I may be superseded—my employers think me dead!'
'Then come with me,' said SOMERS, 'and taste indigo instead.'

But all their plans were scattered in a moment when they found
The vessel was a convict ship from Portland, outward bound!
When a boat came off to fetch them, though they felt it very kind,
To go on board they firmly but respectfully declined.

As both the happy settlers roared with laughter at the joke,
They recognized an unattractive fellow pulling stroke:
'Twas ROBINSON—a convict, in an unbecoming frock!
Condemned to seven years for misappropriating stock!!!

They laughed no more, for SOMERS thought he had been rather rash
In knowing one whose friend had misappropriated cash;
And PETER thought a foolish tack he must have gone upon
In making the acquaintance of a friend of ROBINSON.

At first they didn't quarrel very openly, I've heard;
They nodded when they met, and now and then exchanged a word:
The word grew rare, and rarer still the nodding of the head,
And when they meet each other now, they cut each other dead.

To allocate the island they agreed by word of mouth,
And PETER takes the north again, and SOMERS takes the south;
And PETER has the oysters, which he loathes with horror grim,
And SOMERS has the turtle—turtle disagrees with him.

PATIENCE; or BUNTHORNE'S BRIDE

Enter BUNTHORNE, *who changes his manner and
becomes intensely melodramatic*

RECIT AND SONG—BUNTHORNE

Am I alone,
    And unobserved? I am!
Then let me own
    I'm an æsthetic sham!

This air severe
    Is but a mere
        Veneer!

This cynic smile
Is but a wile
Of guile!

This costume chaste
Is but good taste
Misplaced!

Let me confess!
A languid love for lilies does *not* blight me!
Lank limbs and haggard cheeks do *not* delight me!
I do *not* care for dirty greens
By any means.
I do *not* long for all one sees
That's Japanese.
I am *not* fond of uttering platitudes
In stained-glass attitudes.
In short, my mediævalism's affectation,
Born of a morbid love of admiration!

SONG

If you're anxious for to shine in the high æsthetic line as a man of
culture rare,
You must get up all the germs of the transcendental terms, and plant
them everywhere.
You must lie upon the daisies and discourse in novel phrases of your
complicated state of mind,
The meaning doesn't matter if it's only idle chatter of a transcendental
kind.

And every one will say,
As you walk your mystic way,
"If this young man expresses himself in terms too deep for *me,*
Why, what a very singularly deep young man this deep young man
must be!"

Be eloquent in praise of the very dull old days which have long since
passed away,
And convince 'em, if you can, that the reign of good Queen Anne was
Culture's palmiest day.
Of course you will pooh-pooh whatever's fresh and new, and declare it's
crude and mean,
For Art stopped short in the cultivated court of the Empress Josephine.
And every one will say,
As you walk your mystic way,
"If that's not good enough for him which is good enough for *me,*
Why, what a very cultivated kind of youth this kind of youth must be!"

Then a sentimental passion of a vegetable fashion must excite your
languid spleen,
An attachment *à la* Plato for a bashful young potato, or a not-too-French
French bean!
Though the Philistines may jostle, you will rank as an apostle in the
high æsthetic band,
If you walk down Piccadilly with a poppy or a lily in your mediæval
hand.
And every one will say,
As you walk your flowery way,
"If he's content with a vegetable love which would certainly not suit *me,*
Why, what a most particularly pure young man this pure young man
must be!"

At the end of his song PATIENCE *enters. He sees her*

BUN. Ah! Patience, come hither. I am pleased with thee. The bitter-
hearted one, who finds all else hollow, is pleased with thee. For you
are not hollow. *Are* you?

PA. No, thanks, I have dined; but—I beg your pardon—I interrupt you.

BUN. Life is made up of interruptions. The tortured soul, yearning for solitude, writhes under them. Oh, but my heart is a-weary! Oh, I am a cursed thing! Don't go.

PA. Really, I'm very sorry——

BUN. Tell me, girl, do you ever yearn?

PA. (*misunderstanding him*). I earn my living.

BUN. (*impatiently*). No, no! Do you know what it is to be heart-hungry? Do you know what it is to yearn for the Indefinable, and yet to be brought face to face, daily, with the Multiplication Table? Do you know what it is to seek oceans and to find puddles?—to long for whirlwinds and yet to have to do the best you can with the bellows? That's my case. Oh, I am a cursed thing! Don't go.

PA. If you please, I don't understand you—you frighten me!

BUN. Don't be frightened—it's only poetry.

PA. Well, if that's poetry, I don't like poetry.

BUN. (*eagerly*). Don't you? (*Aside.*) Can I trust her? (*Aloud.*) Patience, you don't like poetry—well, between you and me, *I* don't like poetry. It's hollow, unsubstantial—unsatisfactory. What's the use of yearning for Elysian Fields[1] when you know you can't get 'em, and would only let 'em out on building leases if you had 'em?

PA. Sir, I——

BUN. Patience, I have long loved you. Let me tell you a secret. I am not as bilious as I look. If you like, I will cut my hair. There is more innocent fun within me than a casual spectator would imagine. You have never seen me frolicsome. Be a good girl—a very good girl—and one day you shall. If you are fond of touch-and-go jocularity—this is the shop for it.

PA. Sir, I will speak plainly. In the matter of love I am untaught. I have never loved but my great-aunt. But I am quite certain, under any circumstances, I couldn't possibly love *you*.

BUN. Oh, you think not?

PA. I'm quite sure of it. Quite sure. Quite.

[1] In classical mythology, the abode of the blessed after death.

BUN. Very good. Life is henceforth a blank. I don't care what becomes of me. I have only to ask that you will not abuse my confidence; though you despise me, I am extremely popular with the other young ladies.

PA. I only ask that you will leave me and never renew the subject.

BUN. Certainly. Broken-hearted and desolate, I go. (*Recites.*)

> "Oh, to be wafted away
> From this black Aceldama[2] of sorrow,
> Where the dust of an earthy to-day
> Is the earth of a dusty to-morrow!"

It is a little thing of my own. I call it "Heart Foam." I shall not publish it. Farewell! Patience, Patience, farewell!

[2] Scene of the suicide of Judas Iscariot; cf. Acts i.18.

Oscar Wilde

1854-1900

Epigrams

✣ "Would you like to know the great drama of my life?" Wilde once asked. "It is that I have put my genius into my life—I have put only my talent into my works." The speaker was certainly entitled to his reputation as the wittiest man in late Victorian England; and while many of his best sayings wilt when transplanted from the rarefied atmosphere of the comedies and fictions, the following selection from his published works and recorded conversations will illustrate his mastery over epigrammatic statement, as well as the attitudes towards life and art which informed his spectacular, but tragic, career.

Formerly we used to canonize our heroes. The modern method is to vulgarize them. Cheap editions of great books may be delightful, but cheap editions of great men are absolutely detestable.

We live in an age when men treat art as if it were meant to be a form of autobiography.

Gossip is charming! . . . History is merely gossip. But scandal is gossip made tedious by morality.

One knows so well the popular idea of health. The English country-gentleman galloping after a fox—the unspeakable in full pursuit of the uneatable.

It is personalities, not principles, that move the age.

Paradox though it may seem—and paradoxes are always dangerous things—it is none the less true that life imitates art far more than art imitates life.

Art finds her own perfection within, and not outside of, herself. She is not to be judged by any external standards of resemblance. She is a veil, rather than a mirror. She has flowers that no forests know of, birds that no woodland possesses. She makes and unmakes many worlds, and can draw the moon from heaven with a scarlet thread. Hers are the forms more real than living man, and hers the great archetypes of which things that have no existence are but unfinished copies. Nature has, in her eyes, no law, no uniformity.

. . . the more we study Art, the less we care for Nature. What Art reveals to us is Nature's lack of design, her extraordinary monotony, her absolutely unfinished condition. Nature has good intentions, of course, but, as Aristotle once said, she cannot carry them out.

Find expression for a sorrow, and it will become dear to you. Find expression for a joy, and you intensify its ecstasy.

The one characteristic of a beautiful form is that one can put into it whatever one wishes, and see in it whatever one chooses to see; and the Beauty, that gives to creation its universal and aesthetic element, makes the critic a creator in his turn, and whispers of a thousand different things which were not present in the mind of him who carved the statue or painted the panel or graved the gem.

Art is the most intense mode of Individualism that the world has known.

The true artist is a man who believes absolutely in himself, because he is absolutely himself.

Bad artists always admire each other's work. They call it being large-minded and free from prejudice. But a truly great artist cannot conceive of life being shown, or beauty fashioned, under any conditions other than those he has selected.

The originality which we ask from the artist is originality of treatment, not of subject. It is only the unimaginative who ever invent. The true artist is known by the use he makes of what he annexes, and he annexes everything.

The longer one studies life and literature the more strongly one feels that behind everything that is wonderful stands the individual, and that it is not the moment that makes the man but the man who creates the age.

Literature always anticipates life. It does not copy it, but moulds it to its purpose. The nineteenth century, as we know it, is largely an invention of Balzac.

Laughter is the primeval attitude towards life—a mode of approach that survives only in artists and criminals!

. . . try as we may we cannot get behind things to the reality. And the terrible reason may be that there is no reality in things apart from their appearances.

Life is terribly deficient in form. Its catastrophes happen in the wrong way. There is a grotesque horror about its comedies, and its tragedies seem to culminate in farce.

Science can never grapple with the irrational. That is why it has no future before it, in this world.

If we lived long enough to see the results of our actions it may be that those who call themselves good would be sickened with a dull remorse, and those whom the world calls evil stirred by a noble joy.

A cynic is a man who knows the price of everything and the value of nothing.

Moderation is a fatal thing. Nothing succeeds like excess.

When we are happy we are always good but when we are good we are not always happy.

What we want are unpractical people who see beyond the moment and think beyond the day. Those who try to lead the people can only do so by following the mob. It is through the voice crying in the wilderness that the ways of the gods must be prepared.

All authority is quite degrading. It degrades those who exercise it, and it degrades those over whom it is exercised.

A child can understand a punishment inflicted by an individual, such as a parent or guardian, and bear it with a certain amount of acquiescence. What it cannot understand is a punishment inflicted by society.

As one reads history . . . one is absolutely sickened, not by the crimes that the wicked have committed, but by the punishments that the good have inflicted; and a community is infinitely more brutalized by the habitual employment of punishment than it is by the occasional occurrence of crime.

To become a spectator of one's own life is to escape the suffering of life.

I wrote when I did not know life; now that I do know the meaning of life, I have no more to write. Life cannot be written; life can only be lived.

What people call insincerity is simply a method by which we can multiply our personalities.

Between me and life there is a mist of words always. I throw probability out of the window for the sake of a phrase, and the chance of an epigram makes me desert truth. Still I do aim at making a work of art.

Man is least himself when he talks in his own person. Give him a mask, and he will tell you the truth.

The value of an idea has nothing whatsoever to do with the sincerity of the man who expresses it.

. . . a sentimentalist is simply one who desires to have the luxury of an emotion without paying for it.

Experience is the name every one gives to their mistakes.

SUGGESTIONS FOR ADDITIONAL READING

Although the list could be indefinitely extended, the following novels and plays will serve to provide some idea of the abundance and variety of humor in Victorian fiction:

Thomas Love Peacock, *Crotchet Castle* (1831)

Charles Dickens, *The Posthumous Papers of the Pickwick Club* (1836-37)

William Makepeace Thackeray, *Vanity Fair* (1847-48)

Elizabeth Cleghorn Gaskell, *Cranford* (1851-53)

Anthony Trollope, *Barchester Towers* (1857)

Charles Lutwidge Dodgson ("Lewis Carroll"), *Alice's Adventures in Wonderland* (1865); *Through the Looking-Glass* (1872)

George Meredith, *The Egoist* (1879)

Max Beerbohm, *Zuleika Dobson* (1911)

William Schwenk Gilbert and Arthur Sullivan, *Patience; or Bunthorne's Bride* (1881)

George Bernard Shaw, *Arms and the Man* (1894); *Candida* (1895)

Oscar Wilde, *The Importance of Being Earnest* (1899)

The following collections of comic writing may be recommended:

A Nonsense Anthology, collected by Carolyn Wells (New York, 1903); reissued by Dover Publications (New York, 1958)

A Book of Nonsense, edited by Ernest Rhys and R. L. Green (Everyman's Library, 1927)

Straw in the Hair: An Anthology of Nonsensical and Surrealist Verse, compiled by D. K. Roberts (London, 1938)

A Treasury of British Humor, edited by Morris Bishop (New York, 1942)

The Faber Book of Comic Verse, compiled by Michael Roberts (London, 1942)

Stephen Potter, *Sense of Humour* (London, 1954)

A Century of Humorous Verse, 1850-1950, edited by R. L. Green (Everyman's Library, 1959)

Parodies: An Anthology from Chaucer to Beerbohm—and After, compiled by Dwight Macdonald (New York, 1960)

A Century of Punch, edited by R. E. Williams (London, 1956), contains a good selection of humorous drawings from *Punch*

Selective Bibliography

I. GENERAL WORKS ON THE VICTORIAN AGE

The Historical Setting

Clapham, J. H. *An Economic History of Modern Britain.* 2nd ed., 3 vols. Cambridge, Eng., 1930-38.

Clark, G. K. *The Making of Victorian England.* Cambridge, Mass., 1962.

Cole, G. D. H. *A Short History of the British Working Class Movement, 1789-1947.* Rev. ed. London, 1948.

Ensor, R. C. K. *England, 1870-1914.* Oxford, 1949.

Fay, C. R. *Life and Labour in the Nineteenth Century.* Cambridge, Eng., 1920.

Halévy, Elie. *A History of the English People in the Nineteenth Century,* trans. by E. I. Watkin and D. A. Barker. 2nd ed., 7 vols. London, 1949-52.

Rostow, W. W. *British Economy in the Nineteenth Century.* Oxford, 1948.

Trevelyan, G. M. *British History in the Nineteenth Century, 1782-1919.* 2nd ed. London, 1937.

Trevelyan, G. M. *Illustrated English Social History: Vol. IV, The Nineteenth Century.* London, 1952.

Woodward, E. L. *The Age of Reform, 1815-1870.* 2nd ed. Oxford, 1962.

Young, G. M., ed. *Early Victorian England, 1830-1865.* 2 vols. London, 1934.

Young, G. M. *Victorian England: Portrait of an Age.* 2nd ed. London, 1957.

Young, G. M. and Handcock, W. D., eds. *English Historical Documents, 1833-1874.* London, 1956.

The Intellectual Climate

Appleman, David, and others, eds. *1859: Entering an Age of Crisis.* Bloomington, Ind., 1959.

Bernal, J. D. *Science and Industry in the Nineteenth Century.* London, 1953.

SELECTIVE BIBLIOGRAPHY

Boner, H. A. *Hungry Generations: The Nineteenth-Century Case against Malthusianism.* New York, 1955.

Briggs, Asa. *Victorian People: A Reassessment of Persons and Themes, 1851-67.* London, 1954.

Brinton, Crane. *English Political Thought in the Nineteenth Century.* 2nd ed. Cambridge, Mass., 1949.

British Broadcasting Corporation. *Ideas and Beliefs of the Victorians: An Historic Revaluation of the Victorian Age,* with foreword by Harman Grisewood. London, 1949.

Brown, F. K. *Fathers of the Victorians.* Cambridge, Eng., 1961.

Cassirer, Ernst. *The Myth of the State.* New Haven, Conn., 1946.

Clark, Kenneth. *The Gothic Revival: A Study in the History of Taste.* 3rd ed. London, 1962.

Curtis, S. J. and Boultwood, M. E. A. *An Introductory History of English Education since 1800.* 2nd ed. London, 1962.

Dicey, A. V. *Lectures on the Relation between Law and Public Opinion in England during the Nineteenth Century.* 2nd ed. London, 1914.

Dodds, J. W. *The Age of Paradox: A Biography of England, 1841-1851.* New York, 1952.

Elliott-Binns, L. E. *Religion in the Victorian Era.* London, 1936.

Faber, Geoffrey. *The Oxford Apostles.* Rev. ed. London, 1936.

Faber, Geoffrey. *Jowett: A Portrait with Background.* Cambridge, Mass., 1957.

Gillispie, Charles C. *Genesis and Geology.* Cambridge, Mass., 1951.

Halévy, Elie. *The Growth of Philosophic Radicalism,* trans. by Mary Morris. Rev. ed. London, 1949.

Harrison, J. F. C. *Learning and Living, 1790-1960: A Study in the History of the English Adult Education Movement.* London, 1961.

Heilbroner, R. L. *The Worldly Philosophers: The Lives, Times, and Ideas of the Great Economic Thinkers.* New York, 1953.

Hobhouse, Christopher. *1851 and the Crystal Palace.* London, 1937.

Houghton, W. E. *The Victorian Frame of Mind, 1830-1870.* New Haven, Conn., 1957.

Irvine, William. *Apes, Angels, and Victorians: A Study of Darwin, Huxley, and Evolution.* New York, 1955.

Lewis, Roy and Maude, Angus. *The English Middle Classes.* London, 1949.

Lippincott, B. E. *Victorian Critics of Democracy.* Minneapolis, Minn., 1938.

SELECTIVE BIBLIOGRAPHY

Mack, E. C. *Public Schools and British Opinion since 1860.* New York, 1941.

Magnus, Philip. *Gladstone: A Biography.* New York, 1954.

Mead, G. H. *Movements of Thought in the Nineteenth Century,* ed. by M. H. Moore. Chicago, 1936.

Neff, Emery. *The Poetry of History: The Contribution of Literature and Literary Scholarship to the Writing of History since Voltaire.* New York, 1947.

Pevsner, Nikolaus. *High Victorian Design: A Study of the Exhibits of 1851.* London, 1951.

Plamenatz, John. *Utilitarianism, with a Study of the English Utilitarians.* Oxford, 1949.

Routh, H. V. *Towards the Twentieth Century: Essays in the Spiritual History of the Nineteenth.* New York, 1937.

Simpson, G. G. *The Meaning of Evolution.* New Haven, Conn., 1950.

Somervell, D. C. *English Thought in the Nineteenth Century.* London, 1929.

Steegman, John. *Consort of Taste, 1830-1870.* London, 1950.

Stephen, Leslie. *The English Utilitarians.* 3 vols. London, 1900.

Tawney, R. H. *Religion and the Rise of Capitalism: A Historical Study.* New York, 1926.

Williams, Raymond. *Culture and Society, 1780-1950.* New York, 1958.

The Literary Background

Altick, R. D. *The English Common Reader: A Social History of the Mass Reading Public, 1800-1900.* Chicago, 1957.

Annan, N. G. *Leslie Stephen: His Thought and Character in Relation to his Time.* Cambridge, Mass., 1952.

Baker, J. E., ed. *The Reinterpretation of Victorian Literature.* Princeton, N.J., 1950.

Batho, E. C. and Dobrée, Bonamy. *The Victorians and After, 1830-1914.* Rev. ed. London, 1950.

Beach, J. W. *The Concept of Nature in Nineteenth-Century Poetry.* New York, 1936.

Buckley, J. H. *The Victorian Temper: A Study in Literary Culture.* Cambridge, Mass., 1951.

Bush, Douglas. *Mythology and the Romantic Tradition in English Poetry.* Cambridge, Mass., 1937.

SELECTIVE BIBLIOGRAPHY

Cazamian, Louis. *Le Roman Social en Angleterre, 1830-1850.* Paris, 1904.

Cecil, David. *Early Victorian Novelists: Essays in Revaluation.* London, 1934.

Chesterton, G. K. *The Victorian Age in Literature.* London, 1913.

Cruse, Amy. *The Victorians and their Books.* London, 1935. [Published in U.S.A. under title, *The Victorians and their Reading.*]

Dalziel, Margaret. *Popular Fiction 100 Years Ago: An Unexplored Tract of Literary History.* London, 1957.

Elton, Oliver. *Survey of English Literature, 1830-1880.* 4 vols. New York, 1920.

Evans, B. I. *English Poetry in the Later Nineteenth Century.* London, 1933.

Fairchild, H. N. *Religious Trends in English Poetry: Vol. IV, 1830-1880.* New York, 1957. *Vol. V, 1880-1920.* New York, 1962.

Gaunt, William. *The Pre-Raphaelite Tragedy.* London, 1942. [Reprinted in 1943 under title *The Pre-Raphaelite Dream.*]

Gaunt, William. *The Aesthetic Adventure.* London, 1945.

Holloway, John. *The Victorian Sage: Studies in Argument.* London, 1953.

Hough, Graham. *The Last Romantics.* London, 1949.

Jackson, Holbrook. *The Eighteen Nineties: A Review of Art and Ideas at the Close of the Nineteenth Century.* London, 1913.

James, Philip. *English Book Illustration, 1800-1900.* London, 1947.

Johnson, Edgar. *One Mighty Torrent: The Drama of Biography.* New York, 1937.

Johnson, E. D. H. *The Alien Vision of Victorian Poetry.* Princeton, N.J., 1952.

Kermode, Frank. *The Romantic Image.* London, 1957.

Langbaum, R. W. *The Poetry of Experience: The Dramatic Monologue in Modern Literary Tradition.* London, 1957.

Leavis, F. R. *The Great Tradition: George Eliot, Henry James, Joseph Conrad.* London, 1948.

Leavis, Q. D. *Fiction and the Reading Public.* London, 1932.

LeRoy, G. C. *Perplexed Prophets: Six Nineteenth-Century British Authors.* Philadelphia, 1953.

Maison, M. M. *The Victorian Vision: Studies in the Religious Novel.* New York, 1961.

Pascal, Roy. *Design and Truth in Autobiography.* Cambridge, Mass., 1960.

Praz, Mario. *The Romantic Agony,* trans. by Angus Davidson. 2nd ed. London, 1951.

Praz, Mario. *The Hero in Eclipse in Victorian Fiction,* trans. by Angus Davidson. London, 1956.

Price, R. G. G. *A History of Punch.* London, 1957.

Roppen, Georg. *Evolution and Poetic Belief: A Study in Some Victorian and Modern Writers.* Oslo, 1957.

Spielmann, M. H. *The History of "Punch."* London, 1895.

Stevenson, Lionel. *Darwin among the Poets.* Chicago, 1932.

Tillotson, Geoffrey. *Criticism and the Nineteenth Century.* London, 1951.

Tillotson, Kathleen. *Novels of the Eighteen-Forties.* Oxford, 1954.

Tindall, W. Y. *Forces in Modern British Literature, 1885-1946.* New York, 1947.

Walker, Hugh. *The Literature of the Victorian Era.* Cambridge, Eng., 1910.

Warren, A. H. *English Poetic Theory, 1825-1865.* Princeton, N.J., 1950.

Welland, D. S. R. *The Pre-Raphaelites in Literature and Art.* London, 1953.

Willey, Basil. *Nineteenth Century Studies: Coleridge to Matthew Arnold.* New York, 1949.

Willey, Basil. *More Nineteenth Century Studies: A Group of Honest Doubters.* New York, 1956.

Wright, Austin, ed. *Victorian Literature: Modern Essays in Criticism.* New York, 1961.

SELECTIVE BIBLIOGRAPHY

II. INDIVIDUAL AUTHORS

The following listings will suggest some of the more important primary and secondary sources for further study of the authors represented in this anthology. Wherever possible, standard editions of their collected writings are cited first, followed by notations of the best works of reference, biographical and critical. For biographical information the student should consult either *The Oxford Companion to English Literature, The Encyclopaedia Britannica,* or *The Concise Dictionary of National Biography*; and for fuller bibliographical data, *The Cambridge Bibliography of English Literature.*

MATTHEW ARNOLD (1822-1888)

Poetical Works, ed. by C. B. Tinker and H. F. Lowry. London, 1950.
The Letters of Matthew Arnold to Arthur Hugh Clough, ed. by H. F. Lowry. London, 1932.
Notebooks, ed. by H. F. Lowry and others. London, 1952.
Complete Prose Works, ed. by R. H. Super, under publication by the University of Michigan Press in about ten volumes. To date the following have appeared: *On the Classical Tradition* (Ann Arbor, 1960); *Democratic Education* (Ann Arbor, 1962); *Lectures and Essays in Criticism* (Ann Arbor, 1962).

Brown, E. K. *Matthew Arnold: A Study in Conflict.* Chicago, 1948.
Tinker, C. B. and Lowry, H. F. *The Poetry of Matthew Arnold: A Commentary.* London, 1940.
Trilling, Lionel. *Matthew Arnold.* New York, 1939.

ROBERT BROWNING (1812-1889)

Works, ed. by F. G. Kenyon. Centenary ed., 10 vols. London, 1912.
Complete Poetic and Dramatic Works. Cambridge ed. Boston and New York, 1895.
Shorter Poems, ed. by W. C. DeVane. New York, 1934.

DeVane, W. C. *A Browning Handbook.* Rev. ed. New York, 1955.
Griffin, W. H. and Minchin, H. C. *The Life of Robert Browning.* Rev. ed. London, 1938.
Miller, Betty B. *Robert Browning: A Portrait.* London, 1952.
Raymond, W. O. *The Infinite Moment, and Other Essays in Robert Browning.* Toronto, 1950.

SELECTIVE BIBLIOGRAPHY

SAMUEL BUTLER (1835-1902)

Works, ed. by H. F. Jones and A. T. Bartholomew. Shrewsbury ed., 20 vols. London, 1923-26.
Note-books, ed. by H. F. Jones. London, 1912.
Further Extracts from the Note-books, ed. by A. T. Bartholomew. London, 1934.
The Essential Samuel Butler, ed. by G. D. H. Cole. London, 1950.

Jones, H. F. *Samuel Butler: A Memoir.* 2 vols. London, 1919.
Stillman, Clara G. *Samuel Butler: A Mid-Victorian Modern.* New York, 1932.
Willey, Basil. *Darwin and Butler: Two Versions of Evolution.* London, 1960.

THOMAS CARLYLE (1795-1881)

Works, ed. by H. D. Traill. Centenary ed., 30 vols. London, 1896-99.

Froude, J. A. *Thomas Carlyle: A History of the First Forty Years of his Life.* 2 vols. London, 1882.
Froude, J. A. *Thomas Carlyle: A History of his Life in London.* 2 vols. London, 1884.
Harrold, C. F. *Carlyle and German Thought, 1819-1834.* New Haven, Conn., 1934.
Neff, Emery. *Carlyle and Mill: An Introduction to Victorian Thought.* Rev. ed. New York, 1926.
Roe, F. W. *The Social Philosophy of Carlyle and Ruskin.* New York, 1921.
Symons, Julian. *Thomas Carlyle: The Life and Ideas of a Prophet.* London, 1952.

ARTHUR HUGH CLOUGH (1819-1861)

Poems, ed. by H. F. Lowry, A. L. P. Norrington, and F. L. Mulhauser. Oxford, 1951.
Correspondence, ed. by F. L. Mulhauser. 2 vols. Oxford, 1957.

Chorley, Katharine. *Arthur Hugh Clough: The Uncommitted Mind.* Oxford, 1962.
Woodward, F. J. *The Doctor's Disciples: A Study of Four Pupils of Thomas Arnold at Rugby: Stanley, Gell, Clough, William Arnold.* London, 1954.

SELECTIVE BIBLIOGRAPHY

CHARLES ROBERT DARWIN (1809-1882)

Autobiography, ed. by Nora Barlow. London, 1958.
The Darwin Reader, ed. by Marston Bates and P. S. Humphrey. New York, 1956.
The Living Thoughts of Darwin, ed. by Julian Huxley and James Fisher. Rev. ed. London, 1958.
Barnett, S. A., ed. *A Century of Darwin*. Cambridge, Mass., 1958.
Darwin, Francis, ed. *The Life and Letters of Charles Darwin*. 2 vols. London, 1888. [Contains a list of Darwin's writings.]
Eiseley, L. C. *Darwin's Century: Evolution and the Men Who Discovered It*. New York, 1958.
Himmelfarb, Gertrude. *Darwin and the Darwinian Revolution*. New York, 1959.

CHARLES DICKENS (1812-1870)

Works, ed. by Andrew Lang. Gadshill ed., 34 vols. London, 1897-99.
The Nonesuch Dickens, ed. by Arthur Waugh, Walter Dexter, and others. 23 vols. London, 1938-39.
The New Oxford Illustrated Dickens. 21 vols. London, 1947-58.
Cruikshank, R. J. *Charles Dickens and Early Victorian England*. London, 1949.
Forster, John. *The Life of Charles Dickens*, ed. by J. W. T. Ley. London, 1928.
Gissing, George. *Critical Studies of the Works of Charles Dickens*. Rev. ed. London, 1924.
House, Humphry. *The Dickens World*. London, 1941.
Johnson, Edgar. *Charles Dickens: His Tragedy and Triumph*. 2 vols. New York, 1952.
Miller, J. H. *Charles Dickens: The World of his Novels*. Cambridge, Mass., 1959.

CHARLES LUTWIDGE DODGSON (1832-1898)
(Lewis Carroll)

Complete Works, with introduction by Alexander Woollcott. New York, 1936.
Diaries, ed. by R. L. Green. 2 vols. London, 1953.
The Annotated Alice, ed. by Martin Gardner. New York, 1960.
Collingwood, S. D. *The Life and Letters of Lewis Carroll*. London, 1899.

SELECTIVE BIBLIOGRAPHY

Hudson, Derek. *Lewis Carroll.* London, 1954.
Sewell, Elizabeth. *The Field of Nonsense.* London, 1952.
Taylor, A. H. *The White Knight: A Study of C. L. Dodgson (Lewis Carroll).* Edinburgh, 1952.

WILLIAM SCHWENK GILBERT (1836-1911)

Plays and Poems, with preface by Deems Taylor. New York, 1932.

Pearson, Hesketh. *Gilbert: His Life and Strife.* London, 1957.
Williamson, Audrey. *Gilbert and Sullivan Opera: A New Assessment.* London, 1953.

THOMAS HARDY (1840-1928)

Works. Wessex ed., 22 vols. London, 1914-23.
Collected Poems. New York, 1948.
Notebooks, ed. by Evelyn Hardy. London, 1955.

Duffin, H. C. *Thomas Hardy: A Study of the Wessex Novels, the Poems, and The Dynasts.* Rev. ed. Manchester, 1937.
Guerard, A. J. *Hardy: The Novels and Stories.* Cambridge, Mass., 1949.
Hardy, Florence E. *The Early Life of Thomas Hardy, 1840-1891.* London, 1928.
Hardy, Florence E. *The Later Years of Thomas Hardy, 1892-1928.* London, 1930. [The two foregoing have been reissued in a single volume, *The Life of Thomas Hardy, 1840-1928* (London, 1962).]
Weber, C. J. *Hardy of Wessex: His Life and Literary Career.* New York, 1940.
Webster, H. C. *On a Darkling Plain: The Art and Thought of Thomas Hardy.* Chicago, 1947.

GERARD MANLEY HOPKINS (1884-1889)

Poems, ed. by W. H. Gardner. 3rd ed. London, 1948.
Letters, ed. by C. C. Abbott. London, 1935.
Further Letters, ed. by C. C. Abbott. Enlarged ed. London, 1956.
Journals and Papers, ed. by Humphry House and Graham Storey. London, 1959.

Gardner, W. H. *Gerard Manley Hopkins: A Study of Poetic Idiosyncrasy in Relation to Poetic Tradition.* 2 vols. New Haven, Conn., 1948-49.
Peters, W. A. M. *Gerard Manley Hopkins: A Critical Study toward the Understanding of his Poetry.* London, 1948.

SELECTIVE BIBLIOGRAPHY

Pick, John. *Gerard Manley Hopkins: Priest and Poet.* London, 1942.
Weyand, N. T. and Schoder, R. V., eds. *Immortal Diamond: Studies in Gerard Manley Hopkins.* New York, 1949.

ALFRED EDWARD HOUSMAN (1859-1936)

Complete Poems, ed. by T. B. Haber. Centennial ed. New York, 1959.

Housman, Laurence. *My Brother, A. E. Housman.* New York, 1938.
Marlow, Norman. *A. E. Housman: Scholar and Poet.* Minneapolis, Minn., 1958.
Robinson, Oliver. *Angry Dust: The Poetry of A. E. Housman.* Boston, 1950.
Watson, G. L. *A. E. Housman: A Divided Life.* London, 1957.

THOMAS HENRY HUXLEY (1825-1895)

Collected Essays. 9 vols. London, 1893-94.

Bibby, H. C. *T. H. Huxley: Scientist, Humanist, and Educator.* London, 1959.
Huxley, Leonard. *Life and Letters of Thomas Henry Huxley.* 2 vols. London, 1900.
Peterson, Houston. *Huxley, Prophet of Science.* London, 1932.

EDWARD LEAR (1812-1888)

The Complete Nonsense, ed. by Holbrook Jackson. London, 1947.
Letters, ed. by Lady Strachey. London, 1907.
Later Letters, ed. by Lady Strachey. London, 1911.
Journals: A Selection, ed. by Herbert Van Thal. New York, 1952.

Davidson, Angus. *Edward Lear: Landscape Painter and Nonsense Poet.* London, 1938.
Sewell, Elizabeth. *The Field of Nonsense.* London, 1952.

THOMAS BABINGTON MACAULAY (1800-1859)

Complete Works. Whitehall ed., 20 vols. New York, 1898.

Beatty, R. C. *Lord Macaulay, Victorian Liberal.* Norman, Okla., 1938.
Bryant, Arthur. *Macaulay.* Edinburgh, 1932.
Trevelyan, G. O. *The Life and Letters of Lord Macaulay.* 2 vols. London, 1876.

SELECTIVE BIBLIOGRAPHY

WILLIAM HURRELL MALLOCK (1849-1923)

Principal works:
The New Republic; or, Culture, Faith, and Philosophy in an English Country House (1877); see edition by J. M. Patrick (Gainesville, Fla., 1956).
The New Paul and Virginia; or, Positivism on an Island (1878).
Memoirs of Life and Literature (1920).

Adams, A. B. *The Novels of W. H. Mallock.* Orono, Maine, 1934.

GEORGE MEREDITH (1828-1909)

Works. Memorial ed., 26 vols. London, 1909-10.
Poetical Works, ed. by G. M. Trevelyan. London, 1912.
An Essay on Comedy and the Uses of the Comic Spirit, ed. by Lane Cooper. Rev. ed. Ithaca, N.Y., 1918.

Beach, J. W. *The Comic Spirit in George Meredith.* New York, 1911.
Kelvin, Norman. *A Troubled Eden: Nature and Society in the Works of George Meredith.* Stanford, Calif., 1961.
Sassoon, Siegfried. *Meredith.* London, 1948.
Stevenson, Lionel. *The Ordeal of George Meredith.* New York, 1953.
Trevelyan, G. M. *The Poetry and Philosophy of George Meredith.* London, 1906.

JOHN STUART MILL (1806-1873)

Principal works:
A System of Logic (1843); *Principles of Political Economy* (1848); *On Liberty* (1859); *Considerations on Representative Government* (1861); *Utilitarianism* (1863); *Auguste Comte and Positivism* (1865); *Autobiography* (1873); *Three Essays on Religion* (1874).
Mill on Bentham and Coleridge, ed. by F. R. Leavis. London, 1950.
Hayek, F. A. *John Stuart Mill and Harriet Taylor: Their Correspondence and Subsequent Marriage.* Chicago, 1951.

Anschütz, R. P. *The Philosophy of J. S. Mill.* Oxford, 1953.
Britton, Karl. *John Stuart Mill.* London, 1953.
Packe, M. St.-J. *The Life of John Stuart Mill.* London, 1954.

WILLIAM MORRIS (1834-1896)

Collected Works, ed. by May Morris. 24 vols. London, 1910-15.
Letters, ed. by Philip Henderson. London and New York, 1950.
Selected Works, ed. by G. D. H. Cole. London, 1934.

SELECTIVE BIBLIOGRAPHY

Eshleman, L. W. *A Victorian Rebel: The Life of William Morris*. New York, 1940. [This work was reissued in England under the pseudonym L. E. Grey and with the title: *William Morris: Prophet of England's New Order* (London, 1949).]

Mackail, J. W. *The Life of William Morris*. 2 vols. London, 1899.

Morris, May. *William Morris: Artist, Writer, Socialist*. 2 vols. Oxford, 1936.

Thompson, E. P. *William Morris: Romantic to Revolutionary*. London, 1955.

JOHN HENRY NEWMAN (1801-1890)

Correspondence of John Henry Newman with John Keble and Others, 1839-1845, ed. at the Birmingham Oratory. London, 1917.

Essays and Sketches, ed. by C. F. Harrold. 3 vols. New York and London, 1948.

Letters and Correspondence of John Henry Newman, ed. by Anne Mozley. 2 vols. London, 1890.

Autobiographical Writings, ed. by Henry Tristram. London, 1956.

Culler, A. D. *The Imperial Intellect: A Study of Newman's Educational Ideal*. New Haven, Conn., 1955.

Harrold, C. F. *John Henry Newman: An Expository and Critical Study of his Mind, Thought, and Age*. New York, 1945.

Trevor, Meriol. *Newman: The Pillar of Cloud*. London, 1962.

Trevor, Meriol. *Newman: Light in Winter*. London, 1962. [Completing a two-volume biography.]

Ward, W. P. *The Life of Cardinal Newman*. 2 vols. London, 1912.

WALTER HORATIO PATER (1839-1894)

Works. Library ed., 10 vols. London, 1910.

Selected Works, ed. by Richard Aldington. London, 1948.

Child, Ruth C. *The Aesthetic of Walter Pater*. New York, 1940.

Wright, Thomas. *The Life of Walter Pater*. 2 vols. London, 1907.

DANTE GABRIEL ROSSETTI (1828-1882)

Works, ed. by W. M. Rossetti. Rev. ed. London, 1911.

Poems, ed. by Oswald Doughty. London, 1957.

Family Letters, ed. by W. M. Rossetti. 2 vols. London, 1895.

Ruskin: Rossetti: Pre-Raphaelitism, ed. by W. M. Rossetti. London, 1899.

SELECTIVE BIBLIOGRAPHY

Angeli, Helen R. *Dante Gabriel Rossetti: His Friends and Enemies.* London, 1949.
Beerbohm, Max. *Rossetti and his Circle.* London, 1922.
Doughty, Oswald. *A Victorian Romantic: Dante Gabriel Rossetti.* London, 1949.
Rossetti, W. M. *Dante Gabriel Rossetti as Designer and Writer.* London, 1889.

JOHN RUSKIN (1819-1900)

Works, ed. by E. T. Cook and Alexander Wedderburn. Library ed., 39 vols. London, 1903-12.
Diaries, ed. by Joan Evans and J. H. Whitehouse. 3 vols. Oxford, 1956-59.

Cook, E. T. *The Life of John Ruskin.* 2 vols. London, 1911.
Evans, Joan. *John Ruskin.* London, 1954.
Leon, Derrick. *Ruskin, The Great Victorian.* London, 1949.
Rosenberg, J. D. *The Darkening Glass: A Portrait of Ruskin's Genius.* New York, 1961.
Wilenski, R. H. *John Ruskin: An Introduction to Further Study of his Life and Work.* London, 1933.

ALGERNON CHARLES SWINBURNE (1837-1909)

Complete Works, ed. by Edmund Gosse and T. J. Wise. Bonchurch ed., 20 vols. London, 1925-27.
Letters, ed. by Cecil Lang. 6 vols. New Haven, Conn., 1959-62.

Hare, Humphrey. *Swinburne: A Biographical Approach.* London, 1949.
Lafourcade, Georges. *Swinburne: A Literary Biography.* London, 1932.
Welby, T. E. *A Study of Swinburne.* London, 1926.

ALFRED TENNYSON (1809-1892)

Works, ed. by Hallam Tennyson. Eversley ed., 9 vols. London, 1908-13.
Complete Poetical Works, ed. by W. J. Rolfe. Cambridge ed. Boston and New York, 1898.
Poetical Works. London, 1953.

Buckley, J. H. *Tennyson: The Growth of a Poet.* Cambridge, Mass., 1960.
Nicolson, Harold. *Tennyson: Aspects of his Life, Character, and Poetry.* Rev. ed. London, 1949.

SELECTIVE BIBLIOGRAPHY

Pitt, Valerie. *Tennyson Laureate*. London, 1962.
Tennyson, Charles. *Alfred Tennyson*. London, 1949.
Tennyson, Hallam. *Alfred Lord Tennyson: A Memoir*. 2 vols. London, 1897.

WILLIAM MAKEPEACE THACKERAY (1811-1863)

Works, ed. by Anne Ritchie. Centenary Biographical ed., 26 vols. London, 1910-11.
Works, ed. by George Saintsbury. Oxford ed., 17 vols. London, 1908.
Letters and Private Papers, ed. by G. N. Ray. 4 vols. Cambridge, Mass., 1945-46.

Dodds, J. W. *Thackeray: A Critical Portrait*. New York, 1941.
Ray, G. N. *Thackeray: The Uses of Adversity (1811-46)*. New York, 1955.
Ray, G. N. *Thackeray: The Age of Wisdom (1847-63)*. New York, 1958.
Tillotson, Geoffrey. *Thackeray the Novelist*. Cambridge, Eng., 1954.

JAMES THOMSON (1834-1882)

Poetical Works, ed. by Bertram Dobell. 2 vols. London, 1895.

Dobell, Bertram. *The Laureate of Pessimism*. London, 1910.
Salt, H. S. *The Life of James Thomson*. Rev. ed. London, 1914.
Walker, I. B. *Thomson: A Critical Study*. Ithaca, N.Y., 1950.

OSCAR WILDE (1854-1900)

Works. 14 vols. London, 1908.
Works, ed. by G. M. Maine. London, 1948.
Selected Works, ed. by Richard Aldington. London, 1946.
Letters, ed. by Rupert Hart-Davis. London, 1962.

Ervine, St. John. *Oscar Wilde: A Present Time Appraisal*. London, 1951.
Pearson, Hesketh. *The Life of Oscar Wilde*. London, 1946.
Winwar, Frances. *Oscar Wilde and the Yellow 'Nineties*. New York, 1940.
Woodcock, G. *The Paradox of Oscar Wilde*. New York, 1950.

Notes for Illustrations

GEORGE CRUIKSHANK (*1792-1878*)
was the leading comic artist and illustrator of the first half of the nineteenth century in England. Beginning as a contemporary of Gillray and Rowlandson, he carried over into Victorian times the lustiness of humor and satiric bite of an earlier and more uninhibited age.

1. The Gin Shop. In this somber etching, which should be compared with Hogarth's *Gin Lane,* Cruikshank satirizes the addiction to cheap gin, known as "blue ruin," which was the bane of the British lower classes.

2. Pit, Boxes, and Gallery. In analyzing the class structure of English society in *Culture and Anarchy* (1869), Matthew Arnold discriminated between the Philistines or *bourgeoisie,* the Barbarians or aristocracy, and the Populace or lower classes. Cruikshank's portrayal of a typical Victorian theatrical audience of a generation earlier illustrates the same distinctions in fascinating detail through the dress and deportment which set off the staid middle classes occupying the pit or orchestra in the foreground, from the world of high society in the boxes behind, and the rowdy street-types crowding the balcony overhead.

HABLÔT KNIGHT BROWNE (*1815-1882*)
under the signature of "Phiz," was the chief illustrator of Dickens' novels. So closely did Dickens collaborate with the artist that the resulting plates may be accepted as faithful representations of the immortal scenes which they depict.

3. Doctor Blimber's Young Gentlemen as They Appeared When Enjoying Themselves. Dickens' theories about the education of the young inform this superbly conceived and executed engraving from *Dombey and Son,* which shows the pupils of Dr. Blimber's establishment at Brighton out for a stroll under the funereal escort of their pompous headmaster. The joyless servitude to which the inmates of private schools in the period were condemned is emphasized in contrast to the atmosphere of unfettered freedom inherent in every aspect of their surroundings—the frolicsome onlookers, the kite gaily aloft, the distant beach-scene.

4. Mr. Chadband "Improving" a Tough Subject. Literature presents no more unlovely embodiment of religious hypocrisy than the Rev. Mr. Chadband, the Evangelical clergyman of Dickens' *Bleak House.* In this illustration "Phiz" captures him in all his false piety and smirking conceit as, before an audience of disciples, he delivers a canting sermon over poor Jo, the illiterate crossing-sweeper.

WILLIAM MAKEPEACE THACKERAY (1811-1863)
aspired to be an artist before he entered on his literary career.

5. Authors' Miseries. The interest of this cartoon from *Punch* is twofold. The Old Gentleman's tirade calls attention to the reputation for subversive radicalism which *Punch* enjoyed during the first decade of its existence in the 1840's. In the tall, bespectacled auditor on the extreme left Thackeray drew a self-caricature, while his shrinking companion is identifiable as Douglas William Jerrold (1803-1857), popular dramatist and caustic wit. Thackeray and Jerrold were the leading writers for *Punch* in its early years, and their contributions were instrumental in setting the comic tone of the magazine and in laying the foundation for its enduring success.

JOHN LEECH (1817-1864)
was the first of the great trio of comic artists (the others being Keene and du Maurier) whose *Punch* illustrations span the Victorian age. Although principally remembered for his humorous rendering of sporting scenes, including the illustrations for Robert Smith Surtees' hunting novels, Leech was unexcelled in the vein of acid drollery with which he burlesques the fads and follies periodically sweeping the social scene.

6. The Railway Juggernaut of 1845. Leech here satirizes the "railway mania" which reached a climax in 1845, entailing financial ruin on thousands of infatuated speculators.

7. Bloomerism—An American Custom. In July 1851 the revolution in women's wearing apparel advocated by the American feminist Mrs. Amelia Bloomer reached the shores of Great Britain. Leech's cartoon illustrates the hilarity with which *Punch* greeted the new vogue.

8. A Delicate Attention. This engraving, one of a famous series by Leech entitled *Memorials of the Great Exhibition—1851,* speaks volumes about mid-Victorian "artistic" taste, as nourished by the exhibits in the Crystal Palace.

NOTES FOR ILLUSTRATIONS

RICHARD DOYLE (*1824-1883*)

in 1849 created the cover for *Punch* which has been used ever since. Doyle's high spirits and distinctive style added a new and infectious note of playfulness to the pages of the magazine.

9. A Railway Station. Showing ye Travellers Refreshynge Themselves. This woodblock from Doyle's series entitled *Manners and Customs of ye Englyshe* relates to a time when railway dining-cars were unknown. It exemplifies to perfection the artist's lively sense of the absurd, divorced from any satiric intent.

10. Enjoyment! A Scene upon the Grand Canal. In 1854, after he had parted company with *Punch,* Doyle published a delightful picture book, entitled *The Foreign Tour of Messrs. Brown, Jones, and Robinson,* in which he depicted the ludicrous adventures of three very typical young Englishmen on a continental holiday. The self-conscious nonchalance with which they lounge in their gondola typifies the British traveller abroad in all his supercilious insularity.

CHARLES SAMUEL KEENE (*1823-1891*)

succeeded Leech as the leading comic illustrator for *Punch.* Although he lacked Leech's imaginative exuberance and fertility of invention, Keene was a more sensitive artist, who eschewed caricature in his kindly, yet perceptive, portraits of Victorian types from every walk of life.

11. "High" Life below Stairs! Keene here travesties the factional rivalries which permeated Victorian religious life, filtering all the way down to the servant classes.

12. Misapprehension. Drawing and caption alike testify to the impact of Darwinism on the conventional morality of the day.

GEORGE DU MAURIER (*1834-1896*)

created polished drawings for *Punch* in which the late Victorian world of high fashion survives. Du Maurier's style was well suited to mirror the glittering surface of this world, and at the same time to probe its underlying artificiality and hollowness.

13. The Height of Magnificence. In the overbearing and insufferably vulgar person of Sir Gorgius Midas, du Maurier created an archetypal example of the self-made man, possessed by the snobbish determination to buy social recognition.

NOTES FOR ILLUSTRATIONS

14. The Six-Mark Tea-Pot. Du Maurier relentlessly mocked the devotees of aestheticism, one of whose affectations was the collecting of blue-and-white oriental porcelain. The posture and dress of the bridegroom in this engraving suggest Dante Gabriel Rossetti, who was a connoisseur of the china in question, while the bride is an unmistakable caricature of William Morris' wife, whose Pre-Raphaelite beauty is celebrated in numerous drawings by Rossetti.

SIR MAX BEERBOHM (1872-1956) possessed skill as a caricaturist that matched the brilliance of his prose parodies. With his fastidious art Victorianism expires in self-mockery.

15. Mr. Tennyson, Reading "In Memoriam" to his Sovereign. Queen Victoria derived spiritual consolation from Tennyson's great elegy after the death of the Prince Consort in 1861, and as a consequence summoned the laureate to an audience. This delicious plate from *The Poet's Corner* is Beerbohm's imaginative reconstruction of that historic meeting.

16. Mr. Rudyard Kipling Takes a Bloomin' Day Aht, on the Blasted 'eath, along with Britannia, 'is Gurl. During the 1890's Kipling imperialist poetry contributed to the frenzy of jingoistic patriotism that found vent in the Boer War. To the popular image of the poet as a great national bard, sounding blasts on the trumpet of empire, Beerbohm responded with one of the most devastating caricatures in *The Poet's Corner,* in which Kipling appears as a bumptiously festive Cockney, cavorting with a tin horn.

Index of Authors

ARNOLD, MATTHEW
Stanzas from the Grande Chartreuse 72
Dover Beach 79
The Study of Poetry 305
Literature and Science 360

BROWNING, ROBERT
Fra Lippo Lippi 284
Andrea del Sarto 296

BUTLER, SAMUEL
The Musical Banks 447

CARLYLE, THOMAS
Signs of the Times 37
Democracy 113
Natural Supernaturalism 203

CARROLL, LEWIS (see under DODGSON)

CLOUGH, ARTHUR HUGH
The Latest Decalogue 425

DARWIN, CHARLES ROBERT
Autobiography 380

DICKENS, CHARLES
Podsnappery 437

DODGSON, CHARLES LUTWIDGE
A Mad Tea-Party 461

GILBERT, WILLIAM SCHWENK
Etiquette 484
Patience; or Bunthorne's Bride 489

517

INDEX OF AUTHORS

HARDY, THOMAS
Nature's Questioning *230*
In Tenebris II *231*

HOPKINS, GERARD MANLEY
God's Grandeur *247*
That Nature is a Heraclitean Fire . . . *248*

HOUSMAN, ALFRED EDWARD
"Terence, this is stupid stuff . . ." *233*

HUXLEY, THOMAS HENRY
Science and Culture *345*

LEAR, EDWARD
Limericks *470*

MACAULAY, THOMAS BABINGTON
Southey's *Colloquies* *11*

MALLOCK, WILLIAM HURRELL
The New Republic *476*

MEREDITH, GEORGE
Hard Weather *243*
Prelude to *The Egoist* *455*

MILL, JOHN STUART
Of Individuality, as One of the Elements of Well-Being *93*

MORRIS, WILLIAM
Useful Work versus Useless Toil: The Socialist Platform *143*

NEWMAN, JOHN HENRY
History of My Religious Opinions to the Year 1833 *176*

PATER, WALTER HORATIO
Preface *318*
La Gioconda *323*
Conclusion *325*
The Child in the House *404*

ROSSETTI, DANTE GABRIEL
The Portrait *329*

INDEX OF AUTHORS

RUSKIN, JOHN

The Nature of Gothic *127*
Of the Real Nature of Greatness of Style *263*

SWINBURNE, ALGERNON CHARLES

Prelude to *Songs before Sunrise* *236*
The Higher Pantheism in a Nutshell *444*

TENNYSON, ALFRED

Ulysses *62*
Locksley Hall *64*
In Memoriam *214*
The Higher Pantheism *445*

THACKERAY, WILLIAM MAKEPEACE

How to Live Well on Nothing a Year *427*

THOMSON, JAMES

The City of Dreadful Night *222*

WILDE, OSCAR

Epigrams *494*

ILLUSTRATIONS ACKNOWLEDGMENTS